The Age of Dissent

Diálagos Series
Kris Lane, Series Editor

Understanding Latin America demands dialogue, deep exploration, and frank discussion of key topics. Founded by Lyman L. Johnson in 1992 and edited since 2013 by Kris Lane, the Diálogos Series focuses on innovative scholarship in Latin American history and related fields. The series, the most successful of its type, includes specialist works accessible to a wide readership and a variety of thematic titles, all ideally suited for classroom adoption by university and college teachers.

Also available in the Diálogos Series:

From Sea-Bathing to Beach-Going: A Social History of the Beach in Rio de Janeiro, Brazil by B. J. Barickman, edited by Hendrik Kraay and Bryan McCann
Gamboa's World: Justice, Silver Mining, and Imperial Reform in New Spain by Christopher Albi
The Conquest of the Desert: Argentina's Indigenous Peoples and the Battle for History edited by Carolyne R. Larson
From the Galleons to the Highlands: Slave Trade Routes in the Spanish Americas edited by Alex Borucki, David Eltis, and David Wheat
A Troubled Marriage: Indigenous Elites of the Colonial Americas by Sean F. McEnroe
Staging Frontiers: The Making of Modern Popular Culture in Argentina and Uruguay by William Garrett Acree Jr.
A Woman, a Man, a Nation: Mariquita Sánchez, Juan Manuel de Rosas, and the Beginnings of Argentina by Jeffrey M. Shumway
The Origins of Macho: Men and Masculinity in Colonial Mexico by Sonya Lipsett-Rivera
Mexico in the Time of Cholera by Donald Fithian Stevens
Tides of Revolution: Information, Insurgencies, and the Crisis of Colonial Rule in Venezuela by Cristina Soriano

For additional titles in the Diálogos Series, please visit unmpress.com.

The Age of Dissent

Martín Bowen

Revolution and the Power of Communication in Chile, 1780–1833

University of New Mexico Press · Albuquerque

Printed in the United States of America

ISBN 978-0-8263-6480-7 (cloth)
ISBN 978-0-8263-6481-4 (paper)
ISBN 978-0-8263-6482-1 (e-book)

Library of Congress Control Number: 2022950298

Founded in 1889, the University of New Mexico sits on the traditional homelands of the Pueblo of Sandia. The original peoples of New Mexico—Pueblo, Navajo, and Apache—since time immemorial have deep connections to the land and have made significant contributions to the broader community statewide. We honor the land itself and those who remain stewards of this land throughout the generations and also acknowledge our committed relationship to Indigenous peoples. We gratefully recognize our history.

Cover illustration: "Una chingana," ca. 1830, Gay, Atlas de la historia física y política de Chile, 1:29. Courtesy of Memoria Chilena, Biblioteca Nacional de Chile.
Maps by Isaac Morris
Designed by Isaac Morris
Composed in Meno 10 | 13

For Josefina and Eloy

Contents

Illustrations

Maps

Figures

Acknowledgements

It is perhaps ironic that one of the main lessons I learned after the years researching and writing about dissent is how invaluable support, love, and collaboration are. I would like to begin this book by expressing my gratitude to the family, friends, colleagues, and mentors who helped and encouraged me throughout this process.

In distant 2007, Christophe Prochasson saw an earlier formulation of this project and agreed to take me under his supervision at the École des Hautes Études en Sciences Sociales in Paris. By then I was a recently graduated Chilean student with only a basic ability to communicate in French. Were it not for Christophe Prochasson's faith in me, this book would not exist. Once I joined the PhD program at the École two years later, I had the privilege of working with a second dissertation adviser, Jean-Frédéric Schaub. His lively seminar became the core of my graduate education. Both Christophe and Jeanfred are models of intellectual curiosity, scientific rigor, and scholarly engagement. I would like to thank as well Annick Lempérière, Frédérique Matonti, and Clément Thibaud for their helpful commentary and suggestions on my doctoral thesis.

My gratitude additionally goes to the colleagues in Paris who offered me their time and support over the years, especially Juan Carlos Estenssoro, Antonella Romano, and Silvia Sebastiani. I had the honor of discussing some aspects of this project with the late António Manuel Hespanha, who generously listened to me and shared with me his own vision of the period. I am also grateful to the friends that made my Parisian years unforgettable: Nicolás Angelcos, Javiera Azócar, Joaquín Bascopé, Yuritzi Becerril, Kenya Bello, Javiera Bonnefoy, Laura de la Rosa, Josefina Echeñique, João Pedro Gomes, Francisca Gutiérrez, Claudia Jordana, Cristóbal Maino, Sébastien Malaprade, Diego Milos, Amarí Pielowski, Pablo Rivas, Camila Valenzuela, and Matías Wolff. To Marcela Letelier and Sergio Letelier for their generosity and hospitality.

After graduating I was lucky to meet a wonderful group of scholars and friends at NYU Abu Dhabi and the broader NYU network. Special thanks to Martin Klimke, Pedro Monaville, Erin Pettigrew, and Mark Swislocki for their friendship as well as their help in turning a monstruous *thèse de doctorat* into a viable book project. Sinclair

Thomson, Zeb Tortorici, and Barbara Weinstein read portions of the manuscript and offered invaluable support and advice. In New York I additionally benefitted from the insightful comments and warm reception of Jane Burbank, Frederick Cooper, Nicole Eustace, Ada Ferrer, Stefanos Geroulanos, Rebecca Goetz, David Ludden, and Andrew Sartori. I am also grateful to the students who have taken my classes both in Abu Dhabi and New York. They have been a source of inspiration and a constant reminder as to why I chose this career.

I am honored to have my first book in English published in the "Diálogos" series of University of New Mexico Press. My earnest gratitude to Michael Millman for his dedication and support. He was a true champion of this project. Series editor Kris Lane offered invaluable feedback and editorial advice. Andrés Baeza similarly provided useful comments and corrected a few factual mistakes. Kristin McMillan helped clarify my writing and get the manuscript ready for production with admirable patience. Finally, I would like to extend my gratitude to all the staff at UNM Press and especially to the production team for preparing the maps included in this book.

I presented parts of this work at Cambridge University, the Instituto de Historia Argentina y Americana "Dr. Emilio Ravignani" in Buenos Aires, the Venice World Multidisciplinary Conference on Republics and Republicanism, and the Latin American Studies Association Congress. I would like to thank the organizers, presenters, and audiences in these events for their feedback. María Elena Barral, Ernesto Bassi, Guillaume Boccara, Alex Borucki, Gabriel di Meglio, Marcela Echeverri, Anne Eller, Sybille Fischer, Noemí Goldman, Elena Schneider, Kirsten Schultz, Ángela Vergara, and Charles Walker gave me their advice and thoughtful comments. I am indebted as well to Julio Pinto, Fernando Purcell, Claudio Rolle, Rafael Sagredo, Sol Serrano, and Jaime Valenzuela for supporting me in the early stages of my career and transmitting to me their love of history. To my friends Sergio Durán, Camila Gatica, Joaquín Hernández, and Daniel Silva for gifting me with their time and help throughout the elaboration of this book. Santiago Conti, Gabriel Nachar, and Camila Sanhueza did fantastic work locating documents in Chile and Argentina, while Danay Mariman Catrileo generously shared with me resources concerning the spelling of words in Mapuzugun. I was lucky to work with two wonderful editors, Sarah Watkins and Dan Geist, who polished my writing and helped me find my voice in English.

This project was supported by funding from Chile's National Commission for Scientific and Technological Research (CONICYT),

New York University Abu Dhabi, New York University, the École des Hautes Études en Sciences Sociales, and the French Embassy in Chile. I would also like to thank the staff of the Archivo Nacional Histórico in Santiago, the Archivo General de Indias in Seville, and the Archivo General de la Nación in Buenos Aires for their help. I am particularly indebted to Emma de Ramón and Pedro González, Director and Coordinator, respectively, of the Archivo Nacional Histórico, for having facilitated access to the institution's materials. My gratitude goes as well to the Biblioteca Nacional Digital, the Bibliothèque Nationale de France, the Centro Nacional de Conservación y Restauración, the Getty Research Institute, the John Carter Brown Library, Memoria Chilena, the Museo de Artes Decorativas, and the Museo Histórico Nacional for providing the illustrations for this book.

My deepest gratitude to my mother, Rosario Silva, for her endless love and unshakable belief in my work. My father, Felipe Bowen, has also been a constant source of inspiration and support. To my siblings, extended family, and in-laws in Chile, thank you for your help, patience, and encouragement.

I will always be grateful to Josefina Raña for her immense generosity and companionship. Without her labor and support I would not have been able to finalize this book. Eloy came into this world as I was writing it, making the process both more chaotic and more enjoyable and offering a vivid and permanent example that communication transcends words. This book is dedicated to them.

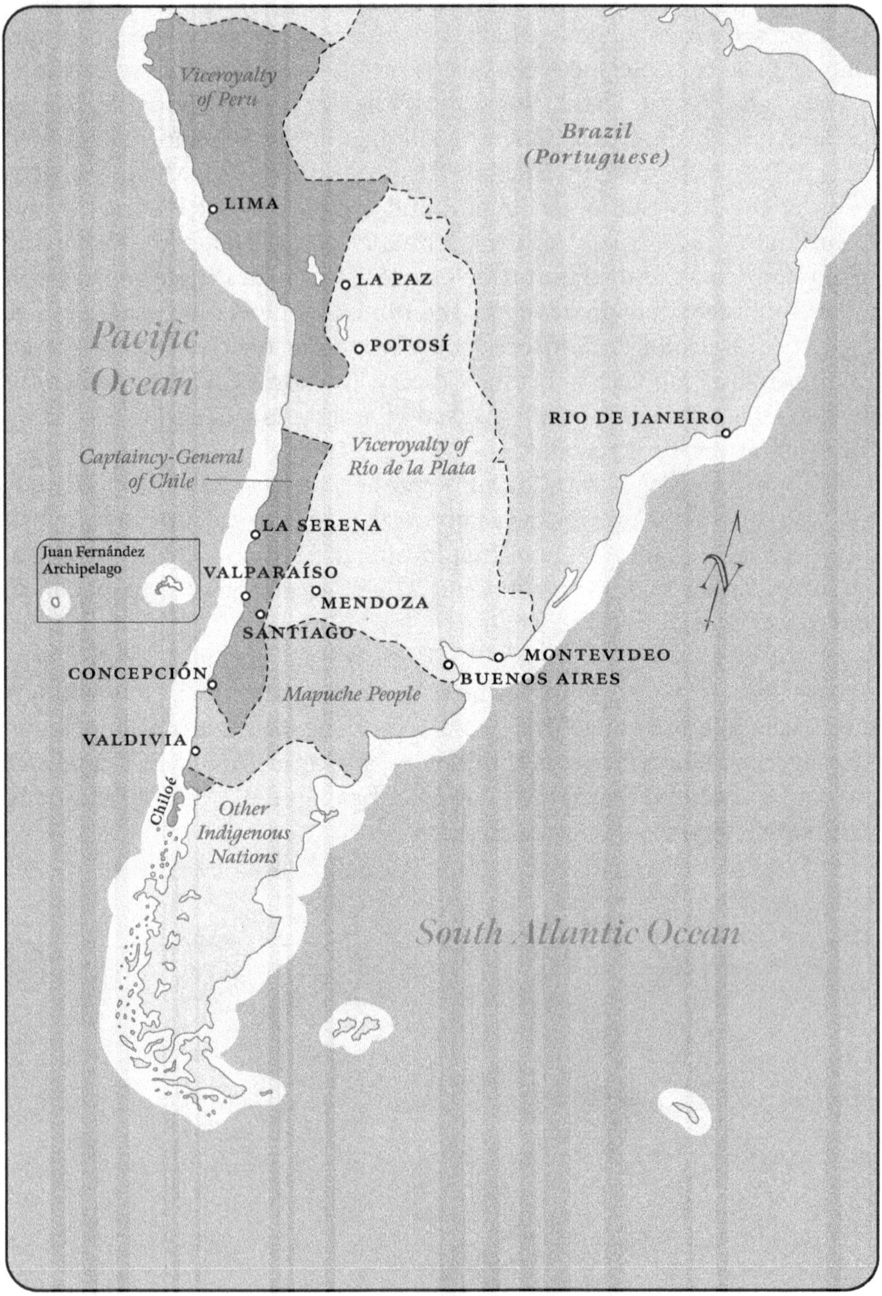

Map 1. Chile and the Spanish southern border, 1800.

Introduction

In early 1814 a woman named Dolores Reyes publicly challenged Chile's military and political authorities. While residents of Concepción, Chile's second-largest urban center, were used to the presence of armed forces—the city was located on the border between the Spanish empire and the sovereign Mapuche people who lived south of the Biobio River—this time the troops occupying the city were fighting a different enemy (see map 1). Since 1813 this sparsely populated Spanish colony on South America's Pacific coast had been torn apart by a bitter civil war pitting the forces of Chile's autonomous government (called insurgents or revolutionaries) against supporters of imperial or viceregal authority (called royalists). The conflict had affected in one way or another the lives of the nearly five hundred thousand people estimated to have been living in Chile at the time. The majority of these were poor women and men of mixed ancestry, followed by a significant minority of Natives and enslaved Africans and African-descended people.

Dolores Reyes came from a prominent family in Concepción—that is, she belonged to the comparatively small group of elites from Spain or of Spanish descent who occupied most positions of power in the colony. She and her relatives had been deeply involved in the imperial civil war. When the insurgent army took control of Concepción in mid-1813, military authorities jailed Reyes and her mother, Josefa Salcedo, in a spiritual retreat house that had been turned into a women's prison. Salcedo stood accused of exchanging letters with her husband, Martín Reyes, who had left Concepción and collaborated with the royalist army. Dolores was charged with having fired a pistol in March of 1813 to celebrate the arrival of the royalist army to the city.[1] On January 14, 1814, while Dolores and her mother were still in prison, the commander of the revolutionary army hanged Dolores's uncle, José María Reyes, for the crime of treason.[2]

A few days later a new insurgent leader named Bernardo O'Higgins reached Concepción. Seeking local support, O'Higgins freed Dolores Reyes and Josefa Salcedo, along with other alleged royalists. It was at this moment that Reyes—after months of imprisonment and the public execution of her uncle—decided to visibly question the legitimacy of Chile's new authorities. Shortly after her release, she paid a visit to

Isabel Riquelme, Bernardo O'Higgins's mother, while wearing on her chest a miniature portrait of the Spanish king, Fernando VII (see fig. 3.2 for an example of such portraits). This was an obvious provocation. Together with his father, Carlos IV, Fernando had abdicated the crown in 1808 to Napoleon Bonaparte, who kept him prisoner in France until March 1814. The royal abdications precipitated a war in the Iberian Peninsula against the French and their supporters and created a political vacuum in the wider Spanish empire. While most revolutionaries in Chile before 1814 claimed they were loyal to King Fernando, royalists doubted their sincerity and considered them rebels against the crown. By wearing a portrait of the captive king, Dolores Reyes was thus openly showing her support for the royalist army in the presence of relatives of Chile's revolutionary commander. Her action, though performed inside a private residence, was remarkable enough to reach the ears of at least one other insurgent official, who heard of it from O'Higgins's sister, Rosa Rodríguez.[3]

Reyes certainly knew her public display of loyalty to Fernando VII would shock the revolutionaries. Hers was an antagonistic manifestation of allegiance to the monarch: it was as much an assertion of her own convictions as it was an indictment of those of her rivals. She used an emblem of unity—the monarch whom most actors professed to support—to make visible her dissenting opinion and to insist on the division of the political community. With her action, Reyes also assumed the right to express her own views about political legitimacy. Her public challenge to the insurgent authorities was all the more striking considering that, because of her gender, she was also excluded from formal political participation. Through her public performance, then, Reyes wielded the power of visible communication to intervene in the political arena.

But Reyes's action had even greater political significance. While she voiced her disapproval of Chile's regime change, she inadvertently helped widen the gulf that separated Chile's revolutionary present from its colonial past. As this book shows, the antagonistic manner in which Dolores Reyes asserted her own agency contributed to the emergence of a political landscape openly and irremediably marked by dissent. Based on an examination of Chile's conflicted history between the first known local anticolonial conspiracy in 1780 and the installation of an authoritarian postcolonial constitution in 1833, *The Age of Dissent* contends that the most revolutionary dimension of this period in Chile was the opening of politics to radical political dissension. Political contestation and experimentation—regardless of whether it derived from monarchists such as Dolores Reyes or from republicans, from liberals or conservatives, from elites or marginalized groups—directly questioned the principles of unity and transcendence that ruled colonial politics and created a new profane and pluralistic political world.

This process implied more than the simple adoption of new institutions, concepts, or practices: it was a revolution in what politics meant and what could be achieved through politics. If politics concerns "the many and the world that arises between them," as Hannah Arendt argues, then this revolution impacted the very nature and shape of that world between people.[4] To bring this dimension of the revolution to light, I focus on the power of communication. By this I do not mean that this dramatic change in politics was the result of the dissemination of radical ideas or information but that it involved finding new ways of conceiving and using the power of communication. This is precisely what Dolores Reyes did when she decided to wear the portrait of the king to challenge Chile's revolutionary leaders: she turned the realm of visible communication into an antagonistic and profane political arena. By reshaping and disputing the power of communication, Reyes and others like her reimagined the very nature of politics.

As I show in this book, notions of communication were essential to how men and women in Chile described and discussed politics. *The Age of Dissent* centers on two such conceptualizations: visibility and propagation (I return to them later in this introduction). In official colonial discourse, the purpose of these two forms of communication was to manifest unity and to protect and secure society's sacred foundations. In other words, their role was supposed to be limited to reinforcing existing social and political structures. Starting around 1780, however, clashing political agents began using visibility and propagation to advance their antagonistic views and to combat those of their rivals. Following the activities of a varied set of actors, including elite women and men, the urban poor, and African descendants, I show how people in Chile turned the realm of communication into a site for the manifestation of disunity and an arena for competing social and political programs. Through their dissenting actions, ordinary and elite individuals changed the function and scope of visibility and propagation, adapting them to a new, fractured reality. No longer limited by an indisputable source of authority nor reserved for the expression of unity and concord, communication became both the engine and the scene of a revolutionary experience in political plurality.

Dissent and the Opening of the World of Politics

Since 1780 the Spanish empire—Chile included—experienced multiple social and political disturbances, including popular uprisings, civil wars, and eventually the disaggregation of most of its possessions in the Americas. But whether these developments represented a radical break with the past remains controversial.[5] The most sophisticated arguments that favor conceptualizing this process as a revolution have come from historians of politics and political culture such as François-Xavier Guerra and Hilda Sábato. In their view, while the Spanish imperial crisis did not witness the takeover of the state by revolutionary factions or the replacement of the ruling classes, it nevertheless involved a political revolution in both Spain and Spanish America. Although they disagree over the exact causes, characteristics, and chronological extent of this transformation, these historians concur that it consisted in the relatively sudden replacement of traditional, monarchical political frameworks by new and modern ones.[6] Chile's political evolution would apparently conform to this interpretation: after the royal abdications of 1808 prompted a series of civil wars in the colony, by 1825 Chile, though still dominated by the same landowning elite, emerged as an independent republic based on ideas of popular sovereignty and equality before the law.

Scholars have criticized this political approach to the Hispanic revolutions for dismissing previous radical experiences in the region, privileging the ideas and activities of white elites, and downplaying the importance of alternative political projects and experiences. Recent literature has focused instead on how—between the second half of the eighteenth century and the early decades of the nineteenth—marginalized actors such as Native and African-descended people negotiated power relations, promoted their interests, and advanced their own radical ideals.[7] The picture of the age of revolutions in Spanish America that emerges from these works is that of an era of multiple and open-ended struggles over the social and political order.

Yet this again raises the question about what—if anything—was revolutionary about the age of revolutions in the Spanish monarchy. As François-Xavier Guerra pointed out as early as 1992, the revolutionary nature of this period cannot be attributed simply to the pace and magnitude of social and political contestation. Guerra argued that neither the institutional transformations, nor the social and economic upheavals, nor the spread and implementation of revolutionary ideals that could be observed during the crisis of the Spanish empire constituted breaks with the past.[8] One could similarly appraise more recent scholarship, as neither the emergence of radical political imaginations, nor the negotiation and open contestation of royal sovereignty, nor the active shaping of power relations and political structures by marginalized actors were unique to this period.[9]

Based on the case of Chile, in this book I argue that what was radically new about the age of revolutions in Spanish America was the emergence of a profaned and pluralistic political landscape. This represented an absolute departure from colonial politics, which was organized around the principles of transcendence and unity. As I show in the following chapters, the Spanish monarchy grounded its social and political order on a transcendent source of authority, God. According to this political philosophy, the world had an intrinsic, God-given order that served as the reference point for human societies. The fundamental norms of society derived therefore from an instance that was external to society itself. This instance was sacred in that it was supposed to be indisputable and beyond human reach. Subjects could challenge norms and their application, but they could not question their ultimate foundation. The primary mediator between society and this external dimension was the monarch, who had privileged access to this truth. Politics thus had a sacred core, as the act of grounding social and political order was ultimately tied to a source of authority that lay beyond the reach of ordinary subjects.[10] Associated with this idea was the principle of unity. This consisted in the assumption that society's proper and desirable state, as dictated by its transcendent point of reference, was union in hierarchy. In this view, society, as could be observed in everyday life, did not correspond to its true, perfect form, and it was the role of politics to adjust it to this normative vision of itself.

This hegemonic vision of politics did not concern merely the relationship between society on the one hand and the government or the state on the other. In colonial and revolutionary Chile, authority was institutionally distributed among multiple actors, including government officials, leaders of religious and secular corporate bodies, magistrates, hacienda owners, and household heads. In the official discourse, the power of these figures flowed directly from the same indisputable source as the king's and constituted a reflection of society's transcendent order and hierarchy. This political philosophy therefore had an enormous social relevance. Irrespective of their status, gender, and race, actors in both colonial and revolutionary Chile encountered this philosophy not only when they openly negotiated or contested power, such as when litigating in court, but also when they engaged in more mundane activities, such as walking in the streets or hearing a sermon during Mass.

These conventions were not simply imposed from above. In everyday life, royal authority—and the notions of transcendence and unity that sustained it—was the product of permanent negotiation and accommodation between different parties across the empire.[11] This vision of politics was not monolithic either, generating instead a series of pressing problems and questions. For example, the very idea of transcendence invited discussions over the identity of the primary mediator between society and its sacred source of order. Early modern Spanish jurists such as Francisco Suárez argued that the people were the original mediators between the monarchy and God and that they had permanently delegated their sovereignty to the king (a position revolutionary elites in Spanish America adopted to justify autonomous rule after 1808).[12] Actors similarly clashed over the ultimate will of the sovereign, society's proper hierarchical structure, and the nature of the fundamental laws according to which the sovereign was to rule.[13] Yet, despite its flexibility, this official approach to politics constrained legitimate political action by sacralizing society's source of order and hailing unity as its ultimate goal.

Between 1780 and 1833, ordinary women and men such as Dolores Reyes called these official norms into question, profaning the realm of politics and forcing it to embrace open expressions of division. Through their dissenting actions, they canceled the distance between themselves and society's exterior point of reference. This resulted not in a secularized political arena, but a profaned one. Actors continued to ground the social order on outside instances such as God or nature, but in doing so, they desecrated the position of mediator between society and its transcendent source of order. They thus rendered society's ultimate foundation a matter of dispute and assigned to politics the power to transform (rather than reflect) the social order. Because it lacked an indisputable source of authority, this profaned political landscape was also pluralistic in that it had to embrace division and antagonism as ineradicable and even legitimate components of political life. The revolution studied in this book, then, consisted not so much in a regime change, the lifting of barriers to political participation, or how social groups used politics as an instrument to advance their own goals and objectives. Rather, it was a disclosure of the political dimension; that is, a process by which actors simultaneously created and became aware of new forms of articulating their shared world.[14]

Although philosophers and legal theorists have long argued that the end of conventional sacralized mediators between society and its transcendent source of authority represented a major political development in the Western world, only recently have historians begun extending this interpretation to the Spanish American revolutions.[15] Often assuming or mentioning this process in passing, this literature has mainly focused on its effects on institutional politics and ideological disputes. *The Age of Dissent* is the first detailed exploration of how ordinary actors in revolutionary Spanish America both produced and reacted to an antagonistic and profaned political landscape.

To study this "opening of the world of politics"—to borrow

Michael P. Costeloe's phrase—I follow the proliferation of radical political dissent between 1780 and 1833.[16] By radical political dissent I mean open discord over what actors considered essential elements of social and political order. These dissenting activities rendered core aspects of society a matter of contention, asserting explicitly or implicitly that they could be changed through concerted human action. As Dolores Reyes's performance in 1814 exemplifies, these actions often involved framing the community in antagonistic terms and highlighting the contingent nature of its social and political structures. Dissent, then, was both the symptom and the cause of the desacralization of social and political authority and of the transgression of the normative ideal of unity.

Dissent is a particularly flexible category of analysis: it has no predetermined or preferred shape. It is not a property inherent to actions or ideas but a measure of differentiation or dissimilarity. As a concept, dissent interprets politics from the point of view of its intrinsic negativity, focusing on how society's political dimension is structured by exclusion and antagonism.[17] This book, then, offers what philosopher Nicole Loraux once described as a political anthropology of negativity: it seeks to understand how actors produced and processed division and disagreement and how they experienced political plurality.[18] For this reason, radical dissent should not be identified solely or even mainly with anticolonial aspirations or ideas of independence. From the point of view of the hegemonic political discourse, any challenge to authority was political in that it explicitly or implicitly concerned the proper order of the world. Dissent could be everywhere.

Communication, Publicness, and Fields of Political Action

Politics is as much about grounding the social order as it is about composing and disputing worlds in common.[19] To examine how dissension transformed politics in revolutionary Chile, I thus turn to communication. Communication features prominently in histories of the age of revolutions: scholars often invoke it to discuss the dissemination of the revolutionary gospel across frontiers, the empowerment of subjects and citizens through public deliberation, and the multimedia landscape that shaped revolutionary political cultures.[20] Recent scholarship has dramatically improved our knowledge of the information networks Indigenous and African-descended peoples constructed in the Atlantic world, and how they used communication and media to pursue their own objectives.[21] Taken together, these studies show that communication was essential to how actors during the revolutionary era framed their political agency and goals.

Yet to fully consider the relationship between communication and politics, it is necessary to challenge the assumption that communication naturally consists in the exchange of information or ideas. Notions of communication vary dramatically across time and place. As John Durham Peters has shown, in the West alone communication has referred to radically different experiences, from the transmission of data to the communion between lovers.[22] The meaning of communication is never settled: people constantly discuss and negotiate what communication is and how it affects others.[23] In this book, I propose to study communication as a site of contention, an arena in which past actors elaborated and discussed the worlds they shared as well as the kinds of interactions that took place within them.

In colonial and postcolonial Chile, politics and communication overlapped, not because communication put in circulation politically sensitive information but because both politics and communication concerned how people acted on each other. This connection was made explicit in the realm of activities contemporaries labeled as public. What was public were simultaneously the actions that affected others and the matters that were of concern to the community. This was a fundamentally political category: as François-Xavier Guerra and Annick Lempérière have observed, the notion of public during this period "always refers to politics."[24] But "public" was also always about communication, as notions of communication were essential to determining the social impact of people's actions. In the concept of public, then, politics and communication were fundamentally intertwined.

Studies of the category of "public" in Spanish America during the age of revolutions have only partly acknowledged this relationship. While rich and sophisticated, this literature—which includes scholarship on the modern public sphere, civic life, and definitions of "public" and "private" in law and everyday life—has not yet fully considered the multiple parameters actors used to construct and evaluate the public impact of any given action.[25] This in turn results in a partial rendering of the intersection between publicness and politics. By expanding our understanding of what constituted communication during this period, *The Age of Dissent* uncovers the broader range of coordinates that women and men in Chile used to determine what was public and sheds new light on the political dimension of publicness.

People in revolutionary Chile, I show, relied primarily on two modes of communication to establish what was public: visibility and propagation. In the official discourse, actions performed in crowded areas were presumed to be of common knowledge because they had been witnessed by many. What was visible was public and thus concerned society as a whole. Propagation, on the other hand, described the potential of an action or behavior to disseminate across society and affect others. This form of communication operated mainly via two mechanisms: imitation and contagion. Spreading through these means, people's words, behaviors, and actions also gained public import.

Visibility and propagation structured fields of political action. Take the example of imitation. From the perspective of the official discourse, society was an arena in which different models of behavior coexisted and competed. Children imitated their parents, subordinates their superiors, ordinary people their neighbors. To intervene in this field of mimetic exchanges, authorities promoted what they considered good examples and combated negative ones. Thus, for instance, colonial officials hailed religious laywomen as providing the population positive examples that served to counteract the bad ones set by unruly women. Rival groups similarly saw in imitation a political battleground. While some intellectuals and political figures in postcolonial Chile hailed secular theatrical performances as providing audiences examples of morality and good behavior, members of the church rejected them for promoting dishonesty and irreligiosity. To neutralize these vectors of irreligious contamination, church figures considered it necessary to reinforce the social power of nuns and regular clergy, counting on their positive influence to check the impact of the secular theater. From the point of view of mimetic relations, then, religious laywomen, stage productions, prostitutes, nuns, and priests, although of different natures and occupying highly dissimilar social locations, participated in the same field of interactions, one held together by the force of imitation.[26]

According to the official colonial political philosophy, visibility and propagation needed to be channeled and controlled in accordance with the principles of transcendence and unity. What was visible had to correspond to the transcendent order of society, which visibility also helped actualize and render manifest. Thus, clothes and other visible distinctions were expected to reflect the hierarchies that emanated from society's exterior source of authority. People's public, visible actions similarly had to manifest veneration and obedience toward the monarch, as he was the mediator between society and the transcendent truth that dictated this order. On the other hand, authorities relied on propagation to foster what they considered proper respect toward the sacred source of their power as well as to frame conflict and division as unwanted anomalies. Mimesis and contagion provided colonial politics with a much-needed explanation for dissension, a description of its power to negatively impact society, and the instruments to fight it.

Starting around 1780, social actors in Chile began engaging with visibility and propagation in new and original ways, sometimes to combat the proliferation of dissent, sometimes to adapt to it, and sometimes to produce it. Ordinary men and women increasingly turned both fields into arenas for the pursuit of antagonistic visions of social and political order, in which formerly sacred principles of authority were profaned, and dissension and division reigned. By appropriating the powers of visibility and propagation, people in Chile reimagined their political agency and imposed plurality as politics' inescapable horizon. As a result, by 1833, official concerns with safeguarding unity and authority coexisted in practice with a new experience of the public arena, one marked by the profanation of sources of order and the ineluctability of dissent.

This book explores these changes in a thematic rather than chronological manner. Chapter 1 introduces visibility as a field of political action. Based mostly on evidence from Santiago, Chile's capital, it analyzes the relationship between visibility and urban spaces and shows how actors used visibility to assign political power and relevance to social phenomena. Chapter 2 studies the relation between visibility and the transcendent social order. It shows how, after Chile's first independent junta or revolutionary committee was installed in 1810, different political factions and groups began using clothes and accessories to question as well as to create inequality. By emancipating visible publicness from the task of simply representing society's transcendent order, these actors turned visibility into an instrument of social and political engineering. Chapter 3 focuses on how women and men in Chile transformed the relationship between visibility and the principle of unity. After 1808, people from different social backgrounds used objects such as portraits, flags, and rosettes to make their political affiliations visible and identify those of others. Through these actions, they turned visibility into an antagonistic field in which division and difference were on permanent display. Chapter 4 analyzes the destruction of secular signs of power in urban Chile between the collapse of the Spanish empire in 1808 and the consolidation of independence around 1825. Through their actions, a wide range of iconoclasts—from elite women to free African-descended artisans—transformed visibility into an instrument of profanation, rendering disputable and questionable the figures and principles colonial and postcolonial regimes tried to promote as sacred.

Chapter 5 turns to propagation, examining the relationship between political plurality and the power of imitation. It shows how, after 1808, partisan groups and political figures sought to use imitation as a political instrument, channeling its power to both produce and combat dissension. Through the example of self-proclaimed royalist hero María Ana Pérez de Arza, the chapter examines how the power of imitation became essential for how individuals understood their political agency in an era marked by antagonism and division. Chapter 6 analyzes how political agents relied on contagion (as a concept and as a set of related practices and institutions) to understand, combat, and create dissent—and thus political plurality. It focuses particularly on how people used the notion of contagion to position themselves as actors in a world of proliferating disagreement and division, as well as to explain and tolerate radical dissension.

Chapter 7 further examines the connection between political plurality and the field of propagation. It analyzes the institutions and practices authorities used to prevent the propagation of dissension and insubordination after 1780. The chapter focuses on the enormous impact these institutions and practices had on the lives of women and subaltern men, as well as on how these groups challenged them. The eighth and final chapter studies the emergence of a neutral notion of communication in revolutionary and postcolonial Chile, one not characterized by the powers of visibility or propagation. It shows how ordinary individuals and lawyers questioned the relationship between visibility, propagation, and publicness to allow for different expressions of political dissension to be considered legitimate—or at least not seditious. These views, rather than reflecting coherent doctrines of liberalism, pluralism, or the modern public sphere, were practical responses to a profaned and pluralistic experience of politics, to which they also contributed. Dissension and political plurality, then, invited actors to reconsider both the power of communication and the nature of the public sphere to make space therein for irreducible division and conflict.

Taken together, these chapters show how the fields of visibility and propagation were instrumental to the "opening" of politics in revolutionary Chile. Women and men wore accessories such as portraits and rosettes to display their antagonistic, partisan views; they chose specific clothes to make visible their position regarding social inequalities; they carried and spread incendiary documents and information they hoped would help bring down the government; they accused rivals of contaminating others with their contagious ideas and behavior. Their engagement with these fields had powerful consequences for them—from Romualdo Antonio Esponda, a modest merchant brutally flogged in Santiago's central square for weaving a royal flag in 1814, to Mercedes Arias, a woman imprisoned in a detention house in the city of Concepción in 1817 for allegedly setting a bad political example for others. Through their efforts to, by turn, create and combat antagonism and division, people like Esponda, Arias, Dolores Reyes, and countless others shaped new ways of grounding the social order and composing the political space between them.

Chile between 1780 and 1833: A Brief Overview

In this final section, I offer a brief description of the social, military, and political developments that took place in Chile between 1780 and 1833. I also discuss the book's chronological framework and introduce the period's key figures, events, and factional and military struggles.

While I begin with the year 1780, dissent was hardly unknown in Chile or the broader Spanish monarchy before that date. The eighteenth century began with an inter-imperial and civil war, the War of the Spanish Succession (1701–1713), and episodes of dissension were common across the empire afterward (one scholar has calculated that, in the Andean zone of South America alone, there were ninety-five revolts between 1750 and 1781).[27] Chile was no exception: a Native Mapuche insurrection erupted on the island of Chiloé in 1712, tax riots rocked Santiago and surrounding areas in 1766 and 1776, and there was widespread opposition to the royal decision to expel the Jesuit order from the Spanish empire in 1767. Additionally, during the second half of the eighteenth century, many poor, Indigenous, and African-descended individuals directly or indirectly challenged the colony's hierarchical order by asserting their honor and bodily dignity, fighting enslavement, and challenging the payment of the Indigenous tribute. Taken together, these activities demonstrate, as I show throughout this book, that local actors were willing to "profane" royal decisions and render the social and political order a matter of dispute.

But something distinctive occurred in late 1780: a group of men in Santiago conspired to overthrow the government and make Chile an independent republic. The main conspirators were two Frenchmen, Antonio Vergne and Antonio Gramusset, joined by a lawyer named Mariano Pérez de Saravia from the neighboring Spanish colony of Río de la Plata. People in Chile were at the time discussing both the Indigenous revolution led by José Gabriel Condorcanqui (Tupac Amaru II) and Micaela Bastidas in Peru and the American (US) revolution. There were also rumors of an imminent British attack against the colony. The Santiago conspirators likely believed this hemispheric uncertainty, combined with earlier expressions of social discontent, set the stage for a revolution in Chile. To garner popular support, Vergne, Gramusset, and Pérez de Saravia developed a political program that included the abolition of slavery, of the death penalty, and of social hierarchies. They also contemplated the equal distribution of land

and protecting the Catholic Church against government intervention. This project responded as much to European radical ideologies as to what the conspirators perceived were the goals of disparate groups in Chile—African and African-descended people, be they enslaved or free, the urban and rural poor, and Indigenous peoples. But the plotters never got the chance to make their plan public. In late 1780, when only a handful of individuals knew about the conspiracy (and it is difficult to establish whether they participated in it), Pérez de Saravia denounced Vergne and Gramusset to the colony's highest court, the royal Audiencia. In early 1781, the tribunal imprisoned and deported the two Frenchmen to Lima, ignoring the other alleged conspirators.

I have chosen to begin this study in 1780 because, although ineffective, the conspiracy of Vergne, Gramusset, and Pérez de Saravia symbolizes a change in the status of dissension within the colony. The plot brought together the aspirations of different actors and processed them for the first time into a revolutionary political program—which implicitly meant framing politics as a mechanism with the capacity to transform the existing order. The plan made patent that social hierarchies were a matter of contention and that royal authority was not beyond dispute. The year 1780 also serves as a marker because of the global circumstances that encouraged the conspirators. The conspirators likely saw the Tupac Amaru and American revolutions as indicators of imperial weakness and the emergence of alternative forms of rule. While part of their project was ideologically linked to the European republican tradition, these men also considered the need to invite the independent Mapuche groups who lived east of the Andes and south of the Biobio River to appoint their own representatives to the government—a gesture toward Indigenous sovereignty that echoed the issues raised by the Tupac Amaru revolution. The year 1780, then, exemplifies the experimental and open-ended nature both of the Atlantic revolutions and of Chile's revolutionary experience in particular. While manifest expressions of radical dissent were rare in Chile for years after 1781, colonists were aware of the monarchy's mounting political, financial, and military difficulties as well as of the challenges posed to the existing order in other regions of the Atlantic world. Efforts to reinforce the sacrality of social and political structures now took place against a local and global background marked by the existence—avowed or disavowed—of radical social and political alternatives.[28]

Although 1780 marked the onset of an era of rising challenges to the official colonial discourse in Chile, the final opening of politics came only decades later, as the imperial crisis of the 1790s and 1800s culminated in the collapse of the Spanish monarchy in 1808. I divide this period into two phases: a "revolutionary" one, between 1808 and the insurgent victories of 1817, and a "postrevolutionary" one, between 1817 and 1833. The first corresponds mainly to the downfall of the monarchy and the imperial civil wars in the colony, while the second is primarily identified with the organization of Chile as an independent country. These two labels serve solely as chronological signposts: for contemporaries, both the nature of the revolution and its outcome remained uncertain at least until the late 1820s. How dissension transformed politics during these years is explored in the following chapters. Here I will limit myself to listing the most relevant social and political developments.

When news arrived in Chile of the royal abdications of 1808 and the war against the French, two main factions formed among local elites. Some supported the establishment of an autonomous collegiate government—a junta—while others rejected the need for any institutional innovations. For the sake of simplicity, I will call the former insurgents or revolutionaries and the latter royalists. While the colony's highest-ranking official, the governor, sided with royalists, members of several other institutions joined the ranks of insurgents. This division also extended to the Catholic Church, whose members split into antagonistic political factions for the entire revolutionary period. In Chile as in the rest of the Spanish empire, the ideological bases of monarchical order became the subject of much contention, and political vocabularies and concepts changed dramatically. Heated political discussions were a constant in Santiago as well as in towns and cities such as Concepción. Subaltern actors such as enslaved and free African-descended people participated in these debates and attendant political machinations.[29] Tensions in the colony grew, and in July 1810 the Spanish governor, Francisco Antonio García Carrasco, was forced to resign. After a brief intermediate government, on September 18, 1810, an assembly of some four hundred elite men in Santiago proclaimed a junta.

Initially headed by seven members, the junta represented Chile's first autonomous or revolutionary government. While overtly proclaiming its loyalty to King Fernando VII, then captive in France, the junta also engaged in radical measures and sided, although cautiously, with the revolutionary government of Río de la Plata (which was at war with the royalist government of Peru, Chile's powerful and influential neighbor to the north). The junta also advanced several administrative and religious reforms, prepared the installation of a national Congress in Santiago, and eventually abolished the Audiencia. The Congress, which met in 1811, although dominated by moderates, also took radical measures, most notably issuing a law banning the slave trade and declaring free all children henceforth born to enslaved mothers in Chile.

The revolutionary period that started around 1808 was one of widespread confrontation that cannot be reduced solely to the conflicts between royalists and revolutionaries. Rival insurgent factions battled for control of the government. The most enduring of these rivalries pitted supporters of the Carrera—a powerful family from Santiago led by military officer José Miguel Carrera—against followers of Bernardo O'Higgins, the illegitimate son of a former Spanish governor whose main base of support came from the frontier area near Concepción. The monarchy's collapse also generated debates over how sovereignty would be distributed between the different territorial units that composed the colony. Clashes between the elites of Santiago and those of Concepción, in particular, almost led to a civil war between revolutionaries in 1812. Dissent also arose from below. Individuals belonging to categories excluded from active participation in the official political discourse—women, the urban poor, Indigenous and African-descended peoples—openly asserted their political agency and aspirations, breaching the norms of hegemonic politics. More than ever before, aspects of social and political order became a matter of dispute, from the role of the Catholic Inquisition in enforcing religious conformity to the codification of racial and social inequalities.

In late 1812, the viceroy of Peru sent a small military expedition to Chile, thus involving the colony in the ongoing imperial civil war between revolutionaries and royalists. The expedition conscripted soldiers in the southern provinces of Chiloé and Valdivia before moving to Concepción, where they met only limited resistance. Having raised an army of over two thousand men, the royalists then marched toward Santiago but soon reached a stalemate with insurgent forces. In January 1814, the viceroy of Peru dispatched a new military force to Chile, and royalists again conscripted soldiers in Chiloé and the region around Concepción. By then, the independent Indigenous Mapuche groups that lived south and east of the colony joined the conflict on both sides and provided most of the soldiers in the Concepción area. After almost two years of war, in October 1814 royalist general Mariano Osorio took control of Santiago. Many insurgents, including Bernardo O'Higgins and most of the Carrera family, fled across the Andes to Río de la Plata.

The royalist administration—led by generals Mariano Osorio and Francisco Marcó del Pont between 1814 and 1817—reinstated monarchical rule in Chile, reestablished the Audiencia, and annulled the measures insurgents established since 1810. Meanwhile, across the Andes, José de San Martín, the governor of the province of Cuyo in Río de la Plata (centered on the city of Mendoza), began organizing an army with the support of émigrés from Chile. He distanced himself from José Miguel

Carrera and his supporters and sided with General Bernardo O'Higgins, whom he appointed as an army commander. San Martín's plan was to take control of Chile, leave O'Higgins in charge, and launch an attack from there on Lima.

In early 1817, San Martín crossed the Andes with an army of more than 4,000 men (most of them free Black men), defeated the royalists in the battle of Chacabuco, and had the people of Santiago acclaim O'Higgins as Supreme Director of Chile. On February 12, 1818, O'Higgins issued a declaration of independence, which officially ended Chile's status as a Spanish colony. He then defeated a new royalist expedition from Peru, securing insurgent authority. But the war was far from over, as O'Higgins needed to provide men and resources for San Martín's expedition to Lima. San Martín's army left Chile for Peru only in 1820, and it did not manage to deliver a final blow to the royalists. Meanwhile, in the south, Valdivia and Chiloé remained under royalist control until 1820 and 1825, respectively, and royalists and revolutionaries fought a guerrilla war in the frontier area beyond Chillán. The Mapuches played a predominant role in this conflict; one scholar has even claimed that by 1819 this was fundamentally a Mapuche war.[30] In any event, it did not end quickly. Although by 1824 the revolutionary government had the royalist guerrillas on the run, the last of them were defeated only in 1832.

Trouble at Chile's farthest periphery was matched by trouble at the core. O'Higgins's authoritarian and reformist rule won him many enemies, and they came from all quarters: Santiago's aristocracy, ranking clergy, elites in Concepción, and factions in cities and towns across the country. In late 1822, General Ramón Freire, the intendant of Concepción, led a rebellion against the government, and in January 1823 O'Higgins was forced to resign. The new government exiled him to Peru, where he would unsuccessfully conspire to return to Chile. He died in 1844.

Between 1823 and 1830, an array of openly antagonistic political groups emerged, including conservatives, liberals, federalists, *o'higginistas* (supporters of O'Higgins), and *estanqueros* (a group of merchants united primarily by their commercial interests). A particularly potent source of confrontation was the issue of territorial sovereignty, which led multiple cities, towns, and provinces to assert their autonomy. Artisans, soldiers, militiamen, peasants, and the urban poor actively shaped this political landscape, which was rife with dissent. They voted, supported parties or political figures, and participated in demonstrations, mutinies, and rebellions. The 1820s also marked a period of increased political freedom and experimentation. In 1823, Chile's Senate abolished slavery despite fierce opposition from the government and slaveholders. A year later, legislation significantly expanded male access to citizenship, which became practically universal in 1828. A Liberal administration tried to enact sweeping reforms to the Catholic Church in 1825, and in 1826 a federalist-controlled Congress allowed citizens to elect their own parish priests. These innovative measures and the disputes they generated show that actions formerly framed as beyond the pale of politics—such as transforming the social order and allowing communities to choose spiritual guides—were now subject to contention.

General Ramón Freire resigned in 1826. After several short-lived administrations, in 1827 Liberal leader Francisco Antonio Pinto became president. His government faced the relentless opposition of conservatives, o'higginistas, estanqueros, and federalists. During the presidential elections of 1829, the government's adversaries accused liberals and the administration of violating the constitution (which had been redacted and approved by Congress the year before). General José Joaquín Prieto, a reputed o'higginista, led yet another group of rebels out of Concepción and, with the support of the opposition, waged war against the Liberal administration. In early 1830, Prieto emerged victorious.

Soon, political infighting erupted among the new governing factions. General Prieto sided with the estanqueros and was elected president in 1831, yet the true political force behind his administration was an estanquero merchant named Diego Portales, who would remain Chile's leading political figure until his assassination during a military insurrection in 1837. Until Portales's death, the new regime was marked by the persecution of liberals, the exclusion of federalists, and the neutralization of all other rivals. The new administration rejected the reformist spirit of the previous years and aimed to reinforce (or reinstate) social hierarchies and the role of the church. It also sought to curb subaltern groups' political participation and to limit access to citizenship. A new constitution, approved in 1833, enshrined these principles and gave Prieto, Portales, and their associates the means to legally enforce their authoritarian rule. Prieto would serve two full five-year terms as president of the republic, leaving office in 1841.

I have chosen to end this study in 1833 because, seen retrospectively, the new constitution represented the consolidation of Prieto and Portales's authoritarian regime. It also serves to demarcate (although symbolically) the end of Chile's postrevolutionary civil experiments and the start of a different phase in the country's politics. As I show over the course of this book, the era between 1780 and 1833 can be interpreted as one of mounting dissension, antagonism, and profanation of transcendent authority. While this process began during colonial times, it accelerated dramatically after 1808. The sources of division and dispute after that date included such issues as which political regime to adopt, the role of the church, racial and social inequalities, and territorial political representation. Some of the pillars of Chile's colonial social structure were either abolished (slavery, race legislation, and legal inequality) or questioned (the elites' control over land, the power of the church). Additionally, subaltern actors such as the urban poor and Indigenous and African-descended people overtly challenged the relations of subordination that were so essential to the hegemonic discourse. As will be seen in the following chapters, these developments were inextricably tied to radically new ways of imagining and using the power of communication.

CHAPTER ONE

Visible Publicness, Urban Space, and the Politics of the Gaze

In late colonial and revolutionary Spanish America, the concepts of "public" and "visible" were intimately bound. The dictionary of the Spanish Royal Academy in 1735 defined the adverb "publicly" (*públicamente*) as describing an action carried out "openly and patently, in plain sight," while "publicness" (*publicidad*) encompassed the nature of public affairs, actions performed without secrecy, and "a place or location in which many people gather." The same dictionary defined "in public" (*en público*) as referring to things done "publicly, in everyone's sight."[1] These definitions remained stable at least until the early decades of the nineteenth century.[2] Through the concept of "public," then, the Spanish empire's official language established a chain of equivalencies between politics (public affairs), the gaze (actions performed in plain sight), and space (places gathering many witnesses).[3] This set of correspondence suggests that the visible was a threshold of sorts, marking the transition of actions and behaviors from nonpublic to public. An action performed in a location where several people met was more public than one executed in a secluded, less crowded area. Visibility—these definitions seem to suggest—brought people's actions into the sphere of politics.

There is a wealth of literature on the role of optics and the gaze in structuring racial and gendered politics in Latin America.[4] Although inspired by this scholarship, my goal in this chapter is not to establish how effective the gaze was in shaping social and political structures in late colonial and revolutionary Chile. My aim is to map the points of contention and power dynamics that emerged from the relationship actors drew between visible phenomena, publicness, and space. My argument is that, through their interactions, people in Chile constructed visibility as a specific social and political arena. When a woman of mixed ancestry covered most of her face to attend a ball to which she was not invited or when men from Santiago's subaltern classes settled a conflict in one of the city's most crowded streets, they were simultaneously participating in, actualizing, and shaping this sphere of activities. I call this field "visibility" or "visible publicness."

To investigate the nature of visibility as a field of social and political action, this chapter focuses on urban Chile—especially Santiago,

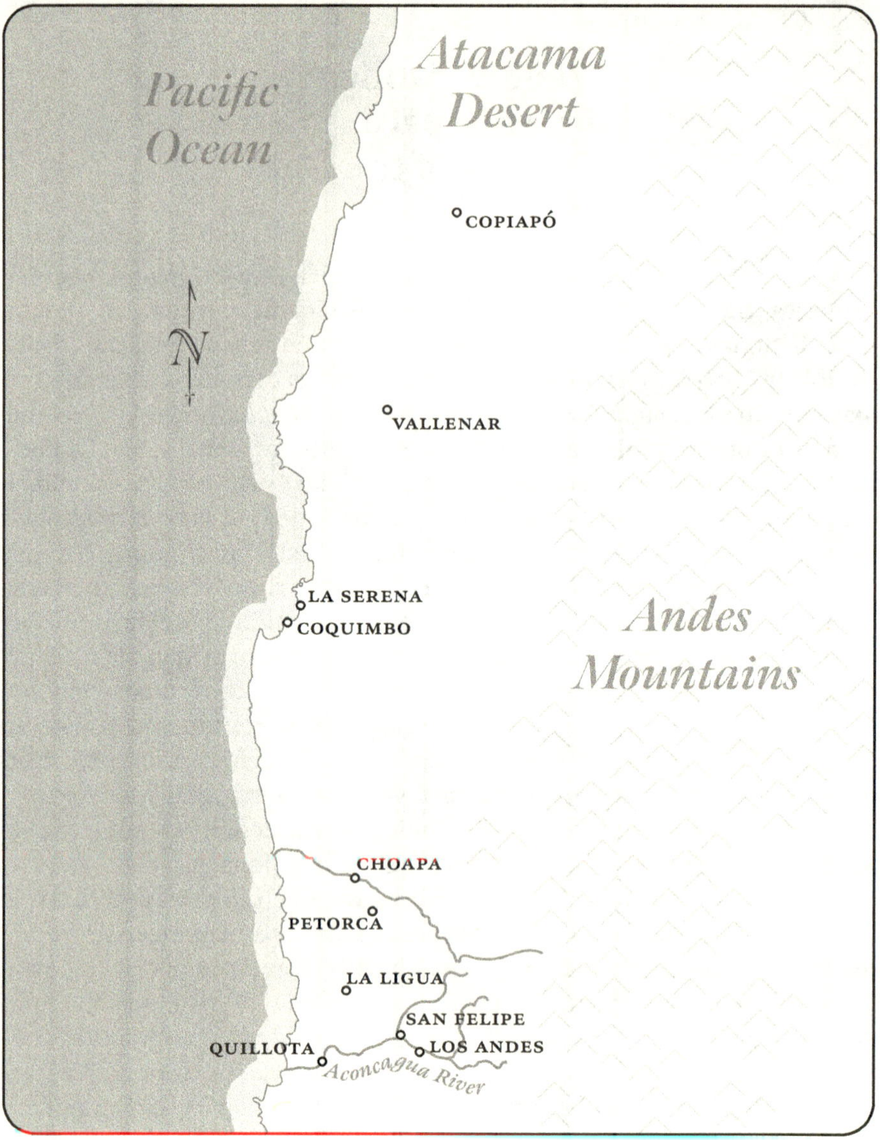

Map 2. Chile between the Atacama Desert and the Aconcagua River.

Chile's capital. I begin with an exploration of official definitions of visible and how they informed government policies and power dynamics. I focus primarily on how different observers established a set of parallels between urban life, publicness, and the visible, and how this was supposed to grant cities or towns a certain power over people. I then examine urban infrastructure and its connection with visibility, showing how cities and towns were expected to project a visible image of the political community, how they served as theaters of hierarchy and power, and how they provided the spaces where social visibility was performed every day. The chapter then analyzes the ways in which ordinary people negotiated visibility. Studying the activities of Santiago's plebeian population, I show how non-elite actors challenged the official distribution of visibility, contested and negotiated the values associated with it, and used visibility for their own purposes. The final section, on the practice of covering one's face, provides an example of how the field of visibility both molded and was molded by ordinary subjects.

The City and the Rule of Law

During the eighteenth century, Spanish authorities actively promoted the foundation of cities in the Americas, including in Chile. Only a handful of small towns existed in Chile in the early years of the century, including Santiago, Concepción, La Serena, Valdivia, Chillán, and Valparaíso.[5] These urban centers constituted the colony's administrative and political pillars, their sphere of influence often extending to the vast rural areas that surrounded them. Yet most of the colony's population lived and worked in haciendas and small properties in the countryside. In 1703, peninsular authorities ordered the creation of new towns to relocate this dispersed rural population. Local officials, hacienda owners, and ordinary people alike initially resisted such orders, but by the 1740s this opposition had largely been overcome, and new towns were formed throughout the countryside.[6] One historian counts ninety-nine villages and forts founded in Chile between 1742 and 1800. After subtracting those destroyed by the Mapuches during the war of 1766–1771 (discussed below), approximately sixty new villages were established by 1801 (see maps 2 and 3 for a map of Chile and its main cities and towns in the early nineteenth century).[7]

The frenzied foundation of new towns after 1740 reflected the civilizational and political power authorities attached to visibility. In the early modern Spanish Atlantic, visibility was inextricably tied to public information and the collective sanctioning of reality. This connection was encapsulated in the legal formula "public and evident" (*publico y*

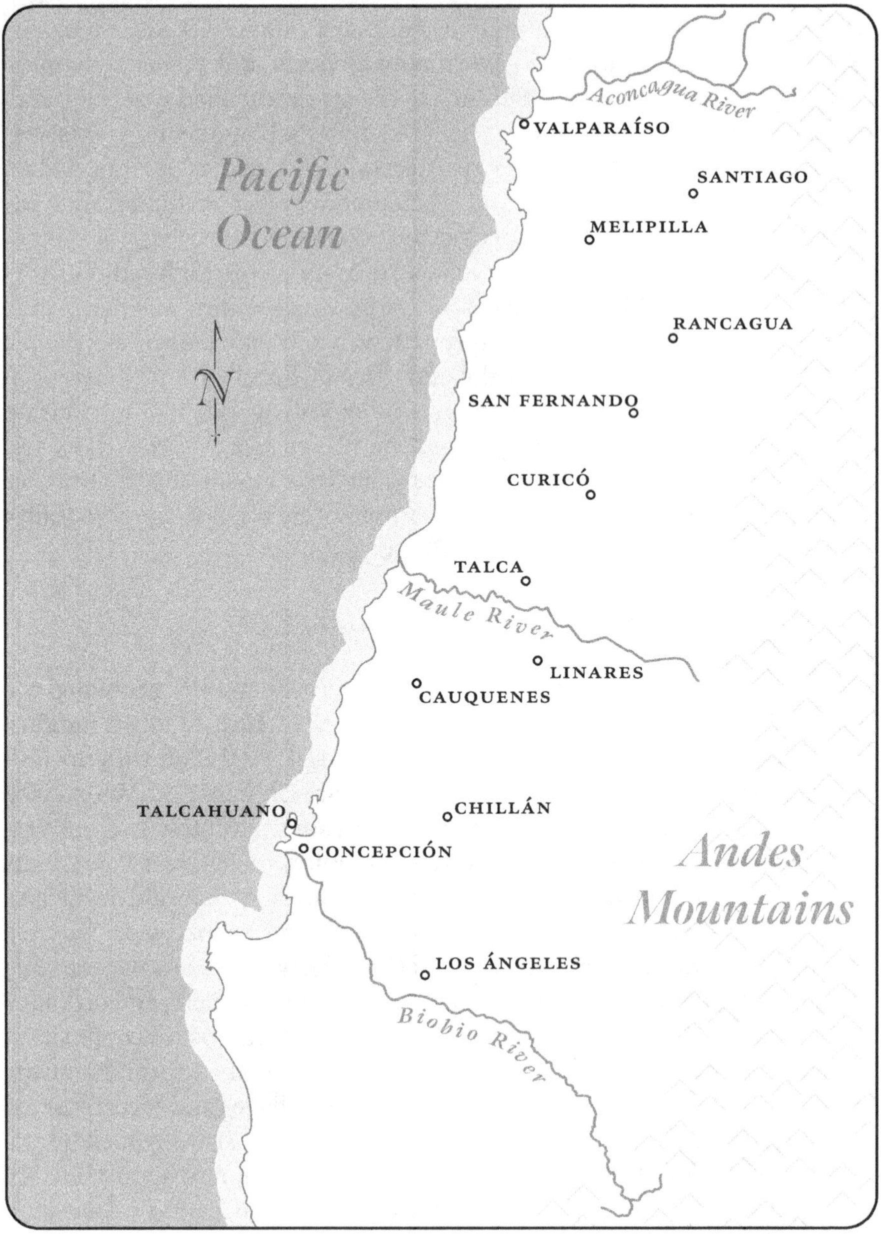

Map 3. Chile between the Aconcagua and Biobío Rivers.

notorio), which authorities and ordinary people alike used in official documents and trials to describe facts of common knowledge. This category construed certain aspects of reality—such as someone's reputation—as being validated by an entire community and constituted for this reason a powerful type of legal evidence.[8] Witnesses regularly evoked the category of "public and evident" to characterize both the events that took place in visible, urban spaces, and the information that could be derived from them. For example, in a criminal investigation conducted in 1809 against a colonial officer accused of corruption, a witness testified that it was "public and evident" that the officer was close friends with other powerful men, as they could regularly "be seen" walking together in Santiago.[9] The witness thus associated an action performed in a visible space (Santiago's urban setting) with it being "public and evident." This relationship was so strong that ordinary people and authorities alike used "visible" as a synonym for "public" or "well known."[10]

As the concept of "public and evident" suggests, people living in Chile's cities, villages, and towns paid close attention to the actions carried out in the public space. Testimonies from witnesses and litigants involved in various types of legal action show that community life was marked by an intense exchange of gazes and that ordinary people perceived visibility as one of the main characteristics of "public" actions or behaviors.[11] This connection between publicness and the gaze was quite literal. In 1815, Santiago's bishop sentenced a young couple who had married in secret to receive the nuptial blessing during Mass while holding "candles in their hands, so that with the publicness of this act they may purge the sort of secrecy" of their marriage.[12] In the bishop's sentence, publicness was achieved through light and communal witnessing.

Visibility was the sine qua non for the rule of law. By rendering people's behavior public, officials argued, visibility prevented crimes and transgressions. Activities carried out in public or well-lit spaces were consequently presumed to be innocent and lawful. In his report written in 1793 on Santiago's public entertainments, Judge Juan Rodríguez Ballesteros argued that theater audiences in the capital behaved honestly because the establishment was appropriately lit.[13] From this point of view the opposite of the "public" was not the "private" but the "hidden, clandestine."[14] Limited visibility—as could be found in shadows or during the night—was the harbinger of illicit actions, the stamp of most sins and crimes. In 1800, for example, Santiago's bishop banned all nighttime meetings in churches because people could engage in unlawful behavior under the shroud of darkness.[15] Merchants and colonial authorities in Santiago and Concepción often cited the immorality associated with the lack of visibility to justify the prohibition of nocturnal commercial activities (in which plebeians and the enslaved played a central role).[16]

If one place captured the connection between visibility, publicness, and the rule of law, that place was the city. By producing relations of visibility, cities enforced lawful behavior, promoted the principles of Catholicism, and ensured the correct functioning of society.[17] The urban, visible space transformed people. In the Spanish legal and political traditions, cities were portrayed as both products of civilization and civilizing instruments. Their sphere of influence even extended beyond their physical boundaries, as colonists saw towns and cities as centers that radiated civilization and religiosity toward nearby areas.[18]

The opposite to the city was *el monte*. Although monte can be directly translated as a "mountainous area," the concept of el monte described in general any unsettled, relatively inaccessible area. El monte constituted a sort of negative image of the urban space. In administrative documents and legal testimonies alike, el monte was presented as a space where there was no visibility or publicness and where the rule of law was suspended.[19] Colonial officials and elites often complained that outlaws and criminals took refuge in el monte to avoid the authorities' vigilant eyes.[20] The association between el monte and the suspension of law was so strong that ordinary people commonly referred to unmarried couples—even those residing in a town or city—as living al monte (like in the wilderness).[21] Lacking the social and political relations that emerged from visible publicness, people in el monte supposedly lived uncivilized and unruly lives.

Urbanism, Discipline, Colonialism

As a result of their association with visibility and the rule of law, cities and towns were considered by authorities to be powerful political instruments. Officials believed people congregated in cities and villages were easier to control and rule than dispersed populations. This seemed particularly important in eighteenth-century Chile. The colony could by then be divided into three distinct socioeconomic regions: the north (between the Copiapó and Aconcagua rivers), the center (between the Aconcagua and Maule rivers), and the south (between the Maule and Biobio rivers). The northern region, while less populous than the other two, hosted an important copper mining industry. The central and southern regions were primarily agricultural districts marked by large estates or haciendas.[22] A floating workforce constantly poured from the two latter districts. Composed mainly of young men and women of mixed ancestry, this population followed seasonal job opportunities in the countryside, labored and traded along the southern frontier, traveled long distances for employment in the mine districts, and camped in the outskirts of towns and cities, where they performed all kinds of work.[23] Authorities characterized these individuals as rebellious and unreliable, and complained about their alleged immorality, criminality, and idleness.[24] The founding of towns all across the colony was a means of enforcing a degree of control over these dangerous "plebeians," as they were often described.

Reflective of the disciplinary role attributed to the urban landscape were the numerous edicts issued during the second half of the eighteenth century regulating the everyday activities, work discipline, and morality of town and city dwellers.[25] The government put special emphasis on controlling the behavior of Santiago's subaltern men and women.[26] In 1778 the capital was divided into four different barrios (neighborhoods), each under the supervision of its own district magistrate or *alcalde de barrio*. The alcalde de barrio's main task was to monitor the neighborhood's inhabitants and bring their transgressions to the attention of higher authorities. Their work of urban vigilance seems to have been at least partly effective. Historian Verónica Undurraga credits the alcaldes de barrio for the net increase in criminal investigations initiated by the government during the last two decades of the eighteenth century.[27]

Colonial officials also sought to utilize the power of urban life to transform Chile's Native population. After the Spanish invasion in the sixteenth century, the colonial government resettled Indigenous peoples living north of the Biobio River in special jurisdictions known as *pueblos de indios* or "Indian towns." Despite their names, these communities often had a low population density, the inhabitants living thinly distributed through their territories. One historian estimates that 393 Indian towns were either created from scratch or recognized from previous, precolonial settlements.[28] By the second half of the eighteenth century, some twenty to thirty thousand people lived in these jurisdictions according to a generous estimate (which likely includes non-Native dwellers).[29] Most of the Natives in these towns belonged to the Mapuche nation, though other national groups were represented as well, such as the Diaguita in the northern districts.[30] Normally, these communities owned a number of protected, communal lands, had their own authorities, or caciques, and paid tributes.

During the eighteenth century, the number of tributary individuals officially classified as "Indians" declined in most of Chile's Indian towns, prompting hacienda owners and royal officials to question the amount of land that had been granted to them in previous centuries. By recalculating the amount of land Indigenous communities were entitled to, authorities were able to dispossess them of part of the territories they had historically occupied and sell them to neighboring landowners.[31] Significantly, some of these lands were dedicated to the formation of new towns, such as Rancagua and Melipilla, both founded in 1743.[32]

By end of the eighteenth century, colonial authorities and hacienda owners sought to completely dismantle some Indian towns. In 1785, for instance, the government tried to sell the lands of seven Indigenous communities near Santiago—Talagante, Lampa, Carrizal, Llopeo, Macul, Gallardo, and Chiñigüe—and to relocate their inhabitants to two other Indian towns, Pomaire and El Bajo. To justify this decision, officials claimed that the towns did not conform to the standards of urban, civilized life and had become hotbeds of criminality. As the royal committee in charge of overseeing the formation of new urban settlements in the colony argued in 1797, these Indian towns were but *rancherías* (collections of huts) occupied by idle, alcoholic, and otherwise dissolute people. Relocating them to proper towns would make the Natives adopt "civil and Christian lives" and enforce on them "order and subordination."[33] Legal complications, logistic challenges, and Native resistance made it difficult for officials and landowners to follow this plan through, but they eventually managed to remove some of these communities and seize their lands.[34] The dispossession of Indigenous lands was carried out in the name of promoting urban, disciplined, visible life.

Royal authorities also sought to make the independent Mapuche people adopt an urban lifestyle. In the eighteenth century, the Mapuches controlled the Andean zone between Rancagua and Concepción, the vast plains and mountain regions south of the Biobio River, and a portion of the pampas on the other side of the Andes. Their total population is unclear, although Spanish observers estimated there were some one hundred thousand Mapuches living south of the Biobio River by 1800. This Indigenous nation comprised different groups who spoke Mapuzugun (the Mapuche language), shared the same cultural practices, and responded to common political structures. The Mapuches lived widely dispersed through their territory and were organized around kinship, territorial, and political units. Authority in each of these interlocking spheres was exercised by male family heads and wealthy men, generally referred to herein as *logkos* ("heads" in Mapuzugun). Though excluded from these positions of authority, women exerted much political influence and wielded considerable spiritual power. During the eighteenth century, some Mapuche leaders had managed to establish a relatively stable frontier with Chile based on a complex system of interethnic diplomacy and the threat of war. Armed conflicts between the Mapuches and settlers, as well as between different Mapuche groups, were nevertheless common in frontier areas.[35]

By the mid-eighteenth century, Spanish officials had become convinced that to colonize the Mapuches they needed first to reform their way of life. To do so, they relied on the power of visible publicness. They thus asked the crown to create new villages in Indigenous territory to "civilize" and in this manner conquer the Natives. After much consideration, the royal government put the idea into practice. During the general parliament (or meeting) celebrated in the fort of Nacimiento in December 1764, Governor Antonio Guill y Gonzaga and the bishop of Concepción, Ángel de Espiñeira, communicated the crown's plan to erect towns in Mapuche territory to the almost two hundred logkos and two thousand warriors who were present at the occasion. The logkos reacted with caution and asked the Spanish for time for further consultation. Colonial authorities, arguing they had obtained the consent of the Mapuches, began implementing their plan nonetheless until a group of logkos organized a massive uprising to stop them in 1766.[36] By 1767 all the villages that were being constructed in Indigenous territory (around eighty in total, thirty-nine of which had already obtained the official title of "town") were destroyed. Peace was restored only in 1771.[37]

Visible Cities, Visible Power

During the eighteenth century, Chile's major cities increased in size and population. Although available estimates are often unreliable, by 1800 Santiago likely had over thirty thousand inhabitants, and the number would perhaps reach forty thousand around 1830.[38] The colony's other cities were significantly less populous. By 1810 Concepción had somewhere between six and ten thousand inhabitants, while La Serena counted some five thousand.[39] The most dramatic demographic change took place in the city of Valparaíso, which became the dominant port in Chile after 1811. According to contemporary estimates, the city's population grew from five thousand to seventeen thousand between 1813 and 1822.[40] While sparsely populated compared to the surrounding countryside, Chile's late colonial cities exerted much political and economic influence over their hinterlands.[41] The rest of the colony's towns were very modest in size and population and in many cases were characterized by economic activities and ways of life almost indistinguishable from those of the surrounding rural areas.[42]

Although neither populous nor rich, following the Spanish imperial imagination these towns and cities were meant to give concrete physical expression to the ideals of order, rationality, and hierarchy that

Figure 1.1. Santiago's central square, ca. 1830. The government palace and the former siege of the Audiencia can be seen to the right. The central square continued to be Santiago's most symbolic place after colonial times. Gay, *Atlas de la historia física y política de Chile*, 1:11. Courtesy of Memoria Chilena, Biblioteca Nacional de Chile.

underpinned the colonial regime as well as to provide visible evidence of the community's loyalty to the king and adherence to Catholicism.[43] The central square (*plaza mayor*) was the Spanish American city's most prestigious location. In Santiago, the buildings of all the major local institutions were situated around the plaza mayor (see fig. 1.1 and map 4). There was located the palace of the colony's top-ranking official, the governor, as well as the seat of the highest local court, the Audiencia. The square also hosted the residence of Santiago's bishop, head (along with the bishop of Concepción) of the Catholic Church. Finally, there was Santiago's city hall or *cabildo*, which together with the colony's other municipal councils represented the interests of local elites.[44] Buildings on this square were meant to manifest the power and prestige of colonial institutions. According to historian Gabriel Guarda, officials even forbade trees to grow in the central square to leave a clear view of the buildings and the political and religious ceremonies that took place in it—that is, to ensure their visibility.[45]

During the second half of the eighteenth century, efforts were taken to improve Chile's towns and cities and make their built environments

Figure 1.2. "The Mint of Santiago," 1824. Schmidtmeyer, *Travels into Chile*, pl. 24. Courtesy of the John Carter Brown Library.

reflect the important place they occupied in the official discourse. New hospitals, churches, promenades, barracks, and jails were built across the colony and monumental buildings constructed in La Serena, Santiago, and Concepción.[46] The grandeur of some of these projects is exemplified by Santiago's mint, the most spectacular building erected in Chile during this period. The project, financed with public funds and carried out under the supervision of Italian architect Joaquín (Gioachino) Toesca, began in 1780 and was practically finished by 1800. A vast compound enclosing more than eighteen thousand square meters, La Moneda was a sign of the city's wealth and power as well as one of the most sumptuous neoclassical public edifices built in all of Spanish America (see fig. 1.2 and map 4).[47]

Staging Status

The urban landscape was also a stage on which to display signs of wealth and prestige. Building facades, in particular, provided colonists with a highly visible surface to exhibit and reinforce status. The preferred manner to do so was by affixing coats of arms to institutional and particular buildings. The royal escutcheon adorned the governor's palace in Santiago's central square (later replaced with Chile's national coat of

Figure 1.3. Royal coat of arms sculpted by Ignacio Andía y Varela during the first decade of the nineteenth century. Cerro Santa Lucía, Santiago. Photograph by the author.

arms) as well as the edifices of secular and religious organizations supported by the royal treasury.[48] Establishments financed with municipal funds enjoyed the privilege of exhibiting an inscription of their respective city's blazon.[49] Similarly, prestigious bodies such as Santiago's Royal University of San Felipe had their own coats of arms installed on their buildings' fronts.[50] Officials saw these objects as important reflections of institutional prestige. In the early nineteenth century, the director of Santiago's mint went so far as to commission a colossal—and very expensive—royal coat of arms over three meters high to be installed atop the edifice's main entrance (see fig. 1.3).[51]

Colonists also used these surfaces to show their families' honor, wealth, and status. As they did in other Spanish American cities, Santiago's powerful, especially those who enjoyed noble titles, placed stone and wooden versions of their families' coats of arms above their houses' main entrances (see fig. 1.4).[52] Composed mostly of the descendants of Spanish migrants, these elites were constantly competing over control of the colony's land, people, and institutions. Visibly inscribing their status in the urban landscape was one of the means they used to assert influence and power. There was apparently a significant market

Figure 1.4. Colonial house in Santiago, 1872. Tornero, *Chile ilustrado*, 8. Courtesy of the Getty Research Institute, Los Angeles.

for sculpted family blazons in colonial Santiago. An artisan named Ambrosio Santelices achieved fame in late colonial times by creating the coats of arms that adorned the houses of the capital's titled nobility.[53]

Dominant groups also used urban spaces as theaters to visibly manifest their wealth and status. The most notable of these stages were Santiago's two public walks or promenades: the *Alameda* or promenade of the *tajamares* (literally, "cutwaters"), and the promenade of the *cañada* ("cattle track"). The first, built in 1745 and renovated in 1804, consisted of a walkway along the Mapocho River on the eastern side of the city, while the second was a broad street that was completely refurbished into a public walk between 1817 and 1825 (see map 4).[54] The ruling classes used these places to meet and talk. For them, all of "the people"—in the

Figure 1.5. “Tajamar, or Public Walk,” 1824. Schmidtmeyer, *Travels into Chile*, pl. 12. Courtesy of the John Carter Brown Library.

Figure 1.6. “Tajamar, or Public Walk,” 1824. Schmidtmeyer, *Travels into Chile*, pl. 12, detail. Courtesy of the John Carter Brown Library.

restricted sense of those they deemed worthy of consideration—could be found in these locations. In 1831 Vicente Claro, a supporter of exiled General Bernardo O'Higgins, informed the general that he had given orders not to sell a new edition of the newspaper *El O'Higginista* until 5 p.m., so that "most of the people would be gathered in the promenade of the *Alameda*."[55] Similarly, in 1813, José Santiago Rodríguez Zorrilla, Santiago's royalist interim bishop, informed his superior in Lima that a rival bishop named Rafael Andreu y Guerrero surprised everyone by appearing "in the public walk of the *Alameda*" wearing a tricolor rosette, the symbol of Chile's insurgent authorities, on his hat. This scandalous behavior, Rodríguez Zorrilla insisted, had been perpetrated "in front of an immense audience."[56] Performed under the eyes of "the people" or an aristocratic "audience," actions carried out on these promenades immediately became public.

Elites made no secret of their desire to gaze and be gazed on in Santiago's chief promenades. In 1813 military officer Ambrosio Rodríguez claimed he stayed in his room every day between 9 and 11 a.m. looking from his window at the passersby on Santiago's cañada.[57] Likewise, those gathering or strolling the promenades were aware their actions were being observed by the crowd. All wore their best attire, knowing they would be inspected and evaluated by others.[58] Travelers visiting Chile during the first half of the nineteenth century left us evocative visual testimonies of these public walks, which they represented as hosting both small and large crowds of wealthy and influential men and women (see fig. 1.5).[59] In some images, these groups appear to be engaged in intense social and visual exchanges. For example, in the promenade of the tajamares, women stayed inside their carriages, in the promenade's center, observing the men who walked around them (and who tried to observe them in return) (fig. 1.6).[60]

The promenades' visible publicness made them politically relevant. Wealthy women, for instance, used these spaces to gain social recognition and to participate in public life.[61] Adriana Montt told her son in a July 1826 letter that she had crossed paths with the president of the republic in the promenade of the tajamares, and that she had invited him to visit her house (which the president subsequently did).[62] Chileans were well aware of the role these walks occupied in local politics and thus took great interest in watching and interpreting everything that happened on them. Both elite and non-elite men and women evaluated political alliances and factional and familial alliances based on observing who talked to whom and who walked with whom in such places.[63]

Urban Publications

The first modern printing press arrived in Chile in late 1811. Newspapers proliferated over the years, but the publishing industry remained concentrated in Santiago. The relative rarity of printed materials before 1812 did not mean that the written word was unimportant. Manuscript letters, gazettes, newsletters, reports, pasquinades, and manifestos played pivotal roles in both colonial and postcolonial times. But the act of publication was not confined to the written word. As defined by the dictionary of the Spanish Royal Academy in 1803, "to publish" (*publicar*) was not only to print something but to make it "patent" and "manifest," "revealing" it to the public.[64] More than disseminating information, publication was seen as an act of revelation that made an aspect of reality widely known while also incorporating it into the realm of publicness.

A wide set of urban practices was aimed precisely at making things public. Governments used urban spaces to make orders, news, and information available to the population. Streets and squares were the scene of what Michèle Fogel has called "ceremonies of information," ritual performances that informed the community of important events (such as a birth in the royal family or a military victory).[65] Town criers—many of them of Indigenous or African ancestry—walked through main squares, announcing official orders and news. Placards presenting the authorities' rulings, manifestos, decrees, and other relevant information were affixed in visible sites such as church doors, the corners of central squares, the doors of each city hall, and the governor's palace in Santiago.[66] The urban setting was so intensely associated with official publications that judges considered people living in towns and cities to be thoroughly informed of the government's provisions.[67]

Authorities also relied on urban publicness to ensure the impact of official punishments. Since early colonial times, capital punishment in Chile involved parading the offender through what was commonly referred to as the jurisdiction's "most public streets" before putting them to death.[68] The execution itself needed to take place in a visible public space. In Santiago, public executions were regularly carried out in the central square or, more rarely, on a hill or other clear or elevated space where the corpse could be easily seen.[69] In some cases, the offender's severed body parts were exhibited in well-attended or otherwise significant places, such as the central square, the city entrance, or the location where the crime had been committed.[70] Other punishments such as public lashes were similarly performed in "visible" streets and squares.[71]

While these forms of urban publication were in principle the exclusive prerogative of the state and church, ordinary people were

Figure 1.7. Church and central square of the town of Andacollo, near La Serena. Johann Moritz Rugendas, 1838–1839. Women can be seen walking toward the church with their heads covered. Men—including both workers and wealthier individuals—form groups in the central square. Courtesy of Biblioteca Nacional Digital de Chile.

far from being merely their passive recipients. Individuals sometimes asked the government to engage in urban forms of communication. In September 1814, Santiago's revolutionary police discovered merchant Romualdo Antonio Esponda weaving a royalist flag. In Esponda's words, after storming the room he rented in the capital, the police escorted him to prison with his "hands tied . . . through the most public streets." A few days later, he was publicly paraded on top of a donkey in Santiago's central square, where he received two hundred lashes while naked. When royalists took control of the capital, Esponda wrote a petition to the government asking for a "public satisfaction, correspondent to the publicness of the insult" he had received.[72] The Council of the Indies in Spain agreed and devised an elaborate ceremony to be celebrated in Santiago's central square. On November 30, 1816, a large crowd, which included the capital's main authorities and military companies, gathered in Santiago's plaza mayor to witness a ritual celebrating Esponda's loyalty. The merchant thus obtained what he had requested: a public compensation for a public offense.[73]

But people in Chile did not need official intercession to use the urban space as an instrument of publication. Between 1808 and 1809, merchant Juan Jiménez Guerra on his own initiative celebrated positive news from Spain (then at war with France) by making noise with whistles and drums, tossing fireworks, and placing illuminations in front of his house in Santiago.[74] Similarly, established merchants and other commercial enterprises used cities' built environments to attract the attention of passersby and communicate commercial information through inscriptions, placards, signs, and decorative figures.[75] In small towns and villages, people conducted their disputes, settled accounts, and executed other significant actions in the area in front of the local church—the most public space in their respective jurisdictions, especially when town residents and people from surrounding areas attended Sunday Mass (see fig. 1.7).[76] Others across the colony even appropriated the urban landscape for argumentative and sometimes illegal forms of publication. Disgruntled groups and individuals posted pasquinades and documents, affixed caricatures, and wrote graffiti on church doors and city walls to ridicule, insult, and threaten officials and rival factions. Groups of people also shouted, sang, and otherwise voiced their views about public affairs in streets and squares, especially during the night.[77]

A case from 1831 offers an interesting example of how nonofficial actors used the urban landscape as a "space of publication."[78] Around March of that year, political agitator Vicente Claro received an official order to leave Santiago. The government wanted him out of the capital to neutralize his campaign in favor of exiled General Bernardo O'Higgins in the upcoming presidential elections. The administration gave him only four hours to leave the city. According to an account he later wrote, Claro took a series of actions explicitly designed to make public the government's orders, which he considered arbitrary: "I got angry and decided to walk my way out of the city, to make the government's conduct more visible [*marcable*]." By walking instead of riding a horse or using a carriage, as would have been expected from someone of his social standing, Claro sought to attract the attention of the city's inhabitants. He departed his house at 9 a.m. with suit and cane, accompanied by a "peon" he did not identify by name, who carried his luggage. "To make this tragedy more public," he wrote, "I crossed the Plaza [the central square] and the city twice" to get to the house of Santiago's military commander. There, he asked the commander to inform the government of the time and manner in which he was leaving the city. "From there, I got out again to cross the streets, looking for the most public ones, and the central square, in order to get to the alameda." The reference is to the cañada, where the road that would lead him to his destination, the town of Melipilla, began. "I can't recall how many times nor how many people interrupted my march in the city to gather information and to regret my situation. The same thing happened in the alameda, as I stopped in many houses to say goodbye."[79] Claro thus relied on the visibility of Santiago's streets, squares, and promenades to make public what he considered an unfair and scandalous official decision.

The Plebeian City

Visibility and publicness were not equally distributed along the social spectrum. "Visible" was synonymous not only with "public," as dictionaries stated, but also with prestige and power. People often used "visible" to describe those who were important, relevant, worth caring about. In his chronicle of events in Chile in 1810, for example, engineer Manuel Olaguer Feliú wrote of how a group of elite men decided to convene a meeting of "up to three hundred persons of the most visible [part] of the people."[80] The meeting took place on September 18, when these "visible" individuals agreed to establish Chile's first autonomous government. Conversely, the elites repeatedly characterized ordinary citizens, plebeians, people of mixed ancestry, and the enslaved as "obscure." In trials and official documents, those seeking to delegitimize rival witnesses or political figures might describe them—to take one instance—as "obscure men from the negligible rabble."[81]

The nominally obscure were, in fact, a conspicuous presence in the urban space, including the colony's political and administrative center. A significant share of the five to six thousand enslaved people estimated to have lived in Chile by 1800 resided in the capital.[82] The city also hosted a large number of free African-descended and Indigenous people. A 1778 census estimated that, of Santiago's nearly twenty thousand inhabitants, around a half were "Spanish" (here meaning primarily of no discernible Indigenous or African ancestry), 25.7 percent were "blacks" and African-descended people, 14.4 percent "mestizos," and 13.5 percent Natives. The capital overall was less white than the surrounding rural areas. The majority of Santiago's African-descended and Indigenous population (around 60 percent of each group) were registered as living in the city's historic center, its only district where nonwhite people outnumbered those classified as Spanish.[83] Other sources maintain that nonwhites constituted a much smaller share of the city's population, prompting questions about the rigor and validity of the 1778 racial classifications as well as about the invisibilization of nonwhites in Chile's colonial and postcolonial documentation.[84] Be this as it may, Santiago was undeniably filled with what elites termed obscure and negligible people.

The capital's diverse demography shaped a complex and heterogeneous social landscape. For example, according to the 1778 census, Santiago's nonwhite population was predominantly female, whereas in surrounding rural areas the opposite was true. Beyond gender dynamics, there was also a great diversity of language and culture. Between 1780 and 1833, Santiago hosted Mapuche leaders, ambassadors, students, and diplomatic missions; theater troupes composed of African-descended, European, and Spanish American performers; enslaved persons brought from Africa and Brazil; artisans, engineers, merchants, captains, and sailors from Europe and the United States; Indigenous people from Peru and Quito; and Mapuzugun-speaking servants and forced laborers.[85]

Santiago's population grew steadily in the late eighteenth century, and the city expanded correspondingly. In the new neighborhoods on the city's edges lived a heterogeneous population of artisans, small business owners, seamstresses, tavern keepers, peddlers, laundresses, and workers of all kinds. Some suburbanites, usually migrants from the countryside, had no permanent occupation and built improvised dwellings their contemporaries called rancherías (the same word the royal committee in charge of the urbanization of the colony used in 1797 to describe Indian towns near Santiago). Most rancherías were located close to the Mapocho River and on lands north and south of the city's historic center (see map 4). Such dwellings were often situated on public or unclaimed properties, although in some cases residents paid a landowner a fee for the right to remain.[86]

For authorities and elites, these neighborhoods were the home of—in the words of one Spanish governor in 1758—an unruly and "insolent rabble" composed mainly of mixed-race people.[87] Elites considered their visible presence in the city both an annoyance and a hazard. In 1802, Governor Luis Muñoz de Guzmán sought to destroy 743 suburban "shacks," as he called them, on the basis that they were an affront to the city's image and decency and generated criminality and disorder.[88] Their inhabitants, moreover, performed their everyday activities in the same spaces authorities and aristocrats considered theaters of power and status. Santiago's central square, for example, was long home to the city's main market, attracting enslaved men and women, street vendors, domestic workers, Indigenous artisans, and many other members of the lower classes.

With their ordinary practices, subaltern individuals produced an urban space that seemed to defy desires for legibility, civilization,

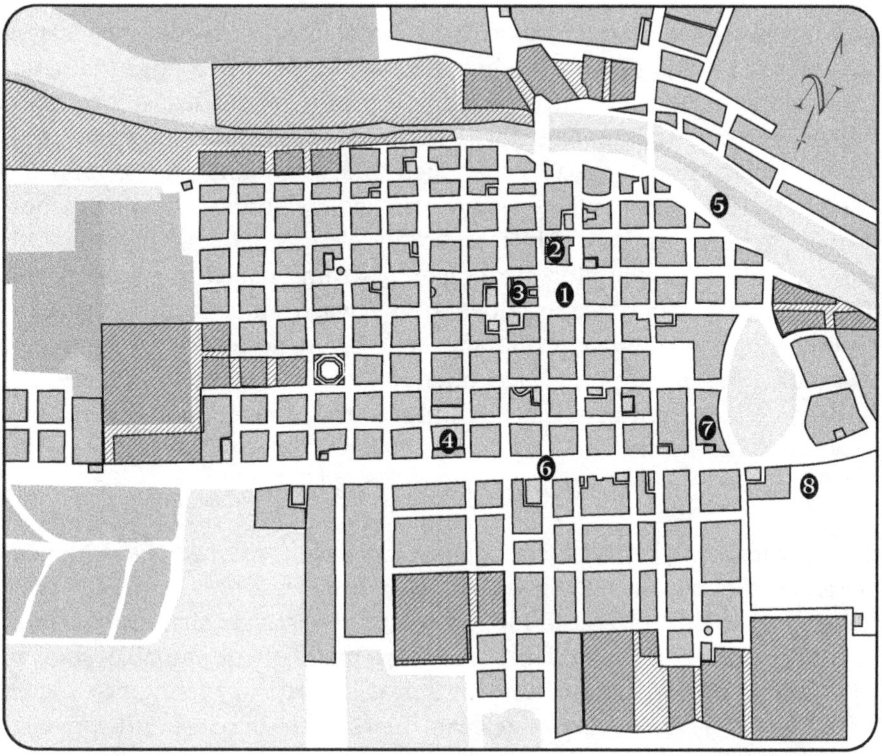

Map 4. Map of Santiago, ca. 1820. Based on Schmidtmeyer, *Travels into Chile*; and De Ramón, *Santiago de Chile*, 90.

and discipline voiced in the official discourse.[89] Urban regulations issued during this period provide a glimpse of the kinds of activities that common people performed in the capital's streets, promenades, and squares. These included selling vegetables, fruit, fish, and other food products; slaughtering animals and drying their hides; making shoes; tailoring garments; feeding animals; washing and drying clothes; cleaning dishes; playing games with balls, kites, and other objects; singing; fighting with knives and rocks; drinking alcohol; and bathing naked in the Mapocho River. As a result of these activities, animal waste and all kinds of garbage littered Santiago's most prominent spaces, including the promenades. According to contemporary accounts, it was not uncommon to see men and women use Santiago's streets, and even the central square, as toilets.[90]

The Plebeian Public

By appropriating urban space, ordinary people fashioned the urban experience of publicness and constituted themselves into relevant publics.[91] Passersby, onlookers, and children playing in the streets shared comments about current events, which sometimes made them valuable sources of information for authorities.[92] In Santiago, ordinary men and women often served as conveyors of relevant news. Elite families and convents dispatched domestic workers—especially African and African-descended women—to buy products in the city's markets and shops, where they obtained and transmitted all kinds of information. These women also served as trusted messengers, spreading the talk of the city between houses and institutions. Female servants additionally accompanied elite women to Mass, using the opportunity to observe and talk to others.[93]

The omnipresence of enslaved people in the city and the facility with which they shared information provoked anxiety among elites. A manifesto published anonymously in 1811 accused former Spanish governor Francisco Antonio García Carrasco of having used the enslaved women of Santiago as political spies before being deposed in September of 1810. According to the document (published anonymously but likely written by insurgent politician Manuel de Salas), enslaved women in elite houses reported their masters' activities to an unidentified Black woman, who served as García Carrasco's personal cook.[94] The woman in question, named Magdalena, seems to have wielded much political power: in December of 1809, an hacendado from Talca sent her a letter, now lost, in which he apparently asked her to convince the governor to elect his brother José Ignacio Cienfuegos as Chile's delegate to the Spanish Junta Central (Central Committee).[95] Though clearly seeking to exploit anti-Black and misogynistic sentiments, the 1811 manifesto relied on its readers recognizing the depth and relevance of the communication networks constructed by enslaved women in the city. That same year, after the revolutionary government issued a law freeing newborns, Santiago's enslaved population not only shared and discussed the news immediately, but—according to merchant Manuel Antonio Talavera—over three hundred enslaved men joined forces and hired a lawyer to offer the government their military service in exchange for their freedom. Following Talavera's account, authorities reacted with fear and imprisoned seven individuals accused of being the movement's leaders. Although Talavera perhaps exaggerated the total number of people involved, the episode suggests Santiago's enslaved population had built social networks that allowed them to act with a certain level of coordination.[96]

These relations help explain, in the particular context of Santiago, the importance urban space held for ordinary citizens. As examined in more detail in the following chapter, the city's subaltern groups cared greatly about their public presentation, especially about the clothes they wore, when walking Santiago's streets and squares. The attention they dedicated to their appearance reveals both the importance they assigned to other people's gaze and the association they established between publicness and the urban space. This connection led individuals of different social positions to use streets and squares to make information and actions public. In 1767, for example, a tavern owner of African descent named Manuel Fernández decided to shout insults at his neighbor while in a "public street," likely with the goal of giving his offenses against his rival a public stamp.[97] Historian Paulina Zamorano argues that much of the violence men inflicted on their female partners in Santiago during the eighteenth century was done in a similarly "public" manner.[98] Through visible and open demonstrations of force, men sought to assert their masculinity and reassure their peers of their adherence to conventional gender codes.[99] In her analysis of over one hundred honor disputes among ordinary people in eighteenth-century Santiago, Verónica Undurraga likewise found that plebeian men usually took their violent confrontations over matters of honor to public spaces such as squares and streets. Most of the public honor face-offs among Santiago's lower ranks took place in such crowded spaces as the central square, its adjacent streets, and the cañada.[100]

Contesting and Negotiating Visibility

While officials praised the positive effects of visibility, other members of Chile's population seemed to reject it. Perhaps the most dramatic repudiation of the model of official visibility was the perennial escape into el monte. Court records indicate how various actors perceived mountainous and inaccessible zones as a refuge from oppressive laws and norms. These included couples facing the opposition of their parents or communities, men fleeing the military draft, enslaved persons escaping servitude, Indigenous peoples pursuing greater autonomy, young men seeking to live free from external supervision, and people evading political persecution.[101] Evidence suggests that the spaces referred to as monte sometimes harbored communities of mixed people (poor Spaniards and people of African and Indigenous descent) who lived beyond the reach of authorities and hacienda owners.[102] El monte was not therefore just a place to escape from the rule of (urban) law, but what Stephanie H. Camp calls a "rival geography"—that is, an "alternative [way] of knowing and using" the colonial space.[103]

Subaltern actors also negotiated the limits of visibility with authorities. This was the case of the *chinganas* and *pulperías*. Chinganas were temporary taverns located in both urban and suburban areas, where customers (mostly but not exclusively men) drank alcohol, listened to music, and watched couples dance.[104] Pulperías were permanent stores inside cities and villages that also sold alcohol to a mostly male and popular audience. In places such as Santiago and Valparaíso, chinganas and pulperías were managed and sometimes owned by entrepreneurial plebeian women, whom one magistrate defined in 1763 as "mulattas, zambas, Indians, and others of this kind."[105] Authorities and elite intellectuals had a negative opinion of these establishments, which they often characterized as brothels and hideouts for criminals—that is, as places where people could elude governmental control. Customers apparently agreed on the latter point. According to scholars, the word chingana comes from the Quechua *chinkana* and means "hiding place."[106] Based on this etymology, it seems that clients perceived chinganas as places where they could enjoy themselves while avoiding official surveillance.[107] It is likely that pulperías offered a similar service to their patrons.

Given the popularity and economic success of chinganas and pulperías, authorities thought it best to bring them into greater visibility rather than suppress them.[108] In 1763, 1773, and 1799 the government ordered all pulperías in Santiago to leave their doors open "so that magistrates may be able to see from the outside" what was going on inside. It also mandated that each establishment consist of a single room, forbidding any additional areas removed from the public eye.[109] Nineteenth-century representations of chinganas, which usually portray them as open spaces with no backrooms or doors, suggest this regulation

Figure 1.8. "Una chingana," ca. 1830, Gay, *Atlas de la historia física y política de Chile*, 1:29. Courtesy of Memoria Chilena, Biblioteca Nacional de Chile.

was extended to these shops (see, e.g., fig. 1.8). As Santiago's intendant reminded the city's officials in 1823, before granting permits to chingana owners they needed to make sure that the establishments would "be installed in public and honest places."[110] A newspaper article in 1827 explained the logic behind these measures, arguing that if chinganas were banned, their customers would continue to gather "in hidden places that cannot be seen: there, alone, without any respect and with no one to control them, they will abandon themselves to all kind of excesses."[111] Authorizing and regulating chinganas and pulperías, then, served to prevent their customers from finding other, even less visible spaces.

The accelerated social and political crisis in Chile after 1808 allowed an increasing number of actors to challenge the "elite allotment" of visibility. Military mobilization and open struggles over political power offered many plebeians and *castas* an opportunity to gain new social recognition. In Santiago, crowds of poor and nonwhite people actively participated in factional clashes, political demonstrations, and military coups.[112] These occasions offered plebeians the latitude to dramatically intervene in the urban space. Richard Longeville Vowell, a British officer who lived in Chile for most of the 1820s, noted that Santiago's destitute, "though rarely seen in times of tranquility, when they lurk in the recesses of Guangali and La Chimba [Santiago suburbs], swarm like wolves in the streets, in hopes of plunder, when there is any prospect of a riot or a revolution. The appearance of their gaunt, wild looking figures, in the Plaza and other places of public resort, is a sure indication to the inhabitants of Santiago, of some approaching political explosion."[113] Vowell's prejudiced observation illustrates how, through their political actions, Santiago's nonwhite and non-elite population breached hegemonic norms of visibility.

One of the individuals who gained visibility through his military and political engagement was José Romero. Born in 1794 allegedly from the union of an enslaved woman and an aristocratic man, Romero had been emancipated at an undetermined age. At age thirteen, he joined Santiago's free Black militia, and as a young man he went on to play an active role in the War of Independence. He was a well-recognized figure in Santiago during the following decades, being particularly renowned in his later life for his philanthropic work. Although by the time of his death in 1858 some elites hailed him as a virtuous man and an exemplary citizen, in the 1820s many derided his social and political visibility.[114] Members of the dominant groups gave Romero the nickname *Peluca* ("wig") due to both his appearance and their presumption that he craved visibility and recognition.[115] In July of 1824, Romero and other Santiago inhabitants, including African-descended artisans and main square vendors, stormed the city hall and demanded the suspension of Chile's constitution. In his account of the events, lawyer Juan Egaña—the constitution's main author and advocate—deplored these men's involvement in the demonstration and stressed that no more than a handful of "visible" persons participated in it. What seemed to scandalize Egaña was that Romero had illegitimately claimed political visibility, adopting a leading role and daring to demand, alongside other people of color, a different constitution for the country.[116]

The One-Eyed Public and the Female Gaze

Of all of this period's practices, none is more revealing of the optic nature of public space than that of the *tapadas* and *tapados* ("covered" women and men). This practice involved leaving home with most of the head, face, and body covered. Tapadas enveloped themselves in long black veils, leaving uncovered only one eye, with which they observed others (see fig. 1.9). Tapados—also called *embozados*—covered themselves with ponchos, handkerchiefs, and long hats. Although these parallel practices shared a

Figure 1.9. "The usual walking costume of Lima," 1825. Caldcleugh, *Travels in South America*, vol. 1. Courtesy of the Getty Research Institute, Los Angeles.

similar concern about visual relations in the urban space, gender norms and expectations gave them entirely different purposes and connotations.

Men in Chile disguised themselves with ponchos and hats to engage in illicit actions associated with the assertion of masculinity and male honor codes. As a lawyer argued in 1811, it was customary for young men from respectable families to go about at night with their faces covered to avoid exposure of their love affairs.[117] When Juan Egaña, acting as a lawyer, sought to demonstrate that two Santiago women were sex workers, he presented as evidence that "covered men" were seen leaving their house every night.[118] Covered men not only visited their love interests thus disguised but also performed other transgressive actions such as attending nocturnal gatherings to drink alcohol or battering rivals in the dark of night.[119] Between 1811 and 1813, partisans of the Carrera family in Santiago disguised themselves in this way to assault and whip women reputed to be royalists or from royalist families. One of their victims, María Ana Pérez de Arza, claimed to have had a miscarriage as a result of being hit by a horse during such an attack.[120]

While men seemed to have covered their faces regularly, it was covered women who captured the attention of authorities and foreign travelers. Although predominantly associated with Lima, the capital of the viceroyalty of Peru, women had worn the tapada costume in parts of Spain and Spanish America since at least the sixteenth century. Historians have argued—with little supporting evidence—that this practice existed in Chile in the seventeenth century.[121] Regardless of the date of its first appearance there, the tapada costume was well known in Chile during the eighteenth and nineteenth centuries. Sources occasionally mention the presence of tapadas in theater houses, bullrings, chinganas, and religious processions, and they were apparently a common sight at nocturnal balls and celebrations.

Authorities and foreign visitors in South America thought women disguised themselves this way to flirt and engage in other forms of sexual misconduct.[122] The problem with the costume, elite men argued, was that it allowed women to walk through the city's visible spaces without male supervision and without being held accountable for the morality of their actions. The logic behind these fears illustrates the power contemporaries gave to visibility in enforcing conformity and disciplining people's behavior. Authorities thus repeatedly tried to end the practice. Chile's governors forbade the tapadas *de cara* ("women with covered faces") along with masks and other disguises in 1760, 1770, 1788, and 1799.[123] At the beginning of the nineteenth century, municipal authorities prohibited tapadas from attending Santiago's theater, arguing that their disguises were incompatible with the "decency and formality that should reign in every public gathering."[124]

The truth is that women adopted the tapada costume for a variety of reasons, all related to the role of the gaze in producing and enforcing publicness. Sources concerning the practice in Lima suggest that women chose to cover their faces to avoid the judging gaze of other members of their communities and to cope with what María de la Luz Hurtado has called the "exigencies of presentation"—that is, the demands imposed on women by social visibility.[125] According to a military officer who served in the Chilean occupying forces in Lima in the late 1830s, women used the disguise to avoid making public their economic straits. Covering their faces and clothing, they could leave home even if they lacked the proper attire to be seen in public or could remain anonymous while buying cut-rate products in the streets.[126] An earlier account based on the writings of British General William Miller—who was part of San Martín's army in Peru in the early 1820s—provides additional information. Miller observed that women of "rank" in Lima covered themselves either because they were "elderly, or unprovided with a proper dress, or not liking the trouble of dressing, or slightly indisposed, or in deep mourning." Others went "thus disguised in consequence of not being of a rank in life to appear otherwise, and it is maliciously supposed that some few attend for purposes of flirtation." In Miller's words, covering their faces allowed women to become "unseen spectators"—that is, to observe others while avoiding their judging gaze.[127]

In Chile, both men and women attended major social events with their faces covered. Their presence was not always welcomed and could be framed as an attack against morality and the rule of law. In a long report written in the last decade of the eighteenth century, Judge José Rodríguez Ballesteros noted that the private celebrations of Santiago's "distinguished citizens" customarily involved arrangements for music and dances. "But," the judge continued, "*tapados* and *tapadas*" would often turn up in such numbers "that they block the yard's doors, the hall, and the dormitory, not allowing the house's owners to use these spaces." The covered attendees' lack of shame and respect was so profound that they sat among the formally invited and attired guests, even at events held in the governor's palace or the houses of royal officials. Defying any who tried to stop them, tapadas and tapados forced the doors and destroyed "everything" in their path. The judge asked that severe actions be taken to end the practice, or it would "continue" for "many years."[128]

Confirming Rodríguez Ballesteros's apprehensions, the practice remained popular well into the nineteenth century. José Zapiola, author of a remarkable memoir of his childhood, recalled being a part of such crowds of anonymous partygoers almost a decade after Rodríguez Ballesteros completed his report. Ironically, he attended thus covered one of the renowned concerts that the judge organized in his own house in Santiago.[129] C. E. Bladh, a Swedish traveler who visited Chile during the 1820s, recounted the "weird and unpleasant custom" local elites had of allowing "acquaintances and strangers into the courtyard, where a ball was held, to observe the dance." He noted that "even decent ladies attended covered, along with ordinary people, to satisfy their curiosity."[130] In the city of Coquimbo, men and women still adopted this costume to visit elite houses as late as the 1840s.[131]

The tapadas of Chile were more than passive groups of onlookers. Adopting this costume allowed women to intervene in visible publicness in spite of gender, racial, and social barriers. A striking example of this can be found in a letter María del Carmen Vial wrote to her daughter Josefa Bruzual in 1816. Vial described to her daughter the excitement caused by the arrival of a group of Russian officers in the town of Linares. Three balls were organized to celebrate the illustrious visitors, and Vial shared with her daughter plenty of commentaries and anecdotes about the first one. But she did not have as much to say about the second, which took place at the governor's residence, because "the *cholas* meddled their snouts first" and "the governor was distracted with some *tapadas*." The pejorative word *chola* designated both socially and racially inferior women and suggested that the covered women were poor, of impure ancestry, and unworthy of attention. According to Vial, their unwanted presence at the ball ruined the evening for her and the other aristocratic women, who soon left the event.[132] Although we do not have sources that give the tapadas' point of view, this episode shows how, by concealing their identities, covered women managed to transgress the racial and social boundaries associated with visibility and penetrate spaces other social actors believed were beyond their reach.

The practice of covering one's face reveals the multiple ways in which people negotiated visibility in Chile during the revolutionary period. By covering their faces, men and women suspended at least partly the idea of discipline and rule of law associated with visible publicness; they questioned the social and racial hierarchies that separated obscure from visible people; they navigated and even transgressed accepted gender norms; and they coped with the social demands associated with visibility. In doing so, they also reinforced the power of visibility. The essential characteristic of the tapada costume was that it allowed those who wore it to see without being seen. As part of the public that gathered in the courtyards and rooms of aristocratic houses, chinganas, and theaters, covered women and men reminded everyone that they were being observed. This anonymous public confirmed that visibility was a structural condition of the public space, the element that defined social standing, morality, and power. And yet, by refusing to show their faces, they also demonstrated that the hierarchies and rules associated with visibility could be challenged and subverted.

CHAPTER TWO

Signs of Difference

Clothes, Badges, and the Visual Construction of Inequality

On September 4, 1811, young military officer José Miguel Carrera led a coup d'état against Chile's first National Congress in Santiago. The Congress had been inaugurated exactly two months before, and, together with the revolutionary junta formed in September of 1810, it presided over Chile's first autonomous government. By September 4, 1811, the political climate was extremely tense, as multiple elite factions fought for control of the state. Congress in particular was divided between revolutionaries (who sought to implement reforms and move Chile toward a position of increased autonomy within the empire), royalists (who opposed the revolution and rejected further innovations), and moderates (who supported only limited changes to the colonial regime). That day, after positioning his troops in Santiago's central square, Carrera handed Congressmen a list with the names of the representatives that "the People" demanded be expelled from Congress as "enemies of the system."[1]

But Carrera was unfamiliar with the names on the list. He had left Chile in 1807 and lived in Europe until July of 1811. "I did not have enough information about my country, as I had only recently arrived," he wrote later about the weeks before the coup. Although the conspirators publicly claimed they wanted to purge Congress of moderates and royalists, their movement was truly aimed at eliminating rival political figures independently of their ideological positions. The day of the coup, the list of "enemies of the system" had been given to Carrera by a group of co-conspirators who gathered in Santiago's central square. According to his journal, upon looking at the congressmen, Carrera decided to replace the name of Congressman Juan Agustín Alcalde with that of his colleague Agustín Eyzaguirre. "I fancied," Carrera wrote, "that Eyzaguirre, with his golden buckle, his snuff box, his big cane, his deep red cape, and his velvet shoes had to be more royalist [*godo*] than Alcalde, who, although as dumb as the former, was at least young." Based on these observations, Carrera grabbed a pen, crossed out Alcalde's name, and scribbled in Eyzaguirre's.[2] What Carrera did not know was that Agustín Eyzaguirre was one of Santiago's most prominent revolutionary figures.[3]

Unfamiliar with local politicians, Carrera judged Eyzaguirre's political position based on certain visible evidence (clothing, accessories, age). As the anecdote reveals, Carrera considered these phenomena to be *signs*—visible manifestations of an invisible characteristic. In this he was not exceptional: for people in Chile during the Age of Dissent, visible phenomena almost always signified something. More specifically, the realm of visibility—the world of public, urban interactions described in the previous chapter—was crowded with signs of difference, visible expressions of dissimilarity in hierarchy, authority, and prestige. Questions about inequality were thus intimately tied to questions about visible signs.

During the revolutionary era, Chileans reimagined the power of visible signs, attributing to them the ability to produce rather than reflect social and political hierarchies. This constituted a departure from late colonial notions of order and visibility in which objects such as clothes, badges, and uniforms were supposed to render public (not construct) social differences. In both colonial and postcolonial Chile, local elites used dress to distinguish between the upper classes and the rest of society, and people wore badges, uniforms, and other distinctions as means to compete for social prestige. But starting in 1810 a discourse critiquing nobility and racial difference emerged in Chile, according to which signs of difference were at the same time false and powerful. As revealed by a series of debates that occurred in Santiago in 1823, postcolonial political agents began to consider clothes and badges not as manifestations of a reality that transcended them but as producing the differences they were purported to represent. Instead of reflecting real distinctions in merit or patriotism, signs of difference now came to express competing views about the origins and nature of social inequalities. From being a mirror of transcendent hierarchical differences, the realm of visible publicness became a stage in which actors disputed a mutable, openly contested social order.

Recognizing Difference

In colonial legal discourse, humans were fundamentally unequal. The concept most often used to characterize their differences was *calidad*. A protean category, calidad encompassed a person's skin color, ancestry, gender, wealth, trade, piety, merits, and honor, among other variables.[4] As some of the personal attributes linked to calidad were also considered inherited and inheritable, differences in calidad were implicitly or explicitly racialized.[5]

According to this philosophy, calidad, being unequally distributed among people, should give birth to a hierarchical social order in which those of higher calidad were at the top of the pyramid, and those of lower calidad were at the bottom. The role of government and the law was to uphold and protect this hierarchical structure.[6] In both colonial and postcolonial Chile, for example, parents had the legal right to object to their children's marriage choice if the potential spouse was found to be "inferior."[7] Similarly, individuals were subjected to different legal expectations and entitled to different privileges depending on the group to which they belonged or were ascribed. For instance, legislation protected people considered "worthy" from dishonorable bodily punishments such as public whippings.[8] This legal and political framework explains why litigants regularly constructed identity narratives about each other in court, as establishing their calidad was fundamental to define the legitimacy of their claims and dispute those of their rivals.[9]

Enforcing these differences was bound to be controversial, particularly in times of social and political transformation. During the eighteenth century, elites across the empire clashed over the definition of "merit" and its role in society. Bourbon officials and reformers, for example, claimed that the main component of merit was individual talent, whereas other groups emphasized the importance of ancestry and lineage.[10] In Chile, as in other Spanish American colonies, persons of African, Indigenous, and otherwise "impure" descent sought and obtained social and political elevation, challenging the allegedly immobile nature of the colonial order. Men and women from all walks of life—including castas and the enslaved—also framed themselves as honorable subjects, questioning elite ideas of fixed and self-evident hierarchies of merit and worth.[11]

Competition over rank and hierarchical difference generated a constant demand among all kinds of actors—from wealthy noblewomen to humble militia officers—for the government to "recognize" their worth, merits, and patriotism. For powerful families, this recognition could take the form of honorific (and often lucrative) posts in the administration, nobility titles, entailments, and access to military orders. By 1780, there were twenty-one nobles, ninety-eight members of military orders, and twenty-six entailments and entail-like privileges in Chile.[12] Colonial elites were eager to obtain these distinctions, as they served as visible markers of status that helped them cement their position against adversaries.[13] For ordinary people, the recognition of merits and patriotism could come in the form of financial benefits and visible distinctions—including medals and uniforms, which I discuss below. In 1792, for example, the commander of Santiago's Black militia, a prosperous barber named José Gregorio Arenas, requested a salary in recognition of his services to the monarchy.[14]

Like their peers elsewhere in the Spanish empire, late colonial Chileans expected inequality to be publicly evident. Struggles for recognition thus often took the form of battles over the visible expression of superiority and subordination. For example, men and women of all social origins demanded that others perform gestures of respect such as removing their hats in their presence, especially if others were watching. Failure to carry out such manifestations of deference could result in altercations and legal actions.[15] Similarly, elite colonists regularly disagreed and litigated over questions of preeminence and etiquette during public festivities and ceremonies.[16] As these examples show, individuals in the urban, public space needed to be permanently alert to potential threats to the visible expression of their worth and status.

Crucially, the people involved in such controversies presented themselves as preserving existing inequalities between them and others, not as creating them. In a perfect world, colonists seemed to suggest, there would be no clashes over preeminence and distinctions, as these would be publicly transparent and everyone would occupy their proper place in society. Thus, when individuals and groups demanded the king to visibly and publicly uphold their status and calidad, they were usually expecting the sovereign—the figure with the most direct access to the foundations of the social order—to simply confirm a preexistent difference between them and others.[17] They acted as if the visible world needed only to sanction forms of dissimilarity that transcended it. For subjects, then, existing visible hierarchies never fully corresponded to the real, authentic differences between them, and it was the task of politics to correct this discrepancy.

Regulating Dress

In Chile, as in the broader Atlantic world, clothing played important economic, political, moral, and religious roles. Its relevance derived directly from its visibility: clothes were among the most visible signifiers of an individual's social identity. As the hygiene practices of the period indicate, people thought of their clothes as visible extensions of themselves. An early nineteenth-century educational manual reminded children that personal hygiene consisted in washing their hands, heads, and clothes—that is, those parts and trappings of the body that others could immediately see.[18] People in Chile indeed paid much attention to dress, and used it regularly to describe and identify others. Clothes constituted a sort of social language, one that was expected to reflect "all the differences in the social fabric."[19] Dress and accessories were in particular supposed to visibly manifest an ordered and hierarchical society, identifying the population along racial, gender, and social lines.[20] Wearing given types of clothing was therefore not universally permissible. Dressing as someone of the opposite gender, as people did during carnival in Santiago in the early 1770s, was a crime.[21] It was also a crime to wear a religious habit without having professed or use a blazon without authorization. According to early modern European penal thinking, transgressing such laws was a crime akin to perjury or falsifying coins—it was an attack on truth and the natural order of things.[22]

In late colonial Chile, many worried about the reliability of conventional signs of personal identity such as dress and honorific treatments. When called on to determine a person's calidad in court, authorities and ordinary individuals often noted that signs of difference were no longer trustworthy and lamented that there was confusion between people of different statuses and "colors." These actors were not just voicing a paranoid fear of social disorder: during the second half of the eighteenth century, ordinary people seeking social promotion did indeed manipulate codes of dress (and the uncertainty surrounding them) to their advantage.[23] This reinforced the notion that signs of difference needed to be protected for them to reflect a transcendent social order.

In many colonial territories, these and similar concerns led to sumptuary laws prohibiting castas (especially African and African-descended women) from wearing certain clothes and accessories. In seventeenth-century Chile, the government expressly forbade Indigenous and African-descended people from wearing clothes other than those accorded to them by law.[24] Authorities passed similar regulations during the following century. The 1744 synod of Concepción ordered women of "noble" condition to wear mantles instead of simple shawls when attending church, cautioning them that failure to do so could lead them to be "mistaken" for "plebeian people, and servants, and Black and Mulatto women, whom the royal law [forbids] from wearing mantles." This order, the synod stated, was meant not only to regulate the morality of church attendees but also to enforce "the political distinction of their calidad."[25]

As described in chapter 1, during the second half of the eighteenth century the government repeatedly outlawed "disguises," forbidding people from wearing, in the words of one such edict, a "dress that does not correspond to their status, sex, and calidad."[26] These prohibitions were not abandoned during the republican era. In 1830, Santiago's intendant ordered that "no person shall be allowed to circulate in disguise or wearing clothes or insignia that do not correspond to them."[27] Although these edicts were not sumptuary laws explicitly designed to control upward mobility, they were nevertheless based on the assumption that certain clothes "did not correspond" to certain individuals. They were efforts to maintain society in what actors claimed was its proper order and to reinforce the role of dress as a visible marker of difference.

Binary Classifications

Elites and officials in Chile during the Age of Dissent used clothing to classify people primarily as either decent or indecent. According to this binary view, society was structured in two fundamental groups: the worthy few and the contemptible majority. During the late eighteenth and early nineteenth centuries, local elites considered themselves as honorable, respectable, and good people, while describing the rest of the population as dangerous, despicable, insignificant, and base.[28] In this context, each person's calidad, in the specific sense of whether they belonged to the decent or indecent segment of society, was supposed to be made visible in the quality of their clothing. This correlation between dress quality and calidad was not meant in principle to identify people on a scale of wealth but rather in accordance to differences in honor, merit, genealogy, and preeminence. As Cynthia E. Milton has shown for colonial Quito, in their requests for financial assistance from the government, individuals of presumed high status could cite their substandard clothing as evidence of their financial difficulties and the ensuing mismatch between their "real" calidad and their visible appearance.[29]

The ruling groups in Chile operated under the assumption that the majority of the population had access only to poor-quality clothes. This association was so strong that the word *roto* (worn out, ragged) came to designate, in a pejorative manner, the urban and rural poor.[30] According to the dominant groups, ragged and worn-out clothes reflected not only people's wealth but also their behavior and personality. Dress marked both a social origin and a way of life. Late eighteenth- and early nineteenth-century Spanish dictionaries thus defined roto as a man characterized by his licentious behavior *and* his tattered clothes.[31] Postcolonial newspapers reinforced this idea, arguing that ragged and dirty clothes contributed to the wearer's degradation and shaped his or her character.[32]

Along with quality, observers used fashion to differentiate between the dominant groups and the rest of the population. In Chile, as in similar colonial and postcolonial settings, donning what were considered fashionable clothes was a sign of social distinction, an indication that the wearer belonged to "civilized" society.[33] This mode of differentiation was

Figure 2.1. "Costumes des habitans de La Conception," Milet-Mureau, *Atlas du voyage de La Pérouse*, pl. 5. The woman on the right—who is of low social status, as indicated by her lack of footwear—nevertheless wears a dress similar in style to those of the elite women to the left. Notice also the two men wearing ponchos. Courtesy of Bibliothèque Nationale de France.

hypothetically reserved for those in the upper echelons of society. Visual evidence suggests, however, that other groups (likely prosperous artisans and petty merchants) competed to wear fashionable clothing similar to that of the elites (see fig. 2.1). The rural and urban poor, meanwhile, wore *ponchos* and other garments produced in domestic and Mapuche textile industries as well as cheaper clothes imported from Europe and Quito.[34]

Restricted availability of fashionable and decent clothing supposedly allowed for the easy visual recognition of social difference in both colonial and postcolonial Chile. For example, while on trial for conspiracy in 1840, soldier Juan de Dios Castillo declared he had attended a secret meeting with other "poor" people and some undetermined "gentlemen," whom he identified as such because they wore "tailcoats and jackets."[35] Conversely, elites regularly identified local dress and fashion styles such as the male poncho with non-elite people.[36] The binary classification implied by such distinctions, however, did not represent the full range of sartorial choices nor all the values social actors invested in their and others' clothing. Elite men wore exclusive and expensive ponchos,

Figure 2.2. "Arribano," Johann Moritz Rugendas, ca. 1838. This man's dress identifies him as an "arribano," a man from the southern frontier. Rugendas included this drawing in his *Album de Trajes Chilenos*. Courtesy of Biblioteca Nacional Digital de Chile.

for example, especially when in rural areas.[37] Traditional clothing, on the other hand, conveyed much more complex information than simply who belonged to the elites and who did not. Visual evidence from the nineteenth century suggests that people read garments such as ponchos and hats as signifiers of gender, geographic origin, occupation, and social status. In 1838 Bavarian painter Johann Moritz Rugendas published in Santiago a collection of lithographs titled *Album of Chilean Costumes*, which included representations of a peasant from the southern frontier, a muleteer, and a cart driver, all wearing distinctive clothes (see fig. 2.2).[38]

Subaltern people asserted their self-worth through clothing, showing that they did not think of themselves (or their clothing) as indecent. In 1753, an enslaved man named Pedro asked his owner, Bernardo Pintado, to provide him with a pair of shoes, as he claimed even animals in Santiago wore footwear. Seeing that Pintado dismissed his petition, Pedro requested the mediation of a local magistrate named Gregorio Blanco. Pressured by urban visible publicness, Pedro must have felt that shoes would reflect something important about him—about his honor and his worth—to have taken the effort to appeal to authorities and run the risk of enraging Pintado.[39] When in 1776 a free African-descended man named José María Rodríguez took money from the mail, he spent it immediately on visible signs of calidad: a good poncho for himself, a shawl for his wife, and some high-quality tack for his horse.[40]

Despite the many and varied exceptions and gradations to convention, this polarized system of signs had profound consequences on how people were treated in everyday life. Sometimes individuals misread others' clothes, classifying them in the "wrong" social group and treating them with what they retrospectively viewed as undue respect or scorn. In 1821, as commander José Bernardo Uriarte prepared to dispatch a group of conscripts from the town of San Felipe to Santiago, an unnamed woman approached the crowd and requested the liberation of a recruit. According to Uriarte, he was enraged to see this woman in "poor dress" challenge his orders at such a sensible occasion, so he "said to her whatever came to [his] mind" and sent her to prison. Only later would he learn that the woman came from a distinguished local family, making him fear for the legal repercussions of his actions.[41] Individuals of modest means resented the difference in treatment their lack of proper attire afforded them. In 1807 the cacique of the Indian town of Chiñigüe was reported as saying—in the context of a conflict with a wealthy aristocrat and hacienda owner—that officials favored his rival over him "because he didn't have a good poncho."[42] As such episodes confirm, the binary reading of clothing constituted a fundamental aspect of people's everyday experience in the realm of visible publicness.

The Privilege of Uniforms and the Politics of Ostentation

During the second half of the eighteenth century, military uniforms became a preferred marker of prestige and patriotism in Chile. Since the Seven Years War (1756–1763), the colony seemed increasingly vulnerable to attacks from rival empires, leading the Spanish crown to appoint military officers to the highest positions in the administration. The government also created new military units to complement the almost two thousand soldiers stationed in Concepción and its surrounding area. Between the 1760s and 1810s, the number of men enrolled in Chile's militias increased almost fivefold from thirty-six hundred to seventeen thousand. Reformers expected new units to resemble the regular army and allowed their officers to wear uniforms.[43] In this militarized context, colonial officials such as the governor and members of Santiago's city council routinely appeared in public wearing military garments.[44] Powerful men joined the militias partly to enjoy the privilege of wearing uniforms in public ceremonies and even secured military titles for their children.[45]

The prestige of military uniforms also attracted the less fortunate. Many of Santiago's artisans and craftsmen of African descent, for example, joined the city's free Black militias. Although the expense of a uniform was often burdensome, they were an integral part of the prospect of upward mobility that attracted prosperous and entrepreneurial artisans to the militia. Authorities in fact used the aspiration to wear military uniforms among African-descended men as a means of attracting them to the militia.[46] In Santiago after 1777, only soldiers of the free Black militia units and those of the Battalion of Commerce (integrated by "nobles" and poor Spaniards) had the privilege of wearing uniforms.[47]

Santiago's non-elite male population used military uniforms to identify themselves as *hombres de bien*, that is, as honored and virtuous men.[48] In July of 1787 the commander of Santiago's Black militia, José Gregorio Arenas, complained to authorities about Rafael Oré, an Indigenous man from Huancavelica, Peru. According to Arenas, Oré "describes and titles himself Captain of the Indians of Peru [. . .], wearing the respective uniform, without having a single document to prove it."[49] Oré seems to have worn this uniform frequently enough for others to notice he was captain of a militia unit that did not exist in Chile. Similarly, José Romero, an African-descended officer who, as we saw in chapter 1 was criticized by some because of his social visibility, seems to have considered his uniform an integral part of his self-understanding as a patriotic and meritorious subject. For his depiction in the 1850s by an unknown portraitist, Romero, who had a distinguished military career, chose to appear in full military costume—a visible marker of his honor and patriotism (fig. 4.7).[50]

Officers and soldiers were not the only men to wear uniforms. By the end of the eighteenth century, public employees, such as those of the Royal Treasury, wore government-regulated attire.[51] Students in Santiago's elite colonial schools such as the Convictorio Carolino and the Royal Seminary School also had the privilege of wearing uniforms and emblems.[52] After independence, legislative and executive authorities created detailed dress codes for civil servants, hoping these would properly reflect the hierarchies of preeminence and prestige between them.[53]

Along with uniforms came all sorts of badges, medals, pins, and inscriptions. Men belonging to military orders, as well as those serving in the Inquisition, wore exclusive badges representing their titles and honorific employments. The government also bestowed this privilege on individuals of distinguished merit and patriotism. In 1777 José Gregorio Arenas requested and obtained the "medal of the royal effigy," which was awarded to distinguished African-descended and Indigenous men in the Americas for their services to the crown. Arenas, a militia commander and the only man in Chile to have ever obtained this distinction, apparently wore this medal until the day he died in 1792.[54]

Authorities believed uniforms and badges could shape people's conduct. As external manifestations of preeminence and prestige, these objects were supposed to inspire obedience and respect in others.[55] Competition over these signs of difference could also be of service to the crown. Governor Agustín de Jáuregui, for example, saw uniforms and medals as a means to promote interpersonal emulation. When in 1777 the crown granted José Gregorio Arenas the medal of the royal effigy, Jáuregui organized an elaborate ceremony in his Santiago palace. As he informed his superiors in Spain, he decided to bestow the medal on Arenas in front of several military officers from both the regular army and the militias so that "it would serve as an incentive for them." "This, I believe," said the governor, "is the most effective way to make them try to be worthy of the same" distinction.[56] By visibly marking Arenas's services to the monarchy, the governor hoped to encourage others—including white officers—to compete for similar honors.

Producing Difference

Authorities and scholars attributed additional power to visible signs of difference when dealing with independent Mapuche groups. While colonial actors framed civilian dress, uniforms, and badges as reflecting preexisting and even transcendent differences between individuals and groups, in their interactions with the Mapuches they also conceived of these objects as capable of producing the differences they were supposed to represent. As mentioned in chapter 1, Mapuche society was structured around kinship groups and territorial and political alliances. While some leaders or logkos were more powerful than others, there was no single political, spiritual, or military authority, and alliances between different groups often shifted. Colonial authorities perceived this lack of centralized structure as detrimental to their efforts to colonize the Mapuche, as negotiations with some leaders could easily be rejected or overturned by others. Additionally, the central government in Santiago felt the need to establish direct relations with Mapuche leaders to bypass frontier colonists and military commanders who had their own dealings with Mapuche groups and often profited from armed conflict in the region.[57]

To improve the social standing and influence of those Mapuche leaders perceived to have positive relations with the central government, colonial officials gave each a cane or staff that represented their privileged relationship with the Spanish crown.[58] These canes had handles of silver, a metal that held important spiritual meaning for the Mapuches and which Spaniards associated with prestige and power. These objects played a central ceremonial role in Spanish-Mapuche parliaments or councils, more than ten of which were celebrated variously in the Concepción area, Santiago, and Valdivia during the second half of the eighteenth century. On these occasions—crucial events for Spanish-Mapuche relations—Spaniards distributed hundreds of such silver-tipped canes to Indigenous leaders.[59] Spanish officials also felt the need to provide the logkos with pieces of clothing such as felt hats and short pants.[60] In principle, clothes and canes were meant to foster the authority of these leaders—that is, to distinguish them from others—and to make their position enviable. In practice, colonial officials often complained that, rather than seeing the gifts as gracious concessions from the crown, Mapuche authorities felt entitled to this and similar largesse.[61]

After the war of 1766–1771, Governor Jáuregui and Indigenous leaders agreed on the establishment of a Mapuche embassy in Santiago. Spanish officials believed the ambassadors would allow for direct communications with the Mapuches (thus avoiding distortions produced by political and military actors in Concepción) and, most notably, would be a voice of authority in their own communities. While the ambassadors were expected to be important logkos already, Jáuregui sought to amplify their power by providing them with visible distinctions. In 1773, when he was still discussing the embassy's establishment with Mapuche headmen, he was already planning to give them "silver medals" with the king's "portrait."[62] The governor also decided to give the ambassadors a special "dress," which he claimed together with the medals would "greatly influence" other Mapuches, who would seek to obtain these "honors and distinctions."[63] When the five ambassadors and their retinue arrived in Santiago in 1774, Jáuregui celebrated them with a three-day "public parliament" to which the capital's "nobility" as well as royal and church officials were invited. On the third day of this parliament, Jáuregui gave each ambassador a silver medal with the royal effigy, intended as a distinctive reminder of the fidelity they owed to the Spanish king.[64] In 1782 Governor Ambrosio Benavides ordered the minting of fifty-two new medals "to distinguish the ambassadors who [currently] live in this capital" as well as those who would come in the future (the institution was in fact abolished shortly thereafter at the request of Mapuche leaders).[65]

During his tenure Jáuregui also established a school for Natives in Santiago to provide the sons of independent Mapuche logkos a Spanish education. Believing the prospect of wearing a distinctive uniform would attract candidates to the academy, in 1777 he allowed advanced students to don a gown. A year later, he informed the crown that the students "held in high esteem" this uniform and that it would motivate independent

Figure 2.3. "Araucanos," Gay, *Atlas de la historia física y política de Chile*, 1:5. "Araucano" is the name Spaniards gave to some Mapuche groups. Courtesy of Memoria Chilena, Biblioteca Nacional de Chile.

caciques to send their sons to Santiago.[66] The school spent large sums providing students with clothes, and when a group of Native parents requested to see their children in 1783, ten "well-dressed" students were sent to the frontier to both appease and impress them.[67]

Some colonial officials thought clothing could help subjugate the Mapuche. Although there was considerable cultural exchange between the sovereign Mapuches and the inhabitants of colonial Chile, the Mapuches had their own clothing styles that corresponded to their own systems of social differentiation (see fig. 2.3). In a long report sent in 1793 to Spain's minister of finance, Governor Ambrosio Higgins (who adopted the last name "O'Higgins" after the Spanish crown granted him the nobiliary title of Baron of Ballenary in 1795) advanced an ambitious plan to conquer the Mapuches. The plan involved prevailing on them to abandon their clothing styles and adopt Spanish dress, even rewarding those who excelled at the metamorphosis.[68]

These plans and measures reveal that, when dealing with the Mapuches, colonial officials believed signs of difference, rather than reflecting preexisting dissimilarities in hierarchy or calidad, could instead contribute to creating or abolishing them. This apparent contradiction with the conception of visible signs they applied to their own society may be explained by the fact that, for colonial observers, Indigenous social and political systems were not ultimately connected to a transcendental order dictated by God but were rather an expression of barbarism and incivility. It therefore seemed plausible that a superior power—as they claimed to be—could alter or modify Mapuche power structures and collective behavior through the use of signifying visible objects. This colonial view of the malleability of the Mapuche social world would eventually prove to be prophetic, although in an unexpected manner: during the following decades, it would be Chile's society that would be increasingly perceived as open to transformation through the manipulation of visible signs.

Questioning Nobility and Race

Although people continued to value uniforms and badges as evidence of male patriotism and merit during the long imperial crisis and wars of independence, some Chileans also began to challenge the basic assumptions about difference, privilege, and hierarchy on which much of these objects' power rested.[69] They openly questioned the benefit of having a social system built on difference and hierarchy and gave radically new meanings to distinctions in dress. Between 1810 and 1819, in particular, several prominent elites called for the abolition of nobility titles and racial categories. Although diverse in scope and nature, their critical discourses advanced two basic arguments that affected the way visible difference was framed in the country. First, they argued that legally sanctioning race and nobility had negative effects on society, including the reinforcement and replication of unfair privileges and discrimination. More than acknowledging previously existing inequalities, these categories produced them. Second, critics of nobility and race contended that both concepts were founded on patently false premises. They were illusions, fictions introduced by colonialism and based on meaningless *exterioridades* (visible but inessential elements). The critique of nobility and race, then, involved an evaluation of the origins of difference and the power of its visible signs.

People in Chile, as in the rest of the Spanish Atlantic world, advanced ideas of equality long before the revolutionary process started in 1808. During the eighteenth century, enslaved and free African and African-descended people, together with their legal agents, argued for the position that all humans were entitled to basic, natural rights.[70] There was the case, for example, of Juana Manuela Jáuregui, an enslaved woman who in 1757 went to court in Santiago to purchase her freedom—an action she asserted was grounded in natural law.[71] Similarly, artisans and craftsmen, people of mixed ancestry, rural migrants, domestic workers, Indigenous peoples, the enslaved, and many other subaltern people considered themselves worthy and virtuous, and defended their honor in court.[72] Their legal actions, although not necessarily demanding equality for all, challenged the elites' division of society between the honored few and the contemptible majority.

Perhaps aware of these trends, anticolonial conspirators Vergne, Gramusset, and Pérez de Saravia in late 1780 and early 1781 included in their revolutionary program—never made public nor put into action—the redistribution of land, the abolition of all legal differences between people, and the implementation of natural law.[73] Their goal was likely to garner the support of poor, African-descended, and other marginalized people. In the following decades, dominant groups continued to identify a desire for equality among the lower classes. In a manuscript dated July 10, 1810, aristocrat Manuel de Salas accused Governor Francisco Antonio García Carrasco of supporting and exacerbating plebeian demands for material and legal equality.[74]

As the Spanish monarchy collapsed, people in Chile began to openly promote civic equality, challenging in particular aristocratic distinctions. During the inauguration of Chile's first National Congress on July 4, 1811, Congressman Juan Martínez de Rozas defended "equality before the law" and deplored the existence of legal "privileges."[75] In Concepción later that year, a Franciscan friar named Antonio Orihuela, a member of Martínez de Rozas's faction, wrote a manuscript proclamation addressed to the "People of Chile." In it, he denounced rivals in both Concepción and Santiago, whom he characterized as aristocrats and nobles. Orihuela asked his readers "to remember that you are men of the same nature as the counts, marquises, and nobles." He added that "difference in rank and class was invented by tyrants" who used "the nobles" to keep the lower classes under control, and he called for the abolition of "badges, crosses, and other distinctions," which did not reflect true differences in merit. Directly addressing the country's poor (although not mentioning enslaved or Indigenous people), Orihuela asked them to "wake up" and "erase from the living, if possible, these evil beings . . . and [to raise] over their ruins an eternal monument to equality."[76]

Orihuela was not the only one who believed that nobility titles needed to be eliminated.[77] He shared this objective, most notably, with another early member of Martínez de Rozas's clique in Concepción, Bernardo O'Higgins—a man local elites mocked because he was born out of wedlock. Acting as Supreme Director of Chile, in early 1817 O'Higgins decreed all family arms to be taken down from house entrances, claiming that these visible signs did not correspond to true differences in "virtue and merit."[78] The regime's official newspaper celebrated this as a measure in favor of equality and against unnatural distinctions.[79] In September of that year, O'Higgins went one step further and abolished nobility titles. "It is forbidden," the edict read, "to give titles to the men formerly known as counts, marquises, nobles, and knights, nor are they allowed to admit them."[80] Close advisers warned O'Higgins that the measure might harm the administration's relationship with Santiago's elite as well as the revolutionary army's chances to win allies in royalist-controlled Peru. Some in the government even tried to prevent its publication, which they managed to delay until November of that year.[81] Despite this unenthusiastic response, O'Higgins pressed forward. On June 5, 1818, he signed a decree abolishing entails (*mayorazgos*). The decree was so polemical that its publication was permanently blocked by Congress and the courts. When O'Higgins was forced to resign in 1823, it was partly because Santiago's aristocracy opposed his rule.[82]

Some revolutionaries also rejected racial categories in the name of equality. Philosopher and lawyer Juan Egaña believed republican regimes were incompatible with racially divided societies. But while he explicitly framed racial prejudices as baseless, he also considered them too powerful for the government to erase. Instead of fighting racism, Egaña thought the state should focus on making Chile's population racially homogeneous—which in practice meant eradicating African, African-descended, and Indigenous peoples. In 1810, for example, he advocated the abolition of the slave trade as a means to limit the number of African people entering the country.[83] In a constitution he drafted in 1811, Egaña declared that it was "convenient . . . that no differences exist between [the country's] citizens, not even accidental ones." His draft constitution therefore included a mandatory program of racial miscegenation designed "to destroy" these differences by forcing nonwhites to marry whiter partners.[84]

Others were more concerned with correcting the racial prejudices Egaña believed were impossible to eliminate. An educational text written anonymously around 1814 characterized the preeminence given to whiteness as a colonial product. The document asserted that "all men are equal" and that physical differences between humans were merely "accidental." The document went on to accuse "Spaniards" of basing their oppressive rule on the "miserable and ridiculous" argument of "white color." Equality, in this view, meant recognizing merit—understood as moral and intellectual qualities—beyond external signs of difference, such as skin color and racial labels.[85]

During these early stages of the revolution, Chile's new authorities adopted measures to dissociate skin color and ancestry from ideas of honor and merit and erase some racial distinctions and hierarchies. Between 1811 and 1819 the state proclaimed Natives and citizens of Chile to be equal before the law, abolished the Indigenous tribute and legal privileges, and replaced the legal categories of "Indian" and "Spaniard" with that of "Chilean."[86] The abolition of the Indigenous tribute was likely much desired by the Indigenous communities, many of which had petitioned not to pay it for decades (and sometimes actively refused to do so).[87] But statutory equality was ultimately harmful to Indigenous communities, as it deprived them of important legal protections. After declaring their equality, the Chilean state enacted laws in 1826 and 1830 to survey Indigenous lands and assign individual property titles to them.[88] It is hard, therefore, not to see behind much of this egalitarian rhetoric a project intended to favor large hacienda owners, who—as seen in chapter 1—had for decades wanted to seize Indigenous communal lands.

Elites were reluctant to extend full legal equality to Africans and people of African descent. This was likely due to colonial notions of casta difference (according to which the offspring of Natives and Spaniards could eventually become Spaniards, while people with African ancestry could never claim purity of blood) and the continuation of slavery until 1823.[89] The government did nevertheless adopt some measures it claimed promoted equality, such as the renaming of Santiago's Black militia in 1813 (erasing any reference to skin color) and the granting of the honorific title of "don" to its officers in 1814.[90] These measures also had an underlying political purpose—in this case, obtaining the support of free Black people, who, as elsewhere in Spanish America, valued declarations in favor of equality.[91]

Between 1810 and 1819 politicians and government officials denounced racial and aristocratic distinctions as irregular and unfair forms of assessing merit and assigning honor. Although their criticisms were often more strategic than dogmatic, they shared certain common features. On the one hand, they proposed that true distinctions between humans were to be found not in "external" manifestations such as family arms, badges, skin color, or racial titles, but in more immanent qualities. On the other hand, they claimed that these exterioridades, while meaningless in and of themselves, had relevant social effects, including reproducing unjust forms of inequality and dividing the political body. Discourses against aristocratic and racial categories often coincided in that these artificial yet influential forms of distinction were inventions of Spanish tyranny and the colonial regime. Following this line of reasoning, signs of difference were not reflections of real inequalities but remnants of an unnatural, harmful, and outdated social and political system.

Challenging Signs of Inequality: The 1823 Debates

The most explicit debates over the relationship between signs and inequality in revolutionary Chile took place in Santiago in 1823. Early that year, a military uprising forced General Bernardo O'Higgins to resign from his post as Supreme Director of the Republic. With the fall of the reformist O'Higgins administration, new political voices emerged, some of them demanding radical social and political change. Their aspirations found sustenance in a most unlikely institution: Chile's provisional senate. This interim body began work in April 1823 and was composed of nine men appointed by the provincial assemblies of Santiago, Coquimbo, and Concepción. Its members included relatively conservative politicians like Agustín Eyzaguirre (the man José Miguel Carrera expelled from Congress in 1811) as well as reformers such as José Miguel Infante and Manuel de Salas. The senate's original purpose was to serve only until the incoming administration of Supreme Director Ramón Freire could organize elections for a new, permanent legislature. In an unexpected turn of events, the new senators launched a set of radical reforms directly aimed at ending some of the most dramatic expressions of inequality in Chile. Of greatest consequence, they abolished slavery and banned whipping as legal punishment.[92]

The 1823 provisional senate also openly addressed the relationship between inequality and its exterior manifestations. That May it passed an act mandating the abolition of a civic-military order known as the Legion of Merit. This institution had been founded by the O'Higgins government in 1817 to replace the Spanish military orders and nobility titles it had eliminated. The Legion was meant to distinguish those men who contributed to Chile's independence, granting them honorific titles, legal privileges, access to the administration, and financial aid. Although O'Higgins likely created the Legion to consolidate his and his army's power, the government declared that its objective was to encourage men—be they in the military or not—to compete for virtue, honor, and glory.[93] By 1823 the institution included around 170 members.[94]

The Legion's power and prestige was intimately tied to the visible assertion of inequality. According to its founding decree, its members were required to wear badges that publicly signified both their membership in the Legion and their position within its internal hierarchy.[95] Portraits of members of this order made during this period show them proudly exhibiting these distinctions in their suits and uniforms.[96] The O'Higgins administration explicitly presented these and other decorations it created as superior versions of colonial distinctions. In October 1817 the state newspaper, *Gazeta de Santiago*, compared the Legion, a distinction of "personal virtue" and "merit," to "the vain and fantastic titles" and "insignificant decorations" of colonial times.[97] In this view, the Legion replaced false and harmful modes of distinction with a new set of visible insignia that represented true differences in patriotism.

The provisional senate did not agree with this interpretation. In a communication to the government dated May 28, 1823, the senators argued that the Legion was "an aristocratic order" that privileged "only a few," when in fact "thousands of men" had helped secure Chile's independence.[98] In a second communication, the senate described the Legion as "medieval" and likened its abolition to that of nobility titles.[99] The senate was not the only political actor to openly criticize the institution. In March of that year, *El Tizón Republicano*, a newspaper published by adversaries of O'Higgins, had argued that "distinctions and hierarchies such as Chile's Order of Merit" were "an invention of tyranny." Using "exterior decorations" to divide society, the newspaper claimed, was incompatible with a republican regime.[100]

These arguments echoed the criticisms of racial categories and nobility titles voiced in previous years. Unlike in those cases, however, the senate's decision sparked a public discussion over inequality and the need to eliminate all exterior decorations.[101] Some men in postcolonial Chile—whom we can label conservatives, though they did not describe themselves as such—worried about the spread of egalitarian doctrines in the country. To them, visibly upholding hierarchies was essential to reconstitute what they regarded as a broken social order. This was the case of lawyer and philosopher Juan Egaña. After the battle of Maipú in April 1818, which shored up Chilean independence, Egaña wrote a report for Santiago's city council on how to restore order in the country. In it he claimed that the government had to maintain "external and political decorum," and he proposed that all officials adopt "a ceremonial dress" and serious manners and that the population be forbidden from treating authorities with familiarity.[102]

In 1823, among the Legion's members and supporters, was Juan Egaña's son and collaborator, Mariano Egaña, then secretary of government. Mariano cared about visible difference as much as his father: in May that year he signed an edict mandating that citizens treat public employees with deference and requested the latter wear their exclusive uniforms and distinctions at all times.[103] In two communications to the senate from June 1823, Mariano Egaña defended the Legion as a useful instrument for rewarding citizens and incentivizing patriotism.[104] Newspapers supportive of O'Higgins expressed similar views, claiming that the Legion did not create new inequalities but only reflected those produced by nature, education, and hard work.[105] The senate did not press the matter, but further political developments soon rendered the Legion obsolete.[106]

The issue of visible distinction was at the core of Secretary Egaña's disagreement with the senators, as a second and simultaneous controversy shows. On May 26, 1823, the senate declared that only the Supreme Director would be called "Your Excellency." All other authorities were to be addressed in the third person singular. The senators had concluded that the traditional honorific treatments for civil authorities were incompatible with "the liberal principles of the republican system adopted in Chile."[107] Mariano Egaña again challenged the senate's resolution. On June 5, the same day he signed his first defense of the Legion, he informed the senate that the administration opposed the measure. Echoing concerns expressed in his father's 1818 report and his own edict of May 1823, Mariano Egaña argued that extinguishing honorific titles "would cause disorder" and "insubordination." "Even in the most democratic republics," the secretary contended, "there cannot be equality" when it comes to obedience. While abolishing honorific treatments would have no effect on the well-educated, the same could not be said of "the inferior classes." For Egaña, it was "irrefutable" that exterior forms such as speaking manners and "dress" had an enormous influence on the public. Denying honorific treatments to authorities would expose them to the insults of the plebe.[108] A newspaper that weighed in, supporting Egaña's position, argued that these exterioridades did not create inequality but simply recognized true, existing differences in merit.[109]

The senators responded vehemently. They accused Egaña of believing that the "moral force" of institutions depended on "purely exterior formalities" such as honorific treatments and "dress." Real authority, they declared, did not derive from mere appearances. With reasoning similar to that which they had advanced against the Legion, the senators argued that honorifics, as exterior signs of respect, were artifacts of the monarchical past unsuited to the nineteenth century.[110] Not hearing back from the administration, the senate declared that its silence would from then on be considered tacit approval and proceeded to publish the law.[111]

A new, regular senate replaced the provisional one in August of

1823. The incoming legislators, among whom Juan Egaña played a leading role, were far more skeptical of reformist initiatives. On November 12 Senator Pedro Arce, a priest, submitted a bill to forbid members "of the regular orders" from "publicly wear[ing] their sacred habits in profane spaces."[112] The senate unanimously rejected Arce's bill the same day it was presented.[113] Still, despite its swift rejection, Arce's bill opened a new discussion about visible inequality.

While we cannot be sure of what Arce wanted to achieve with his bill, some context can help in determining his intentions. Since the late eighteenth century, reformers in the Spanish Empire had seen the regular orders as corrupt and in need of change, such as allowing priests to renounce their vows. Following this line of reasoning, in May of 1823 the provisional senate tried to establish some oversight of the country's convents, sparking another confrontation with the government and generating a heated debate in the press.[114] As a Dominican friar, Arce was particularly invested in this campaign. In 1817 the O'Higgins administration appointed him commissary of regulars, in which capacity he sought to expand secular control over the regular orders. Arce even questioned his own membership in the Dominican order. By 1823 Santiago's ecclesiastical authorities had denied his request to "secularize" (abandon convent life and renounce his order's vows).[115]

Considering these antecedents, Arce's 1823 bill was probably aimed at diminishing the regular orders' social visibility and promoting a kind of practical secularization for their members. Some observers certainly interpreted it in this way. A few weeks after the bill was debated in the senate, another Dominican friar, Tadeo Silva, indirectly denounced it as an attack on the church in his newspaper, *El Observador Eclesiástico*. In Silva's view, reformers wanted to force regular priests not to wear their habits to erase a positive form of inequality, one that granted priests their social prestige.[116] An anonymous pamphlet likely published around this time also argued that religious habits could not artificially create differences in reputation; they only manifested the honor and distinction that those sporting them had already obtained.[117] In the eyes of his adversaries, then, Arce was trying to intervene in the realm of visibility to subvert a natural form of social inequality and curb the regular orders' influence.

On November 17 the senate asked its Committee on Religious Affairs to comment on Arce's rejected bill. The committee—composed mostly of priests—produced a lengthy report that it presented to the senate on December 4. Although the committee found the bill to be absurd and contradictory, it also felt the need to defend dress hierarchy and its role in visible publicness. "Nothing contributes more to [social] order than our ability to recognize each other," they argued. "These are the origins of dress, insignia, preeminence, and distinctions, [all of which] announce the character, profession, and even the conduct of one another, and serve to create the respect each one deserves." Dress, insignia, and uniforms reflected preexisting differences (they helped people "recognize" one another), while they also created hierarchical relations of respect and obedience. "Thus," the committee continued, "the soldier is permanently reminded, because of his uniform and that of his officer, whom he must obey." Like Juan and Mariano Egaña before them, the members of the committee associated exterior signs with the preservation of social order. Dress constituted a "holy illusion" that helped capture other people's "attention, and that predisposes [them] to trust the orders they hear." Visible signs, the committee concluded, had always been instruments of power, and getting rid of them was "impracticable."[118] Arce's bill was archived and never discussed again.

As these debates show, once the O'Higgins regime collapsed in 1823, the visible expression and production of inequality became a matter of much contention. The main issue bearing on all these discussions was whether there was room for legally mandated visible signs of dissimilarity in a republican regime. Two positions emerged. The first group contended that visible recognition of hierarchy was a useful political tool as well as an essential aspect of social order. Some among these argued that signs of respect and hierarchy not only accurately represented differences in merit and patriotism but that they created relations of obedience and deference necessary for society to function correctly. Others held that these signs were powerless by themselves and that their influence derived from the fact that they represented real and not artificial differences. The second group started from the opposite assumption. Instead of representing true, existing differences in honor and prestige, they argued, these visible signs created artificial and unfair distinctions, dividing the social body. Recognizing merit and virtue through exclusive orders and signs of hierarchy was anachronistic and incompatible with a republican regime. Some of those who advanced this argument also maintained that signs and other external manifestations of hierarchy had no intrinsic power; nevertheless, they cared enough about them to seek their extinction.

Those on both sides tended to recognize in visible publicness the capacity to create and shape power relations. In this they differed little from their colonial predecessors. But the attitude toward notions of difference and their visible expression had shifted dramatically. Visible signs no longer reflected a reality that transcended them, even for those who defended their accuracy. They were now explicitly presented as instruments of social and political engineering capable of producing—and erasing—the same differences they were supposed to reflect. The disagreement over how to use visibility as a political tool was so pivotal that it became a central aspect of Chile's emerging postcolonial partisan identities. Parallel to the 1823 debates, a realignment of political forces was taking place in the country. Two main groups emerged from this process, conservatives and liberals, each increasingly identified with one of the two positions described above. Signs of difference were now at the core of Chile's postcolonial political fracture.

Pipiolos and Pelucones: Fashion Trends and Partisan Identities

To understand how signs of difference became so important for Chile's postcolonial partisan identities, we must first return briefly to the early stages of the revolution—specifically, to José Miguel Carrera's identification of Agustín Eyzaguirre during the September 1811 coup. Carrera based his judgment of Eyzaguirre's political identity on a set of signs that denoted his social position. He saw in Eyzaguirre's golden buckle, red cape, and velvet shoes (items that supposedly distinguished the most prestigious and meritorious men in the colony) signs of reactionary politics. Evaluating Eyzaguirre in this way, Carrera seems to have been the first to use clothing as a means of partisan identification in revolutionary Chile. By establishing a correlation between social position and political identity and cataloging those at the top of society as enemies of the revolution, this mode of identification relied on the colonial binary system of classification while inverting its values. Objects that formerly identified the worthy few were now politically suspicious precisely because they betrayed an anachronistic view of social difference and its outward manifestation.

Around 1800 new French- and British-inspired fashion trends became popular among Chile's elites. Thereafter, the aristocratic style of previous decades coexisted with simpler, more "bourgeois" sartorial choices. These new clothing styles were still markers of distinction, as they reinforced elites' sense of belonging to the "civilized" world.[119] Nevertheless, they also represented a radical change in how clothing signified difference. More homogeneous visually, these new trends were not in principle structured around the display of multiple signifiers of status and hierarchy. This contrast is especially evident in the portraits of male members of Santiago's elite by painter José Gil de Castro during the time royalists controlled the city (1814–1817). While some royalists chose to be represented in the old aristocratic style to manifest their calidad, others adopted much less ostentatious forms of dress (see figs. 2.4–6).

Figure 2.4. Portrait of Judas Tadeo Reyes, José Gil de Castro, 1815. Reyes was an influential civil servant and a staunch royalist. He is portrayed wearing an elaborate uniform, a cane, golden shoelaces, and two badges, one representing his role in the Inquisition and the other his membership in the Order of Calatrava. His choice of being represented with so many signs of difference contrasted with newer and simpler fashion trends. Only his *Brutus* hairstyle is reflective of the latter. See Majluf, *José Gil de Castro*, 155 and Cruz, "El traje como signo de los nuevos tiempos," 208. Courtesy of the Museo Histórico Nacional (Chile).

Figure 2.5. Portrait of Vicente García Huidobro y Morandé, José Gil de Castro, 1815. García Huidobro y Morandé was marquis of Casa Real. He is represented wearing a relatively sober but luxurious tailcoat and jacket, a cane, the badge of the prestigious Order of Carlos III, and, according to historian Isabel Cruz, a powdered wig. See Majluf, *José Gil de Castro*, 157 and Cruz, *Patrimonio artístico en Chile*, 378. Courtesy of the Museo Histórico Nacional (Chile).

In postcolonial Chile, people began associating these different clothing styles with political identities that, in turn, were defined by their respective attitudes toward inequality. This was true of the two main political groups that emerged in Chile in the 1820s: liberals, also called *pipiolos* ("novices"), and conservatives, also referred to as *pelucones* ("bigwigs"). Crucially, both pipiolos and pelucones were nicknames given to these groups by their rivals. Although it would be anachronistic to conceive of pipiolos and pelucones as modern political parties, they were nonetheless more than merely pragmatic and interest-oriented factions. While the boundaries between them were fluid at times, they were nevertheless loosely organized around competing and sometimes mutually exclusive views on politics and society.[120]

Observers had used the labels "pelucones" and "liberals" since the early stages of the revolution. Pedro Arce, for example, criticized the "indecent *pelucones*" in a letter he sent to General O'Higgins in 1817.[121] But such references were brief and did not necessarily indicate defined partisan identities.[122] It was not until 1823 that these identities emerged more clearly in a process concurrent with, and informed by, the debates about signs of inequality. In May of 1823, the same month the provisional senate decided to abolish slavery, the Legion of Merit, and honorific treatments for government authorities, *El Tizón Republicano*, the anti-O'Higgins newspaper, published a poem that seems to be the first full description of the pelucones on record. The poem began with a portrait of the colonial pelucones as men who carried genealogical books and wore wigs, golden-threaded clothes, velvet shoes, and tricorn hats. Pelucones, then, designated the old colonial elite and its obsession with visible difference. Present-day pelucones, the text continued, no longer wore the same clothes. They preferred simpler garments, such as black suits, silk buttons, and English-style shoes. But even if they dressed differently, they were the modern-day version of those colonial men who "fought over blazons" and were in "perpetual war" over their genealogies. Modern pelucones could not accept that "today the law treats as equal the noble and the plebeian" and that now only "merits and virtues" decide each person's standing in society.[123]

For *El Tizón Republicano*, the label "pelucones" identified a partisan group characterized by its attitude toward inequality and its exterior manifestations, precisely at a time when signs of difference were being debated in both the provisional senate and the press. This description echoed earlier efforts to identify and describe this faction. In 1820 a satirical dictionary published in Santiago mockingly identified as "gentlemen" (*caballeros*) those who valued inequality and rejected the "revolution in

Figure 2.6. Portrait of Ramón Martínez de Luco and his son, Fabián Martínez de Luco, José Gil de Castro, 1816. A wealthy royalist, Martínez de Luco's garment is relatively sober. The only distinction he wears is the scapular of the Virgin of Carmen—perhaps an invocation for divine protection. The text to his right describes the painting as a "memory" addressed to his children. See Majluf, *José Gil de Castro*, 171. Courtesy of the Museo Histórico Nacional (Chile).

hierarchy" taking place in Chile.[124] But unlike caballeros, the moniker "pelucones" clearly struck a chord and soon entered into popular use. In September of 1824 the newspaper *El Liberal* described pelucones as a group that based people's worth "upon nobility titles, family connections, and money." "Arrogant" and "presumptuous," the pelucones were the opposite of the liberals, whom the newspaper described as "true republicans" who valued real "merits" and "services to the nation."[125]

In the liberals' minds, the category of pelucones connected a fashion style, a social position, and a political affiliation—particularly the defense of social inequality.[126] This directly affected the way in which signs of difference were now interpreted. Pelucones, as noted above, meant "bigwigs," referring to the powdered wigs that distinguished men in positions of power and wealth during colonial times (see fig. 2.5). By referencing the colonial wig, liberals used the category of pelucones to denounce the visible ostentation of hierarchy and the construction of difference based on superficial elements such as clothing, genealogy, and accessories.[127]

Pelucones, whose ranks comprised men such as Juan and Mariano Egaña, felt they were the voice of reason in a country that was descending into chaos. They believed that radical change would bring only trouble and that hierarchy and obedience were fundamental for steering the country away from anarchy. They insisted that they needed to keep Chile safe from their ignorant, hot-headed, and corrupt rivals, the pipiolos.[128] We do not know exactly why conservatives gave liberals this nickname, although according to the latter it was meant to deride them for their supposed lack of means.[129] Liberals even accused pelucones of seeing them as *despedazados* (torn apart, which referenced ragged clothes) and *rotosos* (from the deeply pejorative *roto*).[130]

Some conservatives did indeed suggest a connection between what they perceived to be their rivals' poverty and their political affiliation. Pointedly, they and other adversaries of liberals gave the latter the additional nickname of *descamisados* (shirtless), perhaps suggesting that they could not afford proper attire.[131] Aware of this, some liberals tried to use the label to their own advantage. In 1827 a group of radical liberals published the newspaper *El Descamizado*, in which they contended that descamisado was the Spanish equivalent of *sansculotte*.[132] The newspaper, of which only one edition was released, featured a woodcut of a Phrygian hat on its masthead (see fig. 2.7). Revolutionaries in Chile and other regions of Latin America had adopted this accessory, also known as a "liberty cap," to symbolize the revolutionary commitment of those who did not have the means to wear sumptuous, expensive hats.[133] *El Descamizado* hailed equality and was directly addressed to Chile's artisans and poor urban and rural workers, much like Orihuela's 1811 proclamation. By adopting "shirtless" as a form of identification, the faction behind the newspaper inverted the political values traditionally associated with clothing, turning a sign of indecency into a symbol of political virtue.

These partisan identities were not purely elite affairs, as the scholarship on the subject has assumed.[134] Subaltern individuals were not only aware of the existence of these and other factional identities but actively participated in their emergence. Luis Ambrosio Morante, an actor of African descent, used the word *pelucón* in a deriding manner during a

Figure 2.7. *El Descamizado*, 2 May 1827. Photograph by the author.

theater performance in 1823, an offense for which he almost spent a night in prison.[135] We can imagine other non-elite individuals similarly contributing to establish and popularize these terms in their daily interactions, such as when sharing the news in the urban space; going to church or the theater; attending social gatherings with their faces covered; or working as house servants, tailors, seamstresses, barbers, and laundresses—occupations that required familiarity with elite sartorial choices. These partisan distinctions could not have been irrelevant to the marginalized people who took part in mutinies and rallies in the 1820s. Take, for example, the demonstration of July 19, 1824, in which elite liberals, together with poor and nonwhite men, demanded the abolition of the 1823 constitution (the work of renowned pelucón Juan Egaña). Though sources barely mention their presence, it seems likely that some non-elite participants in the event, such as tailor José Gregorio Cañas, shared the pipiolos' view that the constitution was too conservative and elitist.[136] He was not alone. A few days after the demonstration, none other than Luis Ambrosio Morante celebrated on stage the fall of the constitution as a victory over the aristocracy.[137]

Popular politics was in fact essential to this fracture. If attitudes toward inequality, real or alleged, were so central to postcolonial political identities and programs, it was in no small measure due to subaltern demands for civic and material equality.[138] For example, in an effort to attract Santiago's artisan organizations and militia members to their ranks (many of whom were of African descent), some political factions in 1829 promised they would support and promote equality.[139] A pamphlet issued that year explicitly called on artisans, former members of Chile's Black militia unit, and soldiers of the national guard to support the "popular" party (the federalists), which was founded on the principle of equality.[140] According to one critical observer, in 1829 conservatives and estanqueros had persuaded barbers, shoemakers, and bricklayers in Santiago that "Chile will become a new Santo Domingo" (referring to the Haitian revolution).[141] The importance of equality in postcolonial partisan politics was therefore not arbitrary, nor did discussions about egalitarianism take place in an elite echo chamber. This did not mean that all or even the majority of Chile's popular classes favored liberals; many ordinary men and women rejected their perceived irreligiosity, and in fact most of Santiago's artisan organizations supported other groups in the elections of 1829.[142]

During the years of political experimentation between 1823 and 1830, Chileans used clothing not only to distinguish between rival political identities but, more importantly, to indicate opposing views about inequality. Liberals' and conservatives' ultimate disagreement was not over how well clothes and accessories matched people's "real" calidad but over the very need to make such visible distinctions. None of these groups framed these objects as reflections of transcendent differences; on the contrary, they used them to make intelligible their disagreement over how to organize social relations in the country. This mode of reading visible signs put in question the values elites commonly attached to garments. The liberal discourse, in particular, inverted the traditional, binary reading of clothing, suggesting that it was but a social convention. Through these controversies, then, political factions contributed to transform visible publicness into an arena in which competing understandings of hierarchy and status collided.

The binary system of identification based on quality and fashion remained in force after 1823 and so did the interest in uniforms, medals, and badges as means of social distinction for both elites and subaltern individuals. But something had changed during the revolutionary era. People now used badges and dress to discuss, reinforce, and denounce inequality and power relations. As a result, the connection of signs to what they were supposed to represent became muddled—not only could they distort "real" social hierarchies, but they could create them. Through the realm of visible publicness, Chileans could now reach and modify a formerly transcendent social structure. For elite and ordinary people alike, this must have represented a radically new experience of the visible public sphere, one in which they permanently encountered and produced plural, antagonistic visions of the social order. Visible signs of difference were now also visible signs of radical dissent—public expressions of the unfixed nature of society.

CHAPTER THREE

Visible Disunity

Material Culture and Partisan Identification in the Public Arena

On September 27, 1814, revolutionary authorities in Santiago stormed the room that petty merchant Romualdo Antonio Esponda rented in the city. The government had received information that Esponda was secretly fabricating a royal flag. In his room, officials found just such a flag as well as a folder containing a Spanish royal coat of arms and a set of letters, both made of enamel, meant to be pasted to the royal flag once it was finished. When assembled, the letters spelled "Long live Fernando the Seventh, King of Spain and Emperor of the Indies." The discovery of these objects presented a serious problem for the merchant. The leaders of the insurgent government felt particularly vulnerable at the time, as the royalist army was advancing from the south toward Santiago. They immediately imprisoned Esponda and, after a hasty two-day trial, sentenced him to publicly make amends for the crime of insulting Chile's new, tricolor flag. He was punished in Santiago's central square, as mentioned earlier in this book, and then forced to cry "Long live the Fatherland" while the public executioner burned his royal flag and hoisted the new tricolor over its ashes.[1]

When royalists regained control of the capital in early October, Esponda wrote a petition to the government asking to be compensated for his suffering. He argued that his ordeal was the consequence of his "public ostentation" of loyalty to the king during "Chile's insurgency." Esponda asked the government to restore his reputation and honor, which had been stained by his public lashing. Santiago's new, royalist city council as well as Crown attorney Prudencio Lazcano backed Esponda's request, framing him as a royalist hero. In 1815 the government sent Esponda's petition to Spain and in the meantime appointed him treasurer of Santiago's customs, an honorable and profitable position.[2] On April 3, 1816, King Fernando VII declared Esponda Knight of the American Royal Order, an extremely prestigious distinction, and conferred on him the status of nobleman.[3] The king also ordered a ceremony to be celebrated in Santiago's central square in which Esponda would be covered with royal flags to signify the crown's protection. On November 30, 1816, in the presence of an "attentive and large crowd [*pueblo*]" that included some of Santiago's most important political and military authorities, the celebration took place according to the monarch's instructions.[4]

Before revolutionaries discovered his unfinished royal flag, Romualdo Antonio Esponda was but a modest merchant, son of a Navarrese surgeon whose orbit did not extend to elite circles.[5] Because of what he claimed was his visible royalist commitment, Esponda was both punished and rewarded, transitioning from ordinary subject into knight and nobleman. Yet, sadly for him, his story did not end there. Like many other royalists, when the revolutionary forces of General José de San Martín defeated the royal army in Chile in early 1817, Esponda and his family fled to Lima. We know of his ultimate fate thanks to a petition that his mother, María Mercedes Sánchez, dispatched to Spanish authorities in November of 1818. According to Sánchez, her son joined a military expedition from Peru to Chile in early 1818. At the decisive February 12 battle of Chacabuco north of Santiago, the royalist army was again defeated, and Esponda—his name well known among revolutionaries, his mother claimed—was executed.[6] Probably to highlight her son's merits to obtain financial compensation from the government, María Mercedes Sánchez tied the death of Esponda to his fame as a royalist and thus, indirectly, to that fateful day on which he had been discovered preparing a royal flag.

Esponda's reversals of fortune and ultimate demise reveal the risks and possibilities of visible political identification in Chile during the Age of Dissent. By "identification," I mean the ways in which individuals both self-presented and were classified by others.[7] In revolutionary and postcolonial Chile, observers judged actions such as preparing a royal flag or wearing a tricolor rosette as signs of people's internal political affiliations—evidence of their political loyalties or sympathies. At the same time, people used or wore such objects in visible urban spaces as well as on visible parts of their bodies or accoutrements (hats, clothes, the chest) to self-identify as supporters of one or another partisan group or figure. This mutually reinforcing process, partly founded in the strong nexus observers established between visible signs and people's social status, is what I call here "political identification."

Political identification during the revolutionary and postcolonial eras was a disruptive practice. According to official political norms, visibility should project an image of unity, and individuals should compete to be identified as loyal and patriotic subjects or citizens. Visible publicness would in this manner confirm and reinforce the government's legitimacy. But with the process of accelerated political decomposition that began in

1808, people like Romualdo Antonio Esponda and the authorities who punished and rewarded him transformed the nature of visibility. By displaying division and attracting antagonism, political actors willingly (and unwittingly) contributed to the destabilization of all official claims to unanimity, turning visibility into a field for the contestation of legitimacy and making dissent an unavoidable dimension of political life.

Visible Unity

In standard colonial politics, visible publicness was officially reserved for the manifestation of society's political and religious unity. During public ceremonies, the colony's most prestigious and visible urban spaces, such as Santiago's central square, were supposed to become stages on which the community would express its unanimous support for the government and joyful acceptance of the king's sovereignty. These demonstrations of popular support were produced by institutions, collective bodies, and individuals alike. Participation in public festivities was oftentimes mandatory and represented a financial burden for those with limited means, such as artisans and militiamen.[8] Foremost among these political rituals during the second half of the eighteenth century were proclamations of a new king or royal accession (ceremonies celebrated in Chile in 1760, 1789, and 1808), receptions or investitures of governors, Corpus Christi, the parade of the royal pennant, and celebrations of news from the royal family (of births, weddings, etc.).[9] According to the hegemonic discourse, the parades and public performances that occurred on these occasions reflected the colony's unity as well as its hierarchical political and social order.[10]

These ritualized expressions of unity and conformity rendered visible the relationship between sovereignty and truth. By the second half of the eighteenth century, the monarchy's official doctrine held that political sovereignty derived from God's will. Humans were not expected to question this absolute truth, which transcended them, rather only to recognize it. Recognition was performed through the visible acclamation of the sovereign, which certified the correspondence between the political community, its religious and political principles, and the government. In this political philosophy, acclamations were not necessarily considered expressions of the people's will but rather a medium through which this harmonious relationship was made manifest. This is why official documents describing public ceremonies contained repeated and often formulaic references to the cheers, fireworks, illuminations, and military salvos that took place in them—these were the conventional, visible signs of the government's legitimacy.[11]

The purpose of this political community sanctioned by God was pursuit of the common good, a course of action that was objectively beneficial for society as a whole.[12] According to this vision of politics, this goal could not be achieved without unity, harmony, and support for the government. The main role of religious and political authorities was therefore to prevent conflict, dissension, and division, including among ordinary subjects.[13] Dissent could not be tolerated, as it represented a dangerous anomaly that disturbed the social order and endangered the body politic. Officials routinely blamed factions for instigating expressions of discord and antagonism within the colony, implying that disagreement necessarily had its origins in groups of disgruntled people who valued their own interests over the objective benefit of the community.[14]

In the hegemonic discourse, then, visible expressions of dissension were undesirable and should not be tolerated. Officials prohibited the manifestation of an alternative to either Roman Catholicism or Spanish royal sovereignty, including in the urban space. Authorities and ordinary people alike required individuals to constantly display religious and political conformity to the point that non-Catholic visitors to postcolonial Chile often complained of the gestures of respect toward Catholic symbols demanded of them in public spaces.[15] The government also had to manage other, less egregious forms of dissension, such as conflicts between officials, to ensure that disputes did not become public or visibly evident and that colonial officials always projected an image of harmony and unity to the rest of society.[16]

Despite official emphasis on concord and harmony, social and political clashes were common in late colonial Chile, and people of different backgrounds openly debated and challenged governmental decisions. Partisan life was equally intense: colonial elites operated in cliques organized around shared economic interests, family ties, and geographical origins.[17] My claim, thus, is not that there was no criticism of state authorities during colonial times or that there was less political or social conflict than occurred during and after the revolution. Rather, it is that the principles of unity and harmony set the parameters of legitimate political action—including in the realm of visible publicness.

The normative role attributed to unity and concord shaped people's political strategies. In late colonial Chile, officials such as governors and Audiencia judges had an interest in portraying their jurisdictions as united under their rule, while other, less powerful agents had an incentive to visibly display their conformity (unless they sought a confrontation). Individuals wishing to be officially recognized as good citizens—as "patriots" in the eighteenth-century meaning of the word—had to present themselves as actively contributing to society's well-being while avoiding visible displays of factionalism and disunity.[18] Props like the royal pennant, the king's portrait, and the royal coat of arms allowed colonists to perform their patriotism and render visible the community's alleged political and religious unity.[19] Perhaps the most important of these objects was the royal portrait. Under Bourbon rule, government officials and the population alike deployed official royal portraits to express the colony's unanimous support for the monarchy. Exemplary ceremonies included the celebrations surrounding the accession of King Carlos IV in 1789.[20] Colonial elites bought copies of the royal portrait and mounted them in their residences as well as on public buildings. Sometime before 1796, a merchant living in Spain named Nicolás de la Cruz acquired copies of the queen's and king's portraits and had them installed in the city hall of his hometown, Talca, where most of his family resided. Royal officials agreed to consider this among the merchant's merits.[21]

The Collapse of the Monarchy and Individual Identification

In August of 1808 alarming news reached Chile: Napoleon Bonaparte had captured King Carlos IV and most of the royal family and was holding them prisoner in France. Moreover, both Carlos and his son Fernando had renounced the Spanish throne, which now belonged to Napoleon's brother Joseph. Although unexpected and unprecedented, these events were the culmination of years of mounting fiscal, political, dynastic, and military problems plaguing the Spanish empire.[22] The two-decade-long rule of Carlos IV had generated much opposition among Spanish elites as well as the wider population, although popular anger remained focused on Manuel Godoy, the king's powerful minister and adviser. Worried about his own succession prospects, Fernando staged a coup against Carlos in March of 1808, prompting the monarch to abdicate. But Carlos almost immediately disavowed his decision, leaving Spain in an uncertain political situation. A few months later in May of 1808, Napoleon put an end to the dispute by forcing both Carlos and Fernando to renounce the throne in his brother's favor.

It is worth noting that when Napoleon attacked the Spanish monarchy and installed a puppet regime in 1808, elites in Spain did not react uniformly. Proclaiming Fernando as their rightful king, most peninsular Spaniards joined efforts to reject the French and their government. This movement was initially led by anti-Godoy political forces who blamed the former minister for causing the crisis. But other Spaniards collaborated with the new, French-supported regime, either because they wished to retain their official appointments or because they believed the new administration represented an opportunity to change the monarchy

Figure 3.1. Coin (2 *reales*) bearing King Carlos IV's effigy, 1791. Courtesy of Museo de Artes Decorativas (Chile).

for the better. This situation left colonists in Spanish America in an awkward position. With limited information about events transpiring across the ocean, officials appointed during the Godoy administration had to navigate suspicions of treason and doubts about which political forces were prevailing at any given moment at the heart of the empire.

Political uncertainty and the ensuing crisis of legitimacy quickly rendered public manifestations of loyalty problematic, even in distant colonies such as Chile. In 1808 Chile was under command of a Spanish military officer named Francisco Antonio García Carrasco. García Carrasco had only recently become interim governor after his predecessor unexpectedly died. While these circumstances shielded García Carrasco from being perceived as a creature of Manuel Godoy, they did not protect him from accusations of treason.[23] In August of 1808 news of Fernando's accession to the throne in March arrived in Chile together with news of the royal family's imprisonment that had taken place two months later.[24] The information was confusing, and proclaiming Fernando as the new king was a risky move. Although García Carrasco quickly followed the example of the viceroy of Río de la Plata in Buenos Aires and announced Fernando as the colony's new legitimate king—swearing loyalty to him on September 20—he apparently hesitated to make other visible commitments. Most notably, he delayed stamping Fernando's bust on newly minted coins until later that year, even though the director of Santiago's royal mint repeatedly requested his authorization.[25] This was not a minor omission, as the presence of the king's likeness on official coins represented his uncontested sovereignty and was officially framed as an expression of loyalty to the monarch (fig. 3.1).[26]

Despite the uncertain situation in the Peninsula, most subjects across Spanish America decided to visibly show their support for the captive king. More than self-evident or traditional displays of loyalty, their actions should be considered efforts to construct and reinforce monarchical legitimacy in a profoundly contested and uncertain political moment.[27] The king's portrait played a major role during this early stage of the crisis. His painted image was paraded and publicly celebrated in places such as Chuquisaca (today Sucre, Bolivia), Buenos Aires, Huamanga (Ayacucho, Peru), and Santa Fé (Bogotá, Colombia).[28] Chile was no exception. For example, the king's portrait was displayed and paraded in Santiago during the proclamation of Fernando VII on September 20, 1808.[29]

The most elaborate of these visible demonstrations of fidelity toward Fernando was held in the north coastal city of La Serena in July of 1809. After obtaining a copy of the king's portrait from a Spanish ship, the local commissioner staged a reception for it as if it were the monarch himself. On July 10 the commissioner issued a proclamation calling on the population to visibly display its "love" for the monarch during the event. The next day, the portrait was brought into the city—which was draped with flowers and other decorations—on top of a magnificent carriage driven by twelve soldiers. The elaborate reception of the portrait was accompanied by traditional expressions of acclamation and joy, such as fireworks and military salvos. After the event La Serena's commissioner ordered two notaries to write a detailed description of the ceremony, which he sent to Chile's governor as evidence of the population's support for the captive king (and, implicitly, of his own loyalty and zeal). The document emphasized the harmonious collaboration between religious, military, and political figures and mentioned how "poor farmers" expressed their joy to see their king. The report paid particular attention to a "poor and wretched" old woman who, as the royal carriage approached, threw incense in front of her house so that the portrait-king should not suffer the foul smells of animals and "waters." "No one told her that her presence was required in that parade, nor did she have any motivation other than the spontaneous impulse of her love and appreciation for the sovereign," the notaries stated. The unnamed woman's alleged spontaneous gesture certified both the authenticity of her sentiments and the unity of the community behind the captive Don Fernando.

Figure 3.2. Miniature portrait of Fernando VII, 7.50 x 6.10 cm, ivory. Courtesy of the Museo Histórico Nacional (Chile).

The document ended by arguing that "everyone" in La Serena wanted to "distinguish themselves as the king's most faithful and loyal vassals."[30]

This need to identify themselves as patriotic subjects was apparently widely felt in the colony. A new way of deploying the king's portrait emerged during this period among those who wished to highlight their personal support for the monarch. According to the memoirs of Francisco Antonio Pinto (born in 1785), between 1808 and 1810 "most of" Santiago's young aristocrats "carried in their hats the portrait of Fernando, in the manner of a rosette" (see fig. 3.2).[31] These miniature portraits, which people in many other areas of Spanish America also wore, allowed individuals to more clearly present themselves as loyal and patriotic subjects. During the proclamation of Fernando VII's accession in Santiago, public servants and military officers attached portraits of the captive king to their hats.[32] In Concepción the intendant ordered all male residents to do likewise.[33] This practice suggests that, given the climate of suspicion created by the imperial crisis, elite men felt compelled—or were explicitly obliged—to visibly and individually display their loyalty to the monarch.

Women felt the same need. According to one source, in August of 1808 elite women in Valparaíso were eager to obtain copies of Fernando's portrait to wear during the official proclamation of the new king's accession the following month.[34] The episode of Dolores Reyes—recounted in detail in the introduction—suggests that at least some elite women in Chile owned and wore miniature portraits of Fernando VII. Pinned near the heart, the miniature portrait was intimately connected to gendered vows of remembrance, love, and fidelity. It thus became an appropriate medium through which women could make manifest their individual, political, and affective attachment to the king.[35]

Producing Unanimity

Behind these visible expressions of unanimous support for an exiled, untested, would-be king, division and mutual suspicion reigned. As soon as news of the abdications at Bayonne arrived in Chile in August of 1808, diverse colonial elite factions accused one another of conspiring against the monarchy.[36] As the situation in Spain evolved into a political revolution and the French appeared to be winning the war, the idea of forming an autonomous junta that would rule Chile in Fernando VII's name gained traction among local but not appointed elites. Many people, including the governor and the judges of the Audiencia, opposed this course of action, which they argued constituted a rebellion against the monarchy. After months of bitter political struggle—which included the forced resignation of Governor García Carrasco in June of 1810—the pro-junta faction finally prevailed, and on September 18, 1810, an assembly of over four hundred men proclaimed and installed a governing junta in Santiago.

Despite its fractious origins—or rather because of them—supporters of Chile's first autonomous government presented it as the product of the people's unanimous will. The edict sanctioning the junta's formation argued that the assembly had been convoked to eliminate "the dangerous differences in citizens' opinions" sparked by the imperial crisis.[37] The junta thus claimed it was not beholden to any faction but was instead the instrument the people had created to bridge their internal divisions. The junta and its followers cited visible expressions of popular support as evidence of the veracity of these claims. The September 18 edict stated that the junta had been "acclaimed" with "uniformity" by all the men who attended the assembly.[38] Two days later, the junta sent communications to city councils across Chile in which it stressed that people had demanded its creation "unanimously and peacefully" and that it had received "universal acclamation."[39] Agents were soon dispatched to all the colony's far-flung districts to secure matching declarations of acclamation and support.[40] The junta would later cite these "uniform" celebrations as proof of the population's consent to its creation.[41]

As one might suspect from these forcibly spontaneous, even defensive, colony-wide displays of unanimous support, profound divisions could not be long suppressed. Those opposed to the formation of the junta left accounts of how they were excluded from participating in the September 18 assembly in Santiago and how the dissenting voices of those who managed to attend this reunion were silenced and erased from official records. They also argued that the junta met with no exclamations of joy and support from the general populace or that any such claims were exaggerated in official documents.[42] Regardless of their veracity, these critiques reveal that subjects started conceiving visible publicness as a site of contestation, a field of political activity through which the government's legitimacy could not only be confirmed but also disputed.

New Signs of Political Identification

The Spanish imperial crisis of 1808 led to a civil war pitting royalists against revolutionaries. Almost immediately after its establishment in May of 1810, the junta of Buenos Aires was drawn into war with the viceroyalty of Peru, which soon became South America's royalist bastion. While Buenos Aires's government expected support from the revolutionary junta established in Santiago in September of that year, Chile remained neutral. Long-standing economic, social, and political ties with Peru made war appear too risky for a financially and politically weak regime. But local moderates could not contain the revolutionary process, and in September of 1811 the Carrera family and their allies took control of Chile's government. Led by military officer José Miguel Carrera, the new administration, which lasted until April of 1813, advanced a more radical political agenda complete with fiery rhetoric, drawing revolutionaries into clearer confrontation with royalists.

On July 4, 1812, amid official celebration of the US independence in Santiago, the Carrera government publicly introduced a patriotic rosette and flag. The new emblems had blue, white, and yellow stripes, and complemented the government's efforts to create a new, national army.[43] During the festivities, the administration demanded civil servants and military officers to wear the rosette and hoisted the tricolor flag, entwined with the US flag, in Santiago's most public places.[44] The innovative symbols, which came to replace the Spanish flag and rosette then in use, were again widely displayed during the celebration of the junta's second anniversary in Santiago in September of 1812. On this occasion, the Carrera government also presented a new coat of arms.[45] The ceremonial contexts in which these objects were first announced and celebrated clearly suggest they were meant to be seen as signs of Chile's national sovereignty—in other words, they represented the idea that sovereignty resided in something called the Chilean nation (however one wished to define it). The flag, rosette, and coat of arms thus embodied a new source of political legitimacy as well as a new mode of expressing patriotism. This had enormous implications for how people participated in visible publicness: instead of automatically relying on a set of objects closely associated with the Spanish crown to signify loyalty and adherence to the common good, individuals now had to consider adopting and displaying new items that represented alternative and even contrasting views of patriotism, sovereignty, and political legitimacy.

The creation of the tricolor rosette forced many colonists to consider the implications of political self-identification (fig. 3.3). Established by decree on July 1, 1812, the government claimed that the new symbol was meant to distinguish "the soldiers of the Fatherland"—that is, that its use was restricted to military men.[46] Fifteen days later, the Carrera administration authorized ordinary people to use it, arguing that the "patriotic emblem" would serve to "distinguish the virtuous citizen."[47] In the following days, authorities extended this authorization to priests and issued a decree ordering public employees to prove their patriotism by wearing the new rosette on their hats.[48] These measures were more radical than they may seem at first glance. According to a chronicle that priest Melchor Martínez wrote in 1815, a heated debate took place among royalists after the publication of the decree requiring public employees to wear the rosette. The order, Martínez wrote, put royalists in a bind, since "it was no longer allowed" for them to "hide their opinion, and their system, by means of an ambiguous conduct." Royalists believed the plan was to force them to come out as enemies of the administration by refusing to wear the rosette. Accepting the rosette, on the other hand, would be the equivalent of "having the mark of the beast written on the forehead." A group of prominent royalists gathered to discuss the issue of whether to abide by the order. Some argued that to display the rosette "was to declare oneself a revolutionary," while others asserted that "the cowl doesn't make the monk, and thus this external sign was by no means a manifestation of disloyalty." Martínez did not report the debate's outcome, scoffing that the whole discussion was pointless, because the government already knew who its enemies were.[49] Later testimonies

Figure 3.3. Tricolor rosette used by Colonel Ramón de la Cavareda around 1830–1840. Courtesy of the Museo Histórico Nacional (Chile).

suggest that most people complied with the government's demand.[50] In any case, the episode reveals how Chileans began to carefully consider the signs of political affiliation they deployed and how they framed visible publicness as strained by antagonistic divisions.

People used the rosette to identify both themselves and others along factional lines. In letters addressed to both the archbishop of Lima and Spanish authorities in 1813 and 1814, Santiago's interim bishop, royalist José Santiago Rodríguez Zorrilla, accused a rival bishop named Rafael Andreu y Guerrero of having strolled Santiago's promenade of the tajamares wearing the tricolor rosette "in front of an immense audience" in 1812. This had "scandalized" and embarrassed the local clergy, Rodríguez Zorrilla argued, and constituted evidence of Andreu y Guerrero's revolutionary sympathies.[51] Rejection of the new rosette came in different forms. Some privately held onto the old rosette, as when in 1813 a group of conspirators in Valparaíso allegedly sported the "royal cockade" to symbolize their royalist commitment.[52] Others refused to wear the new one. In October of 1814 Rodríguez Zorrilla cited as evidence of the local clergy's loyalty to Fernando VII that they "had firmly and constantly rejected to use this insignia of rebellion."[53] Not only royalists rejected the tricolor rosette. Earlier in 1814 Juan Mackenna, a supporter of the revolution who opposed the Carrera faction, wrote that the new rosette was a "brand" used by José Miguel Carrera on his "slaves," adding that he had "always seen it [. . .] as the greatest absurdity" and "never wore it."[54]

The new flag generated similarly heated reactions, being rejected by some and appropriated by others as a new sign of patriotism. The government strongly identified the flag with the war against royalists, which began when forces dispatched from Peru reached Concepción in early 1813. The revolutionary army regularly used it, and insurgent authorities gave it a central role in civic and religious ceremonies.[55] In March of 1814 Spanish colonel Carlos Spano died in the town of Talca allegedly defending the new flag against royalist troops, prompting the government to declare him the flag's first patriotic martyr.[56]

By then Chile's revolutionary factions had become increasingly divided over the need and purpose of the flag and rosette. The armed conflict had forced José Miguel Carrera to leave the government in 1813 to lead the war effort far from Santiago. In November of that year, elites in the capital formed a new government with the aim of negotiating a peace deal with royalists. The new authorities named Bernardo O'Higgins to replace José Miguel Carrera as commander of the Chilean army, also excluding the Carrera faction from government. Thus, soon after Spano's alleged martyrdom in defense of the tricolor flag in March of 1814, O'Higgins and the new government under Supreme Director Francisco de la Lastra signed a peace treaty with royalist General Gabino Gaínza, agreeing to abolish the patriotic rosette and flag and revert to using the traditional Spanish royal insignia.

On May 11 Lastra explained this measure to the revolutionary army, asserting that the creation of "the national flag and rosette" had been "an abuse" perpetrated by "an arbitrary government," going as far as to claim that it had "caused the war" between Santiago and Lima.[57] Abolishing these symbols, Lastra argued, could restore peace between the two warring parties. But the decision was met with resistance by soldiers and officers alike, who trampled, burned, and "hanged" the Spanish flags and rosettes they were sent.[58] Military men continued to wear the tricolor rosette, and those donning the Spanish rosette were harassed and assaulted.[59] The government regarded such reactions as seditious but was forced to concede.[60] Facing opposition from officers and troops, O'Higgins forbade military men from wearing any emblems in their hats until the treaty with Gaínza was ratified by the viceroy of Peru.[61]

Some civilians had apparently also grown attached to the new symbol. In 1817 a new administration led by General O'Higgins accused petty merchant and cigarmaker Santos Arenas of having helped José Miguel Carrera depose Lastra as Supreme Director in July of 1814. In court Arenas denied having participated in that "revolution." But he also added that "he took particular pleasure" in the removal of Lastra's government, as he hoped a new administration would lift the ban on the tricolor flag and "that the Spanish flag would be taken down" from the government's palace.[62] Arenas's declaration is remarkable. Although it would have been easier for him to simply reject the charges, he preferred to remind the O'Higgins administration and its followers of their behavior three years earlier, when they supported the restoration of the Spanish flag. Meanwhile, Arenas—who was likely excluded from formal political participation given the modesty of his trade—portrayed himself as a true patriot: not identified with any specific faction, but politically and affectively attached to the national flag.

The case of Santiago merchant Romualdo Antonio Esponda, as we have seen, reflects the opposite position: that of a man of modest means who rejected the tricolor flag. According to Santiago's chief of police, Bernardo Vera, Esponda's preparation of a royal flag suggested he was involved in "a conspiracy against the Fatherland."[63] On trial, Esponda argued that "as the government proclaims obedience to Fernando VII," it did not seem implausible that it might "adopt the Spanish" flag in a forthcoming religious festival.[64] Unconvinced, Santiago's authorities examined Esponda's papers in search of proof of the alleged conspiracy. Among the papers seized was a manuscript entitled "Prophecy of Saint Rose of Lima," supposedly extracted from a book describing the life of the eponymous seventeenth-century saint. According to the manuscript, in a prophetic vision the miraculous nun "bitterly cried at the loss of the kingdom of Chile, which, having rebelled against God and their King, also raised its banners [*banderas*] against Spain."[65] The "banners" in this prophecy can be interpreted both as a metaphor for the establishment of an independent army and, more literally, as a reference to the creation of new flags. The prophecy would in this case express rejection both of the revolutionary process and of the tricolor flag. Ultimately, while revolutionary authorities could not prove Esponda was involved in a conspiracy, he was nevertheless found guilty of sedition.[66]

Esponda was likely preparing the Spanish flag to display his support for the royal army once it entered Santiago.[67] He was certainly not alone in anticipating their arrival. When royalist forces reached the capital in early October of 1814, they found it almost entirely covered in royalist flags.[68] Apparently even the poor residents of the city's suburbs managed to hoist Spanish flags atop their houses.[69] An article published in a revolutionary newspaper in 1817 stated that more than six thousand flags welcomed General Mariano Osorio when he entered the city in 1814—a tremendous number for a city of no more than thirty thousand inhabitants.[70] Esponda was evidently just one of many who were secretly producing and distributing Spanish flags to receive the royalist army. Displaying the Spanish flag in this manner, to show individual support for the royalist government and its victories, was a new form of political action, one that emerged in response to the revolutionary regime's promotion of the tricolor flag. As one witness said of the widespread residential flying of imperial banners, "these flags were new, as before 1810 it was not customary to use them."[71]

Even the miniature portraits of Fernando VII became a means of expressing the colony's political fracture. As recounted in this book's introduction, in 1814, as war between insurgents and royalists raged in southern Chile, a woman named Dolores Reyes visited Bernardo O'Higgins's mother while wearing "on her chest a beautiful portrait of Fernando VII."[72] While Chile's new authorities claimed to be acting in Fernando's name, wearing the king's portrait was clearly an offensive display of support for the royalist cause. The episode suggests that Chileans excluded from formal political participation such as Dolores Reyes used visible publicness to express their own antagonistic visions of political legitimacy.

The creation of the tricolor rosette and flag, as well as people's reactions to them, turned visibility into a field of contention. As Chile's experience in factional politics during this period did not destroy the "concept of unanimity" that had defined colonial politics, to quote historian Sol Serrano, this new manner of using the field of visibility was revolutionary.[73] The stage once supposedly reserved for displays of unity and harmony became an arena in which royal and revolutionary flags and rosettes competed. While all actors in these struggles claimed to represent true patriotism, their actions shattered the sense of harmony and unity that was supposed to rule visible publicness. Displaying or refusing to adopt these signs became a conscious choice, a marker of one's personal affiliation—a measure of division and dissension rather than unanimity and conformity.

Royalist Reaction

Royalists ruled Chile from late 1814 until early 1817. In their efforts to return Chile to the conditions of the prerevolutionary era, they restored the colonial ritual calendar and revived such festivities as the parade of the royal pennant and the swearing in of Spanish governors.[74] Between November and December of 1814, ceremonies of the "renovation" of the oath of loyalty to Fernando VII took place in cities and towns across the colony.[75] The royal portrait and flag reappeared during these celebrations. In November of 1814 the city council of San Felipe sent a resident to Santiago to obtain a copy of the royal portrait as well as a royal flag for display during the town's renovation of the oath of fidelity to the restored king.[76] In Santiago, Fernando's portrait was also venerated in ceremonies such as the inauguration of General Osorio as governor in early 1815 (see fig. 4.6).[77] People similarly used the royal portrait to highlight their individual loyalty to the monarchy. Sometime between 1814 and 1817, a man named José Antonio Tagle bought a portrait of the king to adorn Quillota's town hall. The portrait was paraded through the town and celebrated with a thanksgiving mass before being installed in the building.[78]

Royalists banned the insurgents' rosette, flag, and coat of arms and persecuted those who had created and used them. These former markers of patriotism now served to identify the revolution's main culprits. In November of 1815 the now-reestablished Audiencia wrote to Osorio's successor, Governor Francisco Marcó del Pont, reminding him that, according to a royal order of June 1814, harsh punishments must be reserved for the main agents of the revolution. The royal order offered no explanation as to how to identify them, so the judges advanced their own views on the subject. The main culprits of Chile's revolution, they claimed, were those who sought to make the colony independent through actions such as hoisting the tricolor flag, removing the Spanish coat of arms and the royal portrait, and commanding insurgent troops.[79] Thus, when pressed to think about how to identify Chile's most culpable revolutionaries, the judges cited their relation to signs of political affiliation alongside overt military actions. Support for an object that visibly represented a new principle of sovereignty and legitimacy, such as the tricolor flag, was evidence enough for the Audiencia to label someone a dangerous insurgent.

Royalist authorities followed this criterion when judging people's past political activities. In June of 1815 an Audiencia judge investigated the actions of insurgent Manuel de Salas, asking witnesses if he ever supported "removing the royal coat of arms" and "portraits."[80] A criminal investigation on the political conduct of Anselmo de la Cruz that same year not only proved that he had been a prominent revolutionary leader but also that "he supported the demand to remove His Majesty's arms and to hoist the tricolored flag."[81] These signs were considered evidence of revolutionary commitment in other contexts as well. In 1817 an anonymous royalist in Valparaíso prepared a list denouncing all of the city's "insurgents." The list included a woman named Carmen Ruiz, with the annotation that "the silverware she uses has the mark of the *Patria*."[82] This suggests that Ruiz—who apparently belonged to the local elites, as the list's author gave her the honorific treatment of "doña"—used silverware engraved with Chile's coat of arms, a form of self-identification sufficient to brand her as one of Valparaíso's insurgents.

Aware of how supporting and displaying the flag and rosette was being used against them, some of the men accused of being revolutionaries argued that these objects did not represent their inner convictions and that they had been imposed on them by the Carrera faction. Agustín Eyzaguirre, who, as a member of the junta, had signed the decree establishing the tricolor rosette in 1812, argued that "the mutation of flags, rosettes, etc., happened at a time in which force was the only ruler."[83] This reasoning was echoed by a group of men who had been exiled to the prison island of Juan Fernández. In an undated exposition they sent to the viceroy of Peru, the prisoners argued that none, not even those who now pretended to be the most fervent royalists, had dared to reject the tricolor rosette.[84]

On the opposite side, the government now recompensed those who had worn and defended the royal insignia during the revolutionary period. This was the case with Romualdo Antonio Esponda, who, as seen earlier, was given a prestigious title and made a noble. In the ceremony honoring him in Santiago's central square in November of 1816, the royalist administration lionized Esponda as an example of patriotism and fidelity, a man who had been openly loyal and visibly faithful to his king—unlike other, presumably less committed royalists. Esponda's apotheosis, when he was covered in royal flags, exemplifies how visibility was haunted by radical dissension. Even as it celebrated unity and loyalty, the ceremony reminded people of Esponda's ordeal at the hands of an adversary faction and implicitly suggested that the monarchy was but one system among multiple alternatives—that it was as "constructed" as others were.[85] Performances of unity now contained an explicit or implicit reference to the community's profound political fracture.

Disputing Legitimacy in Postcolonial Chile

When revolutionary forces regained control of most of Chile in 1817, they sought to be legitimized through ritual acclamations and displays of unanimity. Portraits served to celebrate and endorse the new rulers. In ceremonies such as the proclamation of Chile's independence in 1818, images of military commanders like José de San Martín took the place previously reserved for the monarch's portrait.[86] Portraits were also used outside such official settings to express support for individual political and military figures. After O'Higgins was exiled in 1823, his supporters kept his portrait in "visible" rooms in their houses to show their loyalty to him.[87]

The government of Supreme Director Bernardo O'Higgins (1817–1823) also created new representations of Chile's national sovereignty. The new administration placed an enormous coat of arms on the facade of the government palace, replaced the king's portrait with new symbols on coins minted in Chile, and created new flags and patriotic rosettes.

Although their shape and design changed over the years—the final versions of the flag and rosette were adopted in 1817, while Chile's definitive coat of arms was established by decree only in 1834—these signs eventually became valid representations of Chilean nationality to most political players. I have found only scant evidence of people advancing alternative signs of identification: In 1819 a follower of José Miguel Carrera in Talca hoisted a new flag during a military uprising against the O'Higgins regime.[88] In 1824 supporters of O'Higgins wore a "red and black rosette" in Santiago to make visible their opposition to the new government.[89] It is unclear whether any of these signs was meant to compete with or replace the new flag and rosette.

The rosette continued to serve as a marker of individual political affiliation. During the O'Higgins administration both military and civil officials regularly used it.[90] Like the Carrera government in 1812, the O'Higgins administration also made wearing the rosette mandatory on certain occasions. In February of 1818, as royalist forces from Concepción were marching toward Santiago, the government ordered the arrest and interrogation of every individual "not wearing the national rosette [. . .] with no exception by class or status."[91] By forcing all men to wear the rosette, the government likely sought to create an image of unanimity and union at a critical moment for the administration.

Authorities now wanted compulsory identification applied to as many people as possible. In 1820 Juan Egaña proposed a law obliging "all citizens" to "wear tricolored rosettes in their hats" during official festivals. Women "not wearing their church dresses"—that is, the traditional cowl and mantle—were to adorn their heads with "tricolored garlands."[92] This was the first time a prominent figure thought of extending the use of mandatory signs of identification to most of Chile's adult inhabitants, regardless of status and gender. A year later the government decreed that "all citizens" wear the rosette during the anniversary celebration of the battle of Chacabuco (1818).[93] Santiago's city council established its own regulation for the public festivities, ordering women to wear "a flower garland" or "tricolored lace over their heads." Men, on the other hand, were required to wear liberty caps to express their patriotic sentiments.[94] These directives apparently reflected a desire to expand the social reach of visible expressions of patriotism, as ordinary people had more access to flowers and liberty caps than to fine lace and rosettes.[95] It is difficult to evaluate the impact of these developments, as I have not found evidence of women or non-elite men wearing tricolor garlands or rosettes during this period.

Flying the new Chilean flag atop residences and other buildings became a widespread practice, and governments between 1817 and 1833

Figure 3.4. "Street of San Domingo, Santrago [sic] de Chile," Graham, *Journal of a Residence in Chile*. According to the book's table of contents, this image was "sketched on the 18th September," day of Chile's National Festivity. Houses are adorned with what seems to be Chilean flags.

made displaying flags mandatory during political festivities.[96] Although dictated from above, these expressions were meant to be signs of the citizenry's spontaneous jubilation. Failure to comply with such orders could result in an unwelcome visit by the police.[97] Coerced or not, people across the country flew flags from their houses to celebrate civic and military events and to solemnize political ceremonies and patriotic festivals.[98] When Chile's independence was officially proclaimed in Santiago in 1818, the tricolor flag was "put on the façades of all [the city's] houses" (fig. 3.4).[99] According to official sources, every house in the small town of La Ligua hoisted the national flag during celebrations in 1819 and 1823.[100] During a patriotic festivity in San Felipe in 1821, people allegedly hoisted over two thousand tricolored flags, including in "the most humble huts."[101] These and similar references, though of uncertain credibility, indicate that non-elite actors also displayed the tricolor flag on their houses. Visual evidence suggests that, by the 1830s, the flag had been appropriated by Chile's subaltern classes, who incorporated it into chinganas and popular celebrations (see fig. 1.8).[102]

Postcolonial administrations claimed that the use of flags in official political ceremonies was evidence of their legitimacy and the support they enjoyed among the population. In this they did not break with colonial customs. But Chileans found ways of utilizing the new symbols of unity and unanimity to manifest disunity and perform dissent. For example, observers claimed that the absence of flags reflected the government's lack of popular support or legitimacy. In September of 1829 the opposition newspaper *El Crepúsculo* commented that the recent national festivities had been "insignificant" compared to those of previous years, noting that "the Chilean flag appeared only on three or four houses."[103] Similarly, clashing political actors appropriated the flag as a representation of national unity. In 1828 rivals of the commissioner of the town of San Felipe managed to steal the Chilean flag hoisted during his reception ceremony. They replaced it during the night with a flag "made with animal skin," thus "communicating" to the governor and his followers that this was the flag "appropriated for them."[104]

Visible publicness, in sum, became an arena of partisan disagreement. Although people in Chile no longer used signs that represented entirely different political regimes, as had been true between 1812 and 1817, their adoption of the national flag and rosette did not mean a return to unity. Individuals found ways of using these objects to signal dissent and express radical political difference. People even used the very public ceremonies and national festivities in which these objects were regularly displayed to question the legitimacy of governments and constitutional codes and the degree of support they enjoyed among the population.[105] For Chileans, this evolution of visible publicness was far from a neutral development. These forms of dissidence were enormously relevant to them, as they continued to aspire to unity and characterize factional politics as an illegitimate and dangerous aberration. Beyond their specific, contingent causes, these visible manifestations of disagreement were evidence of the difficulty their country had in achieving unanimity. This was the paradox of postcolonial visible publicness. As a field of political action, it was destined to be a stage for the display of unity, unanimity, and harmony as well as of the distance that separated those aspirations from reality.

CHAPTER FOUR

The Profanation of Politics

Iconoclasm, Emotions, and Historicity

In late 1814, when royalists regained control of Santiago and reinstalled the colony's Audiencia, Crown attorney Prudencio Lazcano wrote an eloquent condemnation of the iconoclastic actions that had occurred across Chile since 1810. According to Lazcano, during the revolution,

> dismounted and stripped, [the] royal portraits were crushed; the paintings [portraying] his royal coat of arms were trampled and stabbed with fury; one of the coats of arms was torn into pieces with axe blows, while others were dragged through the public streets in saddle straps, substituted [with] the tricolor flag and with abstract seals that authorized independence.[1]

Like many of his contemporaries, Lazcano was shocked by these actions. He seemed particularly interested in conveying the physical nature of the violence revolutionaries had inflicted on royal representations—ripping down, stabbing, crushing, trampling, dragging, tearing apart, and utterly destroying them. Lazcano's outrage at these aggressions is palpable in his text.

Iconoclasm, understood as the desecration or destruction of symbols of power, was an impactful form of political contestation during the revolution and its aftermath.[2] Acts of iconoclasm were striking because they responded to (and challenged) the political, emotional, and historical meanings associated with the realm of visibility. The people who defiled the representations of the king and his rule questioned the public performance of emotions that hegemonic norms required from vassals and disrupted the visible perpetuation of the monarchy's official memory. Through these radical manifestations of dissent, iconoclasts not only contributed to the mutation of political principles and the radicalization of the revolution, but they also profaned the sacrality of political power itself.

To understand iconoclasm's profound effects in revolutionary

Chile, it is first necessary to define sacrality in more detail. I see the sacred as a social product "rather than [as] a mysterious religious property."[3] In his book *Profanations*, philosopher Giorgio Agamben describes the sacred as something rendered unavailable or "removed from the free use and commerce of men."[4] Niklas Luhmann, with similar reasoning, considers the sacred as the product of a "communication ban" that makes it inaccessible to the uninitiated. "The sacred," Luhmann contends, "is not to be found in nature, it is constituted as a secret."[5] Sacrality, in this view, is not a quality inherent to certain objects or even fields of experience but the result of an operation. By virtue of its exclusion from ordinary life, the sacred becomes transcendent to the community that institutes it, originating what Hannah Arendt calls a "pre-political" source of authority—one allegedly located beyond human agency.[6] The antithesis of the sacred is not therefore the secular (which could be considered its complementary opposite), but the act of profanation. Profanation cancels the transcendent, pre-political status of the sacred. In Agamben's words, profanation "disenchants and returns to use what the sacred had separated and petrified," putting it within reach of the commons.[7]

In this chapter I argue that iconoclastic actions in Chile after 1808 constituted an irreversible profanation of political authority. While in the hegemonic discourse visibility—as a field of political action—was meant to manifest the transcendent origins of political power and the historical and emotional values attached to it, during the revolution it became a medium to express radical political dissension. This visible performance of dissent transgressed the official boundaries of political participation, questioning the indisputability and unavailability of sovereignty.[8] As Elias Canetti observed, the collective destruction of representations of power entails the abolition of the distance and hierarchy that underpins relations of authority.[9] Because of its historical and emotional implications, in Chile this profanation of politics became associated with the emergence of a new political subjectivity, one irreverent toward tradition and authority and proud of its own capacity to construct the future. Iconoclasm was therefore more than a simple, outward manifestation of revolutionary passions. By unsettling the political role of visibility, iconoclasts revolutionized politics itself.

This chapter first analyzes colonial notions of authority, their evolution during the second half of the eighteenth century, and their relationship with visibility and material culture. I then describe how and why, between 1808 and 1814, institutional actors and private individuals decided to engage in iconoclastic activities. Through the examination of a single iconoclastic event in 1812, I show how gender expectations affected the emerging revolutionary iconoclasm. When royalists regained control of the colony in 1814, they interpreted such iconoclastic activities as the result of the insurgents' pride and insubordination, reinforcing the link between iconoclasm and revolutionary subjectivities. Iconoclasm subsequently became more systematic and radical, as after 1817 insurgents sought to erase an increasingly large number of material traces of Chile's colonial past. Finally, I focus on the political trajectories of two African-descended men, José Gregorio Cañas and José Romero, which reveal the interplay between iconoclasm, the profanation of politics, and new political subjectivities in postcolonial Chile.

Sacrality, Emotions, and History

In 1781, after reviewing the trial of Antonio Vergne and Antonio Gramusset, Crown attorney José Márquez de la Plata advised Santiago's Audiencia to execute the prisoners, burn their remains outside the city limits, and scatter their ashes in the air.[10] The two men had been found guilty of plotting to make Chile independent. Although the conspirators' project included freeing the enslaved, redistributing land, allying with independent Mapuche groups, and abolishing social hierarchies, the legal proceedings focused on their plan to sever Chile from the Spanish empire. Márquez de la Plata considered this attack against the king's sovereignty "a kind of sacrilege." He denounced Vergne and Gramusset's "audacity" as well as their "ambition and greed," which had led them to defile the king's "splendor and decorum." To him, Vergne and Gramusset were more than ideological adversaries; they were insolent and insubordinate miscreants who had profaned the king's majesty. The severe punishment recommended by the Crown attorney for Vergne and Gramusset seems to have been inspired by the *damnatio memoriae*, a legal measure of Roman origins that involved condemning or dishonoring an individual's memory.[11] This extreme sentence (which the Audiencia did not implement) was meant to reaffirm both the king's sacrality and his control over history, which the conspirators had challenged. During their trial, Vergne—an impoverished professor of mathematics who rented a room in Santiago—declared that no blood would have been shed and no property would have been lost during their rebellion, which would thus have been admired "in all lands, and for all centuries."[12] The Crown attorney's proposed punishment seemed thus designed to overturn the conspirators' apparent desires: instead of eternal admiration, Vergne and Gramusset's attempted revolution should grant them only shame.[13]

In 1781 it was probably difficult to imagine that, thirty years later, the objects that represented the king and his rule would be defaced and destroyed around the colony. But these iconoclastic actions emerged precisely in dialogue with, and as a response to, colonial notions of authority and power such as those voiced by Márquez de la Plata. Three of the principles present in the attorney's opinion affected the nature and meaning of iconoclasm in revolutionary Chile: the transcendent origins of royal sovereignty, the regime's demand that subjects be humble and love their king, and the use of history as a source of legitimacy.

As historians María Teresa Calderón and Clément Thibaud have argued, the authority of the Spanish monarchs was founded on an "indisputable basis": the king's access to an "unquestionable," divinely sanctioned truth.[14] In early modern European legal culture, the sovereign was charged with preserving the fundamental order of the world, of which human law was just one expression. This idea, while in principle limited royal power, also legitimized it as a manifestation of divine will.[15] As the ultimate arbiter of justice in his kingdoms, the monarch's decisions were supposedly rooted in his faculty to correctly interpret the transcendent order, which no ordinary human could remake.[16] Thus, the Spanish monarchs conformed to the characterization philosopher Claude Lefort gave of early modern sovereigns as mediators between society and its transcendent point of reference.[17]

While subjects of the Spanish king could object to his decisions, they were not allowed to question his authority. This is why Chile's Crown attorney described Vergne and Gramusset's revolutionary plan as "a kind of sacrilege"—not because it attacked the Catholic Church but because it violated the indisputability of royal sovereignty.[18] As a second Crown attorney argued, Vergne and Gramusset wanted to lay a "sacrilegious hand" over the royal crown, thus likening their conspiracy to a desecrating act of manipulation. The idea of the conspirators' unworthy hands reaching for, and thus desecrating, royal sovereignty was scandalous to royal officials.[19]

Objects such as the royal portrait, the royal canopy, and the royal coat of arms embodied this sacrality. According to official discourses and practices, these were material "representations" (also called "memories") of the monarch, which meant that they carried the king's presence within them. As seen in chapter 3, this was not just an abstract idea: the portrait was, to a certain extent, an extension of the king. As such, these items did not belong to the sphere of mundane life. The royal portrait, for example, was normally treated with great deference, as if it were the monarch himself. To reinforce their sacred nature, these representations of the king were often made of or surrounded by precious or scarce materials, such as silver and silk.[20]

Spanish rule was also founded on an official emotional regime: authorities prescribed certain emotions as desirable and constructed others as inappropriate or negative.[21] According to this official emotional regime, those in positions of power needed to love and care for the people under their command while inspiring in them fear and respect.[22] To make these emotional and power relations possible, church and political figures actively promoted humility, which they associated with obedience and subordination. Thus, humility was required of the penitent before the priest, the wife in front of her husband, and the servant in the presence of the master.[23] These emotions had to be made visible through specific gestures and rituals, which in the political arena manifested, for example, in the love vassals professed for their king.[24]

Performing these emotions was crucial for the political community, as love, fear, and humility were supposed to make conciliation and harmony possible. By contrast, the visible display of pride was officially penalized. In early modern Catholic doctrine, sinners were considered above all proud people who challenged God's will.[25] Pride and arrogance, according to the official political discourse, engendered conflict and insubordination. In 1795 Chile's governor wrote that he would use all the force of the law "to repress" the "pride" of a man accused of disobeying municipal authorities in the town of Rancagua.[26] Those who rebelled against the Spanish monarchy were similarly accused of being "proud," which was how Crown attorney Márquez de la Plata described Vergne and Gramusset in 1781.[27]

Last, the Spanish monarchy was grounded on a regime of historicity—that is, on a specific articulation of past, present, and future.[28] Past events—particularly the so-called conquest—legitimized Spanish domination in the Americas.[29] Colonial elites liked to think of themselves as protecting both a political regime and a religious faith they had inherited from their elders.[30] The dead, especially in the church's discourse, were not entirely gone from this world: they watched over their descendants' actions and benefited or suffered as a result of them. People had the responsibility of helping their ancestors navigate the difficulties of the afterlife.[31] This relationship deeply affected the myriad ways in which colonial actors conceived of their ability to innovate and construct the future.[32] The government thus sought to control political memory and, through it, what could be imagined about the future.[33] This is why Crown attorney Márquez de la Plata felt the need to make Vergne and Gramusset's bodies disappear: with no tomb or physical remains by which to be remembered, their memory would be both dishonored and obliterated, reaffirming the monarchy's control over both the past and the future.

These official norms and expectations faced multiple challenges during the last decades of colonial rule. The boundaries between the sacred and the profane were not always clear, and the indisputability of the king's decisions was occasionally questioned in the colony.[34] Additionally, some emotional communities (groups of people who shared the same emotional norms and expectations) overtly celebrated emotions rejected in the authorities' discourse. Arrogance and boldness, in particular, were often considered appropriate—and even necessary—emotions in men.[35] Finally, the monarchy's regime of historicity faced serious challenges as well. Transimperial competition and the decline of Spain's influence and power led intellectuals and royal officials to adopt a reformist agenda that raised hard questions about the monarchy's control over the future. Lawyer Ramón Martínez de Rozas—who would later become one of Chile's most powerful colonial bureaucrats—argued in 1777 against the application of torture, observing that "this century" was "called the Age of Enlightenment [*Siglo de las Luces*]" precisely because it had seen the abolition of such practices. Torture, he continued, was "unworthy of our century." Arguments such as Rozas's distanced the present from past sources of authority, potentially complicating official claims to historical legitimacy.[36]

The malleable and disputed nature of the regime's principles meant that they needed to be constantly defended, a task in which visible publicness played a prominent role. In the authorities' discourse, urban ceremonies were expected to reinforce official emotional norms and renew the link between past and present that legitimized Spanish domination. Public festivities thus demanded that vassals be humble in the king's representation (or "memory"), reminding them of the historical origins of his indisputable sovereignty. In Santiago the so-called conquest of Chile was celebrated each year by parading the royal pennant during the festivity of the city's patron saint.[37] In 1787 Chile's interim governor hailed this as an extremely important celebration, as it "serves as a reminder [*hace memoria*] of [the city's] Conquest, or foundation."[38] A year later, a new governor ordered all towns and cities under his jurisdiction to celebrate the king's patron saint's day. According to him, these ceremonies were necessary "demonstrations of remembrance and reverence toward the sacred person of His Majesty."[39]

The Imperial Crisis and the Performance of Disaffection

In the Atlantic world, radical political transformations often involved violent destruction of statues, portraits, paintings, and sculptures that symbolized existing social and political regimes.[40] In the 1780s insurgent Natives in the Andes directed their wrath not only toward objects and buildings that represented their oppression, such as textile mills, but also against signs of royal power and sacred religious authority.[41] Similarly, people across the Spanish empire celebrated the fall of Prime Minister Manuel Godoy in 1808 by stabbing his portraits and destroying other objects symbolizing his person and government.[42] But it was only during the monarchical collapse after 1808 that official representations of the king's sovereignty were systematically desacralized, destroyed, and replaced in most of Spanish America.

When Napoleon seized the Spanish royal family in 1808, people used material representations to express their hatred toward the emperor. On learning of the king's captivity, a Spanish merchant in Santiago named Juan Jiménez Guerra paid for the fabrication of "a statue of the infernal Napoleon," which he then hanged and set aflame in front of his house.[43] In the tradition of what Horst Bredekamp calls "substitutive image acts"—the use of images to stand in for absent figures—Jiménez Guerra used this statue to punish a person who was far from his reach.[44] While Jiménez Guerra's action was not disruptive in 1808 (no one in the colony openly supported Napoleon), inflicting violence on the representations of despised political figures would soon become an unexpected and unsettling form of political contestation.

Many people in the Spanish empire felt these were extraordinary, cataclysmic times.[45] Matthew D. O'Hara has argued that the inhabitants of New Spain experienced the Spanish imperial crisis as an "Age of Anxiety," one that unsettled their place in history and their relationship with time.[46] Observers were shocked by the period's unexpected, history-altering events and reconsidered their own capacity to enact historic change.[47] As the imperial crisis unfolded, political actors thus began to openly question official views about politics and history and initiated a groundbreaking transatlantic debate about legitimacy, political representation, and sovereignty.[48]

In Chile the crisis engendered an unprecedented discussion about the future of the colony.[49] Debates between royalists and revolutionaries about the best course of action under critical circumstances implicitly questioned the Spanish official regime of historicity. Royalists rejected the need for any political innovation, arguing that introducing changes to the colony's government was both dangerous and illegal. Rebellious aristocrat José Antonio Rojas perfectly captured this position when, in an effort to convince royal authorities he was a loyal vassal, he stated in 1810 that "it is better to continue with the existing [government], even if defective, than to test the novelty of mutating it."[50] Many regarded the formation of a junta in Santiago in September 1810—which implied a de facto declaration of autonomy within the empire—as a rupture with the traditional order of time. In fact, Santiago's royalists deridingly called supporters of the junta "*novatores*."[51] On the other hand some supporters of the junta imitated French revolutionaries and cast, at least in private, the junta's creation as a foundational moment that effectively inaugurated a new calendar. The day the junta was created in Santiago, insurgent Manuel de Salas dated a letter to Juan Martínez de Rozas in the following manner: "18 September of 1810 of the old calendar, and year one of the establishment of the Junta."[52]

As the crisis progressed and political animosity and factional disputes grew, iconoclasm became an increasingly widespread mode of political expression. In January of 1811 statues representing new revolutionary authorities were hanged in the port of Valparaíso—an action so remarkable that news of it reached the viceregal capital of Lima, where it was interpreted as evidence of the insurgent government's unpopularity.[53] The vocabulary of violent disaffection initially directed toward Napoleon now revealed a radical, emotionally charged breach in the population's support for the government.

Gendered Emotions

The first direct challenges against royal objects of power in Chile took place in 1812. That year the revolutionary junta created a new flag, rosette, and coat of arms (see chapter 3). As Clément Thibaud has argued, inventing new signs of sovereignty, sanctioned neither by official history nor by royal authority, was akin to destroying the old and revered monarchical symbols.[54] The government reinforced the iconoclastic nature of this measure during the celebration of the second anniversary of Chile's junta in September of 1812. On the morning of September 30, the new flag was hoisted for the first time in all of Santiago's public buildings. In the evening the government held an extravagant ball in the city's most imposing building, the mint (map 3).[55] The ball's organizers had noticed earlier an iron royal coat of arms located over a door leading to one of the facility's patios (fig. 4.1).[56] Instead of leaving it untouched, they installed a panel on one of its sides and placed numerous lit candles behind it, backlighting it so brightly that it appeared as if obscured by an eclipse. According to a royalist account, this action represented "the civil death of the Prince and his empire."[57] As the royal coat of arms was literally obscured by light, new patriotic symbols took its place elsewhere at the

Figure 4.1. Iron door adorned with the royal coat of arms. This door used to be located in Santiago's mint. Pereira Salas, *Historia del arte en el Reino de Chile*, 411.

mint. A hymn sung during the ball captured the nature of this symbolic replacement: "the twilight of despotism," it read, "is the dawn of the most beautiful sun."[58] Leaving behind Chile's obscure past was the only way to construct a brighter future.

During this event, Bernarda Acedo, a Spanish woman, and María Mercedes Prieto, an aristocratic lady from Concepción, appeared dressed as "Indians" (sources do not explain what this dress consisted of).[59] This was a political provocation that royalist observers did not fail

Figure 4.2. Lithograph representing Javiera Carrera, in Vicuña Mackenna, *El ostracismo de los Carreras*, detail. Although printed in 1857, the image is supposedly based on a portrait of Javiera Carrera made in Buenos Aires in the early 1820s.

to notice. Indeed, Chile's new coat of arms also featured two human figures, a woman and a man, who according to royalist chroniclers were "dressed" as "Indians."[60] To positively reference Native groups in revolutionary Spanish America was akin to defacing the crown's symbols, as in elite discourses Natives both symbolized the violent and illegal origins of Spanish rule and evoked a local source of sovereignty with which it might be replaced.[61] Dressed as "Indians," these wealthy women implicitly questioned the monarchy's official regime of historicity, denouncing the colonial past and announcing a different future.[62]

During the ball, General José Miguel Carrera and his brother, Juan José (also a military officer), wore in their hats an ornament representing an inverted crown shattered by a sword and shot at by a rifle. The message could hardly be clearer: the military might they wielded overpowered monarchical authority. Another member of the Carrera family, Javiera Carrera (José Miguel and Juan José's sister), also wore an inverted crown on her head (fig. 4.2). This was a strikingly iconoclastic outfit, especially considering her gender. Javiera Carrera played an important political role during Chile's revolution, discussing governmental affairs, advising her brothers, and participating in factional disputes. But her political prominence was controversial. For example, in a bitter letter written to her husband from exile in Mendoza in 1814, Javiera Carrera reminded him of his past "complaints that a woman has no part in government."[63] Thus, by manifesting her disaffection toward monarchical rule in 1812, she not only made visible her support for the revolutionary cause but also asserted her worthiness as a political subject and her determination to renegotiate traditional gender roles.[64]

The actions of iconoclasts such as Javiera Carrera carried great historical and emotional significance. "Iconoclasm," Lynn Hunt writes, "is inseparable from the experience of time."[65] Through their dress and the objects they wore, these men and women became actors of a new time, contesting the monarchy's historical legitimacy and constructing a new future. The scene at the ball was a mold-breaking emotional performance, particularly for the three women involved: Bernarda Acedo, María Mercedes Prieto, and Javiera Carrera. Since 1810 royalists had accused insurgents of being proud, fearless, and vain.[66] But while these emotional attitudes were compatible with popular notions of masculinity—which valued bravery, defiance, and independence—they were certainly considered inappropriate for women. Women, a priest wrote in 1810, ought to restrict their political activities to loving their king and praying for him. He requested them to display sobriety, humility, compassion, and sorrow to attract God's favor.[67] The three women's iconoclastic outfits were a direct transgression of both official and popular gendered emotional prescriptions. Appearing in public wearing an overtly antimonarchical object in 1812 was a declaration of fearlessness, a defiant challenge to those who interpreted revolutionary politics—and particularly women participating in politics—as a sinful form of insubordination.

Javiera Carrera, Bernarda Acedo, and María Mercedes Prieto are the only women I have been able to identify as performing iconoclastic actions during this period.[68] The absence of more women in the documentation is likely due to the incompatibility between gender norms and the emotional resonance of iconoclasm. For women, iconoclasm implied breaking both official emotional regimes and traditional gender norms. For men, on the other hand, iconoclasm, while politically subversive, was a means of asserting masculinity. Gender norms made it easier for men to visibly participate in the profanation of politics, but it is worth keeping in mind that women also found in iconoclasm a relevant political tool to question the sacrality of political power and the emotional regime associated with it.

Desecrating the King

After Viceroy Abascal of Peru sent troops to southern Chile in late 1812, sparking a civil war in the colony, local revolutionaries engaged in increasingly extreme iconoclastic activities. The silver royal coat of arms that adorned the chambers of Santiago's Audiencia suffered an ignominious fate. In 1813, during a public gathering in the chambers of the now abolished court, merchant Nicolás Matorras is reported to have asked, "Until when will this sign of our former enslavement remain here? I will give a thousand *pesos* to extinguish it."[69] The junta promptly accepted his offer. The funds Matorras provided in exchange for the coat of arms in May of 1813 were dedicated to the erection of a pyramid in commemoration of those who had died combating royalist forces.[70] The obsolete memory of the king, which Matorras characterized as a "sign of our *former* enslavement," was erased to make space for the creation of a new entity to be revered and remembered: the revolution and its martyrs. As for the coat of arms, it was partly melted to make silver coins. Its remains, royalist General Osorio wrote two years later, were found "in possession of [Matorras's] widow," a woman named Ventura Pradel, "broken into a thousand pieces, and notably damaged."[71]

On September 11 of that year, Chile's government authorized circulation of coins minted in Potosí by the revolutionary government of Buenos Aires, which displayed "the characteristic signs of freedom and union of the United Provinces of Río de la Plata."[72] Royalists did not miss the iconoclastic connotations associated with this decision. As seen in chapter 3, authorities required that all coins minted in Spanish territories bear the king's effigy. Replacing it was a serious offense against the monarch and his sovereignty. In 1815 Chile's royalist governor pointed out to his superiors in Spain that, on these revolutionary coins, the "respectable portrait of our Monarch and his Royal Arms" had been replaced by revolutionary "symbols."[73]

During the 1813–1814 civil war between royalists and insurgents, the royalist army used the traditional royal flag and cockade as its emblems, while the revolutionary forces adopted the new tricolor signs. As was customary in wartime, soldiers and officers in the revolutionary army desecrated their adversaries' favored symbols.[74] If we are to believe General José Miguel Carrera, by April 1813 insurgent troops had even adopted "death to the king" as their rallying cry in the battlefield.[75] Though Carrera may have been exaggerating, it seems that an antiroyal sentiment eventually spread among the military. Many in the revolutionary army refused to adopt the royal insignia when insurgent authorities, in an effort to reach a compromise with the royalists, attempted to restore them as the army's official emblems in May of 1814. Instead of accepting them, revolutionary soldiers and officers openly mocked the royal cockade and flag. Most dramatic among these actions were the two times unidentified individuals "hanged" the royal flag in Santiago's central square.[76] While it is unclear whether these soldiers and officers meant to explicitly reject royal sovereignty, their actions certainly contributed to profaning its material manifestations.

Revolutionaries also directed their wrath against Viceroy Abascal in the same manner Jiménez Guerra had expressed his anger at Napoleon in 1808. During the civic festivities of September of 1814, a fireworks-stuffed "mannequin" representing Abascal was burned in Santiago.[77] One young witness of this event later claimed it shocked him and led him to believe the viceroy was a bloodthirsty monster.[78] Similarly, according to a list of Valparaíso revolutionaries drawn up by an anonymous royalist, one Pedro Patiño "burnt a statue of Mr. Abascal."[79] The phrase in the original Spanish ("*quemó al señor Abascal en estatua*," which translates literally as "burnt Mr. Abascal in statue") underscores the striking nature of these actions: burning an effigy was akin to burning the man himself. Furthermore, viceroys were officially considered "representations" of the king, much like the king's portrait or the royal pennant.[80] Burning the viceroy "in statue" could therefore be interpreted as a direct, physical affront to the monarch.

Although it is hard to ascertain the impact of these actions, they certainly shocked others. Iconoclasm is an emotionally charged practice: it depends on the affective investment placed in the objects being destroyed.[81] Iconoclastic actions were thus directed not only against the people or principles represented in the desecrated objects but also against the wider audience that loved them and held them sacred. As noted in previous chapters, in late September of 1814, Santiago's revolutionary authorities sentenced petty merchant Romualdo Antonio Esponda to publicly burn the royal flag in the city's central square.[82] The sentence was clearly meant to humiliate Esponda; in having him desecrate by his own hand this sign of royal sovereignty, the punishment recognized, and depended on, his own emotional investment in the flag. With this staged event, revolutionary authorities likely sought to scandalize all royalists, something they apparently achieved. A member of the Audiencia described the burning of the royal flag as an act of "treason" and "infamy" that constituted the revolutionaries' "most execrable affront" against the political order.[83]

Iconoclasm as Political Crime

When the Council of the Indies reviewed Esponda's case, it immediately took notice of the destruction of the royal flag that had occurred during his public punishment. On February 14, 1816, the council's attorney argued that burning the flag "in the public square," as the revolutionaries had done, constituted a crime of "high treason," and demanded that the people responsible for it be prosecuted and punished accordingly.[84] Following a similar line of reasoning, the newly established royal authorities in Chile interpreted iconoclastic actions as "criminal excesses" and evidence of treason.[85] As mentioned in the previous chapter, grappling with a country that had experienced four years of revolution, royal authorities felt the need to distinguish between those who were guilty of being agents of the revolution and those who were simply dragged into it by external influences. Iconoclasm proved key in this task, with royalist authorities considering actions such as participating in the removal of the king's insignia or promoting the new patriotic symbols as proof of revolutionary commitment.

The new administration sought to reinstate the symbols of royal sovereignty and resacralize the monarchy and the king. Authorities similarly sought to restore the prerevolutionary regime of historicity, offering in the government's newspaper an edulcorated vision of the colony's past, which they saw as a source of legitimacy and a model for the present.[86] Their efforts were apparently unsuccessful. The government faced continued actions of iconoclasm in the colony, which it framed as the symptom of an uncured revolutionary disease. More than an ideology, iconoclasm betrayed a persistent criminal political subjectivity. For example, in April of 1815 Governor Mariano Osorio described to Viceroy Abascal the circulation in Chile of defaced coins. On one of them, the portrait of the king had been effaced with the help of a file, with "VLP 1816" carved over it. The initials stood for "*Viva la patria*" (long live the fatherland), the rallying cry of the now marginalized revolutionary faction, and 1816 likely identified the year of the coin's hoped-for validity (thus anticipating a future free of monarchical domination).[87] In his communication to the viceroy, Osorio interpreted these defaced coins as evidence of the local population's unruly "spirit."

In 1816 the decision of the Council of the Indies in Spain to pardon most of the colony's insurgents sparked a major controversy among royalists. The Surveillance Tribunal of the province of Concepción and Santiago's city council expressed their opposition to this measure, both citing how "proud" revolutionaries were.[88] Chile's main organ of political repression, Santiago's Committee of Surveillance and Public Safety, cited as a compelling example of how "evil" revolutionaries were "the attacks they have conducted against the royal insignia, their impudence getting to the point of hanging the royal flag." The committee warned that these proud enemies were still roaming the country, as evidenced by the fact that copies of a caricature mocking "the respectable image of the king" had been posted not long before in an unidentified village.[89]

The royalists' response to the manipulation of representations of royal power by revolutionaries ensured that, for those engaging in these practices, iconoclasm was not an inconsequential action.[90] By insisting on the revolutionaries' sense of pride, royalists in some way created it. It required strong conviction to manipulate and deface objects held in such high regard by a powerful rival faction. Putting an end to the old regime and inaugurating a new one required bold actions, as revolutionaries knew full well.

Erasing the Memory of the Monarchy

On February 12, 1817, insurgent troops led by generals José de San Martín and Bernardo O'Higgins secured a decisive victory over royalist forces in Chacabuco, on the outskirts of Santiago. During the battle, a crowd entered the governor's palace in the city's central square and destroyed the gallery containing the portraits of all of Chile's governors since the Spanish invasion.[91] Although the gallery had only been created in the second half of the eighteenth century, it embodied almost three hundred years of Spanish sovereignty.[92] As Governor Ambrosio Higgins stressed in 1788, the gallery represented an uninterrupted succession of officials and safeguarded their "memory."[93] In destroying this gallery, the crowd desecrated not only the representations of its former rulers but also the very principle of historical sovereignty so central to Spanish colonial discourse. This event announced the radicalization of iconoclasm after 1817. Now the time was ripe to erase the entire memory of the colonial regime.

Only six days after the battle of Chacabuco, the revolutionary government confiscated a new royal coat of arms that the royalist administration had commissioned to replace the one destroyed in 1813. It was promptly melted in Santiago's mint to make coins.[94] A second royal coat of arms—described in more detail in chapter 1—was also ruined. Finished in 1808, this enormous carved stone coat of arms was originally meant to adorn the facade of Santiago's mint, but for financial reasons it lay abandoned in the patio of a house in the capital (fig. 1.3). In 1818, after a second important victory over royalist forces near Santiago, a crowd attacked and mutilated it. The abandoned coat of arms became the preferred target of children and the urban poor, who according to some accounts took pleasure in throwing stones at it. The memory of the king met its final, unceremonious end in 1823 when the family that rented the house where it had been abandoned decided to bury it.[95]

Figure 4.3. Coin minted in Santiago in 1822. Volcanos were a recognized revolutionary symbol since the French Revolution. Courtesy of the Museo Histórico Nacional (Chile).

Chile's coins were also changing in response to the new order. Although for practical reasons coins featuring the king's image continued to be minted after revolutionaries took control of Santiago in February of 1817, soon the monarch's face was replaced with a new set of symbols (fig. 4.3). "In a time when Liberty's august emblems replace everywhere the execrable image of the ancient despots," the government declared on June 9, 1817, "it would be extraordinarily absurd" for Chile's coins to "preserve the [king's] infamous bust." Future generations, the government continued, would not understand such a decision. Authorities thus portrayed the replacement of the king's effigy as part of a larger iconoclastic movement, one that marked the distance between the monarchical past and an independent present and future. The administration cared to add that defacing or rejecting the new coin would be considered treason.[96]

This was no inconsequential measure, at least for those who supported the king. Only a few weeks after the government approved the new coins, military authorities in Concepción investigated a laborer named Ventura Astete, who was reputed to have said in a chingana, "I've got money, but that of the king, and the world continues to turn and the king will return." According to another witness, Astete said "that he only uses the king's coins."[97] After speaking some version of these words, Astete got into a fistfight with a friend of his who apparently took offense. For a non-elite individual like Astete, the erasure of the monarch's portrait also represented a historical break, one he confronted with skepticism and strong emotion.

Despite such cases of resistance, iconoclastic actions continued to reinforce the distance between past, present, and future, even reaching beyond the monarch and his sovereignty. On March 22, 1817, General Bernardo O'Higgins ordered the removal of all family coats of arms from the front doors of aristocratic houses.[98] The edict described these "intolerable" objects as "hieroglyphs," relics of a distant and strange past. "The only one who deserves to be perpetuated in the memory of free men," it stated, was the "true citizen, the patriot." O'Higgins's order directly challenged the local aristocracy's reliance on history and ancestry while reframing the present as a foundational moment that would be projected into the future through the perpetuation of the memory of good citizens. Following the order all of Santiago's aristocratic coats of arms were either removed from their doors or covered with mud.[99] According to historian Benjamín Vicuña Mackenna, over the course of several days a group of young men lassoed these familial emblems and dragged them through the streets.[100]

The new government also sought to replace the traditional signs of monarchical rule with symbols of Chilean sovereignty, creating new national flags, coats of arms, and cockades. A coat of arms produced in 1819 explicitly referenced the violent nature of this replacement, showing a caiman destroying the Spanish royal flag and royal coat of arms.[101] Authorities and postcolonial elites used the national festivities in which these signs were customarily displayed to create a new national memory and to highlight the distance between the present and the past.[102]

Finally, in 1825 Santiago's intendant sought to replace the city's street names with new ones "analogous to our political regeneration."[103] The intendant argued that "there is not a single American who does not wish to see every single vestige bearing the memory of Spanish domination erased from this continent."[104] The previous street-name markers were quickly erased and replaced with new indicia.[105] Although most streets ultimately kept their old names, the intendant's orders reveal a will to overcome the monarchical past through the systematic erasure of all reminders.

This general, iconoclastic condemnation of the colonial past represented a radical expression of revolutionary historicity. By erasing the memory of monarchical rule, people actively contributed to creating a new future. A particularly powerful example of this is the portrait of General Francisco Calderón painted by José Gil de Castro around 1824 (fig. 4.4). Castro, an African-descended painter from Lima, had arrived in Santiago in 1813, where he executed several portraits of members of Chile's ruling class (figs. 2.4–6).[106] His paintings reflected the elites' strong desire to ensure their remembrance by future generations (fig. 2.6).[107] The portrait of General Calderón—a leading military figure in the independence struggle—is highly symbolic of the interplay between the effort to destroy the memory of the monarchical regime and revolutionary historicity. In 2009 X-ray analyses of Calderón's painting revealed that it was painted over a copy of the royal portrait (see figs. 4.5 and 4.6).[108] Imagining Castro and his coworkers erasing, brushstroke after brushstroke, the portrait of the king, only to replace it with a painting meant to immortalize an insurgent general, is a perfect encapsulation of how new historical subjectivities were born out of iconoclastic actions directed against the king's memory.

Iconoclastic Political Subjectivities: José Gregorio Cañas and José Romero

Chile's revolutionary and postcolonial authorities sought to legitimize themselves through means reminiscent of the colonial regime's. Like the Spanish monarchs, the country's new military leaders were hailed as virtuous heroes; the Catholic Church sanctioned the new republic and the heads of government; and authorities claimed to be representatives of transcendent and indisputable principles, such as Chilean nationhood.[109] But this "transfer of sacrality" between the monarchical and the new regimes was not necessarily successful: on the contrary, as the period's social unrest and political instability suggests, recomposing the colonial order—and the subjective elements attached to it—required more than reproducing traditional forms of legitimation.[110] If Chile's social and political landscape eventually became more stable, it was not thanks to the resacralization of figures of power or the imposition of new transcendent principles. Scholars have shown that the driving forces behind this process were the creation of political alliances among elite factional groups and the repression of those of lower social and racial standing (though one could also add the negotiation and mediation between these different groups).[111]

Efforts to restore the colonial regime's sacrality all eventually failed. This was a direct result of the iconoclastic nature of the revolution. While the revolutionary process in Chile did not involve the physical execution of the monarch, it did manage to destroy the king's "other" body, the transcendent one materialized in royal coins and portraits.[112] This profanation of the king's sacrality was simultaneously a profanation of politics: no longer could any political actor indisputably claim to have access to the transcendent principles governing political life. As lawyer

Figure 4.4. Portrait of Francisco Calderón, José Gil de Castro, ca. 1824. Courtesy of the Museo Histórico Nacional (Chile).

Agustín Mardones argued in 1813, during the revolution no one could pretend to occupy the king's former position as unquestionable mediator between society and its external source of order.[113] Access to external references such as religion, nationhood, or the natural order was now in permanent contention.[114]

This profanation of politics was tied to the emergence of new political subjectivities as evidenced by the personal trajectories of two men, José Gregorio Cañas and José Romero, the latter also known by the nickname Peluca (see chapter 1). On July 19, 1824, both Cañas and Romero participated in a noteworthy iconoclastic event. That day, a crowd gathered in Santiago's central square to demand the abolition of Chile's constitution and its senate. The constitution, which had been approved only a few months earlier, had originally been meant to inherit the king's majesty. This legal code, like others produced after 1810, was an effort to

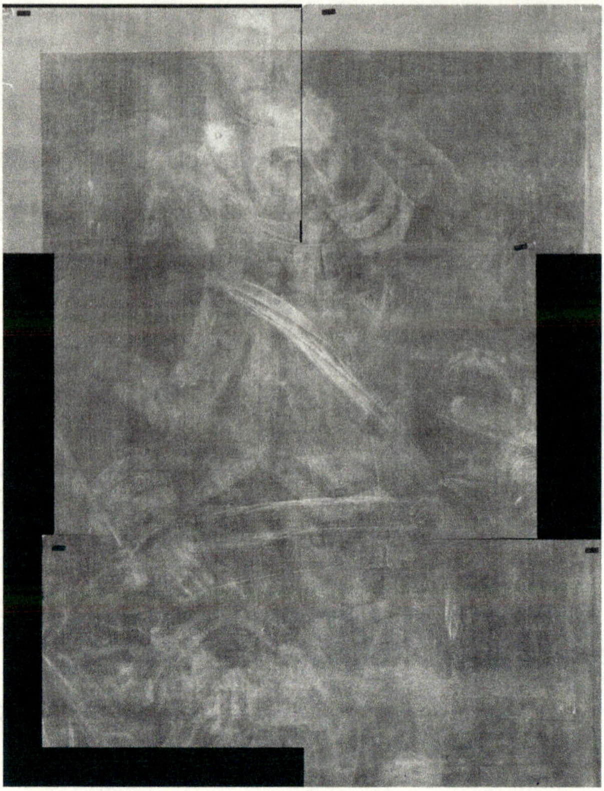

Figure 4.5. Radiography of Francisco Calderón's portrait. Courtesy of the Centro Nacional de Conservación y Restauración (Chile).

restore a transcendent and indisputable source of authority to Chile's unstable postcolonial politics. The government had asked the population to pledge allegiance to the constitution following the same rituals previously reserved for celebrating a new king, invoking God's protection and associating the code with the will and majesty of the Chilean nation.[115]

According to senator Juan Egaña, the constitution's main author and an eyewitness to the event, that fateful July 1824 evening, the crowd—allegedly led by elite politicians—entered Santiago's city hall. As they cried "death to the Constitution, death to the Senate," some of them "striped off the portraits of [Bernardo] O'Higgins and [José de] San Martín, tore them into pieces and threw them to the streets."[116] The group had reason to destroy these portraits. Between 1817 and 1822, General José Miguel Carrera, his brothers, and other members of their faction had been executed in Chile and Río de la Plata in what their supporters saw

Figure 4.6. Portrait of Fernando VII, anonymous. This was one of the many royal portraits produced in Chile after Napoleon toppled the Spanish monarchy in 1808. It was over one such portrait that José Gil de Castro painted General Calderón's. Courtesy of the Museo Histórico Nacional (Chile).

as political assassinations orchestrated by O'Higgins and San Martín. When O'Higgins resigned in early 1823, supporters of the Carrera family (known as *carrerinos*) reorganized, and many of them eventually joined the ranks of the emerging Liberal faction. In July of 1824, as Juan Egaña saw it, most leaders of the crowd that invaded Santiago's city hall were carrerinos.[117] When the crowd destroyed portraits of O'Higgins and San Martín, they were thus physically punishing two of their most hated political enemies and preventing the perpetuation of their memory as alleged heroes.[118]

In a private letter to his son, Mariano, Juan Egaña expressed disdain toward this rebellious "mob." According to him, to bring the constitution down, liberals had "organized the rabble" of Santiago, mobilizing the vendors of the central square and "every indecent man they could attract, with the mulattos Peluca and Cañas playing a principal role."[119] Egaña seems to suggest that these two men were responsible for rallying the street vendors and other members of Santiago's subaltern classes, although he may also have been implying that they represented particularly well the kind of people Liberal leaders attracted. As he stated in a later, unpublished manuscript, these two "ridiculous" men were among "the most abject and clownish" elements of "the rabble."[120] For Egaña, their participation in the event highlighted the movement's scandalous nature—the shocking juxtaposition between a majestic and transcendent constitution and the obscure and wretched people who dared to profane it. Egaña did not attribute to Cañas and Romero any political ideology. In his mind, as castas, they had no political affiliation other than disorder.

But there is reason to believe not only that Cañas and Romero had deeper motivations for joining the assault against the constitution but also that their participation in this event fit with their self-perception as historical agents. The "Cañas" Juan Egaña referred to was undoubtedly José Gregorio Cañas, an African-descended master tailor born some time before 1767 who lived in Santiago.[121] Based on his own account, Cañas had supported the revolution since its inception. In the early stages of the rebellion, the Carrera family hired him to supply boots to the revolutionary army. In July of 1814, when the Carrera brothers staged a coup against the government of Francisco de la Lastra, he helped arm Santiago's Black militia unit in support of the rebellion.[122] His political convictions led him to choose the path of exile when royalists took control of the country later that year, crossing the Andes to the revolutionary-controlled city of Mendoza, where he stayed until early 1817.[123] When Cañas returned to Santiago, the O'Higgins administration accused him of participating in a conspiracy to return the Carrera family to power and thus put him in prison. Cañas vehemently denied the charge, arguing that he was not part of any conspiracy and that the Carrera family had used him and owed him money.[124]

After more than two months in prison, Cañas petitioned General O'Higgins, then Supreme Director of Chile. Instead of assuming a humble position, as was customary in such communications, Cañas forcefully requested his release. While he did not present himself as a worthy Black man, as other African-descended men did in Chile and elsewhere, he did portray himself as a virtuous and patriotic artisan.[125] He claimed his revolutionary commitment was born of a deep inner conviction, not material interests. "Your Excellency knows," he argued, that for royalists and revolutionaries alike "I will never be but a shoemaker," meaning that his social position would remain the same regardless of who ran the government. "In spite" of that, he continued, "my selflessness and patriotism have few rivals." After describing the unjust terms of his imprisonment, Cañas asked O'Higgins, "as first Magistrate of a free people," to release him or to prove he was guilty of a crime. "I am a citizen of Chile, and I have equal rights, and equal representation as a man, as the Nation's first citizen," he boldly asserted. Cañas asked either to be formally convicted or that "satisfaction" be given to him as to why he had been imprisoned.[126] He was soon released, but minus the requested public reparations.[127]

José Gregorio Cañas probably had profound personal and political reasons to participate in the 1824 riot against the constitution. We can only guess whether he felt satisfaction when the crowd destroyed the portraits of O'Higgins and San Martín, the men who had imprisoned him and who had persecuted the political faction he apparently supported. What is certain is that, in spite of his calidad, he considered himself worthy enough to discuss and challenge the country's most fundamental political structures. A few years later, in 1829, Cañas—by then over sixty years old—participated in one of Chile's first political organizations of artisans, the Sociedad de Artesanos del País. This group, which sought to turn artisans into a united and coherent electoral force, was deeply grounded in the notion of equality.[128] But the organization had its own internal contradictions and soon split. While one wing of the Sociedad gave its support to the *estanqueros*, Cañas's faction proclaimed federalist José Miguel Infante as their candidate for the presidency.[129] This suggests a coherence in Cañas's political trajectory, as this section of Santiago's artisans hailed Infante as a champion of equality, citing in particular his leading role as a senator in the abolition of slavery in 1823.[130] By participating in these organizations, José Gregorio Cañas proclaimed his value as a citizen—his almost unparalleled patriotism and selflessness, as he had phrased it back in 1817—and his confidence in his ability to shape the future.

The other African-descended man mentioned by Juan Egaña was Sergeant José Romero. As noted in previous chapters, Romero, born enslaved in 1794, joined Santiago's free Black militia in 1807. This military body played an active political role during Chile's first years of the revolution, as African-descended militiamen embraced the opportunity to display their political convictions as well as to advance their reputations and improve their social standing.[131] Romero, who distinguished himself in a series of battles, was among the militia's most renowned officers. His social prominence in postcolonial Chile generated concern and disgust among some, not least Juan Egaña.

Romero's actions during the 1824 demonstration drew attention. According to one testimony, as darkness fell, advocates and adversaries of the constitution engaged in a heated debate inside Santiago's city hall. At midnight, José Romero presented both groups a portrait of King Fernando VII he had found in a room filled with "old junk." As the story goes, Romero lit the king's image with an oil lamp like the ones used in hospitals to illuminate those who were about to die, and reportedly said: "Sirs, here you have an impartial [arbiter] . . . now go to sleep!"[132]

Romero's reported action, if real, was more daring that it might at first seem. Although Chile had formally declared its independence from Spain in 1818, royalists were still politically and militarily powerful.[133] Romero must have known that his was the kind of action royalists used to identify the most criminal insurgents. He must have felt pretty confident to mock the portrait of a king who likely continued to enjoy the support of an important part of the local population. Romero, a man born enslaved, now desecrated the kingly portrait—explicitly deriding the monarch's role as deliverer of justice—while participating in the abolition of Chile's supposedly majestic constitution.

Romero's political affiliations are difficult to gauge.[134] What seems clear is that, like José Gregorio Cañas, he considered himself a meritorious man. He even preserved his memory in the form of a portrait (fig. 4.7). Like Antonio Vergne in 1781, Romero probably imagined a posterity in which his virtue (and patriotism) would be acknowledged and celebrated. When he participated in the iconoclastic events of July 1824, José Romero was thus not only taking part in a momentous political event—he was also visibly asserting himself as a worthy man with a right to both have and express his own political opinions.[135]

Iconoclasts in Chile boldly laid hands on objects that embodied sacred principles and revered figures, questioning in the process the emotional and temporal dimensions of the colonial regime. Through their iconoclastic actions, individuals like Javiera Carrera and José Romero collapsed the distance that was supposed to separate them—women and castas—from transcendent sources of authority and power. Their rivals, in turn, saw their actions as improper and scandalous. While much of the period's iconoclasm was aimed at replacing signs of monarchical rule with new objects representing alternative political principles, the fact is that no new object could truly replace the king's portrait because no new authority could inherit the king's majesty and prestige. Iconoclastic actions shattered the aura of indisputability that surrounded these material representations of power. As historian Emmanuel Fureix has put it for postrevolutionary France, political signs were now "fragile by

Figure 4.7. Portrait of José Romero, anonymous, ca. 1850. Courtesy of the Museo Histórico Nacional (Chile).

nature"—or at least open to contestation and appropriation.[136] With their daring and sacrilegious actions, iconoclasts contributed to making politics the affair of profane, worldly creatures.

Iconoclasts transgressed the colony's official emotional regime. They broke the chains of affection that supposedly tied them to their sovereign and challenged the position of humility authorities reserved for them. Instead of visibly performing obligatory love and respect toward their superiors, iconoclasts engaged in daring actions. Royalists both acknowledged and reinforced the shocking nature of iconoclasm, accusing revolutionaries of arrogance and pride and pronouncing iconoclastic actions evidence of revolutionary commitment. Asserting oneself as an individual worthy of participating in politics also implied assuming the responsibility of making history. By declaring obsolete all signs of monarchical power and erasing the monarch's memory, iconoclasts marked the revolutionary era as a foundational time.

For individuals such as José Gregorio Cañas, whose participation in politics challenged racial and social boundaries, iconoclasm was not just a way of expressing opinions but a means of reaffirming oneself as a citizen capable of producing historical change. While iconoclasm was a gendered practice reserved mostly for men, women also appropriated it, as exemplified by Javiera Carrera, Bernarda Acedo, and María Mercedes Prieto. The iconoclastic profanation of politics thus involved the transformation of people's perception of their worth and of their historical and political agency.

Iconoclasm was powerful because those who engaged in it (and those who opposed it) shared similar assumptions about visible publicness. It was the transgression of these assumptions—of the political, emotional, and historical values attached to visibility—that gave iconoclasm its political efficacy. As a field of political action, visibility set the conditions for iconoclasm to emerge during the imperial crisis, thus shaping the revolutionary process itself. With their visible performances of dissent, iconoclasts inadvertently questioned the nonpluralistic nature of publicness and contributed to shaping Chile's new and profaned political landscape.

CHAPTER FIVE

Mimetic Publicness, Scandals, and Partisan Heroism

For people living in late colonial and early nineteenth-century Chile, imitation was everywhere. Mimesis seemed to operate at every scale, extending its influence from individuals and corporate bodies to entire societies—even empires.[1] Mimetic relations allowed observers to explain the transmission and reproduction of ideas and behaviors across time and space as well as evaluate their repercussions on the body politic. Much of the power that authorities and the lettered elites attributed to speech, writing, and other, nondiscursive acts derived from imitation. Mimicry thus described a means of communication and a mode of affecting people.

This chapter studies how political actors relied on the notion of mimesis and a series of practices founded upon it to frame, understand, and participate in politics during the Age of Dissent. It is divided into two parts. The first examines how, between the eighteenth and nineteenth centuries, observers used the concept of imitation to render social processes intelligible. I argue that people of this era saw society as being organized around relations of imitation. These mimetic dynamics delineated a realm of communication—a mimetic public sphere of sorts—that was ruled by its own set of values regarding authority and personal behavior. These moral and political precepts were captured in one particular concept, that of "scandal," which described public transgressions that had the potential to propagate and affect others through imitation. The importance of the word "scandal" in this period's social and political language—which will become evident in this and the following chapters—derived from how it articulated mimesis, publicness, morality, and politics.

The second part studies how, between 1808 and 1833, mimesis was put at the service of different—and often antagonistic—social and political projects. This section zooms in on a specific process, the fabrication of heroes. The political relevance of heroes was founded on the idea that they were models of good behavior who affected society through their example. Governments and lettered men tried to create heroes for the population to admire and imitate. Elite partisan groups also saw in heroism a way to celebrate their dead and to promote their causes. But heroism was not reserved for elite men. People officially excluded from politics disputed the meaning of heroism with authorities. Some of them, such as self-proclaimed royalist hero María Ana Pérez de Arza, even created their own pantheon of heroes. The concept of heroism, with its mimetic overtones, allowed people to frame and negotiate their political agency as well as to fight for recognition and power.

Imitation, together with contagion, was part of a complex realm of political action I call the field of propagation, to which this and the following two chapters are dedicated. As a form of communication, propagation (either via mimesis or contagion) designated much more than the simple transmission of information. Men and women of this era used it to describe processes of mutual influence and dissemination that did not always involve discursive material. An individual's actions or behavior, for example, could propagate and thus impact others, even if the person in question never spoke, wrote, or even tried to communicate with others. Imitation was one of the mechanisms that explained this phenomenon and its social impact.

Communicative Examples

People in Chile during the Age of Dissent routinely claimed actions and behaviors propagated through imitation. Political elites, for example, often argued that a dense network of mimetic relations connected the government to society, granting authorities great power over the population. In 1813 while intellectuals in Chile debated the degree to which the state could change the social order, the newspaper *Semanario Republicano* contended that governments had the ability to shape society. Passive governments created apathetic individuals, while wise and active ones engendered virtuous and strong citizens. Imitation explained this influence. Throughout history, the article continued, people have "constantly imitated" their governments, thus acquiring their vices and virtues.[2] Another newspaper, *El Crisol*, described in 1829 the government's effect on society along similar lines. "It cannot be denied," the article read, "that the government has a powerful influence over the people's customs. . . . It seems that even the affections, predilections, and the most ordinary habits of rulers are transmitted to those they rule by some kind of electric communication." This abstract but effective form of communication came from the government's "example."[3]

To discuss their social influence, individuals and institutions often described themselves (as well as others) as "examples." Recounting his merits to the government in 1811, Pedro Lurquin, who was in charge of managing the properties of the expelled Jesuits in Chile, informed revolutionary authorities that, "following my example," his subalterns were joining the junta's army.[4] Similarly, when in 1822 Santiago's city council communicated the merits of priest Diego Antonio Elizondo to the government, it highlighted that "his examples . . . have had a wonderful influence on the morality and civism of the inhabitants" of a rural area near Santiago. According to the city council, this explained why the locals had displayed such "patriotism" during recent conflicts.[5]

Examples not only propagated across the social body, but they also reproduced over time. A religious brochure printed in Santiago in 1824 asked the government to welcome the controversial apostolic vicar whom the pope had sent to South America. The government's exemplary actions on this occasion, the paper argued, would be "followed by posterity," as "he who builds through example, builds for eternity."[6] Mimesis's effect over time could be central to people's understanding of history. In 1824 a man named Ramón Pardo—apparently a former Spanish military officer who arrived in Chile as part of a royalist contingent—finished a rather confusing moral treatise that is today held in Chile's national archives. In his manuscript, Pardo tried to make sense of the wars and cataclysmic events he had witnessed during the revolutionary period. To explain the radical ruptures of this time, Pardo turned to the concept of imitation. He stated that "disciples" reproduce "the bad teacher's example" in the same way that children perpetuate the examples of "bad parents." From this mimetic relation, Pardo concluded that all human suffering, including war, was nothing but the "heritage" of original sin. Pardo's logic can be hard to follow: this evil heritage, he wrote, descended directly from "those who first invented it." These were "Lucifer," "Cain," and "the Romans." "From the latter," he declared, "we (all the nations in the world) have inherited the same example and model." This was the model of war and civil unrest. Pardo saw "examples" as the reason why history both repeated itself and evolved. According to him, contemporary rulers had "drifted away" from the good "example" set by the first kings, with royal families—including Spain's—decaying in "talent" and virtue over time.[7] In Pardo's view, mimetic dynamics connected different eras, explaining the proliferation of vices and the waning of virtue. And though his arguments were rather eccentric, the power he attributed to imitation was not.

Good and Bad Examples

Mimetic relations engendered a system of models and countermodels. By virtue of imitation, words and actions became "examples" capable of influencing others. These were either "good" or "bad," which implied that they were to be judged according to moral and political standards.[8] For this reason, everyone's life was, to a certain extent, of public relevance, as the way in which each person behaved could directly affect others.

First and foremost, people—especially those who held authority over others—were expected to be examples of virtuous conduct. Government officials, such as Audiencia judges during the colonial era and district magistrates after independence, were required by law to be models of virtue and good behavior.[9] The same applied to priests. "Our example," the new bishop of Concepción told the priests under his authority in 1812, has a "highly effective influence" on "our sheep."[10] Schoolmasters, argued a newspaper in 1829, should "give an example" of good behavior "to their disciples."[11] These official notions of what constituted a "good" example followed racial, gender, and class expectations. As discussed below, in the hegemonic discourse, political and military exemplarity was reserved for white elite males, while elite women should aspire only to be examples of religious and domestic virtues.

Individuals actively sought to be considered examples of good behavior. During the second half of the eighteenth century, the officers of Santiago's Black militia often presented themselves as honorable and exemplary men.[12] Late colonial writers, on their side, composed poems for their patrons and friends that hailed them as positive role models. In one such poem, the author praises Manuela Larraín, an aristocratic and influential woman, for her piety and discretion, two virtues traditionally associated with her gender.[13] Elites also sought to manifest their exemplarity in portraits that represented them as religious and virtuous patriots.[14]

With this influence came much responsibility. In fact, expectations surrounding exemplarity were often formulated in the context of their transgression. In 1819 a political conflict erupted in the town of La Ligua, near Valparaíso, pitting two brothers, Juan and Nicolás Orrego, against each other. After an official mediation, the siblings—both prominent local figures—agreed to cease their quarrel.[15] The government congratulated the two brothers for their "reconciliation" and reminded them that the "*vecindario*" (the local community) "always follows the example of its most important citizens." Because the two brothers occupied "military and political positions," the government continued, their "example has an influence over [other people's] conduct."[16]

Like good examples, bad examples were supposed to have a deep impact on society. From the elites' point of view, intergenerational mimesis explained in no small measure the vices and corruption they detected in the majority of the population. Children imitated their parents; consequently, the offspring of racially and socially inferior people adopted and reproduced their alleged bad behavior. Crown attorney José Joaquín Pérez de Uriondo explained in 1804 that "Indians" living in Chile were driven to irreligion and crime because they followed the bad example set by their progenitors.[17] Other observers likewise argued that intergenerational mimesis accounted for the vices they perceived among the enslaved, free Black people, peasants, and the lower classes more generally.[18]

Bad examples threatened the correct functioning of power relations. In 1782 Chile's governor warned authorities in the presidio of Valdivia that deserters and runaways set a "bad example" for the regular troops stationed in the city, which could lead the soldiers to graver forms of insubordination.[19] Censoring actions before they became bad examples was therefore essential to maintaining the country's political and social structures. When in 1801 Santiago's Audiencia issued a royal order granting water rights to two influential miners in the town of Copiapó, a coalition of local hacienda owners, Diaguita people, and other subaltern individuals rose to resist its application. Communicating this news to the Audiencia, a lawyer for one of the miners warned the tribunal that, without swift and proper punishment, Chile's "other [provinces] will receive this terrible example, and due subordination to the sovereign and the superior tribunals will be constantly broken."[20]

Imitation thus configured a field of social and political interaction. Through mimetic relations, people could exert positive or negative influence over others. Being "exemplary" was both a responsibility and a privilege—mimesis supposedly awarded men and women the ability to guide and corrupt others. Because of this power, imitation needed to be regulated. Bad examples were dangerous for society, authorities argued, as they challenged the colony's social, moral, and political order. Through the notion of "example," then, people's lives and everyday behavior became of public relevance, constituting a form of "publicness" that authorities felt the need to monitor and control.

Scandalous Publicness

When in 1816 a judge accused Domingo Sotomayor, a young, enslaved man, of planning "a scandalous attempt against his master," he was using extremely precise language. Sotomayor lived in the house of a slaveholder in Santiago. A few weeks before his trial, he had escaped the house and visited San Isidro Street, near the Mapocho River. There, perhaps in one of the street's famous chinganas, he met a man named José Benavides, with whom he apparently chatted for a while. Sotomayor was soon captured by the police and spent some days in forced public labor before returning to the slaveholder's house. He then resumed contact with Benavides and, after a few meetings in Sotomayor's room, the two men came up with a plan to rob the slaveholder. The day of the robbery, Sotomayor would help Benavides and a group of men enter the house; acting as if they did not know Sotomayor, they would steal as much as they could, leaving the enslaved man's share hidden in his room. The plan was never put into action, as Benavides denounced Sotomayor first.[21]

From the authorities' point of view, the case was alarming. An enslaved man conspiring against a slaveholder in the sacred space of the latter's household was both morally outrageous and politically dangerous. Plotting against a father-like figure in the sanctuary of his own house, and leaving him and his family at some bandits' mercy, was to the elites a form of treason, a violation of the ties of love and loyalty that should bind the enslaved to their holders. Sotomayor's plan questioned the slaveholder's patriarchal authority and set a bad precedent for others to imitate. All these attributes—treachery, insubordination, and bad example—were encapsulated in a single word the judge used when questioning Sotomayor: "scandalous." Through the notion of "scandal," the judge measured the social and moral impact of Sotomayor's behavior. Although we do not know what happened to Sotomayor, as the file on his case remains incomplete, similar legal cases against enslaved women and men during colonial times show that authorities justified severe punishments—including the death penalty—against them based on the idea that their actions set scandalous examples for other enslaved people to imitate.[22]

If there was one concept that defined the realm of mimetic publicness, it was that of scandal. In Spanish political discourse, this word described the publicness of bad and socially dangerous examples.[23] This notion can be traced back to European medieval law, which conceptualized scandal as a visible example of bad behavior that gave other people the inspiration and opportunity to sin. The concept of scandal allowed medieval priests in particular to assess the propagation of faults and judge the amount of damage a person had done with his or her actions.[24]

People in Chile mobilized the notion of scandal to evaluate a person's impact on others. In an itemization of his sins written between 1799 and 1804, elite lawyer José Ignacio Eyzaguirre repeatedly used the word "scandal" to measure how public his bad actions were and how much damage they had caused others.[25] Similarly, in 1823 an anonymous pamphlet denounced priest Camilo Henríquez for conducting "a scandalous and sacrilegious life." Henríquez's behavior, the tract argued, had caused "the ruin" and "perdition" of many "souls."[26] Scandals therefore had public repercussions associated with their ability to propagate sin. A priest from

Colchagua accused a man in 1770 of "going from place to place infecting people with his scandals."[27] The notion of scandal designated the impact of human actions as measured against a transcendentally sanctioned order—scandals were attacks against both the social order and God.[28]

More broadly, individuals also used the words "scandal" and "scandalous" to describe flagrant crimes and public faults that caused shock and outrage. Litigants thus mobilized this concept to frame their adversaries' actions as both public and consequential. In 1767 Ignacio Milán, a merchant living in Santiago, complained that an African-descended ("*pardo*") tavern owner named Manuel Fernández shouted at him that he was a "mulatto" and that his father was a "mulatto baker." According to Milán, Fernández repeated these remarks "time and again in the middle of the street, which led many scandalized persons to show up in their houses' doors." Milán used the concept of scandal to present Fernández's "insolence" as a public affront to his honor.[29] In 1783 an enslaved woman named María del Carmen reported to authorities the mistreatment to which she had been subjected by slaveholders Brianda Manso and Bernardo Altolaguirre. The latter interpreted María del Carmen's denunciation as an act of insubordination, accusing her of having caused "scandal and bad example . . . not only to my house's other servants, but to all [the servants] of the city."[30]

Due to their publicness and impact, scandals were a menace to social and political order. As one official stated in 1813, "scandals" were "the origins of insubordination."[31] One of the main duties of secular and religious authorities was therefore to prevent and eradicate scandals.[32] This gave public relevance to a wide set of phenomena, from specific actions and events to patterns of behavior and even entire lifestyles. In official documentation, people decried the existence of "scandalous disobedience," "scandalous gatherings," "scandalous conduct," and "scandalous life."[33] Through the concept of scandal, then, Chileans constructed what others did and how they conducted their lives as a public matter concerning the political and spiritual well-being of the community.

The Sources of Heroism

In late colonial Chile, history books, religious treatises, sermons, and oratory pieces abounded with models of exemplary conduct. These examples—taken from diverse sources ranging from Scripture to the recent past—were meant to shape people's behavior. Heroes provided the most powerful examples of good conduct, as they were men and women who had pushed the limits of virtuous behavior to almost superhuman extremes, thus setting a standard by which particularly meritorious actions could be evaluated. The monarchy's paramount hero was the king. Official images, ceremonies, and discourse portrayed the Spanish monarchs as heroic figures, both virtuous and mighty.[34] The apogee of this royal propaganda in Chile came in the second half of the eighteenth century.[35] Impressive official ceremonies, such as the 1789 proclamation in Santiago of Carlos IV's accession to the throne, reinforced the idea that the monarch was a military and political paragon. But the king was not the only official colonial hero. Men of letters also highlighted the heroism of Spanish governors in poems, sermons, and public speeches.[36] As governors constantly rotated and were immersed in the colony's contentious factional politics, this heroic propaganda was more formulaic and likely less effective than that which surrounded the monarch.

With the revolution, these models of heroism became obsolete. As Javier Fernández Sebastián has noted, the collapse of the Spanish monarchy and the imperial civil wars led to the emergence of a disparate set of heroes in the Spanish Atlantic.[37] In Chile iconoclastic actions contributed to this process by destroying not only the monarchy's symbols of power and legitimacy but also its official heroes. In this context the country's postcolonial authorities and emerging partisan groups sought to create new role models to replace the monarchical ones. To make Chileans virtuous citizens capable of defending independence and supporting their new regime, men of letters turned to history. In 1817 the revolutionary government considered creating two newspapers that would be tasked, among other things, with finding heroes in the past who would "inspire civic or military virtues" in the population.[38]

For the ruling classes the most prestigious repository of such heroic models of political virtue was classical antiquity. During the proclamation of Chile's independence in February 1818, José Gregorio Argomedo, the state attorney of the Court of Appeals, gave a speech filled with historical examples taken from ancient Greece and Rome. At the time, independence was more aspiration than reality; in fact, at that very moment, the civil war still raged and a royalist army was marching on Santiago. In his speech, delivered from an improvised stage in Santiago's central square, Argomedo likened the Chilean revolution to the historical experiences of Rome, the Dutch Republic, and the United States. He then offered a series of heroic models for different segments of the population to imitate. He argued that the military should imitate Brutus and George Washington, while civil servants should follow the steps of Horace, Curtius, and Decius. As if preparing the audience for the upcoming clash with the royalists, Argomedo finally mentioned the battles of Thermopylae, Plataea, and Marathon as examples of patriotic and civic engagement.[39] This was just one among countless speeches and writings that drew on classical antiquity to propagate heroic models of conduct.[40]

It is hard to evaluate the impact these erudite and male-centered references had on ordinary men and women. But, at least for elite men, this was more than empty rhetoric. Revolutionary leader Juan Martínez de Rozas wrote a private manuscript titled *Dichos y Sentencias de los Antiguos* (Sayings and Maxims of the Ancients) in which he expressed his desire to imitate the heroes of antiquity.[41] Lettered men acted on the belief that following these examples could transform them and others. Around 1831 a group of supporters of General Bernardo O'Higgins tried to convince General Joaquín Prieto, then allied to a rival faction, to switch sides. To persuade him, they thought it would be a good idea to search for examples of similar behavior in the lives of Cicero and Pompey.[42]

Classical antiquity was not the only reservoir of republican heroes. As Argomedo's 1818 speech suggests, other republican experiences also provided examples of heroism. The United States stood out among these. The construction of Washington as a hero in the United States resounded powerfully in Chile, where revolutionary elites presented him as an example of republican virtues.[43] Washington was a patriot, an institution builder, and, most importantly, a man capable of renouncing power—thus an example to local strongmen.[44] As an article published in the newspaper *Semanario de Policía* stated in 1817, Chileans, finally free from Spanish domination, could now aspire to imitate "Washington, Tones [*sic*, perhaps John Paul Jones], Hancock, Jefferson, Pueyrredón, Belgrano, and San Martín."[45] The last three were contemporary military leaders from the United Provinces of Río de la Plata, of whom more below.

Chile's men of letters also appropriated Mapuche history to transform it into a local version of European antiquity.[46] Since colonial times, elites across Spanish America constructed idealized versions of past Natives to foster their own ideas of patriotism and criticize imperial rule.[47] In Chile, it was the war between the Spaniards and the Mapuche people (whom Spaniards called *Araucanos*) during the sixteenth century that captured the elites' attention. According to Francisco Antonio Pinto's recollections, when the British attacked Buenos Aires in 1806, young men like him gathered to read fragments from Alonso de Ercilla's *La Araucana*, a sixteenth-century epic poem that narrated the struggles between the Mapuches and Spaniards. Pinto claimed he and the other aristocrats admired both the Mapuches and the Spaniards depicted in the book, but his narrative suggests that their admiration was focused on the former. According to Pinto, "it was impossible" to read about the "great actions" of Mapuche warriors and leaders such as "Caupolicán, Colo-Colo, Lautaro, and other colossi from our history without feeling our hearts burn in the desire to imitate them."[48]

With the collapse of the Spanish monarchy, the heroization of Natives acquired new political meanings all across Spanish America. Insurgents denounced the Spanish invasion of the Americas as illegal and criminal and presented colonial domination as a permanent war between Spaniards and Natives.[49] In Chile the celebration of Mapuche heroes became part of a wider critique of the colonial regime aimed at legitimizing political autonomy and finding new models of sovereignty. Starting in 1812 references to the so-called Araucanians and their virtues and heroism could be found in official declarations, patriotic iconography, theatrical productions, and newspapers.[50]

Although Ercilla's poem depicted a number of idealized and heroic "Araucanian" women, lettered men in revolutionary Chile chose not to promote them.[51] A relevant exception was Juan Egaña's *Almanak* for the year 1824. In it Egaña described the feats and accomplishments of over thirty Mapuche men, most of them taken from Ercilla's *La Araucana*. But, more surprisingly, he also celebrated two women, Fresia and Janequeo (fig. 5.1).[52] These figures provided striking examples of heroism: in Egaña's description, the two sixteenth-century Mapuche women were warriors who stood up to the Spaniards. While Fresia conformed to conventional gendered norms in the colony—she was famous for pushing her husband, Caupolicán, to fight against the Spaniards, serving thus as a source of inspiration for a male leader—Janequeo did not. As Egaña related, Janequeo was both a warrior and a military commander who obtained several victories over the Spanish. While she was allegedly inspired by gendered sentiments of piety (avenging her spouse, murdered by Spaniards), Egaña praised her not as a devout wife but as the most accomplished military leader of her region's history. Her gender—given the deep-seated expectation that women be weak and passive—rendered her example even more impressive.

This heroization extended exclusively to past Mapuche people. Spanish American elites generally considered contemporary Indigenous peoples to be unfit for civilized life, and Chileans continued to wage war against the Mapuches and capture and force Mapuche children and women to serve as domestic servants. Although in the 1820s some intellectuals and politicians considered the Mapuches to be an independent nation, the predominant attitude among political elites was that they needed to be incorporated into the new Chilean nation and eventually disappear as a distinct group.[53] Thus, as Rebecca Earle has argued, elite *indigenismo* in

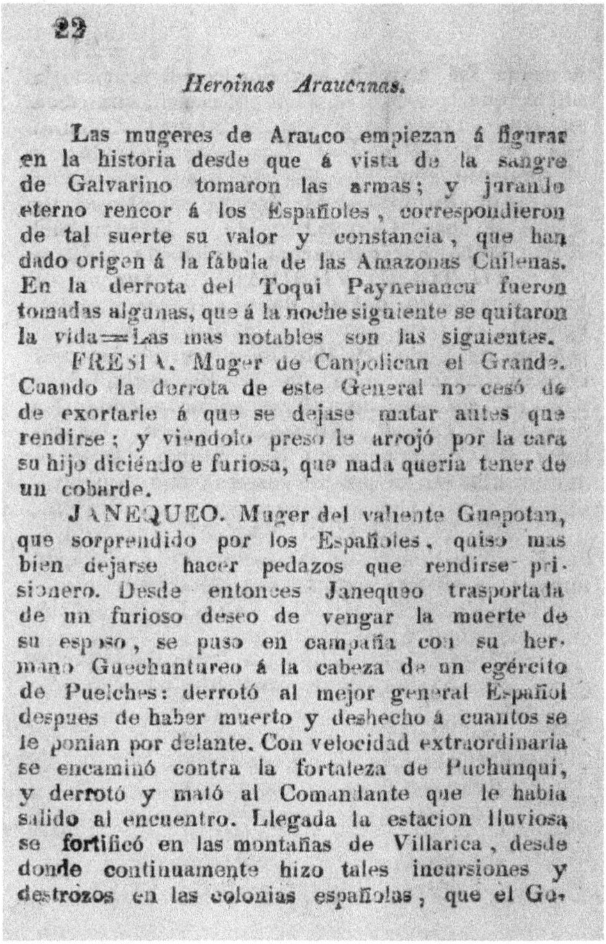

22

Heroinas Araucanas.

Las mugeres de Arauco empiezan á figurar en la historia desde que á vista de la sangre de Galvarino tomaron las armas; y jurando eterno rencor á los Españoles, correspondieron de tal suerte su valor y constancia, que han dado origen á la fábula de las Amazonas Chilenas. En la derrota del Toqui Paynenancu fueron tomadas algunas, que á la noche siguiente se quitaron la vida=Las mas notables son las siguientes.

FRESIA. Muger de Caupolican el Grande. Cuando la derrota de este General no cesó de exortarle á que se dejase matar antes que rendirse; y viendolo preso le arrojó por la cara su hijo diciéndole furiosa, que nada queria tener de un cobarde.

JANEQUEO. Muger del valiente Guepotan, que sorprendido por los Españoles, quiso mas bien dejarse hacer pedazos que rendirse prisionero. Desde entonces Janequeo trasportada de un furioso deseo de vengar la muerte de su esposo, se puso en campaña con su hermano Guechuntureo á la cabeza de un egército de Puelches: derrotó al mejor general Español despues de haber muerto y deshecho á cuantos se le ponian por delante. Con velocidad extraordinaria se encaminó contra la fortaleza de Puchunqui, y derrotó y mató al Comandante que le habia salido al encuentro. Llegada la estacion lluviosa se fortificó en las montañas de Villarica, desde donde continuamente hizo tales incursiones y destrozos en las colonias españolas, que el Go-

Figure 5.1. Section on "Araucanian female heroes" in Egaña, *Almanak nacional para el Estado de Chile en el año bisiesto de 1824*. Photograph by the author.

Spanish America was founded on a process of "appropriation" and "dissociation" in which elites of Spanish descent appropriated the Native past while dissociating present-day Indigenous people from it.[54]

Political groups constantly manipulated examples of heroism for partisan purposes. When the newspaper *Semanario de Policía* invited Chileans in 1817 to imitate men such as Washington, Hancock, San Martín, and Belgrano, it was clearly seeking to legitimize the latter two leaders of Río de la Plata, allies of the O'Higgins regime. Heroes from the past also played a role in ideological and partisan disputes. Defenders of a unified, republican form of government usually referred to classical antiquity, while those favoring federalism tended to emphasize the example of the United States. In the late 1820s ardent federalist José Miguel Infante claimed that the Mapuche people, who had provided Chileans with heroic models of virtue and resistance against the Spaniards, were also an example of the superiority of federal regimes.[55]

Partisan Heroes

Although all heroes served partisan purposes, some were explicitly created as partisan tools. From the early stages of the imperial civil wars, competing factional groups sought to promote their own heroes and martyrs. Unsurprisingly, most of the individuals officially celebrated as heroes during this period gained this status thanks to their involvement in the revolutionary wars. They were usually officers who found glory (some an honorable death) on the battlefield. As these were wars of imperial scale, men from all the Spanish territories could be seen as heroes worth imitating. For example, in 1811 Santiago aristocrat José Antonio Rojas celebrated the "heroes" of Buenos Aires who were fighting royalism.[56] Similarly, sometime between 1810 and 1814, a priest named Juan José Uribe gave a funerary sermon in Santiago's cathedral in honor of the "heroes of Caracas," who (given the context) were probably revolutionary martyrs who died in defense of the revolution.[57]

The first concerted efforts to create heroes from local armies occurred during the civil war between royalists and revolutionaries in 1813 and 1814. In May of 1813 the insurgent government ordered the construction of a pyramid in Santiago that would immortalize the names of all the men deceased fighting the royalists. When news reached Santiago of aristocrat Joaquín Alonso de Toro's death while laying siege to Chillán, the junta ordered that his name be inscribed in the pyramid so that citizens may aspire to "imitate" this "heroic young man."[58] On March 4, 1814, Spanish colonel Carlos Spano died in the town of Talca, reportedly defending the revolutionary flag from royalist troops. Just a few days later, Santiago's revolutionary government published an official account of his death in the newspaper *El Monitor Araucano* and announced the creation of an enormous monument in his memory in Talca's central square.[59] Although the memorial was never built, liberals continued into the 1820s to commemorate Spano as a martyr for freedom. In February of 1825, for example, his name was inscribed in a temporary pyramid that authorities erected in Santiago's central square to celebrate Chile's independence.[60]

Royalists also created their own heroes. In August of 1813, for example, Chile's official newspaper lamented that some people celebrated José Antonio Ezeiza and Manuel Lagos—two men executed for participating in a royalist rebellion north of Santiago—as heroes.[61] Another figure briefly emerged as a royalist hero the following year: merchant Romualdo Antonio Esponda. As seen in chapter 3, in September of 1814, Santiago's revolutionary authorities subjected Esponda to flogging and other public humiliations for embroidering a Spanish royal flag. Soon after, royal authorities sought to make him a hero, a model to be imitated. In a report issued in December of 1814, Santiago's city council explicitly stated that Esponda was a "hero" and that publicly restoring his honor, as the merchant requested, would be "to publicize [*patentizar*] an example of true loyalty."[62] The ceremony held in Esponda's honor in Santiago's central square in November of 1816 and the written account of it published in the official gazette a few days later were meant not only to restore the merchant's honor but also to promote his example among the citizenry.[63]

During the royalist government of 1814–1817, the heroization of colonial authorities was reestablished. Governors Mariano Osorio and Casimiro Marcó del Pont, together with the viceroys of Peru and Spanish King Fernando VII, were celebrated as virtuous and powerful heroes in newspaper articles, religious celebrations, public festivities, and theater spectacles.[64] The regime similarly sought to turn Colonel Tomás Figueroa (executed in 1811 after attempting to overthrow the revolutionary government) into a monarchist hero.[65] When insurgents gained control of most of the country again in February of 1817, these royal officials were of course no longer celebrated. But the heroization of political and military leaders continued. Generals San Martín and O'Higgins were portrayed as glorious heroes in official ceremonies, plays, portraits, and newspapers.[66] It was only after General Ramón Freire seized power in 1823 that this official machine of heroization lost much of its force. Political pluralism—which involved the potential rotation of heads of state and open contestation over their alleged virtues—together with the reserved temperament of leaders such as Freire made it difficult to institutionalize new authorities as heroic figures.[67]

A new phenomenon developed between 1823 and 1830: the opening of mimetic publicness to the competition of antagonistic heroes. Political factions, particularly the supporters of General O'Higgins and of the Carrera family, openly clashed over which people should be celebrated as heroes. After O'Higgins was sent into exile in 1823, his supporters continued to refer to him as "our hero," sometimes even in public pasquinades against the new administration, while critics questioned his heroic status.[68] Followers of the Carrera family, for their part, reclaimed Manuel Rodríguez and the Carrera brothers—whose deaths between 1817 and 1822 they blamed on O'Higgins and his faction—as national heroes. In banquets, theater performances, phantasmagoric spectacles, newspaper articles, ephemeral monuments, and public addresses, the former supporters of the Carrera family celebrated their martyrs as revolutionary heroes worth imitating.[69] This process culminated in 1828 with the repatriation of the remains of the Carrera brothers and the celebration of state funerals for them in Santiago.[70]

Politicians and men of letters tried to incorporate these partisan figures into the more traditional pantheon of historical heroes. For radical liberal Santiago Muñoz Bezanilla, one of those behind the initiative to repatriate the Carrera brothers' remains, the three brothers resembled Lautaro, Galvarino, and Caupolicán, three Mapuche heroes praised in Ercilla's *La Araucana* for fighting and dying for their fatherland.[71] Similarly, in 1828 philosopher and professor José Miguel Varas called on Chilean youth to imitate the great heroes of antiquity as well as Manuel Rodríguez. He even asserted that Rodríguez was more "useful" as a role model for Chileans, as he was "from our own country." "Young people," Varas adjured, "imitate [Rodríguez's] example [and] your glory will be eternal like his."[72]

The importance of these partisan heroes derived directly from the fact that they were models to be imitated. Heroes would propagate and reproduce over time their virtues and ideological choices. Crafting heroes was a political strategy not only because heroes inspired admiration, and thus attracted more people to partisan causes, but also because heroes gave a specific direction to society's mimetic drive.[73] Revolutionaries and royalists, supporters of O'Higgins and those of the Carrera family, all factions competed to advance their own heroes, using imitation to influence politics and transform society. As a result, they established in revolutionary and postcolonial Chile a pluralistic mimetic public sphere in which multiple heroic figures clashed and competed.

Promoting Women's Heroism

In colonial and postcolonial Chile, official discourse celebrated women either as virtuous wives, mothers, and matriarchs or as pious women devoted to God.[74] While these roles seem essentially "private" or nonpublic today, for contemporary Chileans they granted women the power to positively affect society. Nuns, for example, were supposed to radiate their beneficial influence and good example throughout the body politic in spite of living cloistered lives.[75] Scholars and politicians were nevertheless reluctant to consider women as political and military heroes. While there were some attempts at fabricating female revolutionary heroes, such as Egaña's celebration of Fresia and Janequeo, these were isolated episodes. The only government that actively promoted women as heroic role models was the O'Higgins administration (1817–1823). Worried about the support royalism enjoyed among elite women, the government advertised patriotic and heroic women to inspire others to imitate them.[76]

Between 1817 and 1820, Chile's official newspaper presented its readers with several examples of women heroes. Revealingly, in June of 1817, the very first issue of the *Gazeta de Santiago de Chile*, the administration's official organ, opened with a celebration of "citizens" María Silva, Francisca Araya, Juana Latapia, and María de la Cruz Aguilera. The newspaper praised them not for their own actions but because they were relatives of victims of political repression during the royalist regime. Only one of those victims was a woman herself, Águeda Monasterio. Although the article expressed a traditional view of women's role in official politics—not as actors, but as faithful companions to men—it nevertheless revealed a desire to reach women with heroic examples to imitate. As the article stated, its objective was to "publicize" these women's merits so that they might serve as an "incentive for heroism."[77]

It is unclear whether these four women had previously requested a reward from the government, but other women certainly did. Carmen Ureta, Rafaela Riesco, and María Mercedes Matorras, for example, petitioned the government for some kind of financial support before being praised in official documents and newspapers.[78] The government not only acknowledged their merits and accepted their requests but also explicitly promoted them as models to be imitated. In 1818 officials declared María Cornelia Olivares a "citizen" to reward her for having visibly displayed her patriotism in the town of Chillán during royalist rule. The government publicized her case in Santiago's *Gazeta* hoping it constituted "an example worthy of being imitated."[79]

Women even set the standards by which their heroism was to be judged. In late 1817 a young woman from a wealthy background named Mercedes Rosales del Solar donated lint to the government (lint was badly needed in Chile's military hospitals). In her accompanying communication, she advanced the idea that in Chile, like in other countries, "women" should also participate in the fight against "tyranny."[80] The government not only thanked Rosales del Solar but also ordered her letter to be published in Santiago's *Gazeta* "so that the heroism and virtuous sentiments of this distinguished citizen could serve as a perfect model" for all Chilean women.[81]

This acclamation of heroic women was not a mere official creation; it emerged because women themselves pressed authorities to acknowledge their heroism. These women clearly conceived of themselves as politically engaged and exemplary individuals, and official recognition did in fact help spread their fame. In 1825 an anonymous author published a book in Paris about heroic Spanish American women that mentioned several of their names. The book narrated their stories based on official orders published in Chilean newspapers between 1817 and 1820—the very same documents these women helped create through their petitions and requests to the government.[82]

Negotiating Heroism: María Ana Pérez de Arza's Heroic Pantheon

Establishing who was a hero was not the exclusive prerogative of male elites. Men and women of different calidad also created narratives about heroism and sometimes even sought to negotiate them with authorities. This was the case of María Ana Pérez de Arza. Pérez de Arza was an elite woman married to a merchant who fled Santiago during the early stages of the revolution and died in Lima soon after. She took control of her husband's trade and stayed in Santiago with her children.[83] A few weeks after royalist General Mariano Osorio entered Santiago with his troops in 1814, Pérez de Arza wrote to the government, describing her sacrifices during the revolutionary period. She asked the new administration for financial support and to arrange employment for her son.[84] General Osorio accepted her request, noting that she "deserves to be rewarded," and gave one of her sons a government job.[85] Pérez de Arza was unsatisfied with Osorio's response, as she considered the position granted to her son insufficient to meet her family's financial needs. In a new petition, written in February of 1815, Pérez de Arza stressed the unparalleled nature of her merits. "My heroism," she wrote, "extraordinary to my sensitive sex, and unusual among the women of my country, does not demand any other reward than the Spaniards' gratitude." "No woman in this capital," she continued, "can dispute my merits." Pérez de Arza requested additional financial aid from the government "for the only woman who, exceeding herself," defended her king.[86]

This time the government denied Pérez de Arza's request, and so she wrote a third petition, this one directly to the viceroy of Peru, José de Abascal. In it, she again constructed herself as a female hero. "I was born in a country where women are as beautiful as they are miserable," she stated; "this is an axiom." She claimed to be a "poor woman" and a "miserable soldier [*soldado*, gendered male in Spanish]," but her children, she continued, did not deserve to be as unhappy as she was. Pérez de Arza's petition subverted traditional gendered narratives about heroism. Instead of focusing on her husband's merits, as widows during this period usually did, she drew authorities' attention to her own heroism. In fact, she explicitly dispensed with talking about her husband's merits. As she told the viceroy, her husband "was a virtuous Spaniard. But let's leave this aside. Why me, the only martyr in this story, am I left to perish in misery and humiliation?" This transition, from her husband's unspecified virtues to her own status as the "only martyr in this story" signals her desire to be recognized for her own heroism. To the revolutionaries, she claimed, she was "a scandal"; that is, a public example of resistance and disobedience. She enumerated her sufferings during the revolutionary period: according to her, masked men had assaulted her in the street, as a result of which she took ill and had a miscarriage; she had been sentenced to work "as a slave" for a woman named María Ana Toro; and she had also been condemned to perform public works while in shackles. When the royal army entered Santiago in October of 1814, Pérez de Arza was being held prisoner in one of Santiago's monasteries. Together with her unwavering support for the royalist cause, these actions made her a hero and a martyr. How could "the powerful king of Spain and his representatives" ignore her, she asked.[87]

For María Ana Pérez de Arza, being a woman imposed no limit on her heroic capacity. On the contrary, her heroism was even more remarkable precisely because of her gender. As the fragments quoted above show, Pérez de Arza was entirely aware of the gendered nature of heroic discourse. Her own heroism, she claimed, was "extraordinary" and "unusual" among local women, therefore inscribing herself in an alternative pantheon of women heroes. In her communication to the viceroy, she compared herself to Marie-Anne Charlotte Corday, the French woman who assassinated Jean-Paul Marat in 1793. Like Corday, with whom she shared first names ("María Ana"), Pérez de Arza had decided "to be the opposite of my inhuman countrymen" and fight against revolution. It is unclear where and how she heard about Corday, but the French woman was certainly not among the royalist government's official heroes.

Pérez de Arza also compared her case to that of a Spanish American woman like herself, "Manuela la Tucumana." During the British invasion of Buenos Aires in 1806, Manuela Pedraza, a woman born in

Tucumán, reportedly fought side by side with her husband and killed a British soldier with a rifle. Manuela's deeds featured prominently in narratives of the event published in Buenos Aires, and the king rewarded her patriotism with an official appointment (including a salary) as second lieutenant of infantry.[88] In her letter to the viceroy, Pérez de Arza wrote that "Manuela la Tucumana was rewarded. But they say she took a rifle and I did not. But how, I demand, could I have traveled a hundred leagues [to the battlefield], with four children . . . and without my husband?"[89] This suggests that Pérez de Arza not only compared herself to Pedraza but also discussed the nature of her heroism with others. When these other people questioned whether she was as heroic as Pedraza, she replied with arguments that affirmed her gendered virtues—her position in the family unit as caregiver and her status as a widow—while suggesting that she would have gladly joined the ranks of the royalist army were it not for these gendered expectations.[90] In her view, she was not inferior to Pedraza. In her February of 1815 petition to the Osorio administration, she asserted that Pedraza "was less exceptional than I am, but she was a woman and was rewarded, as I expect to be."[91] Like Corday, Pedraza was not part of the male-centered pantheon of official heroes in Chile. Pérez de Arza thus advanced her own set of heroes, one that served to reflect her own merits and support her demands that they be justly rewarded.

In María Ana Pérez de Arza's gendered view of politics, women could also be wicked. In a second letter to the viceroy, she complained that "the tears of the insurgent women" had moved Governor Osorio to ask the king for an official pardon for their husbands. While in her view she had obtained nothing from the royalist government, these "insurgent women" secured benefits for their "criminal husbands."[92] Revealingly, Pérez de Arza did not describe these women as faithful wives who fulfilled their conjugal duties by caring for their men. On the contrary, her labeling of them as "insurgent women" implied that they had clear political affiliations and were as criminal as their spouses. She thus read the governor's request for a pardon in gendered terms: the colony's patriarchal leader preferred Chile's "insurgent women" over her, a royalist and a hero.

Pérez de Arza's self-understanding as a hero also influenced her political activities. Lacking support from Santiago's government, in 1815 she joined the ranks of a dissident royalist faction that opposed General Osorio's rule. In mid-1815 Osorio summoned Pérez de Arza to the government palace. According to an account of these events she sent to the viceroy, the governor suspected she was the author of a pasquinade critical of authorities that had recently appeared in the capital. When Osorio showed her the piece of paper, she said she had never seen it before. When Osorio pressed as to why she denied her crime (although without specifying what exactly she was being accused of), she responded with a question: "Am I a woman capable of denying my own writing, when I know the punishments that correspond to this crime?" When the governor, still not having accused her of any crime, told her to "get out," she refused and replied: "Is this the way to treat a lady? Is this the reward you save for merit and virtue?" Finally, when the governor informed her that she was suspected of writing the pasquinade, she answered: "And is there anyone in the world who may even believe that I am capable of writing a pasquinade against the General . . . , or against any other individual of the Royal Army?"[93] Pérez de Arza reacted with indignation—even insubordination, refusing to leave the room when so ordered—to accusations she believed were beneath her status as a royalist hero. Although she may have exaggerated the terms of her encounter with Osorio, she was certainly gaining notoriety as a political actor. News of her political activities and clashes with the government reached as far as the prison island of Juan Fernández.[94]

Heroism was for María Ana Pérez de Arza a useful social and political tool. Presenting herself as a hero suited both her personal convictions and her material needs. Her claims to heroism—which in her case implied defining a space for women in politics as well as advancing her own pantheon of heroic women—served her to ask for rewards and voice her political views. When circumstances changed, she was forced to abandon those claims. In 1817, after revolutionaries took control of Santiago, she came to the attention of the newly established administration because of her sarcastic commentaries about families that supported the insurgency.[95] A year later an enslaved man named Faustino denounced her to the government for selling contraband goods, and authorities requisitioned some of her assets.[96] The government then deported her to a rural area (La Ligua) for more than six months, only allowing her to move to the town of Los Andes in May of 1819.[97] This was likely a punishment for her royalist allegiance and criticism of revolutionaries. I do not know when she was allowed to return to Santiago. But in 1828, when she sought compensation for the manner in which the accusation against her for selling contraband had been handled, she chose to present herself in public brochures as an apolitical woman who was the victim of unfair political persecution; she even denied having ever been a royalist.[98] Conditions were no longer favorable for heroic royalist women.

As Pérez de Arza's case illustrates, people in Chile relied on imitation and other associated concepts to explain how humans interacted with and affected each other. Mimetic relations connected individuals, groups, and generations, disseminating ways of life, vices, and virtues. In this mimetic public sphere, communication was understood as the propagation not of ideas or messages but of actions and behaviors. Mimesis transformed people's behavior into a public matter, and it was the authorities' task to control the examples that circulated in this dense network of imitations. But mimetic relations were not under the exclusive control of the government, and during the revolutionary era its power was invoked by antagonistic partisan groups. Additionally, actors marginalized by the standard discourse of heroism could also create their own heroic references and ask for their merits to be recognized, as María Ana Pérez de Arza did during the royalist restoration. Mimesis, in sum, became a force in dispute between multiple groups that responded to competing interests and visions of the future.

CHAPTER SIX

Contagious Politics and the Origins of Conflict

In early 1816 the *Gazeta del Rey*, Chile's official royalist newspaper, published a serial feature aimed at convincing its audience that local revolutionaries were akin to the devil. To a modern reader, this comparison may seem absurd or extravagant, but for people living in Chile during the Age of Dissent, it had a clear political meaning. For them, the devil was more than an abstract force of evil—he was a sower of dissent and division. By comparing revolutionaries to Satan, the newspaper did much more than simply criticize the regime's enemies; it offered a theological and anthropological theory of conflict. In particular, it meant to persuade readers that vicious men were the root cause of the revolution and that they had contaminated Chile with the contagious disease of dissension.

The article, probably written by the newspaper's editor, priest José María Torres, was published in twelve installments between January and April of 1816.[1] Its author first assumed that in any human community there would be men (women were excluded from his interpretation of politics) ruled by ambition, arrogance, egoism, and vanity. These vices would lead them to an interest in causing disorder, as only during moments of chaos would they be able to fully unleash their passions. To foster confusion and dissolution, these corrupted men often adopted the flags of freedom, which they used to seduce otherwise innocent people and trick them into aiding their cause. This was the origin of political conflict and precisely what Chile experienced after Napoleon captured the Spanish royal family in 1808. Before the revolution, the article argued, Chile was a quiet, peaceful, and prosperous place. Then a group of vicious men took over the government, disturbing society's moral, religious, and political order. To maintain their grip on power, they exploited the simplicity, ignorance, and passions of the people. Their lies and false promises found fertile ground, leading many Chileans to support the revolution.

It was at this point in the argument that the author drew a parallel between Satan and local revolutionaries. In the Bible, the article argued, the devil led humans to rebel against God's authority. Like modern-day revolutionaries, he used lies and false promises to lure people into disobedience and disorder. The devil did not just push Adam and Eve to challenge God; he introduced a principle of division in the relationship between them, setting in motion a process of disorganization and disunity that disrupted the state of harmony that had prevailed until then. Revolutionaries had similarly transformed Chile's social and political landscape, tricking the population into supporting them and artificially creating disorder and dissent. The article left unstated the natural conclusion of its thesis: that without these agents of disorder, Chile would return to its normal, peaceful state.

In the *Gazeta del Rey*'s interpretation of the revolution, dissent was an anomaly, a sort of social malfunctioning that had its origins in a limited set of primary agents. This form of understanding the sources of political insubordination was inseparable from a certain idea of communication. Communication explained the transition between a situation in which vices affected only a small number of men to a state of generalized disturbance and disorder. Contagion provided the perfect conceptual tool to describe the process by which conflict proliferated without any structural cause or legitimate justification. This concept was not a mere metaphor for the dissemination of pernicious ideas through speech and writing. Rather, it designated the propagation of insubordination and conflict by vague and often unspecified means.

The depoliticization of the population, the dissociation of insubordination from legitimate causes, and the emphasis on external influences were common features of political discourse in the Atlantic world. During the Age of Dissent, elites across the region believed that poor, Indigenous, and enslaved people were somehow incapable of forming their own political ideas or agendas.[2] Historians studying the Caribbean have been struck by how elite observers attributed slave uprisings and revolutions to the influence of outside actors while failing to recognize that enslavement alone could generate the conditions for rebellion and resistance.[3] This form of understanding discord not only reflects the elites' hypocrisy and their disregard for the political abilities of common people, but it is also fundamentally antipolitical: it assumes that plurality and conflict are both artificial and nefarious.

This chapter analyzes the concept of contagion as key to understanding the intersection between dissension and communication during the Age of Dissent. For Chileans, contagion was a predominantly political notion and preoccupation, not a medical one. The concept combined a particular view of society (as a connected body) with an interpretation of dissension (as a communicable disease). Contagion was a way to make sense of as well as to participate in politics. As historian Gilles Malandain has shown, people from the past were observers of their own reality, and they advanced different explanations for events that took place within it.[4] Finding answers to questions such as what caused the revolution, or who was responsible for it, was a form of political action. Some took direct inspiration in the idea and became agents of revolutionary contagion. Others, however, sought to heal the wounds caused by the contagion of insubordination, devising means of political reconciliation and cohabitation. All of these individuals relied on contagion to both generate and navigate an increasingly fractured world.

Contagion and the Divided Body

The word "contagion," as used in Chile and the wider Spanish Atlantic during the Age of Dissent, should not be considered a medical concept that was somehow imported into the political arena. Nor was it a metaphor meant to describe what today we would simply call the communication of ideas. As historian Arnaud Fossier has shown, the Latin words *contagio* and contagium were regularly used in medieval discourse on the transmission of heresy and original sin to understand the propagation of errors and evil.[5] In the Iberian context, authors such as Isidore of Seville (d. 636) and Vincent Ferrer (1350–1419) conceived of sin, heresy, and non-Catholic religions as communicable infections. Controlling this unholy contagion was an essential religious and political task. Rather than the basis of metaphors, then, diseases served as models to explain both the dissemination of religious and political dissent and its effects on society. For example, in the thirteenth-century Spanish code called the *Siete Partidas* (which partly informed the Spanish empire's legislation), the crime of treason was compared to leprosy. Like this disease, treason spread through the body politic from a single origin, endangering society's unity and health.[6]

Considering this theological and political background, it is not surprising that, in late colonial and postcolonial Chile, contagion belonged more to the political than to the medical lexicon. The interpersonal transmission of certain diseases was of course a source of concern for colonial and postcolonial people, and officials adopted measures such as vaccinating the population and quarantining individuals suspected of having contracted maladies such as smallpox and yellow fever.[7] But concern over interpersonal contagion was mostly limited to the prevention of epidemic outbreaks. Hegemonic medicine in Chile continued to be based on the humoral paradigm in which health was determined by the interplay between the body, its constitutive elements, and the surrounding environment.[8]

This form of reasoning was reflected in the most comprehensive medical treatise published in Chile between 1780 and 1833, Guillermo Blest's 1828 *Ensayo sobre las causas comunes y activas de las enfermedades que se padecen en Santiago de Chile* (Essay on the common and active causes of the diseases suffered in Santiago de Chile). In his work, Blest—an Irish doctor who had recently arrived in Chile—enumerated the causes of the diseases that afflicted Santiago's inhabitants. Among the principal ones were the city's "police" (meaning its hygiene and spatial organization), its miasmas, the influence of the sun, and, surprisingly, the "homicides" that took place in it. Blest did not pay much attention to contagion in explaining the propagation of diseases. Consequently, the methods he proposed to prevent them were not based on the idea of obstructing interpersonal exchanges. To fight the most common diseases in Santiago, Blest suggested that authorities reform the city's "police" and that its inhabitants adopt healthy diets and wear clothes adapted to their skin types.[9]

Though a foreigner, Blest's treatise reflected mainstream medicine at the time, both before and after independence. It is therefore important not to overstate the relevance of contagion as a medical concern or practice, which would then serve as a metaphor for politics. Contagion was more central to political thinking and practice than to medicine, as it reflected core assumptions about the nature and workings of the political. More specifically, the notion of contagion referred to the idea that members of society were highly interdependent and that dissension was a dangerous and communicable anomaly.

For women and men living in Chile during the Age of Dissent, the body offered a "principle of vision and division of the social world."[10] That is, the body served as a prism through which actors apprehended the nature of the social bond and established boundaries between them. Chilean elites often claimed that society was divided into two camps, the healthy and unhealthy, using terms such as *pueblo sano* or *parte sana del pueblo* ("healthy people" or "the healthy part of the people") to distinguish between the two. In 1810, for example, a royalist chronicler argued that the "most healthy and distinguished part" of several pueblos (towns/political communities) in Chile was opposed to the revolutionary government.[11] This implied that members of society, like those of an infected body, could be divided between those who remained clean and those who had been tainted by contagion. Another royalist in 1810 characterized his adversaries as "infected by the same disease," referring to their alleged revolutionary allegiance.[12]

Like the human body, the body politic was vulnerable to being contaminated. As one newspaper article stated in 1839, human societies and the human body were "identical in their vital trajectories," as both entities were menaced by diseases that, if not treated properly, could spread and become terminal.[13] Chief among these diseases was dissension. Observers described people who adopted rival views or political positions as "spreaders of evil" and accused them of introducing, disseminating, or sowing "division and discord."[14] Dissenters were thus cast as analogous to a disease afflicting the body politic—communicating their contamination to others, corrupting an otherwise healthy body. For this reason, political figures and groups often claimed that their enemies were a "cancer" that needed to be "cut."[15]

Contagion and Revolution

Contagion—together with other notions that similarly described rapid and impactful forms of dissemination such as "fire" and "electricity"—helped observers in the revolutionary Atlantic explain the radical political transformations that were taking place in the region. The concept allowed them to frame revolts and revolutions as the result of the propagation of insubordination and revolutionary ideas. Contagion was an explanatory model, one that helped local actors to situate themselves within a larger, interconnected world, while framing dissidence as an anomaly promoted by foreign ideologies and people.

Some observers in Chile considered the colony's distance from Europe as having an important prophylactic effect. Between 1770 and 1808, lawyers, bureaucrats, and hacienda owners advanced the idea that Chile was an oasis of peace and harmony in a troubled world. Although this view misrepresented both colonial factional politics and the lives and political activities of Indigenous, enslaved, and marginalized people, it became a recurrent trope in the discourse of the dominant groups. For example, Manuel de Salas repeatedly argued in the 1770s that Chile was the perfect setting in which to conduct a "philosophical" life. Isolated from Europe, people in Chile lived free from the ambition and misery that plagued the Old World.[16] In a speech delivered at Santiago's Royal University in 1804, lawyer Juan Egaña claimed that, because of its remoteness, Chile was untouched by Europe's wars, hunger, and revolutions. For this reason, only in Chile could the Enlightenment dream of a "city made for wisdom, and entirely inhabited by wise men" ever be realized.[17] Seen from this perspective, foreign actors and influences constituted a threat. When British forces attacked the Río de la Plata area in 1806 and 1807, Juan Egaña penned a lengthy speech in which he characterized the assault as an example of "Europe's turbulences" having finally come to disturb Chile's "mansion of peace."[18]

As Chile entered a phase of widespread political contestation after 1808, local observers began interpreting these developments as the result of a nefarious contagion coming from abroad. Between 1810 and 1812 royalist merchant Manuel Antonio Talavera wrote a chronicle/journal in which he described what he called the "revolutions of Chile." In Talavera's narrative, local expressions of insubordination and rebellion against imperial officials stemmed, at least in part, from Buenos Aires's evil influence. Having installed its own independent junta in May of 1810, Buenos Aires was a contaminating agent that spilled its "poison" into neighboring areas.[19] As the revolution in Chile advanced, Talavera concluded that the insurgents' earlier declarations of loyalty toward the king had been nothing but a carefully crafted charade designed to mask a revolutionary plan orchestrated in Buenos Aires.[20]

Others made sense of the political transformations that were taking place in Chile by attributing them to a limited number of corrupted people. Although not necessarily "foreign" in the sense of crossing borders, these men had become alien to their own communities because of their vices and wickedness. As soon as news of the imprisonment of the Spanish royal family arrived in Chile in August of 1808, a manuscript pamphlet denounced the existence of an unnamed faction that wanted to corrupt the rest of the "body politic" with insubordination.[21] After the establishment of a junta in Santiago in September of 1810, many royalists agreed that a small number of men had contaminated and somehow managed to revolutionize Chile—an argument royalists would continue to advance for years, characterizing insurgents and revolutionaries as being "corrupted" or afflicted by a "patriotic corruption."[22]

The most elaborate vision of the origins of Chile's revolution was composed by Franciscan friar Melchor Martínez. Born in Spain in 1762, Martínez had been a missionary among the Mapuches for several years before moving to Santiago in 1805. He apparently enjoyed an excellent reputation among local elites as a theologian and scholar.[23] In July of 1814 the Spanish government informed Chile's royalist commander, General Mariano Osorio, that it was important to "know the true origins of the disturbances and seditions that have taken place, and continue to take place" in the colony. The government instructed Osorio to put someone in charge of writing a history of the revolution, which would clarify not only the period's "events," but also the "people who started and led those disturbances," including any foreign "support and help" they may have received.[24] In 1815 Osorio tasked Martínez with this work. Martínez began his narrative with an analysis of the "causes" of "the revolution in Chile," inscribing local events since 1808 within a relatively global context. Among the causes of Chile's revolution, Martínez included the "crisis of Europe after 1790"—most notably the "so-called Enlightenment" that was disseminated from Paris—and the "example" of the United States, promoted across Spanish America by American agents and their propaganda.[25] For Martínez, the multiplication of dissent and antagonism in Chile could not be dissociated from a revolutionary contagion coming from abroad.

Contagion was especially important for observers during the early phase of the imperial crisis (1808–1814) because it explained the simultaneity of and similarity between geographically distant movements. Paired with a false idea of Chile as an isolated and peaceful country, the concept of contagion allowed colonial officials, merchants, and religious men to present radical dissent and division as unnatural, foreign products. Their emphasis on revolutionary contagion was their way of erecting imaginary boundaries between Chile and the rest of the Atlantic world while inscribing events in the colony within a larger, transimperial and transnational context.

Agents of Dissent

According to observers in Chile and Spanish America, the revolutionary disease often spread through a specific kind of vector: revolutionary agents. As historian Georges Vigarello has noted, the idea of contagion in early modern Europe implied the "localized transmission" of diseases in contrast to the "indiscernible dissemination" that was the focus of traditional medicine.[26] If contagion was a fundamental political concept in the official discourse, it was because the concept itself implied the existence of specific actors responsible for spreading or propagating the disease. In politics, the figure that best represented this communication was that of the agent. Elites often explained contagion as the result of the activities of (usually secret) agents. Local factions not only feared them, but they also dispatched their own, hoping to spread chaos and dissent among their rivals.

Colonial officials and imperial elites constantly worried about the presence of secret agents in the Spanish empire. In 1790—amid rumors of impending war between Spain and Britain—Ambrosio Higgins, Chile's Irish-born governor, informed his superiors in Spain that he was ready to combat the "seditious opinions" that British "evil or undercover emissaries" might "try to spread" in the colony.[27] While no such agent was discovered, Higgins's communication shows how colonial officials worried (or at least pretended to worry) about the destabilizing work of foreign agitators. The most fearsome of these agents were the French. From 1789 onward Spanish authorities were convinced that French revolutionaries were dispatching agents to both Europe and the Americas to promote their revolution. Their concern increased with the radicalization of the French revolutionary process and the revolution in Saint-Domingue. Spanish royal officials across the empire soon began tracking down French and Haitian "Jacobin agents."[28] Although no such agents arrived in Chile, crown officials and colonists worried about the prospect of French people spreading the revolutionary gospel. When in 1795 a priest named Clemente Morán was accused of praising the French Revolution in the city of La Serena, on Chile's north coast, witnesses cared to mention to authorities his worrisome contacts with French individuals.[29]

After the outbreak of war against France in 1808, Spanish elites feared the presence of Napoleonic agents among them. In the following months and years, the idea spread that Napoleon had sent five hundred agents to revolutionize the Americas.[30] Local authorities and members of the elite were therefore in a state of constant alarm. Sometime between 1808 and 1810, two Frenchmen arrived in Santiago, one of whom worked as a secretary for a local notary and the other as a clockmaker. After following them and observing their behavior, a Spanish merchant named Andrés José García concluded they were Napoleonic agents. García, the Inquisition's *revisor* (book censor) in Chile, promptly denounced them to authorities, though, according to him, the Frenchmen mysteriously disappeared after his denunciation.[31]

Colonists soon interpreted political conflict as the result of the machinations of secret Napoleonic emissaries. In 1810 Governor García Carrasco informed Spanish authorities on multiple occasions that resistance to his rule among local elites owed to the work of Napoleon and his agents in the Americas.[32] Royalists also accused revolutionary leaders of working for Napoleon, giving them the nickname of "Napoleones."[33] After carefully considering the political career and behavior of José Miguel Carrera, merchant Manuel Antonio Talavera concluded in 1812 that Carrera was in fact one of Napoleon's agents in Chile.[34] Inversely, since at least 1810, insurgents and supporters of the junta had advanced the idea that royalists were in fact Napoleonic agents or emissaries who aimed to introduce division and discord in Chile.[35]

The person probably most often accused of being a Napoleonic agent was the consul of the United States in Chile, Joel R. Poinsett.

Between 1811 and 1814 Poinsett played a key political role in the country, advising the revolutionary government—and especially General José Miguel Carrera, who ruled Chile between September of 1811 and April of 1813—on issues of military, domestic, and foreign policy. Royalists, who resented his influence and power, routinely claimed he was one of Napoleon's secret agents. In 1813 Spanish royalist general Antonio Pareja sent an emissary to the headquarters of the revolutionary army to persuade insurgents to surrender. Pareja apparently instructed this messenger to inform revolutionary commander Juan José Carrera (José Miguel's brother) that the US consul was a "French emissary" who would ruin people such as Juan José by compromising them in the revolution. Pareja's objective was likely to incite Juan José Carrera to turn against the revolutionary army before it was too late.[36] The idea that Poinsett was a Napoleonic agent pretending to be a consul persisted among royalists for years.[37]

Royalists also suspected the presence of revolutionary agents sent from Buenos Aires. Colonial authorities in Chile and elsewhere feared that the junta established in Buenos Aires in May of 1810 would try to spread revolution to the rest of the continent. In 1811 the aforementioned Talavera argued that "disorder," "seduction," and "deceit" had been brought to Chile by "foreigners, the perverse sons of the Devil from Buenos Aires."[38] Like the *Gazeta del Rey* describing local revolutionaries four years later, Talavera likened Buenos Aires's agents to the devil, as they used deception and lies to foster pride, insubordination, and division in Chile—that is, to create and propagate dissent.

Agents of other Atlantic polities or personages were also a matter of concern. Soon after the Spanish monarchy collapsed in 1808, King Fernando VII's sister Carlota, who was married to the Prince Regent of Portugal, began maneuvering to become Spain's new monarch. From her headquarters in Rio de Janeiro, where she had moved with the Portuguese court in 1807, Carlota sent emissaries and letters to Spain and its colonies, seeking to establish a network of supporters. Given the relations between Rio de Janeiro and the Río de la Plata, she quickly attracted a following in Buenos Aires. In late 1808 Carlota dispatched English merchant Federico Dowling from Buenos Aires to Chile (I briefly describe his activities below). She also sent letters to individuals of prestige and power in the colony, manifesting in this manner that she would favor them should she become Spain's new ruler. Carlota's plans were not always well received, and various factions in the colony leveled accusations of treason against those who seemed close to her. It was not long before partisan groups accused each other of being controlled by Carlota's secret agents. In July of 1811, for example, a political group issued a pamphlet accusing its rivals of being puppets of "Carlota's agents."[39]

After the insurgent victories over royalists in 1817 and 1818, Chile's revolutionary authorities worried about the intervention of secret agents working for the Spanish government.[40] In 1819 the town council and some citizens of Cauquenes deposed the local governor. Upon hearing the news, the intendant of Concepción, Ramón Freire, informed the rebels that their action constituted a serious crime. While Cauquenes's town council argued that the governor's removal had been an act of patriotism, Freire accused them of having been swayed by "Fernando VII's evil agents." The Spanish monarch, according to Freire, unable to conquer Chile by force, wanted "to foster disunion and disorder among us." The intendant told the council that it had (knowingly or not) acted under the influence of one such agent, Francisco de Paula Prieto.[41] Freire also wrote to the central government, relating that "turbulent men" like Prieto were "undoubtedly Fernando VII's agents," whose mission was "to disturb the progress of our liberty and independence."[42] Political actors continued for years to attribute internal dissension—including partisan frictions and military mutinies—to the intrigues of Spanish agents.[43]

Agents rendered dissent and antagonism intelligible. They explained rebellions and insurrections, revolutions and factional disputes, instability and division. Most of all, they were communicative actors: they carried seeds of dissension and conflict with them, spreading them to new areas. Assertions that political rivals were foreign agents—or at least were under the latter's influence—served of course to delegitimize them, but they were more than cynical lies. Those who leveled these accusations found them plausible and probably thought others did as well. The fear of agents was not unfounded or irrational but the result of a particular understanding of both communication and politics in which dissent was framed as an unnatural phenomenon spread by contaminating vectors.

Communicating Dissent

Agents were not simply the product of people's imaginations. Although observers exaggerated their numbers and power, it was indeed true, for example, that Napoleon sent agents to Spanish America. Similarly, many governments and political groups dispatched agents to distant territories or appointed as agents people already living abroad. These individuals normally worked in a decentralized manner, with ample independence from their sponsoring governments.[44]

One species of agent was the official, diplomatic sort who openly declared their mission of representing a sovereign power or political player. This was the case with the agents appointed by the junta of Buenos Aires in Chile between 1810 and 1814 who actively sought to influence local politics through lobbying authorities, spreading propaganda, spying on rivals, and otherwise molding public opinion. These diplomats thus conformed to the model of the activist revolutionary agent that royalist observers feared.[45] The aforementioned US consul, Joel R. Poinsett, similarly played a crucial role in local revolutionary events, counseling political figures and advocating for transformative measures such as the adoption of Chile's first constitution.[46] Agents representing political figures rather than governments included the aforementioned Federico Dowling, who served as Carlota de Borbón's representative in Chile in late 1808. Dowling was charged with studying the colony's political situation, identifying its most powerful men, and finding potential allies among them.[47]

These agents publicly represented foreign powers or individuals, but others acted in secret, sometimes without official credentials. In 1811 a man named Isidro Castro arrived in Santiago. Rumors had it he came from Lima or Trujillo, in Peru, and that the viceroy himself had expelled him because of his seditious ideas. Royalists in Santiago considered him a charlatan and a man of no talent.[48] Castro had some connections with Buenos Aires's revolutionary government, which sent a letter of recommendation on his behalf to its agent in Santiago, Bernardo Vera. From his communications with Buenos Aires's junta, it appears that Castro was in charge of receiving printed material from that city and forwarding it to (royalist) Lima and other points in Peru. But Castro also sought to influence local politics. His ambitions reveal the power he claimed for himself as a secret agent. As he communicated to Buenos Aires's junta on October 11, 1811:

> So far, I haven't had the chance to obtain anything from this place [Santiago]. I've limited myself to work in favor of public opinion [i.e., generating support for Buenos Aires's government], to foster a military system, and to create ideas previously unknown here. I am like a [metal] founder: in order to make a piece, first I need to create the molds. Your Excellency knows very well the origins of the cold indifference in which some peoples of our America live. Those of us who have had the joy of opening our eyes before others have to multiply our efforts to make the blind see.[49]

In a second communication to the junta, written in December of that year, Castro claimed to be responsible for the installation of a printing press in Chile and to have taken part in the publication of Chile's first newspaper, then in preparation.[50] According to Bernardo Vera, Castro had indeed managed to become "the government's principal confidant" and was now in charge of many tasks, including composing new music for military concerts and directing the creation of a rifle factory.[51]

While Castro apparently appointed himself as a revolutionary agent, others were explicitly dispatched as such. In 1821 the O'Higgins administration charged Antonio Cantuarias, a doctor living in the town of Vallenar, with conspiring against the government. According to authorities, Cantuarias planned to arm the royalist war prisoners held in Vallenar and take control of the town. In an unexpected turn of events, during his trial Cantuarias revealed that his real name was Antonio Luna de Castilla and that he was not a doctor but a secret agent sent by José Miguel Carrera from Río de la Plata to prepare a revolution against O'Higgins's government. Castilla was a professional simulator: before pretending to be a doctor in Vallenar, and even before becoming a secret agent, he had played the roles of Spaniard in Valparaíso (to foster his social position) and of priest in Río de la Plata (to make a living). The administration eventually granted him a pardon, as he apparently provided important information about the Carrera faction.[52]

During military conflicts, agents were often sent to areas under enemy control. Sometime around 1816–1817, a man named Manuel Bazán made two trips to Chile from the revolutionary-controlled city of Mendoza on the other side of the Andes. According to Bazán's wife, Rufina Marín, her husband traveled as a "secret emissary" of the revolutionary army, tasked with encouraging local inhabitants to support the insurgents when they arrived.[53] Like Bazán, several other secret agents worked to stoke the flames of dissent in royalist Chile between 1814 and 1817.[54] The situation was similar in the archipelago of Chiloé, a royalist stronghold that remained loyal to Spain until 1826. Revolutionaries either appointed or dispatched spies and secret agents to Chiloé soon after beating the royalist army in mainland Chile in 1818 and continued to do so as late as 1825. These emissaries and activists gathered vital information about royalist forces and promoted the cause of independence among Chiloé's inhabitants.[55]

Sometimes people presented themselves as revolutionary agents even if they did not appear to be working for any specific party. In 1825 Mapuche logko Venancio Coñuepan sent a petition to Chile's government asking to be rewarded for his contributions to the revolutionary cause.

Coñuepan had actively participated in the revolutionary wars in Chile, establishing himself as a key military ally of the insurgents. But in his 1825 petition, Coñuepan also highlighted his role as a political activist. According to him, soon after revolutionary forces entered Chile from Río de la Plata in 1817, he began educating his warriors about the "rights of man," spreading thereafter this knowledge into neighboring Mapuche communities with positive results.[56] Venancio Coñuepan framed his political activities in a manner that would make sense to revolutionary authorities, presenting himself as having introduced the revolutionary gospel in sovereign Mapuche territory.

While many of these revolutionary agents conceived their political activities in a manner compatible with the principles of unity and unanimity—claiming they were spreading the truth or combating ignorance and vice—others had the explicit objective of communicating dissension and conflict. This was particularly the case during military operations. In 1816 Buenos Aires's revolutionary government instructed General José de San Martín to dispatch "secret agents" to infiltrate royalist troops in Chile to "introduce discontent and division" among them.[57] Four years later, Colonel Jorge Beauchef tasked one such agent with creating confusion, lowering the enemy's morale, and fostering desertion among the royalist garrison in Valdivia. In Beauchef's account, before leaving his camp the soldier had said, "I'm going to introduce disorder."[58]

Acting as agents, people experienced and asserted their agency in a world marked by antagonism and division. Although the effects of their actions are difficult to establish, these activists sought to foster their causes and undermine rival regimes and factions. Their power, real or alleged, was founded on the idea that dissension was a communicable disease. Instead of rejecting or fearing contagion, agents and their allies embraced it as an effective political means in a world that seemed split by radical disagreement.

Explaining Dissent

On the night of November 4, 1764, colonial authorities captured a group of eight enslaved men who were hiding on a rural property near Santiago, apparently waiting to escape across the Andes to Mendoza and Buenos Aires. Once the men were imprisoned, a judicial machine was put in motion, one that had as its main objective not only gathering information about their actions but also bringing them into some sort of legal intelligibility. Based on the ideals of unity and harmony that underpinned Spain's early modern legal culture, the criminal investigation was meant to identify and assign blame to a leader, a primary agent ultimately responsible for this expression of insubordination.[59] Following this view authorities during this period used trials and legal investigations as political instruments to impose the framework of contagion on unwelcome social and political events and to punish the communication of dissent that was allegedly behind them.

Luis Zañartu, the magistrate in charge of prosecuting the 1764 case, repeatedly asked the prisoners to name who had convinced them to join the group.[60] If we are to believe the official record of the investigation, in two rounds of interrogations the judge managed to extract from most of the prisoners the name or identity of the person who had first "disturbed" them. Two men singled out the same individual, a young hairdresser named Valentín Resendo (who witnesses also called "Romero"), as the person who had invited them to join the plot. But Resendo himself claimed in his defense that he had been "disturbed" by Salvador, a shoemaker who was also part of the group. It seems likely that this verb ("to disturb," *inquietar*) did not come directly from the prisoners but was advanced by Luis Zañartu, as it appears in the testimonies of most of the enslaved men as well as in the magistrate's own ruling on the case. The verb suggested that most of the men who participated in the plan had been until then in a state of natural order and subordination until some external agent "disturbed" them. As revealed in their testimonies, some of the prisoners apparently saw this disruption as Satan's handiwork. Ventura, an enslaved man born in Brazil, allegedly declared that, "tempted by the Devil," another prisoner named Manuel "disturbed" him, "telling him to leave for Buenos Aires."

It is unclear whether the prisoners were threatened or tortured before, during, or after their declarations. Linguistic barriers may have additionally existed between the judge and the prisoners, as three of the would-be fugitives came from Brazil, another had been embarked in Guinea, and three others in Angola. Nevertheless, a careful reading of the case suggests that a core group of conspirators was composed of enslaved men embarked in Angola and born in Brazil who had recently arrived in Chile from across the Andes. Following a pattern that can also be identified in other slave uprisings in the Americas, invitations to join the group were then extended from person to person. At some point, the group took a step further and gathered in Santiago's central square, where they agreed to escape the city together. There is much we do not know about how all of this unfolded, as Zañartu was apparently uninterested in establishing an exact chronology of events or even resolving the contradictions between testimonies.

On March 25, 1765, Zañartu sentenced almost all of the prisoners to receive two hundred lashes in Santiago's streets and to either be sold outside Chile or deported for ten years to a penal colony. He dictated a lighter punishment for a young man from Angola named Teodoro, who was legally a minor (he was apparently between fifteen and twenty years old). But he made no such exception for Valentín Resendo. Although also a minor (Resendo declared himself to be eighteen or nineteen years old), Zañartu sentenced him to receive the same punishment as the adults, claiming he had been "the main one to have disturbed others."[61] This sentence was the culmination of a criminal investigation entirely organized around the question of who had "disturbed" whom. Without any conclusive evidence, Zañartu declared Valentín Resendo the "principal" agent of the conspiracy. Like the devil, he was responsible for tempting others to escape, initiating a cascading process of corruption that had resulted in a scandalous example of insubordination to Santiago's enslaved population.

Reading official documents and criminal investigations dealing with conspiracies, mutinies, or rebellions in Chile during the Age of Dissent, one feels as if observing the same drama unfolding over and over again. Facing insubordination and division, authorities immediately sought to identify a main culprit, a source of contagion that would explain the disruption of order and harmony. To do this they usually initiated investigations with the explicit objective of uncovering the "true" instigators. In 1801 in the town of Copiapó, a coalition of elites, plebeians, and Diaguita individuals, disobeying orders from the Audiencia, mobilized to regain control of the district's water from two mine owners. When reports of this insurrection reached Santiago, the Crown attorney stated that it was necessary to conduct a "secret investigation" to find out who the "principal agents" (*motores*) were. These yet-to-be-exposed individuals, he claimed, were "the reason why" Copiapó was in turmoil.[62]

On March 19, 1818, Indigenous Diaguita and non-Indigenous people from the Indian town of Chalinga attacked the neighboring town of Illapel in northern Chile. Shouting "Long live the King," the Natives—apparently led by their cacique, Vicente Paillante, along with a man named Francisco Carvajal—took control of the town, imprisoned government officials, and elected a new governor. This happened as the royal expedition sent from Lima under the command of General Mariano Osorio was marching toward Santiago. On March 20 Chalinga's forces were crushed by a local hacienda owner who managed to kill Carvajal and capture over forty other men.[63] Vicente Paillante could not be found.

Local revolutionary authorities as well as the central government were convinced that royalist "emissaries" or "secret agents" were the real "authors" of this "conspiracy of the Indians." The insurgent government in Santiago appointed a representative in Illapel with the objective of discovering the wealthy, educated, and powerful men who authorities believed must have been behind such an uprising. Even when evidence suggested there were no such connections, the government and its local representative persisted in arguing that the rebellion's true instigators remained in the shadows.[64]

Criminal trials, often the only sources at our disposal through which to study dissenting events during this era, distorted social and political phenomena by applying to them the model of contagion. Their main objective was to separate the healthy from the unhealthy and uncover the agent of disorder and chaos who was to blame for corrupting others. This was particularly the case after 1817, as Chile faced increased social and political instability, and can be appreciated in several trials conducted between that year and 1841 in towns and cities such as Cauquenes, Quillota, Los Andes, San Fernando, Santiago, and Concepción. These trials—which investigated events as different as defiance of official orders, student revolts, and political conspiracies—usually tried to establish a distinction between primary movers or leaders and all other participants who had allegedly fallen under their influence.[65] In the trial of several men accused of sedition in Quillota in 1825, the judge asked one witness if he knew "who was the first author" of the agitation, to which the witness replied: "It is public and evident" that an English man named Enrique Fulner (Henry Faulkner) "was the town's only troublemaker, and first author of all the disturbances that have taken place in it, and that there will never be calm while he remains in this city."[66]

One of the most dramatic examples of this manner of interpreting political communication took place in southern Chile in 1824. On June 21 and 22, a militia unit stationed in Linares deposed the local governor, Pedro Victoriano, and took control of the town. The troops were particularly discontented with the governor because their salaries had not been paid for several months. When military forces reached Linares and disbanded the mutineers, Victoriano immediately questioned a low-ranking officer (*cabo*) named José Barrera, who was reputed to be the rebellion's leader. But Victoriano was not specifically interested in Barrera: he assumed the militia had been incited by powerful local elites and wanted Barrera to confess their names. In his declaration, taken under torture, Barrera identified some of Linares's wealthy men, accusing them of using the soldiers to get rid of the town's governor. On hearing of this, the men Barrera implicated initiated legal actions to clear their names, setting off a lengthy investigation meant to establish exactly who had corrupted the soldiers. Although the trial showed that they had been motivated by their own belief that Victoriano would not pay them their overdue salaries, Barrera was eventually singled out as—in the words of the army's attorney—"the sole cause and author of the crime." Framed as a contaminating agent of insubordination, Barrera was executed in front of his former unit on November 24, 1824.[67]

Adapting to Dissent

Political figures in Chile embraced the idea of contagion not only to delegitimize, produce, and explain dissent but also to adapt to its continued existence. While contagion ascribed the blame for crimes of insubordination to a restricted number of individuals, it also exculpated (at least partly) all others involved. As the Audiencia magistrate José Santiago Rodríguez Aldea stated in 1815, investigations of crimes of sedition were intended to identify and penalize "the heads . . . so that punishment falls over the few, and fear reaches the many."[68] Rodríguez Aldea wrote these comments during one of the many criminal investigations the royalist administration conducted to determine who was responsible for Chile's revolution. Facing a society divided after four years of revolution and almost two years of civil war, officials such as Rodríguez Aldea sought to establish a distinction between the revolution's true agents and those who had simply followed them or their example. This attitude corresponded to what Allan J. Kuethe and Kenneth J. Andrien have identified as the traditional response to expressions of political dissent in the Spanish empire during the eighteenth century. This consisted in dominating the situation by force first, then identifying "suspected ringleaders," and, finally, issuing "a general pardon" to the rest of the people involved.[69]

To assign responsibility for the revolution, royalists opened hundreds of criminal investigations of alleged revolutionaries with the avowed objective of uncovering the revolution's true or main authors. They also established special tribunals to examine the political conduct of thousands more.[70] Authorities also imprisoned and exiled individuals reputed to be the revolution's leaders. As soon as he secured control of central Chile in late 1814, royalist Governor Mariano Osorio—following instructions from the viceroy of Peru—deported over one hundred alleged "motors or heads" of the rebellion to a prison island in the Juan Fernández archipelago.[71]

But by early 1815 it appears both Mariano Osorio and most members of the Audiencia had decided to pursue a strategy of conciliation with local elites, suspending many criminal investigations and lobbying the Spanish government to issue a pardon in favor of Chile's insurgents.[72] In a note sent to the central government in March of that year, Osorio requested a royal pardon for all revolutionaries who remained in Chile. While I have not found this communication, a royal decree summarized Osorio's argument as follows: "The origins of the revolution and its unfolding," he claimed, had been "the work of a limited number of ambitious and corrupted men," who had managed to contaminate "the multitude" with false promises. Most of those being prosecuted in Chile had been the victims of these few men.[73] Members of the Audiencia, for their part, expressed doubt that the hundreds of investigations of alleged revolutionaries would ever uncover who were the revolution's "real authors" or "first agents."[74]

Based on the opinions of Osorio and the Audiencia—as well as the lobbying of the exiles' relatives—on February 1, 1816, the king extended a royal pardon to all but Chile's "first revolutionaries." Given that local authorities had been unable to determine who these men were, the king opted for a pragmatic solution. His decree assumed that the "first revolutionaries" were those who had left the country to neighboring Río de la Plata when royalist forces triumphed in 1814. In practice, this meant pardoning all individuals who were being investigated as revolutionaries in Chile, including those exiled in Juan Fernández and other locations in the colony.[75]

Not all royalists agreed with this strategy. A faction opposed to General Osorio's rule—involving people like María Ana Pérez de Arza and powerful colonial figures such as Judas Tadeo Reyes, María Luisa Esterripa, and Gabino Gaínza—actively opposed pardoning revolutionaries and the return of the Juan Fernández exiles.[76] When the royal pardon reached Chile, the colony had a new Spanish governor, Francisco Marcó del Pont, who (following a common pattern of colonial politics) sided with his predecessor's enemies. He vehemently rejected enforcing the pardon, partly to satisfy his faction and antagonize Osorio's supporters and partly because he faced increased threats from revolutionaries in Chile and across the Andes.[77] This position brought him into conflict with the Audiencia and the relatives of the exiles who wrote the viceroy of Peru and the Council of the Indies denouncing his actions.[78] To justify his reluctance to implement the pardon, the governor argued that many of those exiled in Juan Fernández were in fact Chile's "first revolutionaries."[79] He later gathered and sent the Council of the Indies the opinions of several top magistrates and legal bodies that agreed that the exiles had not repented and would "sow discord" if accepted back in Chile.[80] The controversy regarding the royal pardon came to an abrupt end when the revolutionary forces of generals San Martín and O'Higgins captured Santiago in early 1817.

The source of these controversies was the applicability of traditional politics of reconciliation—which were meant in principle to deal with localized or suppressed episodes of dissent—during an ongoing, empire-wide civil war. Governor Osorio and the Audiencia referred to the logic of contagion to exculpate all revolutionaries in Chile, including former junta members, military commanders, government officials, and men accused of iconoclastic actions. The king and the Council of the Indies agreed, issuing a royal pardon in 1816 that not only refused to identify the "first agents" of the revolution by name but moreover assumed they lived in impunity far from the reach of royal authorities. On the other hand, Marcó del Pont and his supporters similarly refused to identify the ringleaders of the revolution, instead justifying repressive measures against the local population. Even if Chile's insurgent army had been defeated two years earlier, the threat of a revolutionary contagion remained.

The debate among royalists is a telling example of how actors in revolutionary and postcolonial Chile relied on contagion to navigate a political landscape that seemed irremediably plural. If contagion was so central to how Chileans both thought about and practiced politics, it was because it encapsulated a series of assumptions about communication and power. The notion involved likening society to a densely interconnected body. In this analogy, conflict was a disease characterized by its ability to communicate from people to people and region to region. Contagion also implied the existence of contaminating vectors—most notably political agents—who supposedly spread chaos and disorder. It thus offered a framework by which to understand and deal with radical dissent, one that combined the enforcement of unity with the reluctant acceptance of political division. From the point of view of contagion, communication was not an accessory instrument people might bring to the political arena: it was politics itself. It described how people affected each other and how they engendered political change. For this reason, controlling propagation became of particular relevance in revolutionary and postcolonial Chile.

CHAPTER SEVEN

Prophylactic Politics

Sanitary Cordons, Expulsions, and Isolation

In June of 1784 the Spanish warship *San Pedro de Alcántara* made an emergency stop at the port of Talcahuano, near Concepción. The ship had suffered severe damage at sea after departing Callao, Peru, bound for the Spanish port of Cádiz. Its arrival caused much anxiety among local officials. The *San Pedro de Alcántara* had left Peru with forty prisoners, most of whom had been involved in the Tupac Amaru revolution, an anticolonial uprising led by José Gabriel Condorcanqui (who adopted the name Tupac Amaru II) and Micaela Bastidas. Among them were Fernando Condorcanqui, José Gabriel and Micaela's youngest son. The ship's commander, Manuel Fernández de Bedoya, requested that local authorities permit him to unload the ship's cargo and crew (including the prisoners) so that he could inspect and repair it. Although it took weeks to fix the ship, Concepción's military commander, Ambrosio Higgins, refused to assume responsibility for the prisoners and did not even allow them to set foot on land. Worried that the prisoners' presence could unsettle the region, Higgins took severe measures to prevent them from communicating with Mapuche groups, people of mixed ancestry, and Spaniards in Talcahuano.[1]

Higgins was particularly troubled by the prospect of Fernando Condorcanqui—then sixteen years old—somehow joining the Mapuches and disturbing their "tranquility and subordination."[2] Ever since news of the Tupac Amaru revolution reached Chile in 1781, Higgins had been concerned about the effect it could have on the colony's volatile frontier and the possibility of an alliance between Mapuche leaders and Andean rebels. Higgins was aware that the Mapuches knew about the uprising. He reported having personally scolded a group of logkos in November of 1781 for following a Mapuche ambassador named Chicaguala who, according to Higgins, aspired to imitate the example of the Natives of Peru. The group of Mapuche leaders denied having any communication with the rebels but admitted to having heard news of the revolution from "Spaniards." Higgins himself proceeded to describe to them the "punishments" the Spaniards had inflicted on Andean revolutionaries.[3]

Higgins feared not only that the Mapuches might decide to attack the Spanish to capture Fernando Condorcanqui but also that the prisoners on board the *San Pedro de Alcántara* could somehow spark insubordination among them. He saw the prisoners as carrying a dangerous political contagion—the potential to spread disobedience and dissent, precisely at a time when officials feared an imminent British attack. The sanitary cordon he sought to establish between the prisoners and the region's inhabitants was a response to the perceived communicability of their rebellion.

Like Higgins, other colonial and postcolonial authorities tried to control the communication of dissension in Chile. This chapter analyzes the practices and institutions colonial and postcolonial officials used to neutralize what they saw as the propagation of insubordination and division in the country. I show how authorities' efforts were not limited to censoring undesirable ideas or information but also extended to the management and containment of imitation and contagion. The chapter focuses first on the establishment of sanitary cordons. These were protective webs of censorship meant to preserve the community's alleged purity from undesirable contagion. It then studies the practices designed to "purge" society of contaminating agents. Finally, the chapter explores the isolation of people in places such as convents, detention centers for women, and spiritual retreat houses. It reveals how removing men and women from their environment was meant to both protect society from the communication of vices and dissension and transform the people thus isolated. This section first examines three practices and institutions that relied heavily on isolation—*recogimiento*, *depósito*, and *ejercicios*—and then studies how political actors adjusted them after 1810 and sought to use them to combat and punish partisan dissent.

I propose to consider all the institutions and practices studied in this chapter as manifestations of a prophylactic understanding of politics according to which society had to be defended from the dissemination of contagious activities and bad examples. This chapter shows how people in colonial and postcolonial Chile saw in mimesis and contagion two faces of the same problem: propagation. Independent of its specific mechanism or mode of operation, it was the dissemination of unwanted ideas and behaviors that worried them. The prophylactic practices examined in this chapter—such as the deportation of poor men to penal colonies, the enslavement of Indigenous children, and the isolation of unruly women—can be interpreted as forms of censorship adapted to a world in which communication transcended the exchange of information. They were also among the fundamental means through which political actors during the revolutionary period chose to respond to dissent and division. Concerns over propagation, this chapter demonstrates, underpinned racial and gendered power relations and dramatically affected the lives of countless women, men, and children.

Sanitary Cordons

Since the early stages of colonization in the Americas, the Spanish crown tried to shield the New World from contamination by what officials considered the ills of Europe, most notably religious dissent. To do so it regulated migration to the continent and censored unwanted or dangerous books. The Inquisition was the foremost institution in charge of guarding Spanish America's religious orthodoxy. Among its duties was to block any person or book deemed to be infected from entering the region and track down and neutralize those who managed to elude official control.[4]

Concerns over contamination gained a new political meaning during the second half of the eighteenth century. Imperial officials and colonial elites now feared the possibility of a revolutionary contagion coming from other areas of the Atlantic world. While the Spanish government supported the United States in the US War of Independence (1775–1783), it also worried about the example it set for its own colonies in the Americas. In 1779 the crown issued a royal order forbidding the circulation of a book in French titled *Apocalypse de Chiokoyhikoy*, a political tract sympathetic of the American Revolution.[5] The Andean revolutions, led by Quechua- and Aymara-speaking Indigenous people in Peru and Charcas (roughly Bolivia) between 1780 and 1783, also alarmed Spanish authorities, as the episode of the *San Pedro de Alcántara* reveals. Colonial administrators in Spanish America tried to control information about these events, and the crown used official newspapers to spread misinformation about them.[6]

Fears of a revolutionary contagion redoubled after the French and Haitian Revolutions.[7] The Spanish crown reacted to these events by establishing what Lucienne Domergue called a "sanitary cordon" of censorship designed to prevent the spread of revolution into the monarchy.[8] As Claudia Rosas Lauro has noted in her study of the impact of the French Revolution on Peru, this cordon was not limited to written material. In 1791 and 1793 officials in Chile and other Spanish American holdings received orders to block the introduction in their jurisdictions of objects such as clocks, snuff boxes, and medals with engravings or other images indicating support for the French and American Revolutions.[9]

When news of the French Revolution reached Chile, the colony was ruled by Governor Ambrosio Higgins, who, as military commander of the frontier, had dealt with the *San Pedro de Alcántara* in 1784. An ambitious colonial bureaucrat, Higgins poured considerable energy into casting a protective web of censorship around the colony. His main objective was to monitor and control all the routes through which the revolutionary contamination could reach Chile. His initial focus was on the growing number of British, French, and American ships that roamed the Pacific after 1788.[10] Higgins suspected that these ships could not only engage in contraband trade but also spread insubordination and "harmful" ideas and information.[11] His fears were not entirely unfounded: in the following decades, US ships brought cigar cases, snuff boxes, and brushes containing revolutionary images, and merchants such as William Shaler and Richard J. Cleveland carried "subversive papers and books," made "seditious" statements, and distributed copies of the US Declaration of Independence and Constitution in Valparaíso.[12]

To prevent these dangerous interactions, the governor repeatedly reminded coastal authorities that they should restrict all exchanges between the colony's inhabitants and foreign vessels.[13] On January 2, 1792, Higgins issued an edict imposing the death penalty on anyone who communicated with foreign ships, an order he reissued in December of 1794.[14] The arrival of the French frigate *Flavia* at the port of Valparaíso on February 22, 1792, provides a powerful example of how this sanitary cordon was supposed to work. Higgins, together with Valparaíso's military commander, took strict measures to prevent the ship's crew from spreading news concerning the French Revolution. The crew was not allowed to set foot on land, and no one from the colony was permitted to board the ship. The shipowner or captain could purchase supplies only pursuant to written notes addressed to Valparaíso's military commander (or someone appointed by him), thus barring any direct deals with local merchants. To enforce these orders, government troops patrolled the bay day and night and stationed a boat with armed men near the *Flavia*. When a few days later Higgins received orders from the Spanish government to provide support for the *Flavia* and other French ships, he remained cautious, ordering Valparaíso's military governor to monitor and limit all communications between locals and the crew.[15]

Higgins tracked other sources of contagion as well. He censored the official mail—Chile's essential means of communication with the rest of the monarchy—suppressing letters and newsletters that discussed the French Revolution in favorable terms.[16] On April 9, 1795, he sent classified orders to officials in the ports of Coquimbo and Valparaíso, to Santiago's bishop, and to customs officers in the Andes requesting increased control of books, other written material, and "dangerous people" who might want to enter the colony.[17] The governor similarly enforced the expulsion from Chile of two Frenchmen, clockmaker Juan Trimalle and dentist Miguel Porré, who were on their way to Spain after being expelled from Peru for talking openly about the revolution.[18] Higgins also prosecuted priest Clemente Morán in 1795 for having praised the French Revolution and refused to send him back to La Serena, citing the dangers of having him resident in a port visited by many "foreign vessels."[19]

After Higgins left office in 1796, official concern with revolutionary contagion became less evident, but book censorship and bans on communications with foreign vessels continued. The work of Andrés García, a Spanish merchant who held the office of *revisor* (book censor) of the Inquisition in Chile, provides an example of the prophylactic measures officials took to protect the colony from the revolutionary disease. When in 1813 García requested government compensation for his political loyalty, he cast himself as having fought to protect Chile from revolutionary contagion since the early stages of the Atlantic revolutions. The merchant claimed to have burned over two thousand books between 1791 and 1813 and to have "purged" (removed specific content from) many more. While García's censorship primarily affected religious texts—most of the books he censored came from conventual libraries—it is nevertheless possible that he burned revolutionary tracts, novels, and political treatises as well. After 1807 García also made efforts to dismantle political groups he considered to be revolutionary and surveilled men he feared to be French agents. He recounted how, in 1811, revolutionaries "brought from Buenos Aires two small crates with [copies of] Jean Jacques Rousseau's *Social Contract*, which had been translated and printed in that corrupted city." According to García, this book was meant to prompt the youth to question "subordination, and to throw themselves unashamedly into a life of vices." Someone denounced the shipment, and the censor managed to burn over 130 copies. In return, García contended, the insurgent government imprisoned him for twelve days.[20]

While scholars have highlighted the censorship of revolutionary news and ideas during the late colonial era, they have paid less attention to how authorities continued to apply the same logic in later years. Sanitary cordons were not a natural response to the supposed power of radical ideas but a prophylactic practice integral to the official, nonpluralistic understanding of politics. Insurgent and postcolonial actors sought at different moments to extend sanitary cordons around Chile, protecting it from contagious or otherwise dangerous people and written material. After the creation of the first junta in September of 1810, the new government actively censored the mail, and in 1813 it banned Spaniards and other Europeans from entering Chile.[21] The administration of General Bernardo O'Higgins (1817–1823) adopted even more extreme measures, seeking to prevent the introduction in Chile of agents, letters, proclamations, and printed documents from the Carrera faction, then waging war against rivals in Río de la Plata.[22]

Authorities in colonial times also thought of establishing sanitary cordons to protect specific groups or locations from what they claimed were dangerous sources of insubordination and unruly behavior. This was particularly the case with Indigenous communities, which in official discourses were often portrayed as vulnerable to corruption by Spaniards and other groups.[23] The law established that only Native people were allowed to live in Indian towns and charged local caciques and *cacicas* (female Indigenous leaders) with enforcing this measure. Foreigners were blamed for bringing seeds of corruption and dissent. When in 1772 and 1773 the Indigenous community of Choapa rebelled, Spanish observers such as the local priest attributed their actions to the nefarious influence of mixed-race people and foreign and perverted caciques.[24] The way they told it, conflict emerged not from the oppression the people of Choapa experienced but from a flaw in the sanitary cordon that was supposed to keep them safe from external contamination.

Sanitary cordons were therefore far from mere reactions to the power of new Enlightenment ideas or radical activists. They reflected the potential authorities attributed to dissent and insubordination to replicate and disseminate among people. In the officials' eyes these cordons were meant to protect society from negative mimetic dynamics and nefarious forms of contamination. But sanitary cordons were far from being enough to prevent the emergence and propagation of dissent. Most of the time, it was also necessary to purge the body politic of the sources of dissension and disagreement within.

Purges

In March of 1823 a junta recently established in the town of San Felipe decided to banish a man named Francisco Calvo. The junta was one of many created earlier that year in towns north of Santiago to replace government officials appointed by the crumbling O'Higgins administration. In his trial, supporters of the junta presented Calvo's exile as necessary to prevent the propagation of dissent in their community. "While the whole province was unanimously celebrating our freedom [from the O'Higgins regime]," they argued, "an unruly and agitated individual was discovered, who immediately tried to infect this province with the turbulence of his anarchic ideas. This is Don Francisco Calvo."[25] For the junta and its supporters, expelling Calvo was a prophylactic measure explicitly designed to prevent his infectious, dissenting "ideas" from spreading.

Deportation was one of the main ways that authorities in Chile sought to "purge" corrupting elements from the body politic.[26] Purges were a common therapeutic method during this period, which consisted in the evacuation of fluids from the body. Purging reflected a "way of thinking" about health and disease in which expulsion was considered key to maintaining an organism's well-being.[27] From this point of view, bad ideas and bad people needed to be purged from the political body to keep it healthy. In 1810 Manuel Antonio Talavera believed it was necessary to "purge" Chile of the ideas of "independence."[28] Fifteen years later a man wrote in a private letter to a fellow politician that the time had come "to purge our country of evil-doers," meaning their political antagonists.[29]

Authorities saw in deportation a powerful and extremely flexible instrument to purge society of corrupting elements. Colonial edicts and laws regularly listed deportation to penal colonies and expulsion from Chile among the potential punishments for a myriad of crimes, including carrying weapons, singing lewd or satirical songs, and hiding deserters from the Royal Navy.[30] Between the second half of the eighteenth century and the first decades of the nineteenth, people were deported for crimes as varied as sorcery, murder, mutiny, conspiracy, robbery, and writing pasquinades.[31]

One of the main targets of deportation were men who authorities labeled as "vagabonds"—meaning individuals of low calidad who allegedly lacked any permanent occupation. Historian Alejandra Araya found that over 50 percent of the men accused of being vagabonds between 1686 and 1814 were sentenced to deportation.[32] The Spanish crown and local officials used the deportation of so-called vagabonds to round up troops and conscript labor for the colony's strategic military posts (Valdivia, Valparaíso, and Juan Fernández), muster sailors for the Royal Navy, and press men into forced labor for public works.[33] Thousands of men were thus deported during this period. A report by the notaries of the Audiencia established in 1798 that "in the last three years" alone the tribunal had sentenced 290 men to deportation to penal colonies.[34]

The main destination of the men thus punished were the penal colonies or presidios of Valdivia and Juan Fernández.[35] The presidios were military fortresses with a population of inmates who served as laborers (mostly in public works) and soldiers. Valdivia was the colony's most important penal colony. Since its establishment as a presidio in the seventeenth century, it received dozens if not hundreds of prisoners from both Chile and Lima every year. The prison island of Juan Fernández was located in the Juan Fernández archipelago in the Pacific Ocean, more than 600 kilometers from Chile's coast. First found by Spaniards in the second half of the sixteenth century, the previously uninhabited archipelago hosted a penitentiary colony since 1749 and regularly received inmates from Quito, Lima, and Chile. The living conditions in both prisons (and especially in Juan Fernández) were extremely harsh, and prisoners often rebelled and attempted to escape.[36]

Government officials were not the only ones who believed in the need to send disobedient or disorderly men to the presidios. Household heads—both men and women, usually of elite or wealthy backgrounds—sometimes requested the government to deport young male family members to discipline them or separate them from the perceived sources of their vices. Gabriel Valdivieso, for example, wanted his son to be sent to Juan Fernández in 1783 for desiring to marry without his authorization, while the mother (unnamed in the documentation) of Pedro Nolasco Balbontín requested he be sent to Valdivia for disobedience and incorrigibility.[37] Although such men normally received better treatment than ordinary inmates, their experience in the presidios was expected to be harsh enough to reform them. Fernando Urízar sent an "unruly" son to the presidio of Valparaíso in 1789 so that he would be subjected to "the hardships, discipline, and moderation [recogimiento]" of fortress life.[38] The time these men spent in the presidio was often indefinite—they would be set free only once they had fully reformed.

The social and political efficacy of deportation derived from the fact that it allegedly removed bad examples and contagious people from a given location, preventing bad behaviors and dissent from replicating and spreading. In the final decades of the eighteenth century, colonial officials argued that vagabonds constituted a "ferment" of vices that could "contaminate" and "infect" others through their "example" unless they were separated from society.[39] Colonial authorities likewise deported people accused of dissension and insubordination—such as the group of eight enslaved men who tried to flee Santiago in 1764—with the explicit goal of preventing them from setting a bad example and contaminating others with their "scandal."[40] Valparaíso's military governor captured the prophylactic logic behind deportation to penal colonies in an 1841 communication to the interior minister. The governor argued that "when society removes from its interior one of its members because his actions are harmful," its "primary objective" is "not just to punish him physically," but to "isolate him so that his example and lessons do not propagate doctrines and behaviors opposed to those of the majority."[41]

More than an arbitrary form of punishment, deportation was a response to the perceived communicability of certain crimes.

As political clashes and civil wars engulfed Chile between 1810 and 1833, multiple political actors explicitly framed deportation as a way to remove agents of discord and dissent and prevent the further spread of dissension.[42] Government officials and military commanders regularly put this idea into practice, deporting their rivals to penal colonies, other jurisdictions, or simply out of town.[43] When insurgents took control of a good portion of Chile in early 1817, they deported hundreds of prisoners to the other side of the Andes, most of them (although not all) enemy soldiers.[44] Warring parties similarly established political prisons to separate political rivals from society. The penal colony of Juan Fernández served as a dedicated political prison in 1814–1817, 1821–1822, and 1831–1837.[45] During the royalist regime of 1814–1817, when the presidio hosted over one hundred political prisoners, the government explicitly argued that deportation to Juan Fernández separated corrupted individuals from the social body and neutralized their ability to propagate dissent.[46]

Executions served an analogous purpose to deportation. Authorities saw public executions in part as instruments to prevent the reproduction of bad examples and the contagion of insubordination. This measure was supposedly applied to individuals for which there was no hope of reconciliation, either because of their recalcitrant behavior or because of the heinous nature of their crimes. For example, in November 1816 an Audiencia Crown attorney, assessing the case of Santos Tapia, a man he qualified as "incorrigible," recommended separating "him from the living [. . .] so that the corruption of his perverted customs won't propagate."[47] A few months earlier, he had asked the courts to publicly execute a man named Pascual Henríquez, who had been found guilty of "sodomy." This execution was meant to "prevent the negative consequences of his bad example."[48] Countless other individuals (mostly but not exclusively men) were executed on the grounds that the way in which they conducted their lives (their "bad example") was somehow contagious.[49] Starting in the 1820s, some individuals and institutions voiced their opposition to public executions, but even they did not question its communicative purpose, recognizing—as Santiago's city council did in 1827—that public executions "separate from society an infectious member."[50]

Isolation and Recogimiento

In colonial and postcolonial Chile, isolation was a political instrument akin to purgation or the erection of sanitary cordons. Isolation methods interrupted the communication of vices within society by separating contaminated, and therefore contaminating, individuals and (ideally) transforming them. Isolation was supposed to operate in two complementary dimensions: it prevented individuals from corrupting their environment, and it protected the isolated individuals from the nefarious influences that surrounded them. The isolation of men and women would not only interrupt a chain of reproduction of bad examples and contagion but would render them good examples that would spread their positive influence across society. There were three main forms of isolation in Chile during the Age of Dissent: recogimiento, depósito, and ejercicios. This and the two following sections examine these practices and the principles associated with them. A final section addresses how actors used and adapted these forms of isolation to combat political dissent after 1808.

Recogimiento (which can be roughly translated as enclosure and restraint) was an official norm of behavior that associated female isolation with virtue and honor. While permanently evolving and subject to negotiation, this ideal had been influential in the Spanish Atlantic since the early colonial era. According to this vision, women had to remain homebound, avoid exposure to the outside world, and behave with modesty and reserve.[51] The "ideology of recogimiento," Jessica Delgado has observed, emerged from the idea that sin was contagious and "that women were particularly contagious beings by nature."[52] In late colonial times, authorities from different districts—including Concepción, Petorca, San Fernando, and Talca—voiced their concern over the need to enforce recogimiento on women as a prophylactic measure to prevent scandals and the contagion of vices.[53]

In the official discourse, it was customary to assume that women of better calidad were also *recogidas* or socially restrained, while women of lesser calidad were not.[54] But recogimiento was a flexible model of conduct that both affected and could be appropriated by poor and nonwhite women. Slaveholders claimed, for example, that enslaved women would not follow recogimiento rules if granted freedom, thus legitimizing enslavement in the name of this ideal. But some enslaved women turned this discourse upside down. In a legal suit from 1757, Juana Manuela Jáuregui argued that, if allowed self-purchase as she desired, she would "live perhaps in even greater recogimiento" than as an enslaved person.[55]

In late eighteenth- and early nineteenth-century Chile, recogimiento was also celebrated in official models of masculinity. While masculinity was frequently associated with unconstrained behavior—a disposition opposite to recogimiento, as Thomas A. Abercrombie has pointed out—this was not always the case.[56] Secular and religious authorities often praised male candidates for official posts (particularly priests) for their recogimiento. By this they meant prudence, moderation, morality, and—if the candidates were regular priests—the observation of enclosure.[57] Just like enslaved women, enslaved men similarly mobilized this moral standard to appraise their own honor and good behavior. In 1770 Joseph Sosa highlighted his "recogimiento"—which, he claimed, "was the envy of all who know me"—in a petition he made to force his master to sell him.[58]

The ideal of recogimiento was expressed with particular force in asylums for women known as recogimientos or *casas de recogidas*. Literature on Spanish and Portuguese America shows that the manner of administration of casas de recogidas, the sorts of women admitted, as well as the establishments' reputation varied greatly depending on their location, the views of the local population, and how women of different statuses negotiated their nature and meaning.[59] These establishments were founded on a series of "misogynist assumptions," as Nancy van Deusen has argued, most notably that women were simultaneously vulnerable to the contamination of the world and corrupting agents who posed a threat to men and society.[60] In the words of Jessica Delgado, authorities worried particularly about the role of women in spreading the "contagion of sin and scandal," framing them either as "vectors" of communication or as "protective bulwarks against it."[61] Casas de recogidas were among the most notable manifestations of these concerns over women's role in the reproduction of crimes and sins.

In the late 1720s Chile's colonial government established a casa de recogidas in Santiago (see map 4 for its location). The Casa was a prison-asylum dedicated in principle to the enclosure of women accused of prostitution and other deviations from moral and sexual norms.[62] The Audiencia best encapsulated the prophylactic reasoning behind this establishment in a communication sent to the king in 1704. The Audiencia argued that it was necessary to establish a "casa de recogidas" in Santiago to enclose the city's "women of immoral behavior [*de mal vivir*] for as long as needed." The objective was to curtail the "scandal of their lack of modesty" and to rectify their behavior. Deportation was an ill-advised punishment for such women, the Audiencia opined, because—among other reasons—deported women "carry with them their danger and scandal, and do not abandon their bad lifestyle." Enclosing immoral women in convents was likewise inapt, as such women "provide a bad example, and contaminate the nunneries' servants" with their presence.[63] The Casa de Recogidas solved these issues, offering a means not only to prevent disorderly women from communicating their vices but also to reform them.

The Casa's internal regulations, which Santiago's bishop submitted for royal approval in 1735, show how this prophylactic purpose was to be realized.[64] The document stated that the institution's purpose was to "enclose [*recoger*], and confine unruly women" and help them to "amend" their "lives." Any secular authority with proper jurisdiction could send a woman to the Casa de Recogidas with no prior trial or legal investigation. These recogidas did not have the right to be heard by a judge or to know the end of their term. The house was under the responsibility of six laywomen (meaning women who lived communally for religious purposes but who did not take vows).[65] According to the Casa's regulations, these women "of known virtue and exemplary life" would ensure that the recogidas remained isolated and would monitor all their exchanges with the outside world.

With isolation came efforts at transforming the recogidas. As Daniel Nemser has noted, the notion of recogimiento articulated the production of a kind of space (isolated, segregated, disciplined) with the molding of people's subjectivity.[66] Both recogidas and laywomen followed a daily schedule regulating their everyday activities, including their sleep hours and eating times. Women were to remain constrained and silent. The Casa's regulations ordered the recogidas to participate in a series of religious sacraments and ceremonies meant to reform them, including attending mass, praying the rosary, reciting the catechism, and confessing their sins. According to this document, laywomen would also collaborate in the recogidas' transformation, impressing on them "good models" of behavior through their "examples" and piety. The final instrument the regulations addressed in reforming the recogidas was penitence. Their time in the establishment was deliberately indefinite to make their punishment more severe and incentivize them to change. Before leaving the institution, women—especially those accused of being "public whores" or having "scandalous friendships"—had to "change their habits" and adopt a "new life." Only Santiago's bishop could establish when a recogida had reached this stage. Thus transformed, the recogidas would become positive "examples" for the rest of society.

These regulations—although perhaps never fully enforced—show how the institution's primary goal was to interrupt negative forms of communication and replace them with positive ones. The institution certainly imposed on recogidas a harsh enclosure that they experienced as a humiliating punishment. In 1740 the Spanish king received a petition signed by the "recogidas" in which they exposed the abuses they were subjected to (it is unclear whether this document represented the position of all or only some of the recogidas). The recogidas highlighted the lack of due process and the indefinite length of their reclusion, which unduly stained the reputation of those imprisoned for minor offenses.[67] More than sixty years later, in 1802, Francisca Urbano, a woman of modest means who lived in a rural area near Rancagua—and reputed to be of African ancestry, though she disputed this—requested the governor to spare her daughter Mercedes Banda from imprisonment in the Casa, characterizing it as a dishonoring experience that would cast a shadow over the reputation of her entire family.[68]

Authorities used the Casa de Recogidas to imprison women found guilty of adultery and other crimes they associated with prostitution at least until the early decades of the nineteenth century.[69] But the Casa evolved over the years, and starting in the 1770s it became increasingly similar to a secular prison, hosting a rotating number of women serving fixed sentences for a variety of crimes—justice for which was not necessarily associated with the ideals of recogimiento.[70] Recogidas still suffered arbitrary sentences. In August of 1789 after an Audiencia judge requested that local magistrates provide information about all the women they had sent to the Casa, the number of inmates dropped from fifty-two to just eleven. Considering this astonishing reduction, the Audiencia's Crown attorney rightly concluded that, when asked for this information, magistrates had simply set free the women they had irregularly or illegally imprisoned.[71]

During the imperial civil wars, the Casa de Recogidas was again transformed, serving as a military base and prison for women until it was finally closed in 1818. In 1824 the government established the Casa de Corrección for women. Although the new institution was no longer run by laywomen and magistrates, whether secular or religious, and could not submit women to indefinite imprisonment, the Casa de Corrección reproduced the prophylactic model of the Casa de Recogidas.[72] The prison would isolate these allegedly criminal women, particularly sex workers, and reform them through work and devotional exercises. Officials justified creating this institution on the grounds that "scandalous" women should not be held in regular prisons, as they contaminated other inmates with their bad "examples."[73] A list of inmates from 1832 shows that magistrates as varied as neighborhood inspectors and Santiago's commissioner sent to the Casa de Corrección women accused of offenses such as theft, adultery, drunkenness, and "being scandalous." Their sentences ranged from a few days to six months and were sometimes pronounced at the request of the women's husbands.[74]

The Casas de Recogidas and Corrección were not the sole prophylactic establishments based on notions of recogimiento. Other institutions responded to similar concerns and were explicitly modeled after the Casa de Recogidas, including two asylums formed in Santiago in 1760 and 1802–1803 and establishments for the poor created in Petorca and Valparaíso.[75] Other than the Casa de Recogidas, the most important of these institutions was the *beaterio* (house for religious laywomen) established by priest Antonio Zúñiga in Peumo, near Rancagua, around 1761 or 1762.[76] A large number of laywomen lived there in voluntary recogimiento, following a religious lifestyle similar to that of Santiago's Casa de Recogidas but performing a larger number of daily devotional exercises and instructing young girls from the surrounding areas. A second group of women lived in the beaterio as recogidas after repenting their previous conduct. Finally, magistrates sent there women accused of transgressing norms of recogimiento to reform their behavior.[77] By 1790 there were more than forty recogidas in the beaterio.[78] Women experienced harsh and arbitrary imprisonments in the facility until it closed sometime after 1817.[79]

Finally, convents were also a prime destination for women who adopted recogimiento, whether by choice, force, or a mixture of both. Laywomen sometimes joined female convents in Santiago, seeking to live according to the ideals of recogimiento. In an undated letter to Martín Calvo Encalada (probably from the second half of the eighteenth century), an elite woman named Agustina Espejo expressed her desire to join a convent as a laywoman to escape her abusive husband.[80] Magistrates often sentenced elite women found guilty of adultery to live in convents until they were fully reformed. The prophylactic purpose of this measure was evident, for example, in a husband's legal request for his adulterous wife to be put in a convent in 1813. In his words, "if a wife is bad, she must be enclosed in a convent to learn virtue and to correct her excesses in solitude. . . . If this is not done, society remains endangered, as a corrupted being remains within it."[81]

The Depósito

A second form of isolation meant to prevent negative forms of communication and transform people was known as depósito (deposit).[82] In legal terms, "depositing" meant entrusting something of value to the care and vigilance of someone else. In contentious settings—such as bets and legal investigations involving money—the elements in dispute were "deposited" with a trusty individual, who would ensure their integrity. When applied to people, "depositing" meant both protecting someone (placing them in a location where they could not be harmed) as well as containing and enclosing them.[83] Being "deposited" also usually meant being placed in the custody of other individuals or institutions.

Colonial and postcolonial elites conceived of this practice as a means to interrupt the reproduction of unwanted behaviors, particularly through the disarticulation of what they considered unfit families. As seen in chapter 5, Chile's dominant groups believed that children raised in nonwhite and poor families imitated their parents' vices, harming society. The depósito was an answer to this communicative problem, as it sought to extract children from such environments, isolating and supposedly reforming them. This form of depósito usually consisted in the separation of children of both sexes from their family units and their placement in another household (framed as of higher calidad), where they would usually serve as domestic workers until they reached adulthood. Some of these deposits were done with the consent of parents or guardians, who perhaps lacked the means to raise their children and who sometimes received a sum of money in exchange for them.[84] Children were sometimes deposited in institutions, where they also labored. In the second half of the eighteenth century, the beaterio of Peumo held several girls under depósito. They came from all over the colony and were provided with recogimiento and education in exchange for working for the beaterio as well as for local families.[85]

In many cases depósito went against the will of parents or guardians. In 1789 a priest took three children away from Isidora Espinosa near Rancagua, prompting her son-in-law (probably at her demand) to petition the government to get them back.[86] Similarly, in 1800 Dionisio Valladares traveled from Melipilla to Santiago to request the liberation of his daughter, who had been taken away from him by the local commissioner and put to work as a domestic servant in an elite household.[87] The official justification behind the forced depósito of children was that it served to isolate them from bad examples, transforming them into virtuous and productive individuals. In late 1807 or early 1808, two soldiers captured a girl named María Leyton, who lived with her grandmother María Mella on the outskirts of the town of San Fernando. The soldiers were following orders from a local priest, who proceeded to give María Leyton to an official who worked in the royal customs house in Santiago. When in June 1808 María Mella demanded the government return her granddaughter to her, the commissioner of San Fernando initiated a legal investigation with the evident objective of undermining her request. Witnesses he summoned testified that

Mella—a woman over seventy years old who lived in a "shack" in the town's "suburbs"—was a "beggar" who conducted a "bad" and "scandalous" life, setting a "bad example" for her granddaughter. The priest removed María Leyton from this environment, they claimed, to avoid these vices being communicated to her.[88]

Indigenous peoples were particularly affected by the depósito. As officials in the town of Melipilla recognized in 1811, it was customary for them to seize—"recoger," as the commissioner put it—children from the neighboring Indian town of Pomaire and distribute them among local families.[89] Officers and elites justified this form of coerced labor as a prophylactic measure meant to prevent these children from learning bad ways of life from their parents.[90] In 1779 the priest of Peumo, Antonio Zúñiga, together with a local official took two girls from an Indigenous woman named Francisca Mora and her non-Indigenous husband, Esteban Gutiérrez. The priest had previously subjected Mora to an ensemble of prophylactic measures: he had deported her from the Indian town of Peumo, citing her reprehensible behavior, and had almost sent her to the Casa de Recogidas in Santiago. Taking Mora's daughters was a natural extension of his efforts to punish and discipline her.[91] While the colonial government sided with Mora and Gutiérrez, and returned their daughters to them, many others suffered a different fate. In 1790 Zúñiga estimated that in the thirty-three years of his tenure as priest of Peumo he had deported and deposited in different houses and monasteries some five hundred girls and adolescent women (both Indigenous and non-Indigenous).[92]

The forced depósito of children was the source of great suffering in Indigenous communities. On September 14, 1811, an official from Melipilla went to the Indian town of Pomaire to take four children who allegedly lived in extreme poverty and had been seen begging in Melipilla. This sort of uprooting, authorities claimed, was a routine practice that helped save Native children from starving as well as failing to learn the basics of Catholicism. When the official tried to take the children with him to Melipilla, he and three military men who accompanied him were stopped by the local cacique, Tomás Pomaire, who, together with many other Indigenous men and women, drove them out of town. On September 21 the official came back to town, this time with nineteen soldiers, to take Tomás Pomaire prisoner. But the cacique's son gathered dozens of Indigenous men and women, many of them armed and ready to fight back. Community members told the party they were not allowed to take a single person from their town. Outnumbered, the official and soldiers returned to Melipilla, once again empty-handed.

The following day, the commissioner of Melipilla led a force of a hundred men to Pomaire to capture both the cacique and his son. The commissioner found dozens of Native men and women barricaded around the cacique's house and stationed on high ground nearby. They were armed with sticks and stones and were joined by some "Spaniards" (white or non-Indigenous individuals) who also lived in the town. They refused to deliver the cacique and his son to the authorities. A confrontation ensued, which according to the commissioner ended with a few Natives and many soldiers and officers injured. Realizing that in neighboring hills there were additional Indigenous forces (which he later learned came from the nearby Indigenous town of Llopeo), the commissioner retreated.[93] It is unclear what happened next, as the documentation ends with the commissioner requesting government help for an additional expedition against the people of Pomaire. But the episode suggests that this Indigenous community had decided to fully support their cacique for resisting the abduction of these children and had even obtained aid from at least one neighboring Indian town.

Officers and colonists also justified the enslavement and forced deportation of Mapuche people living in the Biobio frontier and Valdivia using the logic of the depósito. Since the sixteenth century, Spanish forces had captured, enslaved, and deported Mapuche individuals after military raids. Although the enslavement of Mapuche people was illegal in the eighteenth and nineteenth centuries, colonists continued to impose it on Mapuche women and children under the guise of depósito.[94] In 1798 Chile's governor even requested that the intendant of Concepción publish an edict stating that captive Mapuche children could be freely sold but were to serve in local houses only until they reached the age of twelve, after which they would be free to move to another house or occupation.[95] In both colonial and postcolonial times, frontier bureaucrats, officers, and soldiers expected to enslave Mapuche children and adolescent or young women as part of their compensation.[96] When a Spanish military force left the fort of Valdivia to punish nearby Mapuche groups in 1792, they captured and enslaved over forty individuals in just the first day of attacks.[97] After several months of violence, they captured many "women and children," who were sold among Valdivia's residents and forced to serve as domestic workers under the rubric of depósito.[98] There was also a persistent demand for enslaved Mapuche women and children north of the Biobio River, which was supplied by Spanish soldiers and officers as well as by some Mapuche groups, who sold the prisoners they took from their rivals.[99] Elite men and women requested Indigenous children to labor in their households, and major postcolonial political figures distributed enslaved Mapuche children as gifts among powerful people as late as 1831.[100]

Elites also used a logic analogous to that of depósito to accuse families of enslaved and free African-descended people of reproducing bad behavior. Before the abolition of slavery in 1823, slaveholders sometimes opposed petitions to grant freedom to enslaved children under the premise that they would not receive proper education if raised by enslaved or formerly enslaved people. These children needed to be isolated from their parents, slaveholders claimed, to avoid their being contaminated by their elders' vices. To navigate these arguments enslaved men and women found new ways to use the depósito in their favor. In 1817 an enslaved woman named Martina Prado requested freedom for her two daughters, Manuela, four years old, and Rosaria, only four months of age (also referred to in the documentation as Rosario). Both had been born after the "free womb" law of 1811, which meant they were legally free. When Martina Prado's master, Felipa Cuvé, argued that Martina did not have the means to care for the children, Martina said she would find a house "of honor" in which to "deposit" them.[101] The depósito was agreed to in a legal document in which a man named Diego Lavaqui accepted "the donation in form of *depósito* of the free *mulatilla* Manuela."[102] While Martina managed to reclaim Manuela thanks to this form of depósito, Rosaria died while still in the custody of Felipa Cuvé.[103]

A different version of depósito affected women involved in premarital disputes (such as facing opposition to their marriage choice) or women in the process of divorcing their husbands. Elite and non-elite women in these situations were "deposited" in so-called honest or decent houses or convents while their cases were resolved. This form of depósito was officially portrayed not as a punishment but as a way to protect women from retaliation from an aggrieved party (e.g., their husbands or relatives) as well as to isolate them from their lovers, suitors, and men more generally.[104] Finally, judges also used the depósito as a legal penalty, especially against poor and nonwhite women accused of not respecting sexual and gender norms. These women were deposited in "houses of honest people," where they were required to work.[105] These depósitos had an explicit prophylactic purpose. In the words of the commissioner of Colchagua, they were meant to prevent "unruly women" who had "scandalous" relationships with men from communicating their vices and threatening the social order.[106] Like institutional recogimiento, this practice continued well into the nineteenth century, when it was not uncommon for judges to sentence women to be "deposited" in private houses as part of their punishment.[107]

While women negotiated the terms and meaning of their "deposit" whenever possible, forced depósito was often a humiliating, dangerous, and cruel experience.[108] In 1785 Manuela Orellana, a peasant woman from Colchagua, testified before the Audiencia that the local priest and judge had warned her that, if she did not marry a man with whom she lived, "she would be put to work [as a domestic servant], and they would take her children away from her."[109] This was probably the primary meaning of compulsory depósito for poor and nonwhite women: forced labor and separation from their immediate families.

Ejercicios

Another practice that relied on the alleged power of isolation were the ejercicios (exercises). According to the 1732 edition of the dictionary of the Spanish Royal Academy, performing an ejercicio meant retreating to a religious house to perform acts of devotion, usually following the methods established by the founder of the Jesuit order, Ignacio de Loyola.[110] Ejercicios were very common in eighteenth- and nineteenth-century Chile. These retreats normally took place in convents or in special houses called casas de ejercicios, although they were also carried out in other religious buildings and settings, including for example in the Casa de Recogidas.[111]

For the years between 1780 and 1833, I have identified casas de ejercicios operating in all of Chile's major cities (Santiago, Concepción, La Serena, and Valparaíso) as well as in towns like Talca, Quillota, and Petorca.[112] The physical layout of some of these houses shows the importance of ejercicios during this period and the role that isolation played in them. During the last decades of the eighteenth century, for example, there were two casas de ejercicios in Santiago, one for each gender (they were built next to each other, as indicated in map 4). These institutions were busy enough to have their own salaried administrator.[113] According to a description written around 1790 by a Santiago merchant, Juan José de Santa Cruz, each of these buildings had twenty-five rooms, each divided into two chambers.[114] These chambers served as individual cells, inside of which participants were to remain isolated while they spent their days praying, meditating, and performing other religious activities. Peumo's casa de ejercicios was similar to Santiago's. Finished in 1760, the casa provided participants with individual spaces distributed in eighteen common rooms. The establishment offered three rounds of ejercicios for women each year, hosting eighty individuals per round. There were also three rounds for men with one hundred men per round. This yielded a total of 540 persons undergoing ejercicios each year.[115] The institution was evidently a success and by 1790 had dramatically expanded its capacity: it now had twenty-six rooms and hosted six rounds of ejercicios for both men and women every year. Each round comprised 150 individuals, who often came from distant parishes.[116]

These religious retreats took place preferably during Lent and normally lasted for eight days. Participants came from all social classes. Some penitents paid to attend the ejercicios—five pesos was the fee in Santiago in 1835—while others were exempted from payment due to their lack of means.[117] Parishioners from distant areas who wished to attend the ejercicios in Peumo, for example, needed to bring only their bed or mattress, as food and even tobacco were provided for them.[118] Daily routines of people in ejercicios included fasting, praying, and meditating as well as self-flagellation and other bodily mortifications.[119] During their time inside the house, penitents heard mass and prepared for important religious sacraments, particularly confession. Lay people apparently helped penitents prepare for this sacrament. An enslaved woman named Hermenegilda worked in Santiago's casa de ejercicios for women in 1822, helping "poor people" polish their confessions before they met with a priest.[120]

This regime of isolation, meditation, and religious sacraments was supposed to have a lasting impact on penitents. A man in 1765 reportedly thanked Chile's governor with tears in his eyes after the official had forced him to enter ejercicios as a penalty for living in adultery.[121] This powerful experience was expected to lead penitents to reflect on the way in which they had conducted their lives and make different choices in the future. After finishing a round of ejercicios in March of 1796, a young Javiera Carrera decided not to become a nun and married a suitor instead.[122] Immediately after undertaking a round of ejercicios in 1808, Juan Tamallanca, a former student of the Royal School for Natives, announced he would become a painter.[123]

Enclosure was an essential aspect of ejercicios, as isolation was the precondition for self-inspection and individual transformation.[124] For this reason, according to Santa Cruz, priests kept a constant eye on the doors of Santiago's casas de ejercicios to prevent the people inside from being distracted by the outside world.[125] As one governor stated in 1787, ejercicios were "a time of recogimiento."[126] While some were skeptical of the ejercicios' touted positive effects—they found the practice to be useless, superstitious, and a financial scam—others insisted on their power to reshape people's lives.[127] In 1819 Juan Egaña described ejercicios as a "religious practice" dedicated "to reforming the life and customs" of people.[128] Colonial and postcolonial judges often commuted women's imprisonment sentences to that of participation in ejercicios.[129] Similarly, in 1827 Santiago's city council prepared ejercicios for the male inmates of the city jail, a practice that according to council members had a deep, positive effect on prisoners, transforming their ways of life.[130]

As with other prophylactic practices, household heads had the prerogative of using ejercicios to discipline those under their authority, including relatives, domestic workers, and the enslaved. Sending them to ejercicios was meant to both discipline them and instill the values of obedience and restraint. Men in positions of power even cast it as their duty to force ejercicios on their subordinates. In 1822 Domingo Eyzaguirre, who was in charge of a large public infrastructure project near Santiago, had the project's workers do ejercicios. Two hundred men and sixteen women participated, and over one hundred men had their confessions taken after the ejercicios were over.[131]

According to those in charge, ejercicios not only interrupted negative forms of communication by isolating individuals, but they also created new, positive examples for people to imitate. A 1762 Jesuit report claimed that ejercicios provided "political" benefits to the entire colony, as individuals who participated in them became good "examples."[132] Similarly, a pamphlet printed around 1823 argued that ejercicios had a positive effect on society, as they produced "good fathers, sons, and husbands," who spread Catholic "moral principles and doctrine" through their "example."[133] Ejercicios were also seen as political instruments partly because of their alleged power to deliver messages to the population. Shortly after a series of disturbances in Madrid in March of 1766 (the so-called Esquilache riots), the Spanish crown ordered priests to use sermons and other spiritual practices, including ejercicios, to inculcate in people "love and respect for their sovereigns." This order was reissued and extended to all Spanish American territories in 1778.[134] In 1793 the administrator of Santiago's casas de ejercicios offered to have participants in ejercicios request God's favor in the war between Spain and France—a manifestation of piety that also served to legitimize the monarchy's war efforts.[135]

Prophylaxis and Dissent

During the Age of Dissent, isolation became a method with which to prevent the propagation of partisan dissension. Political actors isolated rivals whose words, ideas, behavior, and influence over the population they feared. Authorities not only mobilized a combination of recogimiento, depósito, and ejercicios to combat negative forms of communication, but they also contemplated using them to shape Chile's postcolonial society and deactivate some of its sources of conflict and disagreement.

Women were the primary target of this form of prophylactic politics. Santiago's Casa de Recogidas, the beaterio of Peumo, the casa de ejercicios of Concepción, and several other religious establishments became prisons for women accused of political crimes. Most of these episodes of captivity took place between 1813 and 1818, at the climax of the Spanish imperial civil war in Chile.[136] One witness recalled that in 1813 revolutionaries imprisoned over two hundred women in Concepción as suspected royalists.[137] The most common offense authorities cited in confining women for political reasons was communicating with the enemy, particularly sharing letters or messages with relatives who served in a rival army.[138]

But women were also jailed for other dissenting activities. As I recount in the introduction, in 1813 Dolores Reyes was put in Concepción's casa de ejercicios for celebrating the arrival of the royalist army earlier that year. Mercedes Arias, who was imprisoned together with Reyes, stood accused of "perverting public tranquility with her bad example."[139] Such incarcerations took place not only in Concepción. Four years later the insurgent government sentenced María Josefa Ovalle to be imprisoned in the beaterio of Peumo because of her "scandalous conduct" in "matters of opinion"; that is, her support for the royalist cause.[140] At least seven other women were sentenced between 1817 and 1818 to be imprisoned in the capital's Casa de Recogidas for being royalists.[141]

The imprisonment of dissenters was also conceived of in terms of depósito. This was the case with royalist María Ana Pérez de Arza, whose political activities I discuss in chapter 5. In 1814 revolutionary authorities sentenced her to be "deposited" in one of Santiago's convents along with her daughters.[142] In a petition to the viceroy of Peru in 1815, she claimed that the revolutionary government gave her "as a slave" to a woman named María Ana Toro, who was to pay her two *pesos* per month—an arrangement that appears to be a form of depósito.[143]

But political and military leaders also weighed using depósito in new ways as an instrument to defuse sources of conflict in a postcolonial world. Conservative lawyer and philosopher Juan Egaña, for example, believed that depósitos could be used to mold people to a republican regime. In his "Moral Code" of 1823, which was supposed to be applied alongside the constitution approved that year, he envisioned the construction of "houses of domestic correction" where parents and guardians could deposit children who needed to be disciplined. This was an essential step in turning Chile's corrupted population into virtuous and patriotic citizens fit for a republican lifestyle—which meant preventing future political division and instability.[144]

Egaña also saw ejercicios as instruments to deal with political dissension. In 1827 he made plans to build a casa de ejercicios on his hacienda near Santiago.[145] Egaña gave a special purpose to this casa de ejercicios: it would not host crowds of women, as he claimed was common in Santiago, but would be exclusively dedicated to "businessmen, household heads, and other persons with influence over other people's morality." On his hacienda, isolated from city affairs and surrounded by nature and religious books, these important men would become more virtuous—that is, they would transform themselves according to Egaña's expectations of good behavior.[146] Egaña probably hoped that, once their retreat had ended, these men would somehow communicate morality and good behavior to those under their command and influence. The jurist was in a very difficult political situation when he contemplated erecting this building. The constitution he had helped create in 1823 had been abrogated, Chile was wracked by political instability, and his political antagonists were increasingly powerful. Through his new establishment, Egaña likely hoped to combat these negative trends, counteracting them with the positive prophylactic and regenerative power of ejercicios.

If the politically powerful considered using recogimiento, depósito, and ejercicios as instruments to contain dissent, address its sources, and replace it with good behavior, it was because they saw in dissension and insubordination a problem inextricably tied to communication. Their aim was not simply to punish political rivals but to prevent the propagation and amplification of discord across society. These three prophylactic methods based on isolation also offered a model to think about political conversion—how to transform vectors of contamination into vehicles of virtue and how to best utilize the powers of imitation and contagion to curb dissension and disunity.

The prophylactic practices studied in this chapter arose from the perceived communicability of insubordination and dissension. Many of the claims about the dangers of propagation voiced by authorities may seem to modern readers as nothing but attempts by white elites to justify social discipline, forced labor, and patriarchal control. But to conclude that unease over communication was merely a facade would be mistaken. The remarkable affinity between these different practices reveals that communication was a permanent source of distress for officials and people in positions of power, shaping and permeating all kinds of power relations. Worries over the propagation of insubordination and vice were integral to the enslavement of Indigenous children, the deportation of poor men to penal colonies, and the imprisonment of women in the Casa de Recogidas. Notions and ideas regarding communication were not irrelevant for the thousands of men and women who experienced enslavement, coerced labor, and physical and emotional pain in the name of curtailing bad examples and preventing negative forms of contagion.

CHAPTER EIGHT

Divided by Opinions

Communication and the Toleration of Dissent

During the Age of Dissent, Chileans constantly invoked visibility and propagation to assess (and assert) the impact of human actions. Visible iconoclastic performances allegedly violated royal sovereignty; heroes changed society by way of imitation; scandalous women were vectors of vicious moral contagions. As forms of communication, visibility and propagation not only made ideas and behaviors public but also endowed them with power. These were not neutral modes of communication, as their functioning always affected individuals and the community. To observe visibility and propagation in action was to see them impacting others. This link between communication and power justified the existence of sumptuary laws protecting society's visible social structure, the execution of men and women who set a bad example, and the deportation of those who contaminated others with insubordination. Authorities cited the power of communication to justify censorship and punish all kinds of dissent, from resistance against enslavement to partisan opposition to the government.

But starting in 1810 various actors—including male merchants, aristocrats, notaries, soldiers, politicians, newspaper authors, military officers, and their lawyers and legal agents—began to discuss the link between communication and power. When prosecuted in civil and military courts for the crimes of sedition or conspiracy, some questioned the public relevance of their dissenting activities, arguing that they had not been visible or propagated to other members of society. Others went further and advanced an alternative view of communication, framing it as the public expression of inner opinions or thoughts—a form of communication that had no immediate power over others. By either reinforcing or questioning the connection between communication and power, these actors demarcated a space for the legitimate expression of dissent. Their concerns over the relationship between communication and dissension were echoed in Chile's constitutional experiments and the debates surrounding them. Several of the constitutional codes drafted between 1811 and 1833 enshrined individual liberties such as freedom of opinion and freedom of speech. These provisions echoed the same arguments people accused of political crimes raised in court. In these two very different arenas—trials for sedition and constitutional experiments—merchants, lawyers, soldiers, and jurists imagined new articulations between communication and power, making it possible to conceive of limited yet significant forms of political pluralism.

This chapter analyzes how disputes over dissent in revolutionary Chile pushed political actors to reconsider the power of communication and the admissibility of antagonism and disunity. These debates did not take place in isolation. Chile's constitutional experiments were part of a broader "constitutional revolution" in the Spanish world.[1] Similarly, when local actors defended notions such as "individual freedoms," they were participating in the emergence of liberalism as a global political ideology.[2] It is therefore necessary to keep in mind that the discussions taking place in Chile were not confined to the artificial boundaries of the nation-state. This does not mean, on the other hand, that the new ways in which local agents framed the dangers of dissent and the power of communication were merely the result of ideas imported from Europe or North America. More than applying a single and coherent doctrine about liberalism or constitutional rights, political actors in Chile mobilized arguments from different sources, ranging from Italian jurist Gaetano Filangieri to Spanish medieval legislation. Their interventions were more instrumental and born out of necessity than dogmatic. Rather than offering a linear history of political toleration being implemented in Chile due to new and progressive ideas imported from abroad, this chapter examines how actors borrowed from different intellectual traditions to respond to the challenges of radical dissension, rendering political pluralism imaginable in the process.

Public and Nonpublic, Criminal and Lawful

During the second half of the eighteenth century, classifying an action or behavior as public usually involved assessing whether it had (or could potentially have) affected others. As historian Jean-Pierre Dedieu has argued, any action was "public" in the early modern Spanish world if its consequences reached beyond the context of a single individual or family unit.[3] Actions were not public by essence—their publicness was a property that emerged from their social repercussions. From this perspective, the classification of public was casuistic and based on contingent and often shifting notions of social impact.[4] In 1778, for example, the colonial government established the post of alcalde de barrio in Santiago. These new officers were tasked with observing the conduct of the capital's inhabitants and initiating legal actions when they transgressed the law. Article 22 of the "instructions" given to the alcaldes authorized them to intervene in "private" and "domestic" conflicts only when the latter came to "patently disturb the neighborhood's peace and quiet," or could have "sensible consequences."[5] Actions and behaviors stopped being entirely "private" or "domestic" the moment they had an effect on society.

Visibility and propagation were among the main parameters officials and ordinary people used to define the publicness of an action or behavior. Regulations for Chile's alcaldes de barrios were directly inspired by those the Council of Castile issued in 1768 when it created the post in Madrid: there, alcaldes de barrio were not allowed to "interfere with the citizens' private conduct" unless the latter provided "a scandalous, exterior example" to others or engaged in "visible disturbances."[6] In this case visibility and imitation explicitly constituted the thresholds between the public and the private, the harmful and the harmless. Similarly, when Governor Mariano Osorio created the post of Santiago's lieutenant of police in 1816, he defined "private or domestic" actions as those "which cannot influence public tranquility, good example, and government."[7] From this assertion it was possible to conclude that providing a bad example was enough to consider an action of public importance.

Evaluating the social impact of an action was also central to criminal law.[8] Late medieval and early modern Spanish penal legislation was shaped by theology. The law—and of course the jurists and thinkers behind it—considered theological concerns as valid criteria with which to determine the degree of criminality of human actions. These included whether said actions constituted an offense against God or revealed a corrupt moral disposition on the part of the offender. During the second half of the eighteenth century, reformers advanced an alternative mode of measuring the criminality of actions and delimiting the range of penal law. Citing the writings of Montesquieu, Beccaria, and Filangieri, authors such as Manuel de Lardizábal and Gaspar Melchor de Jovellanos argued that laws should be rational and proportional (i.e., the most severe punishments should be reserved for the most criminal actions). As a product of human society, penal legislation should punish only actions that damaged or threatened society. This meant that the criminality of an action had to be established based not on how it affected the transcendent source of social order but on the concrete damage it had done to society.

These reformist views had profound consequences on how

authorities and jurists assessed criminal actions. For example, in early modern Spanish juridical doctrines, the crime of lèse-majesté was such a horrible affront to God that the mere intention to commit it could be considered as criminal as carrying it out. By "intention" jurists meant the determination to execute the crime, which according to Spanish laws could be proven when conspirators wrote down a plan or invited others to join them—evidentiary requirements that would be constantly evoked in cases of sedition in colonial and postcolonial Chile. Reformers, on the other hand, considered it irrational to apply the same penalty to those who only intended to commit a crime and those who actually did so. Although some theologians and jurists rejected these new ideas, the crown initially supported them, and there were serious efforts to reform Spanish penal legislation in the 1770s and 1780s.[9] While the reformation drive was ultimately unsuccessful, this new legal reasoning became extremely influential in the Spanish empire and profoundly shaped political thinking during the revolutionary era.[10]

As a result of these developments, different and competing parameters for establishing the criminality of an action existed in late colonial Chile. This becomes evident when comparing the arguments royal officials used in the only two trials for sedition initiated during this period—the investigation of Antonio Vergne and Antonio Gramusset in 1781 for conspiring against the monarchy, and the trial of priest Clemente Morán in 1795 for voicing positive opinions about the French Revolution, both referenced in previous chapters. The criminal investigation carried out by the Audiencia against Vergne and Gramusset in early 1781 showed that the conspirators had discussed their desire to bring down the government, sought potential allies, and drafted a document laying out their revolutionary plan. After reviewing the case, on January 20, 1781, Crown attorney Joaquín Pérez de Uriondo found the defendants guilty of the crime of lèse-majesté. Pérez de Uriondo focused his decision entirely on Vergne and Gramusset's intention to make Chile an independent republic. Secret conspiracies such as this "undoubtedly" constituted the "crime of lèse-majesté," Pérez de Uriondo argued, "even if [their] effects" had not been actually felt by society, "because [this crime] is perpetrated only with the intention and desire [*afecto*] of perpetrating it."[11] What Pérez de Uriondo meant was that the law punished the intention and desire to commit treason, even if these inner dispositions were never put into practice. A second Crown attorney, José Márquez de la Plata, agreed with his colleague, noting that the mere act of thinking to profane the king's sovereignty was a crime.[12] Disregarding the advice of both attorneys, the Audiencia decided not to prosecute the two prisoners in Chile and dispatched them to the viceroy in Lima. Pérez de Uriondo appealed this ruling, claiming that the proceedings proved that Vergne and Gramusset were guilty of treason, as in cases of lèse-majesté guilt "consists only in the desire" to commit the crime.[13]

The case of Vergne and Gramusset was put on hold before the accused had the opportunity to defend themselves, making it difficult to ascertain whether they or their legal agents would have objected to the Crown attorneys' logic. The two Frenchmen were still awaiting trial in Lima in late 1784, when they were sent to Spain to be judged. Vergne perished in February of 1786 when the ship transporting him to Europe wrecked near the coast of Portugal. Gramusset died a few months later while still in prison. In practical terms, both men were severely punished based solely on their criminal intentions.

Authorities adopted a different strategy when they expected to be legally challenged. In prosecuting Clemente Morán in 1795, Governor Ambrosio Higgins stressed the threat this priest's dissenting activities and intentions represented to society. The government investigated Morán for having praised the French Revolution and for questioning monarchical rule in conversations in the town of La Serena and its surrounding area. The case was initiated by crown officials in La Serena, who first gathered the evidence against the priest and sent the results of their investigation to Santiago. To proceed with the trial, Governor Higgins had to consider the thorny issue of ecclesiastical immunity, according to which members of the church had to be prosecuted in their own tribunals and punished per the church's internal legislation. When he met with Santiago's bishop to discuss the matter, the prelate informed Higgins that he would not support lifting Morán's immunity.[14] The governor was then forced to prove that Morán's actions were exceptional enough to try him in a secular court. On May 27, 1795, Higgins sent a communication to Santiago's bishop in which he claimed that Clemente Morán had tried to "win over others" to his "opinion." This meant Morán's conversations revealed not only his heterodox political views but also his criminal intention to affect others. Higgins reminded the bishop he had orders from the king to act "against any person, be they ecclesiastical or secular," who "tried to disturb with actions or words the calm, tranquility, and security of his empire."[15] The governor stressed the potential harm to society of Morán's actions, which also justified prosecuting him in a criminal trial. Two days later, he instructed authorities in La Serena to continue gathering testimonies about the priest's actions.[16] Facing continued resistance from the bishop, on August 3, 1795, Higgins requested the Audiencia to examine the legality of the measures he had taken against Morán.[17]

The Audiencia determined that it fell within the governor's jurisdiction to conduct legal investigations against priests who "aspired to disturb peace, good order, and public tranquility with seditious plans, or with expressions" that affected "citizens' spirits" and inspired in them "ideas" opposed to the "respect" and "veneration" they owed their sovereign.[18]

It is important to consider the language Higgins and the Audiencia used to assess—one may say exaggerate—the importance of Morán's actions and the danger they represented. Neither the governor nor the judges cited Morán's ideas or thoughts as being criminal. Had they done so the bishop could have asserted that such inner dispositions fell within the jurisdiction of the church, which ruled over people's consciences.[19] What officials spoke of instead were "seditious plans," efforts to "win over" others, and "expressions" that might affect "citizens' spirits." As previously noted, the first two of these actions were explicitly mentioned in Spanish legislation as evidence of the intention to carry out the crime of lèse-majesté. The third referenced not only the content of the priest's words but their alleged effect on others. Morán's case stalled for years as the jurisdictional conflict between the bishop and the governor remained unresolved. The priest died in Santiago in 1800 while still awaiting a definitive sentence.

As these cases reveal, royal officials took a strategic approach to assessing the criminality of people accused of sedition, adopting the doctrines that best served to extend and consolidate their jurisdiction. While in 1781 Crown attorneys mobilized traditional legal reasoning to underscore the criminality of Vergne and Gramusset's inner dispositions, in 1795 the government found it more convenient to stress the public impact of Morán's words. The distinctions between public and nonpublic and criminal and lawful drawn by the government were thus not self-evident and were for this reason potentially open to challenge. While the government prevented this from happening during the second half of the eighteenth century, the situation changed dramatically after 1808.

Opinion between Unity and Division

With the unfolding of the imperial crisis in 1808 and the political instability that followed, observers identified the emergence of a new problem in Chile: that of opinions. Scholars of Chile and the Atlantic world have devoted much attention to the notion of "public opinion," which gained prominence during this period as a new and revolutionary principle of political legitimacy and accountability.[20] Their studies often focus on the printing press, hailed at the time as public opinion's main manifestation and instrument.[21] But as Kirk Wetters has noted in the case of Europe, other definitions of opinion—most notably what constituted a nonpublic or private opinion—have not been similarly examined or theorized.[22] This is perhaps because "opinion" is perceived to be a self-evident and ahistorical concept, one designating an individual's judgment or ideas. But this was not the only meaning people in Chile attributed to the word. What was essential in "opinion," I argue, was that it allowed observers to draw a connection between people's inner dispositions and the destiny of the state, associating the problem of division and dissent with people's interior experiences.

Between 1780 and 1830, political actors in Chile used the word "opinion" to designate social norms, public reputation, individual beliefs, and personal judgments.[23] Despite their differences, all these cases referenced the link between people's actions and their inner worlds. For example, someone's "opinion," in the sense of their reputation, was perceived to be the result of an interior quality as expressed in public actions. From this perspective, a person's "opinion" indicated their credibility and served to predict how they would act in the future. Similarly, when describing social rules, the word "opinion" signified the set of convictions, expectations, and internalized norms that determined people's behavior.

As the imperial crisis unfolded, observers in Chile began connecting the concept of opinion with politics and the dangers of dissent. People often talked of "the opinion" to identify a collective stance regarding political issues, asking themselves, for example, whether the opinion supported a given regime or political leader. This "opinion" was a force in dispute, and political agents considered it one of their tasks to shape it and make it conform to their goals.[24] As a concept "the opinion" invoked the power of unity (a unanimous consensus on political issues) as well as the perils of fragmentation. In 1807 Juan Egaña argued that, once people started commenting freely about politics, a dangerous disconnection happened between the government and the citizenry. He called this "the danger of opinions," by which he meant the absence of a unified opinion to guide the population's conduct.[25] "There is no opinion" in Chile, complained Valparaíso Governor José Ignacio Zenteno in 1825, "because each man has his own, and only disorder and anarchy reign."[26]

Confirming the link between opinion and dissension, elite and ordinary people also began using this word during the revolutionary years to identify a person's reputed political affiliation or position.[27] In criminal investigations, actors as diverse as Mapuche domestic workers, women textile makers, soldiers, peasants, and public employees used the word "opinion"—either prompted or unprompted by judges—to position themselves and others along opposite partisan lines.[28] "Opinion," in this sense, served to locate individuals on a mental map of antagonistic or competing political choices such as "patriot," "royalist," and "insurgent." Individuals who did not express full support for a given faction or regime, for example, could be presented as ambivalent in matters of "opinion."[29] In the early stages of the revolution, being of a dissenting "opinion" was grounds for exclusion from citizenship and state employment, and eventually it became reason enough for criminal prosecution and imprisonment.[30]

Through the notion of opinion, then, observers in revolutionary and postrevolutionary Chile tried to make sense of the central problem of their time: dissent. Either as a collective force or as an individual political affiliation, "opinion" gave enormous relevance to people's inner dispositions—to their motivations, goals, and ideals. These interior states not only played a crucial role in political conflicts but were, so to speak, the primary setting of political plurality. Chileans were divided by their opinions. But, paradoxically, the term "opinion" occupied an uncertain position with regard to the classificatory scheme of public/nonpublic and criminal/noncriminal. Were opinions an inner, nonpublic phenomenon or a public one? Could someone's opinion be considered a danger to society? These were crucial questions on which hung the legal status of dissension.

Establishing the publicness and criminality of opinions was particularly difficult because the concept came associated with its own, neutral view of communication. In court cases and other political settings, people in revolutionary and postrevolutionary Chile talked of opinions as inner dispositions that could be made public preferably through speech and writing. A government decree from 1813, for example, established that people had the right to "manifest publicly their opinions," which it equated with communicating "ideas" and "thoughts."[31] As will be examined later, several constitutions drafted and approved between 1811 and 1833 contained similar declarations. Associated with opinion, then, came a new notion of communication in Chile after 1808. In this view, communication was an intersubjective phenomenon, the public rendering of people's inner experiences and worldviews. What communication communicated, then, were statements or judgments about the world—and nothing else. Unlike arguments based on visibility and propagation, from the point of view of "opinion," speech and writing did not immediately transform reality. Compared with visibility and propagation, this was a neutral form of communication, which limited itself to making public an inner disposition (an "opinion") that until then had a nonpublic existence. While this form of publication could have major social consequences, its impact derived mainly from the statements it made public rather than from the intrinsic power of the medium of transmission. This view of communication thus entailed a new set of parameters by which to establish the publicness and criminality of dissension.

Three forms of communication were regularly presented as media for opinions: speech, the press, and letters. In revolutionary and postcolonial Chile, all three were subjected to official censorship and control, even during the period of political toleration that extended between the fall of the O'Higgins regime in 1823 and the civil war of 1829–1830. Government officials regularly justified censoring or punishing specific acts of speech and writing on the basis that they introduced discord and disunity, corrupted public opinion, and were subversive, seditious, and otherwise harmful to society—that is, because of their alleged effects on others.[32] Sometimes authorities explicitly declared that their goal was to censor the manifestation of a dissenting opinion. In November of 1812 the government decreed that "freedom of opinion" should not "be harmful to society." Those with dissenting views about "the system of government" were to refrain from criticizing the new regime and spreading bad news lest they face deportation.[33] What was radically new about this form of censorship was that, unlike colonial provisions against dissenting speech, it identified as its target the public expression of an inner "opinion." This idea of censorship would prove highly controversial during the revolutionary era.

Disputing the Power of Dissension (1810)

Starting in 1810 those accused of sedition (and their lawyers) began advancing the idea that political opinions were not dangerous, even if manifested in speech or writing, and that they could not be prosecuted as crimes. These individuals followed two alternative strategies: denying that the dissenting opinions they defended were either public or criminal, or claiming that some radical opinions were not seditious, even when made public. Both of these positions concerned the power of communication, albeit in different ways. The first emphasized the absence of communication and delineated a nonpublic sphere in which dissenting activities were permissible and removed from state jurisdiction. The second position claimed that expressing opinions or thoughts in speech and writing was a neutral form of communication, at worst barely criminal. These sorts of defenses were first raised in Chile in mid- and late 1810 during two related trials. In the first, conducted by the Spanish governor, Francisco Antonio García Carrasco, three men—Juan Antonio Ovalle, José Antonio Rojas, and Bernardo Vera—were tried for conspiracy; in the second, carried out by Valparaíso's military authorities, one Damián Seguí was tried for sedition.

The trial of Ovalle, Rojas, and Vera was the culminating event in a series of political conflicts within the colony since news of the captivity of the Spanish royal family and the war against the French arrived in August of 1808. Governor García Carrasco's position in May of 1810 was difficult. News arriving from Spain announced the near complete political and military defeat of the Spanish government on the Peninsula, which reinforced the position of those who believed colonies had to form their own autonomous governments. Informed of the dissenting conversations that were taking place in the colony, García Carrasco felt the need to consolidate his position vis-à-vis local elites.[34] On May 18 he initiated a secret criminal investigation of the attorney of Santiago's city council, Juan Antonio Ovalle. Born around 1750, Ovalle was a rich and powerful man with important family connections. In the decree initiating the investigation, the governor charged him with spreading ideas of independence, "alarming" people, and pushing them to join "the project of a scandalous insurrection." The criminal investigation would be swift and abbreviated, García Carrasco added, to prevent such pernicious ideas from "propagating."[35]

The governor's accusation may seem to modern readers a standard example of official repression of dissenting opinions. But it is worth considering in some detail the charges García Carrasco leveled against Ovalle. Like Higgins in 1795, the governor did not accuse Ovalle of *thinking* about independence but of *spreading* the idea. The language the governor used referenced the existence of a plan and the recruitment of collaborators, elements that Spanish law required to prove the existence of a seditious intention to overthrow the king. He did not accuse Ovalle of having criminal thoughts or ideas—an unorthodox opinion, so to speak—but of impacting society by propagating them and putting them into action.

As the secret investigation against Ovalle advanced, the governor targeted two additional men: José Antonio Rojas and Bernardo Vera. Almost eighty years old, Rojas was, like Ovalle, a wealthy aristocrat with strong family connections in Chile and abroad. Bernardo Vera was a lawyer and university professor around thirty years old. The evidence gathered during the early stages of the trial did not amount to much: witnesses accused the three men of discussing bad news about the war against the French, sharing semi-veiled criticisms of the colonial administration and the Spanish empire, and suggesting they would welcome a change in government. No evidence of a conspiracy was found, forcing the government to frame the questionable conversations of Rojas, Ovalle, and Vera as constituting the crime of sedition.

The government planned to imprison the three men on May 25, 1810. The day before, the administration issued an edict forbidding all criticism of imperial authorities. The document categorized dissenting conversations as criminal because they "spread" a "spirit of insubordination and discontent" among the population, "which would disturb order" and lead to a "conspiracy" if left unchecked.[36] The edict thus not only forbade people from speaking against the government but also tried to provide a rationale for why these conversations should not be allowed, citing the dangers of propagation and how speech might drive some people to participate in seditious plans. Having thus prepared the stage, the government imprisoned Rojas, Ovalle, and Vera on May 25 and seized and examined their personal papers. On May 26 the Audiencia judged there was "merit" in the legal investigation conducted by the governor, noting that vassals should not "disseminate concepts or opinions that are subversive of good order and tranquility."[37] Rojas, Ovalle, and Vera were immediately transported to Valparaíso for deportation to Lima.

As was to be expected, many among Santiago's elites reacted negatively to the detention of three of their own. Dozens of relatives and supporters, along with institutions such as Santiago's cathedral chapter, pleaded in favor of the prisoners and requested the government not to deport them to Peru without trying them first. In their interventions powerful actors such as Santiago's city council—one of the bastions of opposition to García Carrasco—were driven to advance cautious yet significant arguments in favor of political toleration. In a communication dated May 28, 1810, the council shared with the governor the population's shock over his decision to imprison the three men, adding that now "each one doubts whether their words, or even their thoughts, constitute a crime." The council argued that it would happily request the full extent of the law be applied to Vera, Rojas, and Ovalle in case they were guilty of "projects and plans" that would "disturb" the state's "tranquility." "But," they continued, if "these men's crime consists merely in words," then the situation needed to be reconsidered, as words should not be punished in the same manner as actions. Even if the accused had proffered seditious words, the council contended, these could not "have any consequences" in events taking place "three thousand leagues" away (meaning in Spain).[38]

Let us examine the council's arguments. By this time council members probably knew that the government justified the imprisonment of Ovalle, Rojas, and Vera based on the alleged criminality of their conversations. Their strategy therefore consisted in dissociating these dissenting words from danger or power. They asserted that speech was far less criminal than action and indirectly demanded that words be shown to have "effects" on others to criminalize them. They also implicitly advanced a scale of culpability between thoughts, speech, and actions in which thoughts were the least consequential and thus most removed from state jurisdiction, while actions had the greatest effect on society and thus had to be regulated and punished.

This dispute over the dangers of dissension continued as the Audiencia judge Félix Francisco Bazo y Berri examined the three prisoners. During these interrogations conducted in Valparaíso between June 26 and June 28, the judge highlighted the impact of the prisoners' dissenting words, charging them with advancing "plans" and preparing "the spirits" for independence. The accused responded by stressing the legitimate nature of their conversations and their lack of impact on others.[39] After their interrogations, Bernardo Vera elaborated on this idea. On June 29 he sent a petition to the governor in which he distinguished between seditious plans—which were criminal—and simple words and opinions, which were not.[40]

The trial of Ovalle, Rojas, and Vera thus slowly turned into a confrontation over the parameters by which to establish the criminality of dissent. On June 29 Bazo y Berri, perhaps convinced there was not much ground for prosecution, granted the three prisoners house arrest in Valparaíso. However, after receiving in mid-June news of the downfall of the viceroy of Río de la Plata and the formation of a junta in Buenos Aires, Governor García Carrasco decided to carry on with deporting them to Lima. In early July he dispatched a secret emissary to Valparaíso with orders to place the detainees on the first ship leaving for the viceregal capital. He also sent secret orders to a merchant named Damián Seguí asking him to gather (without notifying the port's military commander) a group of armed men the day of the ship's departure to prevent any resistance to the deportation. Rojas and Ovalle were sent to Lima, while Vera, feigning being sick, managed to stay in Valparaíso. García Carrasco's actions during these days—which included lying to Santiago's elites and arming people without informing local military commanders—precipitated his fall. After extensive unrest in the capital, the governor was forced to resign on July 16, 1810.

The trial against Ovalle, Rojas, and Vera shifted dramatically after this event. Witnesses now claimed García Carrasco had distorted and misconstrued their testimonies and that they had never questioned the prisoners' loyalty. The situation for the accused improved even more after a revolutionary junta was formed in Santiago on September 18. On October 6 Vera submitted a lengthy legal defense to the court on behalf of Rojas, Ovalle, and himself (Rojas and Ovalle only returned to Chile later that month).[41] While he denied any of them had committed the crime of sedition, he also pushed his defense of dissension further. According to Vera, having an "interior desire for the independence of the Americas" was not a "crime." These "sentiments" were not "criminal in the eyes of God," and were "exempted [. . .] from men's jurisdiction, as long as they don't leave the chest's cupboard, and are not directed at subverting the correct social order." To support this radical political proposition, Vera quoted a law from the Siete Partidas, the influential medieval Spanish legal code. The law stated that "a man should not be punished for any evil thought which he has in his heart, provided he does not put it in operation." An example of such "evil thoughts" was treason, which was executed by "talking with others to implicate them," taking an oath, or "drawing up some document" with co-conspirators. This was the law judges and authorities had in mind when referencing "plans" and invitations in cases of sedition. The law also distinguished between different phases in the execution of a crime. An individual who initiated a criminal action but repented before committing it was not to be judged with the same harshness as someone who actually carried it out. The sole exceptions to this rule were treason, murder, and rape (if the victim was a virgin woman), which were fully criminal even if aborted before completion.[42]

It was in this piece of medieval legislation that Vera—and several others after him—found an instrument to open a space in Chile's legal landscape for the toleration of radical dissent. In Vera's reading of the law, authorities could prosecute seditious thoughts only if they had already been turned into a plan to disrupt "social peace and order." From this Vera concluded that there existed a sphere of nonpublic thoughts and intentions entirely outside the reach of ordinary justice. This sphere of nonpublic inner dispositions, moreover, went beyond people's minds. Vera characterized the seizure of Rojas's correspondence and papers as a criminal effort to "extend" the government's "jurisdiction" "over the depths of our hearts." He also questioned the criminality of conversations, claiming that "mere words" were not liable if none of the accused was involved in a project to subvert social order. Portraying conversations and private letters as simple manifestations of thoughts or opinions, Vera thus framed them as immune from government intervention.[43]

On October 15, 1810, Chile's junta declared Ovalle, Rojas, and Vera innocent.[44] But while the three aristocrats were absolved, a fourth man met the opposite fate. On July 10 Valparaíso's military authorities had imprisoned Damián Seguí for assembling more than forty armed men in the port per García Carrasco's secret orders. The port commander estimated this action to be criminal, as these men—who were not regular soldiers—had gathered without him or any other local military officer knowing or authorizing it. Seguí, a merchant from Mallorca who had collaborated with the governor in previous criminal enterprises (including seizing a British ship, assassinating its crew, and smuggling its cargo), lost all official support once García Carrasco resigned from office. Found guilty of sedition, he was sentenced to deportation to the penal colony of Juan Fernández for a term of four years.

In November lawyer Juan José Santibáñez wrote in defense of Seguí that his defendant had not executed any seditious actions, as he and his men never had the opportunity to act. No "effective evil or harm" derived from Seguí's efforts to enforce García Carrasco's orders, the lawyer argued. "The crime of sedition is not carried out by intentions," Santibáñez added, "but only by a real fermentation, mutiny, or tumult, which did not take place in Valparaíso."[45] This constituted a radical departure from Spanish legislation, which criminalized the intention to commit treason. Santibáñez's defense echoed some of the arguments advanced in the trial of Vera, Ovalle, and Rojas. Like them, Santibáñez argued that harm to society was the most appropriate criterion by which to judge criminal actions and stressed the difference between having the intention to commit a crime and carrying it out. While these arguments were similar to those Vera had put forward only a month earlier, the junta confirmed Seguí's punishment.

Disputing the Criminality of Sedition (1811–1813)

Confrontations over the crime of sedition proliferated after the junta's establishment in September of 1810. For example, in December of 1811 a man accused of having participated in a conspiracy against the Carrera government, while denying the crime, implicitly defended the "immunity" of "thinking."[46] In 1812 Rafael Garfias admitted to having sent letters containing anti-revolutionary news to royalist-controlled Lima. But, he claimed, this exchange had had no social consequences.[47] While he acknowledged his writings contained dissenting opinions, Garfias suggested they be considered criminal only if they had some sort of public impact.

Other defenses were more elaborate. On December 29, 1811, university professor Domingo Salamanca was put under house arrest in Santiago for posting "letters subversive of public order." Among these was an anonymous missive addressed to an unidentified individual in Lima that contained critical remarks about the Carrera family (Salamanca would later say the recipient was the marquis of Zelada). In January of 1812 Salamanca submitted a long legal defense written by lawyer Juan Egaña, although it did not carry his signature. The document began by establishing four allegedly unquestionable principles. First, "freedom of thought is invulnerable" and born of natural law. Second, "a private document" was barely more liable than "thoughts." Third, punishment was reserved for those whose actions damaged society, for which reason "human laws do not punish a man's opinion" as long as it remains "in the sphere of his private thoughts." Fourth, private letters were sacred and should not be violated by any authority unless in extraordinary circumstances. Based on these principles Salamanca was to be considered innocent of all charges, even though he was the author of a letter critical of the head of state.[48] These were radical ideas. To claim that "opinions" were not criminal was to claim that disunity and dissent had to be tolerated, even if only in the nonpublic sphere. The state attorney was unimpressed by Salamanca's defense and accused him of producing impactful blasphemies and calumnies against the government. It is unclear what happened with Salamanca after this stage of his trial, as the file is incomplete.[49]

The era's most dramatic communication and dissension controversy took place in 1813, when defense lawyer José Gregorio Calderón went so far as to request the death penalty for two state attorneys for having accused his defendant of sedition. The case began in January of 1813, when the government detained thirteen men in Santiago for allegedly conspiring to murder the Carrera brothers and take control of the administration. Like García Carrasco in 1810 or Higgins in 1795, the government found little evidence of a conspiracy other than conversations in which the accused had shared critical comments about the administration and (according to some testimonies) suggested putting an end to it. After reviewing the case, on February 23 state attorneys Agustín Vial and Hipólito Villegas concluded that these conversations constituted a "horrible plan" that endangered society, and they requested that the court apply Spanish legislation pertaining to the crime of lèse-majesté. This meant sentencing the conspirators to death. Vial and Villegas justified this harsh recommendation based on the enormous harm seditious plans could cause if implemented.[50]

In response to these charges, lawyers for the accused submitted several defenses, all of which dealt in their own way with the power of communication and the legitimacy of dissent. For example, José Gregorio Calderón, acting as *procurador de pobres* (state-appointed lawyer for defendants who could not afford to pay for litigation), argued that "every citizen has the right to manifest his opinion," and doing so was not the same as launching a conspiracy.[51] A second procurador, Agustín Mardones, submitted a collective defense for three of the accused—which was again likely written by lawyer Juan Egaña. Inspired by the same law of the Siete Partidas that Vera cited in 1810, the defense claimed that thoughts and words were not as criminal as actions. It was better to tolerate the constant disparaging rumors and conversations about the government, the document stated, than to penalize them and produce an unbearable tyranny.[52]

Even more radical was the file submitted by lawyer José Gregorio Calderón on behalf of well-known politician José Gregorio Argomedo.[53] Like other lawyers, Calderón argued that in civil justice "affects" and words "should not be punished, only actions," and that the intention to murder government authorities was not a crime. But Calderón went still further. While it was always legitimate for men to complain about the government, this was even more true at a time when the "social pact has been dissolved" and sovereignty had returned to each individual. Calderón argued that anyone who studied the "rights of man" could see that being part of "factions" was not "a crime," especially in a "revolutionized or democratic State" in which a new "social pact" had not been "sanctioned by the general will." Calderón here interpreted Chile's revolution as a dissolution of the social contract, which had returned to each person their original rights. Among these recovered rights, he seemed to suggest, was that of engaging in dissenting words and actions, as people surrendered these freedoms in favor of the public good only when they entered into a social contract. This meant that, at least until a new social agreement was reached, both private and public political pluralism were licit and had to be tolerated. The lawyer concluded that the state attorneys had distorted the law in their desire to apply the death penalty to the accused, which was itself an offense punishable by death. "I request them to be put on trial by the people," he added, although he did not specify how this might be done.

Calderón's demand to submit the state attorneys to some sort of popular trial is one of the most extraordinary moments in the disputes over the prosecution of dissent in revolutionary Chile. Challenging the association between dissension and danger drawn by the court, Calderón ended up upholding toleration of radical political disagreement. The government did not engage with Calderón's provocations, instead limiting itself to sentencing Argomedo and the rest of the accused to deportation. But while the ideas of lawyers like Calderón were not necessarily effective in court, they were a testament to how the experience of widespread antagonism made it possible for actors to reconsider both the power of communication and the legitimacy of dissent.[54]

A Widespread Debate (1814–1831)

In the years following the 1813 conspiracy trial, ongoing dissension and political persecution kept pushing people as varied as friars, government officials, priests, public employees, and politicians to consider the need for some version of political tolerance. In newspaper articles, petitions to the government, testimonies in court, and institutional decisions, they argued that dissenting convictions were harmless to society as long as they did not manifest in exterior actions. What was relevant, they claimed, was whether people obeyed authorities, regardless of their inner beliefs.[55] In a brochure published in Santiago in 1817, priest José Manuel Verdugo distinguished between "three classes" of people opposed to the government: those whose "opinion" was against independence but do "nothing else"; those who "not only have an opinion [*opinan*], but speak against [the government] whenever they can"; and those who acted and conspired against it. While the first ones deserved to be pitied, the second and third were "criminals."[56] Even ordinary subjects with no apparent legal training raised this idea. Consider, for example, the case of Romualdo Antonio Esponda in 1814. When Bernardo Vera, now acting as a revolutionary judge, charged Esponda with being a royalist, citing as evidence his personal letters, Esponda recognized that it was "true that he is of contrary opinion to the system of the Fatherland" but that he had not "damaged" the state or any private individual with his "exterior" and "interior" actions. This was not a prepared statement by a lawyer: Esponda, a merchant from a modest background, advanced these ideas in the midst of an interrogation by a hostile judge. He improvised a distinction between "opinions" and "actions" that had far-reaching consequences, as it implied that people with dissenting views could and should be tolerated as long as they had not demonstrably harmed the state.[57]

This argument in favor of toleration was popular enough for the newly installed revolutionary administration to consider addressing it. In 1817 the government contemplated creating two official newspapers, which would be in charge of demonstrating that the war against royalists "is no war of religion"—that is, a conflict in which people could act "in good faith" despite having the wrong "opinions."[58] Perhaps following this directive, in May of that year the official newspaper published an article that essentially argued that people's opinions had to align with the government's.[59]

Trials for sedition and insubordination continued to provide lawyers, judges, and other legal agents with occasion to reflect on the limits of state authority and the legitimacy of dissent. Though less frequently than before, people involved in such cases argued that the law punished only actions, not inner dispositions or their expression in speech or writing.[60] During a criminal trial for sedition in 1816, one government official even argued that pluralism had become an inescapable aspect of political life, adding that opposition to the government was not punishable by law unless it threatened to harm society.[61]

During the 1820s politicians and intellectuals constantly debated under which conditions the publication of an opinion or idea through the press could be considered a crime.[62] In general, they agreed that governments should exercise as much tolerance as possible and allow for the coexistence of people of different ideas or parties.[63] But some went further. José Miguel Infante, for example, argued in his newspaper, *El Valdiviano Federal*, that sedition was not a speech crime, as it could not be accomplished through the press (the public expression of an idea being unable to generate a successful conspiracy or rebellion against the state). This meant that all printed opinions had to be tolerated, including calls to overthrow the government.[64] Political agents even called into question the very existence of the crime of sedition. Between 1827 and 1829, politicians like Infante published newspaper articles seeking to exculpate men involved in cases of insubordination and mutiny. Their core argument was that the crime of sedition did not exist, as only illegitimate regimes faced insurrections (thus making all rebellions by definition licit).[65] These ideas—which echoed José Gregorio Calderón's 1813 legal opinion—reveal how far some people were now willing to go to justify legitimate dissension, not only as an inner experience but as a public, manifest one.

Legal Protections

Legal disputes over dissent voiced between 1810 and 1833 echoed a larger discussion of individual rights and the limits of state authority. One of the main concerns among political elites in Chile during and after the imperial crisis was despotism and how to prevent it.[66] What the ruling groups claimed to repudiate was any regime that systematically abused power and violated public and individual freedoms (even if in practice they seldom extended these freedoms to the majority population). The instrument that seemed most suited to protect these liberties and prevent the rise of despotism was a written constitution. By 1808 the Spanish monarchy did not have a constitution (although imperial elites had long been debating the existence of a nonwritten one).[67] When the monarchy fell, subjects all across the empire expressed their desire to finally implement such a code. Chile was no exception: by mid-1810, a revolutionary manuscript titled *Catecismo político cristiano* (Political and Christian Catechism) called for the establishment of a Congress that would dictate a constitution.[68] Demands to draft a charter or to enforce, improve, or change the existing one became common in the following two decades.

After 1808 Chile (as well as the rest of the Spanish Atlantic) became engulfed in an unprecedented constitutional experiment. New constitutions or codes with constitutional range were approved in 1812, 1818, 1822, 1823, 1828, and 1833, and additional constitutional proposals were officially forwarded (but not approved) in 1813 and 1826. Most of these constitutions were never fully implemented, as governments either ignored some of their provisions or declared states of exception to lift limits placed on their power. But the insistence with which political players drafted and approved new constitutions indicates the importance they attributed to them.[69]

Five of these eight constitutions—the drafts of 1813 and 1826 as well as the codes approved in 1822, 1828, and 1833—combined parameters of publicness and criminality with ideas about communication to make room for the legitimate expression of dissent in revolutionary and postcolonial Chile. The code of 1813 had been originally written in 1811 by lawyer and jurist Juan Egaña.[70] It did not list freedom of opinion as an individual right but declared that citizens could do "everything that does not harm the rights of others."[71] The code also established that "a man's house and writings are sacred" and that they could not "be violated" unless authorities had "a strong presumption" that a crime was being committed. "Papers that have not been communicated [*sin comunicarse*]," another article read, were barely more transgressive "than thoughts" and could not be used as the basis for prosecutions of individuals.[72] Much as in his defense of Salamanca in 1812, Egaña in his constitution implicitly distinguished between thoughts and actions, the former being less criminal than the latter, and delineated a nonpublic realm of activities that lay outside the jurisdiction of the state except in special circumstances.

The constitution of 1822, written by an executive-appointed senate, openly tolerated public expressions of dissent. The code's most striking article read that "no one can be punished because of their thoughts, nor for expressing them." The charter not only followed the idea that thoughts were nonpublic and thus outside the state's jurisdiction but did not see an offense in their propagation—the only exceptions were calumnies, insults, or invitations to commit crimes. It also guaranteed the inviolability of correspondence and added "private" conversations to the realm of nonpublic actions that were outside the state's jurisdiction.[73] The code thus framed as nonpublic and noncriminal phenomena such as epistolary exchanges and conversations and protected public expression of any inner disposition that was not explicitly banned by law.

While this constitution was soon replaced with a new one—the code of 1823—that did not offer the same protections, subsequent regulations framed individual freedoms in similar terms. In March of 1825 the Senate's constitutional commission presented a detailed bill of rights that enshrined the right of "everyone" to "manifest their thoughts by speech or by writing, and to publish them through the press." It also stated that "no one will be persecuted for mere opinions" and protected the inviolability of citizens' houses and correspondence.[74] A proposed constitutional code put forward in late 1826 included provisions protecting homes, personal papers, and private correspondence as well as the freedoms "of thought, speech, writing, and the press."[75]

The constitution of 1828 can be seen as the culmination of this process of increased toleration for the feeling and expression of dissent in Chile.[76] The code effectively protected not only thoughts but also their public expression. It declared that authorities could not violate people's houses or their private correspondence and guaranteed the right of every individual to publish his or her opinions. An article that read "no one will be persecuted or disturbed because of their private opinions" was interpreted at the time not only as advancing religious toleration but also as banning all forms of political persecution.[77] By protecting "private opinions" as well as the manifestation of inner thoughts through speech and writing, the constitution protected dissension as both a nonpublic and public experience.

The 1828 constitution did not have a long life. Growing political confrontations led to civil war in late 1829 between liberals—then in control of the government—and a coalition of conservatives, supporters of O'Higgins, estanqueros, and other factions. The latter won the war and eventually imposed a new, authoritarian regime. After the war many among the winners began questioning the expectations set for constitutional codes and denounced constitutionalism as a failed experiment that had been unable to preserve the freedoms it proclaimed.[78] Some even highlighted the pernicious side effects associated with protecting individual freedoms and recommended their immediate suspension to impose social and political order.[79] In the meantime the government appointed a constitutional convention tasked with writing yet a new code for Chile. Approved in 1833, the charter partly reflected the demands for fewer and weaker protections and more state authority. It established the inviolability of both houses and epistolary correspondence but dropped the protections for people's thoughts and "private opinions" guaranteed in previous codes and regulations. It only granted citizens the freedom "to publish their opinions in the press."[80]

These legal protections, though limited, were not enforced during the following decades, as the government, facing conspiracies and other expressions of resistance and insubordination, repeatedly suspended the constitution under the argument that the state was in danger. As the official newspaper *El Araucano* recognized in September of 1833, this was because subversive plots could not be properly prosecuted in court due to lack of evidence. The newspaper cited the widely held "prejudice" that in such cases "forensic evidence" was needed to establish guilt. Regular trials, the newspaper implied, were unable to contain and punish the proliferation of dissension precisely because of the protections provided by the law over people's nonpublic opinions and ideas.[81] More explicit, as well as more cynical, was the government's leading figure, Diego Portales. In late 1834 Portales asked Mariano Egaña (one of the principal jurists involved in the elaboration of the constitution of 1833) whether the government could imprison a group of men whom he knew were conspiring against it. According to Portales, Egaña answered by invoking the distinction between intentions (an inner disposition) and actions. The law, Egaña claimed, did not authorize the government to arrest conspirators unless they were discovered in the act of carrying out their crime. "Fuck Egaña and his quotes and legal theories," Portales later wrote to a friend, adding that the government should violate the constitution when the situation so required.[82] Through the use of force that such views authorized, the new ruling factions managed to put an end to Chile's constitutional experiment (the code of 1833 was heavily reformed only in the 1870s). But the reach of constitutional freedoms and their enforcement continued to be the subject of much political controversy for decades to come.[83]

Chile's constitutional experiment reflects how subjects and citizens used notions of communication, publicness, and criminality to evaluate the dangers of dissension and promote increased toleration. Most of these charters and regulations delineated a nonpublic realm of sorts composed of phenomena that would not have an impact on society and would thus be immune to state authority. This sphere often included personal papers, private correspondence, and houses. Some codes went further, framing speech and writing as expressions of "opinions" and "thoughts," meaning these were neutral and even protected forms of communication unless their content explicitly violated the law. These developments constituted much more than a simple attempt at implementing transnational constitutional theories and liberal precepts; like the arguments advanced in court at the same time, they were responses to the challenges represented by antagonism and dissension. By transforming how the power of dissent was assessed, these codes implicitly recognized Chile's antagonistic fracture, delineating in response what seemed to their authors and supporters acceptable forms of political pluralism.

In colonial and postcolonial Chile, communication and politics were tightly intertwined. Thinking about political pluralism, then, implied reconsidering this relationship. This chapter has shown how widespread political contestation led actors to generate alternative ways of framing the power of communication. By combining the parameters of public/nonpublic and criminal/licit as well as approaching dissension using the concept of "opinion," they came to conceive of forms of dissent that were tolerable either because they had not communicated enough or because their communication was an innocuous manifestation of an inner disposition. These arguments were unsuccessful in stopping official political persecution, but they represented the emergence of a radical new idea: accepting antagonism and disunity as an inescapable political experience, one located at the crossroads of the public and the nonpublic. They reflected a profane view of politics, in which the transcendent source of social and political order was indeterminate and could not rule people's conscience, and an antagonistic vision of society as divided in different "opinions." Although these particular versions of pluralism do not necessarily conform to the normative definitions modeled after the experiences of other regions in the Atlantic world, they were among the most ambitious and radical efforts made by local actors to face the challenges posed by the Age of Dissent.

CONCLUSION

The Power of Communication in an Age of Dissent

In the years following the civil war of 1829–1830, Chile's conservatives and estanqueros imposed a repressive political regime. The new administration excluded rival factions from the state, purged the army of political dissenters, exiled leading opposition figures, restricted freedom of the press, and effectively banned partisan politics. It also quashed advocacy of religious toleration and reformation of the church, limited access to citizenship, tightly controlled elections, and took a more repressive approach to criminality and social insubordination (insisting, e.g., on the need for physical punishments and the death penalty).[1] As these measures demonstrate, the government and its supporters aimed not only to end the social and political unrest that had reigned in Chile since the fall of the O'Higgins regime in 1823 but to reverse the revolutionary process the country had experienced in recent decades. In broader terms they rejected the radical consequences of political pluralism and the profanation of political authority.

Yet there was no turning back. Factional struggles continued, conspirators regularly plotted to overthrow the new regime, and in 1837 the government's principal figure, Diego Portales, was assassinated by troops who refused to join the recently declared war against Peru (1836–1839). Though controlled by authoritarian governments until 1861, Chile's political landscape remained structured around dissent. It included a vibrant though at times subterranean partisan life, a growing number of civil associations, and an increasingly open sphere of social and political debate. The country's diverse political actors—whether African-descended artisans in Santiago, Mapuche people in Chiloé seeking autonomy or even independence from the republic, peasants who joined the civil wars between liberals and conservatives in 1851 and 1859, or women who participated in religious associations—all lived in a society in which politics explicitly meant division and open competition over the foundations of social and political order.[2] This dimension of disunity was not limited to the world of institutional politics and official doctrines but manifested itself in public life more generally, from the press to collective festivities.

This pluralistic and profaned public arena was the result of the revolutionary transformations Chile experienced between 1780 and 1833.

By engaging in dissenting activities, actors during this era rendered the foundations of the social order a matter of dispute and reimagined their ability to affect others. This opening of the world of politics was thus also a revolution in the coordinates that defined public life. *The Age of Dissent* has focused on two such parameters, visibility and propagation, and the fields of political action associated with them. The realm of visibility emerged from the interplay between urban space, activities performed therein (such as acts of urban publication and public ceremonies), material culture (including clothing, portraits, and flags), and political principles (publicness, hierarchy, unity, and reverence). Propagation comprised the alleged transmission of actions and behaviors between humans via imitation and contagion, the patterned interactions that arose from these exchanges (the mimetic public sphere, contagious politics), the conceptual vocabulary through which actors made this influence and its effects intelligible (using terms such as "scandal"), and the practices and procedures through which they sought to wield and contain its power (e.g., promoting heroic models of conduct, dispatching "secret" and public political agents, initiating criminal investigations, and implementing prophylactic measures).

In late colonial Chile these fields were supposed to be limited and regulated by two fundamental principles: transcendence and unity. In the field of visibility, this expectation was reflected in the association between visible publicness and order and discipline, in the visible expression of hierarchical differences and political harmony, and in public manifestations of obedience, love, and reverence toward the sovereign. When applied to the field of propagation, these principles resulted in the prohibition and containment of undesired forms of mimesis and contagion, the framing of such unwanted actions as transgressions against an indisputable social and political order, and the attribution of dissent to the propagating activities of deviant or external actors. This is not to say that men and women in colonial Chile engaged with these two fields exclusively to uphold unity and transcendence but that these two principles defined the boundaries and goals of legitimate communicative action.

Between 1780 and 1833 Chileans rendered dissent an essential feature of these two fields, making room in them for the experience and expression of radical political plurality. Instead of reflecting a transcendentally dictated social order, visible publicness became an instrument for producing and questioning social difference. Similarly, starting with the imperial crisis of 1808, agents as diverse as government authorities, soldiers, elite women, and modest merchants began using flags, rosettes, and other objects to visibly display their partisan affiliations and their rejection of rival groups. Through their actions, these individuals effectively turned visibility into a means for the expression of division and disunity. Many other men and women also decided to use visibility to profane the sacred sources of political power through iconoclastic actions. By extending the range and scope of visibility as a field of political action, these individuals challenged the nonpluralistic nature of colonial and postcolonial official politics, shaking the very foundations of the political order.

The field of propagation was likewise transformed. People in Chile embraced imitation and contagion to advance explicitly partisan and dissenting political agendas, thus profaning the limits imposed on this field by the principles of unity and transcendence. They also increasingly relied on contagion and associated notions to both explain and contain the proliferation of radical dissent both in Chile and the wider Atlantic world. With the acceleration of political clashes during and after the crisis of the Spanish monarchy, institutions and practices previously aimed at preventing the propagation of undesired behaviors—such as prisons for unruly women—became instruments with which to fight rival political groups as well as means by which to construct new social orders.

Finally, the flood of dissension and political persecution let loose after 1808 led people accused of sedition, as well as legislators, constitutional thinkers, journalists, and politicians more generally, to question the very association between communication and power that underpinned the fields of visibility and propagation. In legal arguments and constitutional projects, political players revisited the notion of publicness and advanced a new understanding of communication (as the neutral expression of inner opinions). By discarding visibility and propagation as parameters to assess the public relevance of dissent, these actors invented their own vision of political pluralism, one in which difference and division were inescapable facts of life and antagonism and dissidence had to be tolerated.

These mutations were not merely a byproduct of the opening of the world of politics—they were a constitutive part of it. By contesting, expanding, and negotiating the power of communication, men and women in Chile participated in the profanation of social and political order and the emergence of division as an inevitable dimension of public life. This was far from an abstract process. As shown throughout this book, visibility and propagation played a crucial role in people's everyday lives, shaping institutions and social relations. For men and women in Chile, opening these fields to dissent involved changing their relationship to the urban space, adopting new objects and finding original uses for familiar ones, developing novel forms of agency, challenging accepted emotional norms and regimes of historicity, and even reconsidering the political status of their inner selves. *The Age of Dissent* has also shown the continuities underlying these mutations. The most apparent one is that visibility and propagation, though called into question, remained essential both for how actors framed publicness and human agency and how they made intelligible their reality. Much of the conceptual vocabulary and political repertoire of the revolutionary age—from notions such as scandal to the isolation of dissenting women—had its origins in colonial understandings of visibility and propagation.

Throughout this book, I have characterized visibility and propagation as forms of communication, even though the interactions these notions described and their underlying mechanics differed greatly from what scholars today usually understand by that term. My goal has been to show that visibility and propagation, while different from our modern idea of communication, had a proximate relation to it: they offered alternative descriptions to the same actions and events. As shown in chapter 8, the idea that some human interactions could be best portrayed as the publication of inner opinions (exemplifying a shift closer to our modern understanding of communication) emerged precisely in competition with notions of visibility and propagation. This approach has also allowed me to highlight the often-problematic assumptions and implications embedded in how sources from this period discuss communication. When colonial officials described the contagious potential of radical ideas, they were not just using a metaphor for revolutionary information networks: they were pointing at a very specific field of action to which they attributed power in order to advance and preserve a non-pluralistic understanding of politics. They were additionally referencing multiple other forms of contagion—such as the contagion of insubordination or of bad behavior—which seem more difficult to associate with the exchange of messages or ideas.

The transformation of politics studied in this book was not the product of a coherent political program, nor did it respond to the wishes of a single political group. It was an adjustment to the multiple ways in which men and women made dissent a fundamental feature of public life. This means that dissenting actions, regardless of their purpose and origins, contributed to bring forth a new experience of politics. It is important to bear in mind, though, that the framework I have advanced in this book considers only a part of the meaning dissenting actions had for those who carried them out. The notion of dissent lumps together otherwise fundamentally distinct political experiences (e.g., the trajectories and aspirations of enslaved people and those of elite political factions). In exchange for this limitation, adopting this broad definition of dissension has allowed me to identify and examine together arenas of antagonism and division that are usually studied separately, such as iconoclasm, detention houses for women, the prosecution of sedition, and the production of heroes. Additionally, by focusing on the unexpected results of discord and disagreement, *The Age of Dissent* has shown that politics is not just a realm where groups clash over well-defined and almost self-evident goals and interests but also one that actors struggle to understand and render intelligible.

Although it did not culminate in the establishment of a democratic regime, the revolution studied in this book constituted a crucial episode in the history of democracy in Chile. This is because modern democracies are not just a form of government but also a form of life. They demand the embrace of both indetermination and division as inherent aspects of the social order.[3] As *The Age of Dissent* has shown, in late colonial Chile this required recomposing the world in between people. To both produce and adapt to radical dissension, men and women of all walks of life in Chile also transformed how they conceived of the power of communication, how they framed the ways in which they were capable of affecting one another. By doing so, they introduced dissent—and with it plurality and division—into the very core of their shared worlds.

Abbreviations

ABO	Archivo de Don Bernardo O'Higgins.
AGI	Archivo General de Indias (Spain).
AGN	Archivo General de la Nación (Argentina).
ANFA	Archivo Nacional Histórico (Chile). Fondo Antiguo.
ANFCG	Archivo Nacional Histórico (Chile). Fondo Capitanía General.
ANFIC	Archivo Nacional Histórico (Chile). Fondo Intendencia de Concepción.
ANFICO	Archivo Nacional Histórico (Chile). Fondo Intendencia de Coquimbo.
ANFIS	Archivo Nacional Histórico (Chile). Fondo Intendencia de Santiago.
ANFJCA	Archivo Nacional Histórico (Chile). Fondo Judicial de Cauquenes.
ANFJCO	Archivo Nacional Histórico (Chile). Fondo Judicial de Copiapó.
ANFJE	Archivo Nacional Histórico (Chile). Fondo Jaime Eyzaguirre.
ANFJLA	Archivo Nacional Histórico (Chile). Fondo Judicial de Los Andes
ANFJLS	Archivo Nacional Histórico (Chile). Fondo Judicial de La Serena.
ANFJSC	Archivo Nacional Histórico (Chile). Fondo Judicial de Santiago, Criminales.
ANFMG	Archivo Nacional Histórico (Chile). Fondo Ministerio de Guerra.
ANFMI	Archivo Nacional Histórico (Chile). Fondo Ministerio del Interior.
ANFMS	Archivo Nacional Histórico (Chile). Fondo Municipalidad de Santiago.

ANFMV	Archivo Nacional Histórico (Chile). Fondo Morla Vicuña.
ANFRA	Archivo Nacional Histórico (Chile). Fondo Real Audiencia.
ANFRB	Archivo Nacional Histórico (Chile). Fondo Reynals Bruguera.
ANFSFL	Archivo Nacional Histórico (Chile). Fondo Sergio Fernández Larraín.
ANFSM	Archivo Nacional Histórico (Chile). Fondo Santa María.
ANFST	Archivo Nacional Histórico (Chile). Fondo Salvador Trucíos.
ANFV	Archivo Nacional Histórico (Chile). Fondo Varios.
ANFVM	Archivo Nacional Histórico (Chile). Fondo Vicuña Mackenna.
BNMM	Biblioteca Nacional (Chile). Sala Medina, Manuscritos Medina.
BNMSBA	Biblioteca Nacional (Chile). Sala Medina, Manuscritos Barros Arana.
BNSM	Biblioteca Nacional (Chile). Sala Medina.
CHDICH	Colección de Historiadores y de Documentos relativos a la Independencia de Chile.
SCL	Sesiones de los Cuerpos Lejislativos de la República de Chile, 1811 a 1845

NOTES

Introduction

1. "Noticia de las mujeres que han estado en captura en la casa de ejercicios," 1813, in CHDICH, 23:191–95.
2. Barros Arana, *Historia Jeneral de Chile*, 9:296–98.
3. Carrera, "Diario del Brigadier," which is also the only source for this event.
4. Arendt, *The Promise of Politics*, 153.
5. Discussions over the revolutionary dimension of this era in Spain and Spanish America extend as far back as the nineteenth century. Some of the critical arguments against considering the crisis of the Spanish empire as a revolutionary process are addressed in Paquette, "Dissolution of Spanish Monarchy," 205–6; and Guerra, *Modernidad e independencias*, 12–13.
6. See Guerra, *Modernidad e independencias*; Rodríguez O., *Independence of Spanish America*; Guardino, *Time of Liberty*; Rodríguez O., *"True Spaniards"*; Ricketts, *Who Should Rule?*; Thibaud, *Libérer le nouveau monde*; Sábato, *Republics of New World*; Fernández Sebastián, *Historia conceptual*.
7. Chambers, *Subjects to Citizens*; Walker, *Smoldering Ashes*; Van Young, *Other Rebellion*; Thomson, *We Alone Will Rule*; Helg, *Liberty and Equality*; Méndez, *Plebeian Republic*; Warren, *Vagrants and Citizens*; Lasso, *Myths of Harmony*; Ferrer, *Freedom's Mirror*; Echeverri, *Indian and Slave*; Soriano, *Tides of Revolution*; Penry, *People Are King*. For a similar argument covering the entire Atlantic world during this era, see McDonnell, "Rethinking Revolution."
8. Guerra, *Modernidad e independencias*, 12–13. Historian Jaime E. Rodríguez O. even proposes to consider revolutionary movements in the sixteenth and seventeenth centuries as earlier "Atlantic revolutions." See Rodríguez O., "Atlantic Revolutions."
9. For examples of discontent, negotiation of power, and radical political innovation in the decades and centuries that preceded the Independence era in Spanish America, see Phelan, *People and the King*; Thomson, *We Alone Will Rule*; Serulnikov, *Subverting Authority*; Serulnikov, *Revolution in the Andes*; Landers, "*Cimarrón* and Citizen"; Patch, *Maya Revolt*; Echeverri, *Indian and Slave* ; López, *History of Paraguay*; Cromwell, *Smugglers' World*; Masters, "Invisible Architects"; Minchom, *People of Quito*; Hamnett, *End of Iberian Rule*, esp. 72–104; Penry, *People Are King*; Austin, *Colonial Kinship*, esp. 129–154; Ponce Vázquez, *Islanders and Empire*.
10. My vision of what constitutes a political organization structured around a transcendent source of authority relies heavily on Claude Lefort's. See Lefort, *Essais sur le politique*. Lefort's argument is further analyzed in Marchart, *Political Thought*, 84–108; Plot, *Claude Lefort*; Poirier, *Introduction à Claude Lefort*, esp. 83–107; and Esposito, *Instituting Thought*, 145–209.
11. Echeverri, *Indian and Slave*; Hamnett, *End of Iberian Rule*, 15–52; Cromwell,

Smugglers' World; Tutino, *Mexico City*, esp. 110–17; Masters, "Invisible Architects"; Blanchard, *Fearful Vassals*.

12. Palti, *Archaeology of the Political*, esp. 19–27 and 96–99.
13. Phelan, *People and the King*; Patch, *Maya Revolt*; Chiaramonte, *Nación y Estado*; Twinam, *Purchasing Whiteness*; Dedieu, *Après le roi*; Hamnett, *End of Iberian Rule*, esp. 18–23; Fernández Sebastián, *Historia conceptual*, 378–88.
14. I take the notion of "disclosure of politics" from Lara, *Disclosure of Politics*, esp. 14–17.
15. This interpretation dates back at least to Carl Schmitt (an antisemitic jurist who participated in the Nazi regime) and has been revisited by authors such as Hannah Arendt, Cornelius Castoriadis, Claude Lefort, and Marcel Gauchet. See Schmitt, *Political Theology*; Arendt, *On Revolution*; Castoriadis, *Institution imaginaire*; Lefort, *Essais sur le politique*; Gauchet, *Le désenchantement du monde*; and Gauchet, *Avènement de la démocratie*. The most sophisticated exposition of this argument—which sees the emergence of a profaned realm of the political as the result of internal contradictions within the baroque vision of politics—is Palti, *Archaeology of the Political*. For instances of these views being applied to the Spanish American revolutions, see Palti, *¿Ideas fuera de lugar?*, 29–31, 52–54; Thibaud, *Libérer le nouveau monde*; Sábato, *Republics*; Cid, *Pensar la revolución*, 19; and Fernández Sebastián, *Historia conceptual*, 169–70. An earlier, similar formulation is in Jocelyn-Holt, *La Independencia de Chile*, 223–33. Political scientist Jason Frank has examined the political and aesthetic challenges associated to immanent rule in the Atlantic world in Frank, *Constituent Moments*; and Frank, *Democratic Sublime*.
16. The quote is from Costeloe's 1993 monograph about postcolonial Mexico. By it, Costeloe meant that, after independence, Mexicans could "for the first time . . . reorder the political, social, economic and cultural structure imposed on them by the all-embracing union of Crown and Church." I find the expression very evocative, though I disagree with Costeloe's interpretation. See Costeloe, *Central Republic in Mexico*, 13.
17. My vision of dissension is inspired by the works of Esposito, *Categorías de lo impolítico*; Esposito, *Diez pensamientos acerca de la política*; Loraux, *Divided City*; Mouffe, *On the Political*; Mouffe, *Agonistics*; Laclau and Mouffe, *Hegemony*; Marchart, *Thinking Antagonism*.
18. Loraux, *La tragédie d'Athènes*, 23–24.
19. Latour, "Monde commun."
20. To give but a few examples, see Rosas Lauro, *Del trono a la guillotina*; Darnton, *Poetry and Police*; Warner, *Protocols*; Polasky, *Revolutions*; Adelman, *Revolutionary Networks*.
21. See, for example, Johnson, *Fear*; Ferrer, *Freedom's Mirror*; Dubcovsky, *Informed Power*; Eller, *We Dream Together*; Scott, *Common Wind*; Soriano, *Tides of Revolution*; Carayon, *Eloquence Embodied*. For studies exploring the performative use of media and communication, see Villa-Flores, *Dangerous Speech*; and Ogborn, *Freedom of Speech*.
22. Peters, *Speaking into the Air*. The same goes for the concept of media. See Peters, *Marvelous Clouds*.
23. Cf. Craig, "How We Talk."
24. Guerra and Lempérière, "Introducción," 7.

25. Most scholars interested in the notion of "public" or "publicness" in Spanish America have devoted their attention to examining or questioning the emergence of what philosopher Jürgen Habermas called the "modern public sphere." See Habermas, *Structural Transformation*. For an overview of the literature on the public sphere in Latin America, see Piccato, "Public Sphere." Guerra, *Modernidad e independencias*; Guerra et al., *Espacios públicos*; and Uribe-Uran, "Public Sphere" are perhaps the most influential publications on the habermasian public sphere in Spanish America during the age of revolutions. Recent critical reassessments are in Torres Puga, *Opinión pública*; and Soriano, *Tides of Revolution*. For studies tracing the history of the habermasian public sphere in Chile, see González Bernaldo de Quirós, "Literatura injuriosa"; Desramé, "La comunidad"; Stuven, *La seducción*; Wood, *The Society of Equality*; Stuven and Cid, *Debates republicanos en Chile*, 2:343–71; Piwonka, "Opinión pública"; and Cid, *Pensar la revolución*, esp. 304–17. For civic life, see Forment, *Democracy in Latin America*; Lempérière, *Entre Dieu et le Roi*; González Bernaldo de Quirós, *Civilidad y política*; Serrano, "La definición"; Serrano, *¿Qué hacer con Dios?*; and Sábato, *Republics of the New World*, esp. 132–68. Works examining how actors understood and used the category of "public" include Twinam, *Private Lives*; Twinam, *Purchasing Whiteness*; Chambers, "Private Crimes"; Mannarelli, *Private Passions*; Uribe-Uran, "Great Transformation"; Uribe-Uran, *Fatal Love*; Sellers-García, *Woman on the Windowsill*, esp. 219–22. I discuss the vast literature about Chile that falls under this category in chapter 1.
26. I cover these examples, with the exception of theater and the regular orders, in chapters 5 and 7. For the parallels between theater and regular orders, see, for instance, *El Observador Eclesiástico*, 21 June 1823.
27. Paquette, *Enlightenment*, 8.
28. The trial of Antonio Vergne and Antonio Gramusset can be found in ANFRA, vol. 1644, p. 2, ff. 156–389v. My view of this conspiracy differs from the recent scholarship, which has emphasized the conspirators' allegedly utopian ideas and their European intellectual sources. See, for example, Guerra Acuña, *Pensar*, 37–73; and Cáceres, "Republicanismo bíblico independentista." For the aspirations of eighteenth-century subaltern actors see Araya, "Sirvientes contra amos"; Araya, "El castigo físico"; Araya, "La fundación"; Araya, "Azotar"; De Ramón, "Demandas por igualdad"; Undurraga, *Los rostros del honor*; and González, *Esclavos y esclavas*.
29. See, for example, Torres to the Junta Central de Aranjuez, 29 January 1809, in CHDICH, 8:3–33; testimony of González, 23 May 1810, testimony of Solar, 24 May 24, 1810, confrontation between Solar and Vera, 10 September 1810, in CHDICH, 30:10–11, 14–15, and 262–64; Salas, "Carta de Santiago Leal a Patricio Español," 10 July 1810, in CHDICH, 8:213–55 (attributed to Salas); *Motivos que ocasionaron*, 8; and Talavera, "Revoluciones de Chile," in CHDICH, 29:20.
30. Guevara, *Los Araucanos*, 97. For the reasons why Mapuche leaders joined the war and fought each other during the revolutionary period, see Pairican Padilla, *Toqui*, esp. 41–92.

Chapter One

1. Real Academia Española, *Diccionario*, 1726–1739, 5:420–21.
2. See Real Academia Española, *Diccionario*, 1780, 772, as well as the subsequent editions of this work published in 1783, 1791, 1803, and 1817.

3. See Uribe-Uran, "Great Transformation," 77–79.
4. See Poole, *Vision*; Andermann, *Optics*; Segre, *Intersected Identities*; and Coronado, *Andes Imagined*.
5. Guarda, *Ciudad chilena*, 10–12.
6. Ibid., 20–40; Guarda, *Historia urbana*, 70–79; Lorenzo and Urbina, *Política de poblaciones*, esp. 25–32; Lorenzo, *Ciudades chilenas*, esp. 17–33. On the continental scale of the Bourbon urbanization project, see Luque Azcona, *Ciudad y poder*, 44–45.
7. Guarda, *Ciudad chilena*, 71 and 82–84.
8. Herzog, *Defining Nations*; Martínez, *Genealogical Fictions*; and Hespanha, *Como os juristas viam*, 652–59.
9. Testimony of Carrera in the investigation of Garfias, 1809, AGI, Chile, 206.
10. See, for example, Bernales to Bernales, 22 August 1795, cited in "La sociedad colonial," 181.
11. Salinas, "Fama pública"; Cornejo, *Manuela Orellana*, 85–115; Undurraga, "El honor." For a similar analysis focused on late-colonial Guatemala City, see Sellers-García, *Woman on the Windowsill*, 168–69.
12. Quoted in Salinas and Corvalán, "Transgresores sumisos," 13.
13. Vicuña Mackenna, *Historia crítica*, 2:512–14.
14. As William F. Hanks remarked of early colonial Guatemala in *Converting Words*, 37. I further analyze (and complicate) this distinction in chapter 8.
15. Vicuña Mackenna, *Historia crítica*, 2:516–18.
16. See the edict of Governor Amat, 18 February 1760, reissued by Governor Jáuregui in 17 May 1775, in ANFV, vol. 111, ff. 80–81; the petition of the merchants of Santiago's central square to the government, 1764, ANFV, vol. 321, ff. 36–37; Alava to Caballero, 25 July 1799, AGI, Chile, 221; Piwonka, "Juan José Echeverría," 150–51.
17. See, for example, Higgins to González, 12 June 1789, ANFCG, vol. 780, ff. 356v–57v; and the report of Pérez de Uriondo, 21 June 1805, in CHDICH, 43:72–84. For the relationship between urban space and the rule of law more generally, see Kagan, "World Without Walls"; Hanks, *Converting Words*, 25–84; and Nemser, *Infrastructures of Race*, 25–64.
18. Morse, "Cities as People"; Lorenzo, *Ciudades chilenas*, 179–86.
19. As Lauren Benton has shown, in the Spanish territorial imagination, areas of difficult access such as mountains and hills had long represented the suspension of sovereign power. See Benton, *Search for Sovereignty*, 222–78. For the opposition between el monte and urban spaces in colonial Mexico, see Lipsett-Rivera, *Gender and Negotiation*, 41–48, 58–60.
20. See, for example, the files concerning the Indigenous town of Choapa, 1772–1777, ANFRA, vol. 1794, pp. 2 and 4; and Chillán's city council to the Ministry of Interior, 17 August 1827, ANFMI, vol. 16, ff. 224–24v.
21. Araya, *Ociosos*, 26, 101–2.
22. Carmagnani, *Los mecanismos*.
23. For general overviews, see Bauer, *Chilean Rural Society*, 3–26; Bengoa, *Historia social*, 1:11–36, 103–15, and 141–62; and Salazar, *Labradores*. The patterns of migration of women during this period have received scant attention by scholars.
24. Araya, *Ociosos*.
25. Ibid.; León, *Plebeyos y patricios*.
26. De Ramón, *Santiago de Chile*, 106–12.
27. Undurraga, "'Valentones'"; Undurraga, *Los rostros del honor*, 66.

28. Guarda, *Edad Media de Chile*, 469. This number includes the towns in the jurisdictions of Chiloé (137) and Cuyo (19). The island of Chiloé and the province of Cuyo were part of Chile until 1768 and 1776, respectively.
29. León, "Monarquistas hasta el ocaso," 283.
30. In using "Mapuche" as a national category, I follow the work of Marimán Quemenado, "La República," 66–67. For the Diaguitas, see Molina, "Pueblos de Indios."
31. León, "Monarquistas hasta el ocaso"; Goicovic and Armijo, "Tierras en disputa."
32. Lorenzo, *De lo rural a lo urbano*, 145–53.
33. Reproduced in Amunátegui, *Mayorazgos i títulos*, 3:327. See also the report of Pérez de Uriondo, 27 June 1805, in CHDICH, 43:72–84 as well as Pérez de Uriondo's earlier criticisms reproduced in Amunátegui, *Mayorazgos i títulos*, 3:324–26.
34. Goicovic and Armijo, "Tierras en disputa."
35. Boccara, *Los vencedores*; Zavala Cepeda, *Los mapuches*; Mariman et al., *¡Allkütunge, wingka!*; Villalobos, *Los pehuenches*; Villalobos, *Vida fronteriza*.
36. For detailed but ethnocentric accounts of this policy, see Guarda, *Ciudad chilena*, 59–61; Guarda, *Historia urbana*, 90–96; Lorenzo, *De lo rural a lo urbano*, 187–204. For studies focused on Indigenous agency, see Zavala Cepeda, *Los mapuches*, 112–40; León, "El malón de Curiñamcu." For a brief but illuminating discussion of this uprising and its connection to the Spanish colonizing and disciplining techniques, see Boccara, *Los vencedores*, 271–72. It is worth noting that Governor Guill y Gonzaga also extended the urbanization plan further south to the Mapuche-controlled area between Valdivia and Chiloé. See Guill y Gonzaga to the Supreme Council, 17 February 1766, ANFCG, vol. 792, ff. 44–46.
37. The numbers are provided in Guarda, *Ciudad chilena*, 60.
38. Estimations vary widely. I have relied mainly on Jocelyn-Holt, *La Independencia de Chile*, 65; Colivoro and Álamos, *Población indígena*, 96–118; and Serrano, Ponce de León, and Rengifo, *Historia de la educación*, 1:93–138.
39. Jocelyn-Holt, *La Independencia de Chile*, 65; Silva Vargas, "Una aproximación," 33 and 39; Guarda, *Historia urbana*, 211.
40. *Mercurio de Chile*, no. 2, 1822. It should be noted that the city had been experiencing significant growth since 1779. See Salinas, "Caracteres generales"; and Guarda, *Historia urbana*, 210.
41. This point is made forcefully by Cavieres, *La Serena*.
42. Goicovic, *Relaciones de solidaridad*, 133–53; and Cavieres, *Sobre la independencia*, 192–93.
43. See Elliott, *Empires of the Atlantic*, 38; Kagan, *Urban Images*, 1–44; Kagan, "World Without Walls"; Kinsbruner, *Spanish-American City*, esp. 49–53; Lipsett-Rivera, *Gender and Negotiation*, 31–67; and Osorio, "National Boundaries," 112–14.
44. After Chile's independence, the governor's palace hosted the new national authorities, and a national High Court replaced the Audiencia. For these buildings, see De Ramón, *Santiago de Chile*, 45–50; Guarda, *Historia urbana*, 111 and 257.
45. Ibid., 112.
46. Ibid., 120–51; Pereira Salas, *Historia del arte*, 153–277; Cruz, *Patrimonio artístico*, 170–222.

47. Pereira Salas, *Historia del arte*, 180–211; Guarda, *El arquitecto*, 184–207.
48. These included schools, convents, and churches. See Avilés to the abbess of the monastery of Nuestra Señora de la Victoria, 22 July 1797, ANFCG, vol. 787, f. 34; Frontaura, *Noticias históricas*, 88, 126, and 135.
49. Guarda, *Historia urbana*, 150.
50. Carvallo y Goyeneche, "Descripción histórico-geográfica del Reino de Chile," 10:40.
51. Due to a financial disagreement between the artist and the mint's administration, the coat of arms was never installed in the building. I discuss the ultimate fate of this object in chapter 4.
52. Descriptions of these coats of arms can be found in Haenke, *Reyno de Chile*, 95; *Semanario Republicano*, 18 November 1813; Pérez Rosales, *Recuerdos del pasado*, 10.
53. Pereira Salas, *Historia del arte*, 309–13.
54. Barros Arana, *Historia Jeneral de Chile*, 6:162 and 165; Guarda, *Ciudad chilena*, 68–69; Guarda, *Historia urbana*, 125–29; De Ramón, *Santiago de Chile*, 100–2; Cruz, *Patrimonio artístico*, 195–98.
55. Claro wrote this comment on a letter Antonio Gundian sent to him, 13 February 1831, ANFVM, 112, ff. 39–39v.
56. Rodríguez Zorrilla to the bishop of Lima, 20 January 1813, AGI, Chile 312. For more on this episode, see chapter 3.
57. List of questions prepared by the legal defense of Ambrosio Rodríguez, 1813, CHDICH, 21:351.
58. See, for example, Chijachov, "Viaje a través de las pampas bonaerenses," in Norambuena and Uliánova, *Viajeros rusos*, 283–84.
59. See also "La cañada, promenade publique de Santiago" in De la Touanne, *Album pittoresque*; and "Paseo de la cañada" in Gay, *Atlas de la historia*, 1:plate 14.
60. Johnston, *Letters Written*, 184–87.
61. De Ramón, *Santiago de Chile*, 88–89.
62. Montt to León, July 1826, in Montt, *Recuerdos de familia*, 586–89.
63. See, for example, the testimonies of Zúñiga, Carrera, and Silva Bórquez in the investigation of Garfias, 1809, AGI, Chile 206; and Muñoz's report dated 4 March 1813, CHDICH, 21:357–59. For similar observations concerning other streets in Santiago and Coquimbo, see Pérez de Saravia to Álvarez de Acevedo, 4 January 1781, ANFRA, vol. 1644, p. 2, ff. 163–64; testimony of Gutiérrez, 6 June 1815, ANFSM, A8495; and testimony of Molina, 25 May 1818, in ANFCG, vol. 334, ff. 23–23v.
64. Real Academia Española, *Diccionario*, 1803, 694.
65. Fogel, *Cérémonies de l'information*.
66. For town criers and places of publication, see the edicts published in Santiago between 1762 and 1768 and 1773 and 1780, and in Copiapó between 1747 and 1773, in ANFV, vols. 111, 321, and 342 respectively.
67. See, for example, the trials of Contreras and Ovalle in 1816, in ANFSFL, vol. 33, p. 52, and ANFSFL, vol. 34, p. 12, respectively.
68. Arancibia, Cornejo, and González, "Estudio preliminar," 24–28. See also Uribe-Uran, "Great Transformation," 77–78.
69. Arancibia, Cornejo, and González, "Estudio preliminar," 30; *La Clave*, 4 November 1828.
70. Most of the evidence for this practice I have found comes from the early

nineteenth century. See, for a few examples, Talavera, "Revoluciones de Chile," in CHDICH, 29:263 and 268; Chopitea to Reynals, 5 November 1814, ANFRB, caja 2; the trial of Cuadra and Ojeda, 1818, ANFJLA, leg. 13, p. 25; *El Censor de la Revolución*, 10 May 1820; *Gazeta Ministerial de Chile*, 19 August 1820 and 23 May 1822; and the communications of Santiago's intendant in ANFIS, vol. 1, and vol. 3.

71. See the legal defense of Rodríguez, 1819, ANFCG, vol. 335, p. 5, f. 251v; and the testimony of Mercado, 2 May 1824, ANFCG, vol. 337, ff. 124–24v.
72. Esponda to the government, November 1814, ANFMG, vol. 6.
73. This ceremony and other details of Esponda's case are further explored in chapter 3.
74. Legal defense of Jiménez Guerra, 1811, ANFSFL, vol. 30, p. 4, f. 15.
75. Vicuña Mackenna, *Historia crítica*, 1:29; Zañartu, *Santiago*, 23–26; Zapiola, *Recuerdos de treinta años*, 82; Pereira Salas, *Historia del teatro*, 64.
76. For examples of such episodes in towns like Valdivia, Petorca, Los Andes, and Linares, see Higgins to the governor of Valdivia, 10 January 1793, ANFCG, vol. 783, ff. 403v–4; petition of Silva, 1817, ANFCG, vol. 334, ff. 123–25; López to the Minister of State, 14 January 1824, and Meneses to the Minister of State, 14 January 1824, ANFMI, vol. 5, ff. 198–99v, and 200–1; trial of Quiroga, 1825, ANFIC, vol. 68, p. 11.
77. Examples of these practices can be found in the trial of Pérez de Saravia, 1786, ANFRA, vol. 2251, p. 1; Higgins to Jara, 2 November 1788, ANFCG, vol. 778, ff. 97–97v; Committee of Surveillance and Public Safety to Marcó del Pont, 13 July 1816, AGI, Chile, 207; edict of Fontecilla, 3 December 1817, in *Semanario de Policía*, 10 December 1817; trial of Marcoleta, 1817–1818, ANFCG, vol. 334, ff. 120–235v; Valenzuela, *Fiesta*, 224; Zapiola, *Recuerdos de treinta años*, 65; edict of O'Higgins, 17 June 1818, in *Gazeta Ministerial de Chile*, 20 June 1818; *El Pipiolo*, 26 June 1827; and Johann Moritz Rugendas's 1843 painting, "View of Santiago," reproduced in Diener, *Rugendas*.
78. I take this notion from Jouhaud and Viala, "Introduction," 7.
79. Comments written by Claro in a letter by Lorca, 1831, ANFVM, vol. 112, ff. 83–84v.
80. Olaguer Feliú, *Relación de lo ocurrido*, 28. More examples in Pinto y Cobos to Infante, 3 January 1791, ANFJCO, caja 69, leg. 77, p. 12, ff. 2–3; testimony of Mandiola, 22 December 1802, ANFRA, vol. 2625, p. 5, f. 113v; Mackenna to the junta, 14 March 1811, ANFMI, vol. 8, ff. 71–72; *El Monitor Araucano*, 2 and 4 September 1813; testimony of Cofré, 20 August 1825, ANFIC, vol. 68, p. 11, ff. 354v–55.
81. Hurtado to the king, 20 August 1789, AGI, Chile, 221.
82. I follow here the (likely conservative) estimation provided by Feliú Cruz, *Abolición de la esclavitud*, 33.
83. For the 1778 population estimates, see Colivoro and Álamos, *Población indígena*, 96–118, which also highlights the difficulties of estimating racial demographics based on the period's documentation. For more on racial classifications in this census, see Araya, "Registrar a la plebe."
84. For example, Haenke, *Reyno de Chile*, 94–95 and 202–3.
85. The Mapuche ambassadors are further explored in chapter 3. For examples of the other groups mentioned, see the trial of several enslaved men in Santiago in 1764–1765, ANFCG, vol. 297, ff. 1–58; trial of Vergne and Gramusset, Santiago, 1781, ANFRA, vol. 1644, p. 2, ff. 156–389v; the suit of Coré against

Arenas, 1787, ANFCG, vol. 530, p. 7, ff. 53–64; *vista* (legal pronouncement) of Rodríguez Aldea, 21 February 1816, in CHDICH, 35:325; Seibel, *Historia del teatro argentino*; Colivoro and Álamos, *Población indígena*; Catepillan Tessi, "Pu peñi"; Urbina, *Población indígena*, 256–58.

86. Salazar, *Labradores*, esp. 49–98; De Ramón, *Santiago de Chile*, 93–100.
87. Ibid., 107–8.
88. Muñoz de Guzmán to the President's legal assistant, 31 May 1802, ANFCG, vol. 789, ff. 15v–16. See Araya, "Sirvientes contra amos," 165, for a similar example.
89. On the production of space and ordinary practices, see Lefebvre, *Production de l'espace*, esp. 165–72; and De Certeau, *L'invention du quotidien*, 139–64.
90. See, for example, *Bando de buen gobierno*; edict of Osorio, 10 April 1815, in Medina, *Bibliografía de la imprenta*, 98–99; *Semanario de Policía*, 10 September 1817; *Gazeta Ministerial de Chile*, 30 September 1820; and Uriondo, *El Ciudadano*. See also Zapiola, *Recuerdos de treinta años*, 62–67; Lastarria, "Situación moral de Santiago en 1858"; Rojas Mix, *La Plaza Mayor*, 17–45; Mellafe, "Alma y utopía"; Salazar, *Labradores*, 276–90; De Ramón, *Santiago de Chile*, 52–58, 93–104, 106–12; and Zamorano Varea, "'Ganarse la vida,'" 67–69.
91. For similar arguments concerning the appropriation of urban space by ordinary actors in Spanish American cities, see Jiménez, *Urban Public*; Trumper, *Ephemeral Histories*. On the self-constitution of publics, see Warner, *Publics and Counterpublics*; Yachnin and Eberhart, *Forms of Association*.
92. See, for example, the trial of De la Vega and others for theft, 1801, ANFRA, vol. 1444, p. 3, ff. 84–123.
93. See the criminal trial of Antonio, Santiago, 1767–1768, in Arancibia, Cornejo, and González, *Pena de muerte en Chile colonial*, 131–212; the references to servants and convent communications in the letters of Dolores Peña y Lillo in Kordic, *Epistolario*; the trial of several men for conspiracy, 1813, CHDICH, vols. 22 and 23; and the trial of José Manuel Bazán and others for conspiracy, 1840, ANFJSC, leg. 1588, p. 1. See also Iglesias, "Las recaderas."
94. *Motivos que ocasionaron*, 8.
95. I deduce this from Cienfuegos to Riesco, 24 December 1809, ANFSFL, vol. 156, p. 40. Salas also decried this woman's influence over the governor in a document he wrote earlier but does not mention her supposed role as leader of a communications network. He also reproduces rumors that Magdalena was García Carrasco's lover. See Salas, "Carta de Santiago Leal a Patricio Español," 10 July 1810, in CHDICH, 8:213–55, esp. 223–24. An anonymous chronicle written in the first half of the nineteenth century similarly alluded to her power over the governor. See "Memorias sobre los principals sucesos de la revolución de Chile desde 1810 hasta 1814," in CHDICH, 2:11. Later historians such as Miguel Luis Amunátegui and Diego Barros Arana made disparaging comments about this woman's political role and alleged love affair with García Carrasco. See Amunátegui, *Crónica de 1810*, 1:168 and 382; and Barros Arana, *Historia Jeneral de Chile*, 8:26. For recent (and contrasting) approximations to the role played by Santiago's non-elite population during the years between 1808 and 1810, see León, *Ni realistas ni patriotas*, esp. 40–65; and Cid, *Pensar la revolución*, 45–47.
96. Talavera, "Revoluciones de Chile," in CHDICH, 29:531. Martínez, writing a few years later and relying heavily on Talavera's notes, claims that twenty alleged leaders were imprisoned by the government. Martínez, "Memoria

Histórica," in CHDICH, 41(1):323–24. Both authors also claimed that the enslaved men were armed and prepared for some kind of violent action. This seems unlikely. As scholarship on rebellions of enslaved people in the Atlantic world has shown, references to potential violence from enslaved people by white colonists were often false or exaggerated. See Sharples, "Discovering Slave Conspiracies"; Soriano, *Tides of Revolution*, 120, 134–38.

97. Testimony of Jiménez, 9 February 1767, in Contreras, "Usos y abusos."
98. Zamorano, "Mujeres," 105 and 110–11, although the author does not clarify the social standing of the men involved in these cases. For the same dynamic in smaller towns, see Salinas, "Violencias sexuales," esp. 18 and 27; and Salinas, "Del maltrato al uxoricidio."
99. I follow here Lipsett-Rivera, *Gender and Negotiation*, 36–40, 120–25.
100. Undurraga, *Los rostros del honor*, 55–58.
101. Molina Otárola and Campos Muñoz, "Confín geográfico"; Goicovic, *Relaciones de solidaridad*, 184, 204, 219; Goicovic, "De la indiferencia," 147; Bengoa, *Historia social*, 1:141–62. For the enslaved, although very outdated, see Vial Correa, *El africano*, 167–72. For political persecution, see, among many other examples, the legal case against Valencia and others, 1819, ANFCG, vol. 339, p. 5, ff. 50–59; and the petition of Esponda, 1814, ANFMG, vol. 6.
102. Ruiz, "Comunidades y cacicazgos," 104–5.
103. Camp, *Closer to Freedom*, 7.
104. For these and similar establishments, see Pereira Salas, *Juegos y alegrías*; Garrido, *Historial de la cueca*, 171–92; Valenzuela, "Diversiones rurales"; Salazar, *Labradores*, 93–96, 122–26; Donoso Fritz, "'Fue famosa la chingana . . . '"; Purcell, *Diversiones y juegos populares*.
105. Quoted in León, *Plebeyos y patricios*, 250. See also Flores, "Mujeres del bajo pueblo"; Salazar, *Labradores*, 277–88.
106. Lenz, *Diccionario etimológico*, 299. Scholars accepting this etymology include Pereira Salas, *Juegos y alegrías*, 255, and Garrido, *Historial de la cueca*, 171.
107. See, for a later period, Purcell, "La chingana."
108. Regulating instead of suppressing the chinganas also promised to turn them into lucrative sources of public revenue. See Purcell, *Diversiones y juegos populares*; Fritz, "'Fue famosa la chingana . . .'"
109. Edict of Guill y Gonzaga, 2 April 1763, ANFV, vol. 321, ff. 17–19v; edict of Jáuregui, 7 June 1773, ANFV, vol. 111, ff. 8–15; "Bando de buen gobierno," 68. For the government's critical vision of pulperías, see León, *Plebeyos y patricios*, 241–70.
110. Intendant of Santiago to Sáez, January 1823, ANFIS, vol. 1, f. 313v.
111. *El Monitor Imparcial*, 14 December 1827. Similar arguments can be found in Zúñiga to Higgins, 19 January 1790, ANFCG, vol. 504, ff. 158–74v, here 165–66; and Petorca's attorney to the government, August 1819, ANFMINT vol. 7, ff. 217–17v.
112. See Grez, *"Regeneración del pueblo,"* 195–204, though he presents Santiago's urban poor as passive instruments of competing elite groups.
113. Vowell, *Campaigns and Cruises*, 1:448. In 1822, Gervasio Posadas, former ruler of the United Provinces of Río de la Plata, made a strikingly similar observation regarding the role of Buenos Aires's lower classes during the revolutionary period. Quoted in Bernand, "Color de los criollos," 32.
114. For a positive appraisal see the poem Mercedes Marín del Solar dedicated to Romero in Marín del Solar, *Poesias de la señora Da.*, 123–31. On Romero,

see Feliú Cruz, *Abolición de la esclavitud*, 117–60; Diggs, "Zambo-Peluca"; and Arancibia, "Soldado de la Independencia."

115. I infer this from Arís to O'Higgins, 25 June 1831, ABO, 33:467. In 1828 a newspaper mockingly described Romero as "intrepid and smug." *El Sepulturero*, 27 September 1828. The following year, a group of men called him "an ignorant charlatan." Espejo et. al. *Contesto*. Elites in post-independence Montevideo reacted in a similarly scornful manner to the public relevance and renown of Black scholar Jacinto Ventura de Molina. See Borucki, *Shipmates to Soldiers*, 183–214.
116. The quote can be found in Juan Egaña to Mariano Egaña, 19 August 1824, in Egaña, *Cartas*, 57. A similarly critical remark about Romero's visibility can be found in *El Sepulturero*, 27 September 1828.
117. See the arguments of Santibáñez in 1811, ANFV, vol. 156, ff. 166–72, esp. 169v–70.
118. [Juan Egaña], "Ynforme á favor de Don Gavino Ureta," n.d., ANFV, vol. 120-A, f. 85.
119. Testimony of Montt, 1778, in Montt, *Recuerdos de familia*, 294; Undurraga, "'Valentones,'" 36.
120. Petition of Pérez de Arza, 12 September 1815, AGI, Chile, 208.
121. Mellafe and Loyola, *Memoria de América colonial*, 89–101; Cruz, *El traje*, 51–52; Salinas, *Chilenas de la colonia*, 122–26; and León, "Entre lo público."
122. See Poole, *Vision*, 85–106; Walker, *Shaky Colonialism*, 133–139; Del Águila, *Los velos*, 127–33.
123. For the quote, see "Bando de buen gobierno," 65. For the other prohibitions, see Rosales, *La cañadilla de Santiago*, 93.
124. "El Reglamento de Teatros," 490.
125. Hurtado, "Cuerpo y mujer chilena," esp. 389.
126. Molina Hernández, *Vida de un soldado*, 72–73.
127. Miller, *Memoirs of General Miller*, 1:400–401.
128. Vicuña Mackenna, *Historia crítica*, 2:460–61.
129. Zapiola, *Recuerdos de treinta años*, 86.
130. Bladh, *La República de Chile*, 46. For a similar event in a chingana in Valparaíso, see Hall, *Extracts from a Journal*, 1:18–20.
131. Domeyko, *Mis viajes*, 1:366–73.
132. Vial y Cevallos to Bruzual, 3 April 1816, ANFSFL, vol. 33, p. 54.

Chapter Two

1. Carrera, "Diario del Brigadier."
2. Ibid. For more information on this coup and the conspiracy preceding it, see Vargas, "Del autonomismo al separatismo."
3. The Congressmen agreed to expel all those whose names appeared on the list, with the exception of Eyzaguirre.
4. Araya, "Registrar a la plebe"; Undurraga, *Los rostros del honor*, 71; Delgado, *Laywomen and Making Colonial Catholicism*, 10–14.
5. On race and calidad, see O'Hara, *A Flock Divided*, 4–6; Martínez, *Genealogical Fictions*; Twinam, *Purchasing Whiteness*.
6. Hespanha, *Ordem do mundo*, 60–63.
7. The definition of what constituted inferiority was contentious and evolved over time, but the basic principle remained the same. See Vial, "Prejuicios

sociales en Chile"; Salinas and Corvalán, "Transgresores sumisos"; Corvalán, "Amores"; Goicovic, "Es tan corto el amor"; Figueroa, "El honor femenino"; Pereira Larraín, *Afectos e intimidades*, 68–79. On how people across Spanish America engaged in complex negotiations over these differences of calidad, see Twinam, *Private Lives*; Twinam, *Purchasing Whiteness*.

8. See Araya, "Sirvientes contra amos"; Araya, "El castigo físico"; Araya, "La fundación"; Araya, "Azotar." A similar logic was applied regarding the death penalty. See Arancibia, Cornejo, and González, "Estudio preliminar," 26.
9. See, for example, Araya, "Petronila Zúñiga"; Araya, "La fundación"; and Undurraga, *Los rostros del honor*.
10. Ricketts, *Who Should Rule?*
11. Undurraga, *Los rostros del honor*; Contreras, "Oficios." As John Garrison Marks has argued, the success of free people of African descent represented in itself a challenge to the ideology of white supremacy in the Americas. See Marks, *Black Freedom*.
12. Guarda, *El arquitecto*, 135–45. For complementary (and competing) numbers, see Donoso, *Ideas políticas en Chile*, 117–21; Barbier, "Elites and Cadres"; Silva Vargas, "Composición social"; Enríquez, "Familia local."
13. See, for example, Martín Calvo Encalada to José Manuel Calvo Encalada, 16 September 1794, ANFSM, C2440.
14. Campo de Alange to Higgins, 6 April 1792, ANFCG, vol. 768, p. 70, f. 157; Higgins to Campo de Alange, 22 September 1792, ANFCG, vol. 768, ff. 239v–40. On Arenas's life and career, see Contreras, "Milicias de pardos."
15. For gestures and honorific treatments in eighteenth-century Chile, see Undurraga, *Los rostros del honor*.
16. Valenzuela, *Fiesta*.
17. Notable exceptions to this attitude can be found in Twinam, *Private Lives*.
18. See Cienfuegos, *Catón cristiano-politico*, 54 (this manual was originally published in 1819). For this understanding of hygiene, see Vigarello, *Propre et sale*, 49–102.
19. Vega, "Trajes del teatro."
20. Abercrombie, *Passing to América*; Edwards, *Hiding in Plain Sight*; Lipsett-Rivera, *The Origins of Macho*; Walker, *Exquisite Slaves*.
21. Edict by Jáuregui, 17 February 1775, ANFV, vol. 111, ff. 76–77.
22. Hespanha, *Como os juristas viam*, 652–59.
23. Undurraga, "Españoles oscuros"; Verónica Undurraga, "Fronteras sociales."
24. Valenzuela, "Afán de prestigio," 1:88–89.
25. Quoted in Araya, "Imaginario sociopolítico," 311.
26. "Bando de buen gobierno," 65.
27. Uriondo, *El Ciudadano*, 8.
28. Araya, "Imaginario sociopolítico," 310–12; Araya, *Ociosos*; Fernández, "'La mano del plebeyo.'"
29. Milton, *Many Meanings of Poverty*.
30. See, for example, Benavides to the Audiencia, 20 July 1785, ANFCG, vol. 776, f. 27; Beauchef to Santiago's intendant, 4 April 1825, ANFIS, vol. 2, f. 210; Claro to O'Higgins, 2 February 1827, ANFVM, vol. 97, f. 52v; and Vowell, *Campaigns and Cruises*, 1:448.
31. See Cid, "Un ícono funcional," 1:223.
32. See *El Mercurio Chileno*, 1 July 1828 and 1 February 1829; *El Mercurio de Valparaíso*, 28 February 1829; *Registro Municipal*, 10 March 1829.

33. See, for instance, Yokota, *Unbecoming British*, 72.
34. Cf. Cruz, *El traje*, 102–9, 187–236; De Ramón and Larraín, *Vida económica chilena*, 165–97; Salazar, *Labradores*, 263–69; Salazar, *Mercaderes*, 246–48; Lacoste and Lacoste Adunka, "Chamantos"; and Pinto, *Formación del Estado*, 29–88.
35. Testimony of Castillo, 18 December 1840, ANFJSC, leg. 1588, p. 2, ff. 4v–5.
36. See, for example, "Ordenes para la Guardia de la puerta principal de Palacio," 3 November 1807, BNMSBA, 103, ff. 139–40; Portales to Blest and Ingram, 12 January 1832, in Fariña Vicuña, *Epistolario*, 2:362.
37. Cruz, *Patrimonio artístico*, 380–83.
38. Rugendas, *Album de Trajes Chilenos*. For similar illustrations, see Diener, *Rugendas*, and Gay, *Atlas de la historia*. Most of these images were produced following the conventions of "picturesque" representation, according to which traveling artists had to identify allegedly local and authentic (non-European) aspects of the countries they visited. See Diener, "Lo pintoresco como categoría estética."
39. The slaveholder claimed indeed that Pedro's actions angered him, though he may have been lying to justify the harsh physical punishment he inflicted on the enslaved man for other reasons. See the case against Pintado, 1753, in González Undurraga, *Esclavos y esclavas*, 43–54. For how enslaved people used clothing for self-fashioning in colonial Lima, see Walker, *Exquisite Slaves*.
40. See the case against Rodríguez and others in ANFCG, vol. 305, p. 9, ff. 297–447v. For Rodríguez being described as African-descended, see the testimony of Palacios, 31 August 1776, ff. 308–8v.
41. Uriarte to the Minister of Interior, 14 June 1821, ANFMI, vol. 4, ff. 215–16. Similar examples can be found in the trial of Avaria or Bueras, 1831, ANFJSC, leg. 1580, p. 3; and Zapiola, *Recuerdos de treinta años*, 70.
42. If we believe the local commissioner, who denounced these words to the colony's governor. See Herrera y Rodado to Muñoz de Guzmán, 12 October 1807, ANFCG, vol. 530, p. 9, f. 79. Herrera y Rodado does not mention the cacique's name.
43. Vergara Quiroz, *Historia Social del Ejército*, 1:54–55; Hernández Ponce, "La Guardia Nacional," 64. According to Anthony McFarlane, there were almost thirty thousand men enrolled in Chile's militias in 1808. McFarlane, *War and Independence*, 17–20.
44. Valenzuela, *Fiesta*, 135–73.
45. See the dispute between the governor and the officers of two of Santiago's militia units over their participation in the city's saint day in 1787: Álvarez de Acevedo to the colonels of the regiments of the Prince and Princess, 18 July 1787; and Álvarez de Acevedo to Carrera and Conde de la Conquista, 18 July 1787 and 23 July 1787, ANFCG, vol. 778, ff. 25–25v, 26, and 27v–28v. Examples of children with military degrees can be found in Amunátegui, *Precursores de la independencia*, 3:199–200. These children also wore uniforms, as can be appreciated in the 1816 portrait of five-year-old José Raimundo Figueroa Araoz, in Majluf, *José Gil de Castro*, 166.
46. See, for example, Higgins to Campo de Alange, 11 March 1791, ANFCG, vol. 786, ff. 144–46v. For the crown's use of military uniforms to attract African-descended men to the militias, see Kuethe and Andrien, *Spanish Atlantic World*, 240–41.
47. The soldiers' privilege to use the uniform is mentioned in Benavides to Gálvez, 12 December 1783, ANFCG, vol. 781, f. 154.

48. The quote comes from a 1763 document referring to Black militia officers. Reproduced in Contreras, "Oficios," 68.
49. See the petition of Arenas, 1787, ANFCG, vol. 530, p. 7, ff. 57–60v, here 59v.
50. Contreras, "Contextos sociales y culturales."
51. See "Expediente formado sobre el uso del uniforme a los empleados en las oficinas de Real Hacienda," ANFCG, vol. 214, p. 2, ff. 12–72.
52. Frontaura, *Historia del Convictorio Carolino*, 45–63; Eyzaguirre, "Don Miguel de Eyzaguirre," 80.
53. See, for example, the decree of 8 February 1817, in *Gazeta de Santiago de Chile*, 21 February 1818; the regulation issued in 1819 in SCL, 3:295–96 and 346–47; and the decree of 2 August 1832, *Boletín de las leyes*, 1846, 156–59.
54. Jáuregui to Gálvez, 16 January 1777 and 27 January 1778, ANFCG, vol. 779, ff. 50v–51 and ff. 116–17v; Contreras, "Oficios," 69; and Contreras, "Contextos sociales y culturales," 33.
55. Álvarez de Acevedo to the governor of Valdivia, 14 July 1787, ANFCG, vol. 778, ff. 370–70v.
56. Jáuregui to Gálvez, 27 January 1778, ANFCG, vol. 779, ff. 116–17v. Government officials advanced similar arguments between 1793 and 1795, when discussing the need to provide Royal Treasury employees with a uniform. See "Expediente formado sobre el uso del uniforme a los empleados en las oficinas de Real Hacienda," ANFCG, vol. 214, p. 2, ff. 12–72.
57. Villalobos, *Vida fronteriza*; León, *Apogeo y ocaso*.
58. The policies discussed in this section were common in eighteenth-century Spanish American frontiers. See Weber, *Bárbaros*, 186–92, and 241–45.
59. Zavala, *Los mapuches*, 151–56.
60. Guill y Gonzaga to the Supreme Council, 1 May 1767, ANFCG, vol. 792, ff. 68–77v. In a communication from 1800 regarding Spanish-Mapuche parliaments, the word "clothing" was used almost as a synonym for "gifts." See Pino to the intendant of Concepción, 5 October 1800, ANFCG, vol. 788, ff. 412–13.
61. Guill y Gonzaga to the Supreme Council, 1 May 1767, ANFCG, vol. 792, ff. 68–77v.
62. Jáuregui to Arriaga, 4 September 1773, ANFCG, vol. 777, ff. 168–70.
63. Jáuregui to Arriaga, 31 March 1774, ANFCG, vol. 777, ff. 179–86v.
64. Jáuregui to Arriaga, 3 June 1774, ANFCG, vol. 777, ff. 197v–205.
65. Benavides to the Royal Treasury, 21 November 1781, ANFCG, vol. 774, f. 234v. More on this embassy and Indigenous diplomatic missions in Santiago in León, *Apogeo y ocaso*; León, *Maloqueros y conchavadores*, 175–80; Colivoro and Álamos, *Población indígena*, 180–88.
66. See Jáuregui to Gálvez, 12 August 1778, ANFCG, vol. 779, f. 182v for the quote. See also Jáuregui to Gálvez, 3 October 1777, ANFCG, vol. 777, ff. 87–88. The uniform is described in Barros Arana, *Historia Jeneral de Chile*, 6:353.
67. Benavides to the commander of the frontier, 10 November 1783, ANFCG, vol. 775, ff. 83–83v. For the school's expenses in clothing, see the files concerning the elaboration of new dresses for the students in 1781 and 1785 in ANFCG, vol. 585, p. 4, ff. 107–12v; ANFCG, vol. 40, pp. 12 and 20, ff. 105–9v and 286–96; as well as Benavides to Álvarez de Acevedo, 1 October 1781, ANFCG, vol. 774, f. 230.
68. Higgins to Gardoqui, 18 November 1793, ANFCG, vol. 786, ff. 519v–30v.
69. For an analysis of elite discussions over equality between 1810 and 1828, see Cid, *Pensar la revolución*, 265–303.

70. See Mejías Navarrete, "Esclavitud doméstica," 135–36; De Ramón, "Demandas por igualdad"; Soto, *Esclavas negras*, 122–23. For the importance of claims to "natural rights," see Premo, *The Enlightenment on Trial*.
71. Her legal case is reproduced in González Undurraga, *Esclavos y esclavas*, 131–56.
72. Albornoz Vásquez "Seguir un delito"; Albornoz Vásquez, *Experiencias de conflicto*; Araya, "Azotar"; Araya, "La fundación"; Araya, "Sirvientes contra amos"; Contreras, "Milicias de pardos"; Contreras, "Oficios"; Contreras, "Usos y abusos"; Figueroa, "El honor femenino"; Undurraga, *Los rostros del honor*; Vial Correa, "Prejuicios sociales en Chile."
73. Pérez de Saravia to Álvarez de Acevedo, 1 January 1781, ANFRA, vol. 1644, p. 2, 157–60v.
74. See Salas, "Carta de Santiago Leal a Patricio Español," 10 July 1810, in CHDICH, 8:213–55, 246–47 for the quote.
75. Juan Martínez de Rozas, 4 July 1811, in SCL, 1:41.
76. "Proclama revolucionaria del padre franciscano frai Antonio Orihuela," 1811, SCL, 1:357–59. There is no evidence that Orihuela's political activities matched his revolutionary rhetoric. Although radical, his text was in all likelihood meant for circulation among the members of his elite political faction in Concepción. For analyses of his document, see Salazar, *Construcción de Estado en Chile*, 105–13; and Grez, *"Regeneración del pueblo,"* 205–9. For the partisan background behind its publication, see Cartes, *Concepción contra Chile*, 193–264.
77. For other examples of anti-aristocratic declarations during the early years of the revolution, see *Semanario Republicano*, 16 October, 10 November, 18 November, 20 November, 25 November, and 11 December 1813.
78. Decree of O'Higgins, 22 March 1817, in *Boletin de las leyes, 1817–1818*, 31. I examine this edict and its consequences in more detail in chapter 4.
79. *Viva la Patria. Gazeta del Supremo Gobierno de Chile*, 26 March 1817.
80. Decree of O'Higgins, 16 September 1817, in *Boletin de las leyes*, 1817–1818, 134.
81. Zenteno to O'Higgins, 1 October 1817, in ANFVM, vol. 92, f. 47; *Gazeta de Santiago de Chile*, 29 November 1817.
82. Donoso, *Ideas políticas en Chile*, 122–23; Collier, *Ideas and Politics*, 247–48. Mayorazgos remained a subject of contention during the following decade. See Cid, *Pensar la revolución*, 293–303.
83. Egaña, "Plan de gobierno," in CHDICH, 19:106.
84. Given colonial notions of purity of blood, no marriages between "Spaniards" and people of African ancestry were considered in Juan Egaña's draft. See Egaña, *Proyecto de Constitución*, 21–22. The code was never put into practice.
85. The document is reproduced in Sagredo, *De la Colonia a la República*, 105–22. The publication of this text was halted while it was being printed, probably due to the war.
86. Egaña, "Épocas y hechos memorables de Chile por el Doctor don Juan Egaña," in CHDICH, 19:53; Session of 5 October 1811, in SCL, 1:119; "Reglamento a favor de los indios dictado por la Junta de Gobierno con acuerdo del Senado," *Boletin de las leyes, 1810–1814*, 253–58; decree of O'Higgins, 3 June 1818, in *Boletin de las leyes, 1817–1818*, 313–14; decree of O'Higgins, 4 March 1819, in *Boletin de las leyes, 1819–1820*, 31–32.
87. Ruiz, "Comunidades y cacicazgos"; Mellafe and Salinas, *Sociedad y población rural*, 70.
88. Molina, "Pueblos de Indios," 85–87.

89. On casta notions, see Martínez, *Genealogical Fictions*.
90. According to the government, the unit's official title was "Batallón de Pardos," which could be translated as "Battalion of Blacks," which the junta changed to "Batallón de Infantes de la Patria" or "Battalion of Children of the Fatherland." Decree of the Junta, 25 April 1813, in *Boletin de las leyes, 1810–1814*, 205–6. Arancibia, "Soldado de la Independencia," 14 suggests a similar change in name had already taken place by 1811. For the honorific titles, see the decree of the junta, 28 March 1814, in *Boletin de las leyes, 1810–1814*, 326–27.
91. See, for example, Lasso, *Myths of Harmony*. This was also suggested in a newspaper article celebrating Chile's Black military units in 1821. See *Gazeta Ministerial de Chile*, 8 September 1821.
92. For the abolition of slavery, see Feliú Cruz, *Abolición de la esclavitud*. For the importance of corporal punishment for ordinary people, see Araya, "Sirvientes contra amos"; Araya, "El castigo físico." Unlike slavery, whippings were soon reinstated. See Grez, "*Regeneración del pueblo*," 241–42.
93. See, for example, the decree of O'Higgins, 1 June 1817, *Boletin de las leyes, 1817–1818*, 50–57; and *El Cosmopolita*, 28 September 1822. For the underlying political and social objectives behind the creation of the Legion, see Rabinovich, "Las órdenes militares"; and Ossa, *Armies*, 140–43.
94. In his 1824 *Almanak*, Juan Egaña included a total of 172. See Egaña, *Almanak nacional*; and, for the calculation, Rabinovich, "Las órdenes militares," 23.
95. See the decree of O'Higgins, 1 June 1817, *Boletin de las leyes, 1817–1818*, 50–57. Although the Legion's regulations changed over time, the requirement that members wear such badges remained. See Contreras, "Contextos sociales y culturales," 30; *Recopilación de los decretos*; "Nuevos estatutos de la Lejion de Mérito de Chile," 15 June 1822, in SCL, 6:64–69; and the incomplete and undated manuscript copy of the Legion's statuses in ANFSFL, vol. 38, p. 14.
96. Majluf, *José Gil de Castro*, 202–3, 228–29, 232, 236, 238, 242, 244; Smith and Rueda, *Retrato en miniatura*, 86–87.
97. *Gazeta de Santiago de Chile*, 25 October 1817. See also *Gazeta de Santiago de Chile*, 19 July 1817.
98. See senate to the Supreme Director, 28 May 1823, in SCL 7:159–60.
99. Senate to the Supreme Director, 16 June 1823, in SCL 7:198. See also senate to the Supreme Director, 30 June 1823, in SCL, 7:239–40.
100. *El Tizón Republicano*, 10 March 1823. For other criticisms of the Legion see *Diario de la Convención de Chile*, num. 2, 1822; *El Cosmopolita*, 28 September 1822; *El Interrogante y Respondente*, 27 March 1823; *El Avisador Chileno*, 21 August 1824.
101. Historians have overlooked these arguments, focusing instead on the Legion's partisan identification with General O'Higgins, its alleged association with hereditary distinctions, and the onerous costs of its operation to explain the senators' decision. See Pinto and Valdivia, *¿Chilenos todos?*, 149–50; Ossa, *Armies*, 140–43; Cid, *Pensar la revolución*, 272–74; Rabinovich, "Las órdenes militares."
102. "Memoria dispuesta por orden del Exmo cavildo al Señor Supremo Director despues de la batalla de Maypu," ANFV, vol. 794, f. 10v for the quotes. A year later, Egaña crafted a law regulating etiquette in the new state in which he observed that "social order" depended on impressing people's "senses." See "Proyecto de Ley sobre el reglamento de etiqueta general para los funcionarios de la Republica de Chile," 1820, ANFV, vol. 121, f. 35.

103. Edict of Ramón Freire, 21 May 1823, in *Boletín de las leyes*, 1839, 143–49. According to *El Crepúsculo*, 19 September 1829, this order was followed through, and after its publication civil servants wore specific canes, suits, and hats.
104. See Freire to the Senate, 5 June and 23 June 1823, in SCL, 7:181–82 and 223–24. Mariano Egaña is undoubtedly the author of these communications. See also the communication sent to the senate by a group of Legion members in 2 July 1823, in SCL, 7:224–25.
105. *El Apagador*, 3 June 1823; *El Amigo de la Verdad*, 14 June 1823.
106. Exactly how and when the Legion ended remains unclear. It is likely that the liberals' accession to governmental control and the abolition of Juan Egaña's constitution in 1824 deprived the Legion of institutional support, abolishing it in practice. A newspaper described it in 1827 as a "monarchical institution" associated with the former O'Higgins regime. *El Insurgente Araucano*, 7 April 1827.
107. Senate to the Supreme Director, 26 May 1823, in SCL, 7:154.
108. Freire to the Senate, 5 June 1823, SCL, 7:180.
109. *El Amigo de la Verdad*, 14 June 1823.
110. Senate to the Supreme Director, 16 June 1823, in SCL, 7:198.
111. Session of 30 June 1823, in SCL, 7:242–43.
112. "Proyecto de lei," in SCL, 8:417–18. Arce's project included some minor exceptions to this rule.
113. "Proyecto de lei," in SCL, 8:417–18.
114. *El Redactor del Senado*, num. 2, 1823; *El Interrogante y Respondente*, 15 May and 6 June 1823; *El Nuevo Corresponsal*, 23 May 1823; *El Tizón Republicano*, 30 June and 28 July 1823; and all twenty-six issues of *El Observador Eclesiástico*.
115. Barros Arana, *Historia Jeneral de Chile*, 14:130; Maturana, *Historia de los Agustinos*, 2:573–74; Figueroa, *Diccionario histórico biográfico*, 1:559; Enríquez, "Reforma de los regulares," 54.
116. *El Observador Eclesiástico*, 29 November 1823. Silva had advanced similar ideas in *El Observador Eclesiástico*, 19 July and 30 August 1823.
117. Bustamante [pseud.], *Paco y Manolo*.
118. The report can be found in SCL, 8:513–18.
119. Cruz, "El traje como signo de los nuevos tiempos"; and Cruz, *El traje*, 187–215.
120. These two main political positions coexisted with various other political factions. A recent synthesis in Wood, *The Society of Equality*, 22–29. For a description emphasizing their difference with modern political parties see Heise, *Años de formación*, 79–92.
121. Arce to O'Higgins, 28 October 1817, reproduced in Vicuña Mackenna, *Ostracismo del Jeneral*, 290.
122. According to historian Benjamín Vicuña Mackenna, the Carrera family coined the term pelucones to describe old Congressmen in 1811. See Vicuña Mackenna, *Introducción a la historia*, 1:12. For examples of the word being used before 1823, see *Viva la Patria. Gazeta del Supremo Gobierno de Chile*, 26 March 1817; *Semanario de Policía*, 1 October 1817; and *La Miscelánea Chilena*, 8 March 1821. On the complex and shifting meanings of "Liberal" and "liberalism," see Moyano and San Francisco, "Liberalismo."
123. *El Tizón Republicano*, 19 May 1823.
124. *Diccionario portatil*, 4.
125. Liberals, the newspaper added, also believed that "our entire old system"

inherited from colonial times was "barbaric and Gothic." *El Liberal*, 4 September 1824.

126. *La Estrella de Chile*, 5 October 1826; *Clamor del Pueblo Chileno*, 15 December 1827; *El Verdadero Liberal*, 13 May 1829.
127. See *El Avisador Chileno*, 11 and 21 August 1824.
128. See, for example, Egaña, "Memorias para la historia de la constitucion de Chile promulgada en 823," ANFV, vol. 792, p. 2, ff. 23–136v; *El Almirez*, 13 May 1828.
129. *El Observador de Valparaíso*, 18 June 1827.
130. *El Liberal*, 4 September 1824.
131. Arís to O'Higgins, 12 April 1826, in ABO, 33:14–15; Claro to Woster, 29 March 1827, ANFVM, vol. 112, ff. 158–59v; *El Pipiolo*, 29 March 1827; *El Observador de Valparaíso*, 18 June 1827; *El Avisador de Valparaíso*, 12 and 27 May 1829.
132. *El Descamizado*, 2 May 1827. This translation was apparently widely accepted across the Spanish Atlantic. See, for instance, Soriano, *Tides of Revolution*, 177; and Di Meglio, *¡Viva el bajo pueblo!*, 256–78. For more on radical liberals, see Collier, *Ideas and Politics*, 361–68.
133. On the Phyrgian hat's association with poverty, see Bustamante [pseud.], *Paco y Manolo*, 2. For its use in Chile during this period, see chapter 3.
134. See, for example, Cid, *Pensar la revolución*; Grez, "*Regeneración del pueblo*"; Heise, *Años de formación*, esp. 79–92; Collier, *Ideas and Politics*, 294–97.
135. Zapiola, *Recuerdos de treinta años*, 181.
136. I discuss this event as well as Cañas's political ideals in chapter 4.
137. *El Correo de Arauco*, 13 August 1824.
138. For similar observations regarding other regions in Spanish America, see Lasso, *Myths of Harmony*; Guardino, *The Time of Liberty*, 156–224; Thibaud, *Libérer le nouveau monde*, 445–512, esp. 493.
139. See Grez, "*Regeneración del pueblo*," 220–26 and Wood, *Society of Equality*, 48–78.
140. Los Populares, *A los pueblos*.
141. *El Fanal*, 17 June 1829. The newspaper also implicitly associated Santiago's artisans and Black men in *El Fanal*, 31 March 1829, and recognized the demand for civil equality among them in *El Fanal*, 6 April 1829.
142. For the political alliances of Santiago's artisan organizations, see the references in the previous notes. For popular attitudes toward liberals and their religious reforms, see, for example, Santiago's intendant to the Minister of Interior, 9 January 1826, ANFIS, vol. 4, ff. 2v–3; Bladh, *La República de Chile*, 54; and Errázuriz, *Chile bajo el imperio*, 159.

Chapter Three

1. See the trial of Esponda, 1814, ANFMG, vol. 6; and Concha's description of these events dated 13 October 1814, in CHDICH, 35:136.
2. See Esponda's 1814 petition in ANFMG, vol. 6; Esponda to the President, 1815, ANFCG, vol. 99, p. 58, ff. 493–93v; and the files related to his appointment as treasurer of Santiago's customs in AGI, Chile, 207.
3. Some of Chile's leading figures, including bishops and Audiencia judges, requested to join this order. See the petitions of Villodres, 1813, AGI, Ultramar, 780; Caspe y Rodríguez, 1816, AGI, Chile, 226; and Rodríguez Zorrilla, 1828, AGI, Chile, 313.
4. For the rewards the king granted Romualdo Antonio Esponda, see the files

concerning his case in AGI, Lima, 759, and Imaz to the Minister of Gracia y Justicia, 10 August 1819, AGI, Chile, 313. The ceremony of November 30 is described in *Viva el Rey. Gazeta del Gobierno de Chile*, 6 December 1816.

5. On Esponda's modest social standing, see the official valuation of his property in 1817 in ANFCG, vol. 898, p. 5, f. 48v, and his mother's views on the subject in Sánchez to Esponda, 18 August 1814, ANFMG, vol. 6. For Esponda's father, see Medina, *Diccionario biográfico colonial*, 285, and Laval, *Noticias sobre los médicos*, 84.
6. Petition of Sánchez, 1 November 1818, AGI, Lima, 759. Esponda also lost all his properties in Chile. Accused of stealing approximately 3,500 pesos from the Treasury, his assets were confiscated and sold by the government in 1817. See the files in ANFCG, vol. 898, p. 5, ff. 26–48v.
7. See Brubaker and Cooper, "Beyond 'Identity,'" 1–47; and Groebner, *Who Are You?*, 27.
8. See, for example, the testimony of López, 31 August 1776, ANFCG, vol. 305, p. 9, ff. 309v–11; and Benavides to the Marquis of La Pica, 27 October 1781, ANFCG, vol. 774, f. 338.
9. To these ceremonies could be added the dozens of religious festivities celebrated each year, which manifested the colony's religious unity. See Cruz, *La fiesta*, 125–27; Valenzuela, *Fiesta*, 189–97.
10. Valenzuela, *Fiesta*; Valenzuela, *Las liturgias del poder*; and Cruz, *La fiesta*. I've also found useful, among a vast literature, Leal Curiel, *Discurso de la fidelidad*; Bridikhina, *Theatrum mundi*; Osorio, *Inventing Lima*.
11. Calderón and Thibaud, *Majestad de los pueblos*, 133–35, 145.
12. The nature of the "common good," however, was malleable and subject to evolution and contention. See Lempérière, *Entre Dieu et le Roi*, 23–62; Paquette, *Enlightenment*, 56–92; Premo, *Enlightenment on Trial*, 175–76.
13. For this political philosophy, see Cañeque, *King's Living Image*, 19–26; and Scavino, "La metafísica."
14. These ideas appear regularly in the communications between the governors and local officials during the second half of the eighteenth century and the early nineteenth century. See ANFCG, vols. 778, 780, 784, 787, 788, 789, 790, and 792.
15. Bladh, *La República de Chile*, 52–53.
16. See, for instance, Higgins to the commissioner and city council of Copiapó, 14 December 1788, ANFCG, vol. 778, f. 202; Higgins to the commissioner of Aconcagua, 9 January 1795, ANFCG, vol. 784, ff. 143–43v; Pino to the commissioner and city council of Coquimbo, 22 December 1800, ANFCG, vol. 788, f. 273; Avilés to the Audiencia, 26 January 1797, ANFCG, vol. 787, ff. 9–10.
17. Barbier, *Reform and Politics*; Ricardo Donoso, *Un letrado*.
18. On patriotism in this legal framework, see Herzog, *Defining Nations*.
19. Amunátegui, *Precursores de la independencia*, 1:81–101; Valenzuela, *Las liturgias del poder*, 315–30; Valenzuela, *Fiesta*; Bridikhina, *Theatrum mundi*, 180–83 and 225–42; Osorio, *Inventing Lima*, 81–102; Cañeque, *King's Living Image*, 124–28.
20. See, for example, "Jura y Aclamacion del Rey N. S. Dn. Carlos 3º," 21 April 1761, ANFCG, vol. 690, ff. 281–87; resolution of the Audiencia, 5 August 1768, ANFCG, vol. 697, ff. 36–37; Valenzuela, *Fiesta*, 27–41 and 261–75.
21. See Higgins to Llaguno, 3 May 1796, ANFCG, vol. 786, ff. 120v–21. For more on the role of royal portraits in Spanish South America, see Engel, *Pictured Politics*, 37–56.

22. Hamnett, *End of Iberian Rule*, 72–104.
23. These accusations were likely insincere and inspired by internal factional disputes. See Torres to Saavedra, 7 November 1808, and to the Central Junta, 29 January 1809; Luco to the Supreme Junta, 9 December 1808, and 20 March and 23 December 1809, in CHDICH, 8:VII–VIII, 3–33, 167–73, 181–89, 189–91, and 203–5.
24. Gundian to García, 18 August 1808, ANFA, vol. 34, p. 21, ff. 188–89v; Torres, "Advertencias precautorias a los habitantes de Chile," 1808, in Amunátegui, *Crónica de 1810*, 1:184–92.
25. Barros Arana, *Historia Jeneral de Chile*, 9:45–53. More on García Carrasco's hesitation in Vargas Cariola, "Reacciones chilenas," 187.
26. Majluf, "Cómo reemplazar," 87–89; and Valenzuela, *Fiesta*, 263–66.
27. Here I depart from conventional interpretations of these manifestations, which can be found in Guerra, *Modernidad e independencias*, 150–56; and Cid, *Pensar*, 32–38.
28. Portillo, *Crisis atlántica*, 83; Calderón and Thibaud, *Majestad de los pueblos*, 59–66; Guerra, *Modernidad e independencias*, 150–56; Landavazo, *Máscara de Fernando VII*, 98–111; Thibaud, "Sacrer la République," 132–34; Majluf, "Cómo reemplazar," 76–77; Bridikhina, *Theatrum mundi*, 240–41; Méndez, *Plebeian Republic*, 95–98.
29. Valenzuela, *Fiesta*, 269–71.
30. ANFSFL, vol. 27, p. 10. This episode is analyzed in more detail in Valenzuela, *Fiesta*, 270–71.
31. "Apuntes auto-biográficos del Jeneral don Francisco Antonio Pinto," BNMSBA, vol. 98, f. 217.
32. Amunátegui, *Crónica de 1810*, 1:215; Barros Arana, *Historia Jeneral de Chile*, 8:52.
33. Godoy Orellana, "Fiestas," 72.
34. See García to Trucíos, 20 October 1808, ANFST, vol. 17, ff. 150–51.
35. Cruz, *Patrimonio artístico*, 67–72; Smith and Rueda, *Retrato en miniatura*.
36. See Torres, "Advertencias precautorias a los habitantes de Chile," 1808, in Amunátegui, *Crónica de 1810*, 1:184–92, and the documents reproduced in CHDICH, vols. 8 and 9.
37. "Acta de la instalacion de la primera Junta de Gobierno," in SCL 1:3–4, here 4.
38. Ibid.
39. The junta to Chile's municipalities, 20 September 1810, ANFMI, vol. 13, ff. 5–6, here 5v.
40. See Barros Arana, *Historia Jeneral de Chile*, 8:228; and Montt, *Recuerdos de familia*, 393.
41. "Convocacion al Congreso Nacional de 1811 por la Junta de Gobierno," 5 December 1810, in *Boletin de las leyes, 1810–1814*, 14. Documents regarding the "recognition" of the junta in the colony's districts can be found in CHDICH, 18:226–336.
42. Talavera, "Revoluciones de Chile," in CHDICH, 29:esp. 84 and 101; Olaguer Feliú, *Relación de lo ocurrido*, 31–34; Manifesto of Concha, 21 April 1813, AGI, Chile, 207; Martínez, "Memoria Histórica," in CHDICH, 41(1):esp. 112 and 117.
43. Vargas Cariola, "Del autonomismo al separatismo," 1:274–75.
44. Johnston, *Letters written*, 74. For an analysis of the political role these objects played during the revolutionary period, see Valenzuela, *Fiesta*, 283–303.

For studies focused on the construction of Chilean nationalism, see Peralta, *¡Chile tiene fiesta!*, 125–27; Silva, *Identidad y nación*, 58–64; Zaldívar and Sánchez, "Símbolos," 2:73–115; Pinto and Valdivia, *¿Chilenos todos?*, esp. 50–64 and 195–205; Cruz, *Patrimonio artístico*, 222–40; Cruz, *La fiesta*, 296–309.

45. See also Talavera, "Revoluciones de Chile," in CHDICH, 29:643–51.
46. Quoted in the junta to the governor of Valparaíso, 30 July 1812, ANFSFL, vol. 29, p. 63.
47. Decree of 16 July 1812, *Boletin de las leyes, 1810–1814*, 169–70.
48. See the decrees of 30 July 1812, ibid., 170–71; and the junta to the governor of Valparaíso, 30 July 1812, ANFSFL, vol. 29, p. 63.
49. Martínez, "Memoria Histórica," in CHDICH, 42(1):75.
50. See the arguments revolutionary figures advanced during the royalist restoration, discussed below.
51. Rodríguez Zorrilla to the archbishop of Lima, 20 January 1813, AGI, Chile, 312; Rodríguez Zorilla to the king, 29 October 1814, AGI, Chile, 453.
52. Johnston, *Letters written*, 109; Valencia Avaria, "Banderas de Chile," 23.
53. Quoted in Valenzuela, *Fiesta*, 288.
54. Mackenna to O'Higgins, 18 June 1814, in CHDICH, 23:383–86.
55. See, for example, the ceremonies in Chillán and Santiago mentioned in *El Monitor Araucano*, 17 April and 17 June 1813, as well as the positive reference to the tricolor flag in *El Monitor Araucano*, 15 June 1813.
56. According to the official narrative of the events that was published in *El Monitor Araucano*, 11 March 1814.
57. *El Monitor Araucano*, 13 May 1814. This line of reasoning had been developed in earlier phases of negotiation with royalists. See "Proposiciones de arreglo del Gobierno de Chile," in CHDICH, 23:352–57.
58. Aldunate to Irigoyen, 14 May 1814, AGI, Diversos, 3; Carrera, *Manifiesto*, 15; Barros Arana, *Historia Jeneral de Chile*, 9:447–48; Gandarillas, *Don Bernardo O'Higgins*, 65–66.
59. Copy of a letter from Fernández to Olaguer Feliú, 16 June 1814, in AGI, Chile, 207.
60. Irisarri to O'Higgins, 30 May 1814, CHDICH, 23:379–82.
61. Mackenna to O'Higgins, 18 June 1814, in CHDICH, 23:383–86. The treaty was never ratified.
62. Testimony of Arenas, 6 October 1817, in CHDICH, 43:506.
63. Decree of Vera, 1 September 1814, ANFMG, vol. 6.
64. Esponda's testimony, 28 September 1814, ANFMG, vol. 6.
65. "Profecia de Santa Rosa de Lima al capitulo 20 de Su vida," ANFMG, vol. 6.
66. Vista of the state attorney, 29 September 1814, ANFMG, vol. 6.
67. Testimonies of Sanfuentes and Esponda, 28 September 1814, ANFMG, vol. 6.
68. See, for example, José Santiago Concha's account of these events in CHDICH, 35:137. The great number of flags is also mentioned in a manuscript probably written by Juan Egaña but signed by Dominican friar Domingo Velasco, ANFV, vol. 794, p. 8, ff. 36–37v.
69. José Santiago Concha's narrative in CHDICH, 35:137.
70. *Semanario de Policía*, 22 October 1817.
71. Zapiola, *Recuerdos de treinta años*, 129.
72. Carrera, "Diario del Brigadier."
73. Serrano, "La representación," 502–3.
74. Valenzuela, *Fiesta*, 62–64, 215–22, 281–83.

75. These included Copiapó, La Serena, Petorca, La Ligua, Los Andes, Quillota, Rancagua, Talca, Linares, and Chillán. See Concha, *Crónica de La Serena*, 130; Pérez to Arnaiz, 14 November 1814, ANFV, vol. 699, ff. 72–72v; the official certificate of the festivities in Talca, 24 December 1814, AGI, Chile, 207; the files concerning these celebrations in AGI, Chile, 206; and the list provided in Cid, *Pensar la revolución*, 94.
76. Certificate produced by the city council of San Felipe, 12 November 1814, AGI, Chile, 206.
77. Osorio to the Ministry of Indies, 16 March 1815, AGI, Chile, 312.
78. See the trial of Tagle, 1817, ANFCG, vol. 336, p. 12.
79. The Audiencia to the President, 28 November 1815, in CHDICH, 35:153.
80. Investigation of Manuel Salas's political conduct, 1815–1816, ANFSM, A8495.
81. Vista of Rodríguez Aldea, 28 November 1815, in CHDICH, 35:220–22.
82. List of insurgents of Valparaíso, 1817, in CHDICH, 35:683–84.
83. Quoted in Valencia Avaria, "Banderas de Chile," 22.
84. "Memorial dirigido al virrey del Perú," 12 December 1814, in *Escritos de don Manuel de Salas*, 1:46.
85. I take this idea from Sheryl Kroen's analysis of politics in Restoration France. See Kroen, *Politics and Theater*, 57 for the quote.
86. Monteagudo, *Relacion de la gran fiesta*, 4. For more examples, see Valenzuela, *Fiesta*, 273–75; and Majluf, "Cómo reemplazar," 93–96.
87. Arís to O'Higgins, 18 March 1834, in ABO, 34:456.
88. Avaria, "Banderas de Chile," 43–44.
89. Aldea to O'Higgins, 30 June 1824, in CHDICH, 36:323.
90. Pinto and Valdivia, *¿Chilenos todos?*, 198–99.
91. *Gazeta de Santiago de Chile*, 28 February 1818, in ABO, 10:350.
92. Egaña, "Proyecto de Ley sobre el reglamento de etiqueta general para los funcionarios de la Republica de Chile," in ANFV, vol. 121, f. 66v.
93. *Gazeta Ministerial de Chile*, 17 February 1821. See also Conservative Senate, session of 9 February 1821, SCL 5:44–45.
94. Session of 27 January 1821, ANFMS, vol. 83, f. 44v.
95. In 1817 the commissioner of the town of Talca argued that "even the most miserable men" wore the liberty cap during a political celebration that October. See Montes y Larrea to the Minister of State, 8 October 1817, ANFMI, vol. 13, f. 34.
96. Concha, *Crónica de La Serena*, 134; *Gazeta Ministerial de Chile*, 17 February 1821; Arís to O'Higgins, 16 June 1824, in ABO, 33:7; Juan Egaña to Mariano Egaña, 29 July 1824, in Egaña, *Cartas*, 51; and Arís to O'Higgins, 27 September 1832, in ABO, 34:89.
97. Santiago's intendant to the Governor of the Bishopric of Santiago, 9 September 1819, ANFIS, vol. 1, f. 302; and, for the late 1830s, Gardiner, *Visit to the Indians*, 170–71.
98. See, among multiple references, *Viva la Patria. Gazeta del Supremo Gobierno de Chile*, 28 May 1817; Montes y Larrea to the Minister of State, 8 October 1817, ANFMI, vol. 13, f. 34; *Gazeta de Santiago de Chile*, 15 November 1817; Monteagudo, *Relacion de la gran fiesta*; Silva to the Supreme Director, 17 September 1821, and Viancos to the Minister of Government, 25 March 1823, ANFMI, vol. 7, ff. 240 and 116–16v; Del Campo to the Minister of War and the Navy, 5 October 1821, resolution of Rancagua's municipality, 25 December 1822, ANFMI, vol. 10, ff. 163–63v, and 177–77v; López to the Minister of State,

28 April 1823, ANFMI, vol. 5, ff. 169–69v; and *El Monitor Imparcial*, 14 March 1828.

99. Monteagudo, *Memoria sobre los principios*, 17.
100. Orrego to the Supreme Director, 23 April 1819, and Viancos to the Minister of Government, 25 March 1823, ANFMI vol. 7, ff. 57–57v and 116–16v.
101. *Gazeta Ministerial de Chile*, 3 March 1821.
102. See also the chingana Johann Moritz Rugendas painted ca. 1843, in which an enormous Chilean flag can be seen hanging outside of the establishment, in Diener, *Rugendas*, 145. Historian Paulina Peralta has shown how postcolonial subaltern actors appropriated and gave new meaning to Chile's national festivities and symbols. See Peralta, *¡Chile tiene fiesta!*
103. *El Crepúsculo*, 19 September 1829. The same argument in *El Sufragante*, 22 September 1829. For a similar observation about the choice to hoist flags, see *El Juicio*, 24 September 1830.
104. Ramírez Beza to Torio Lira, Coinco, 29 February 1828, ANFRA, vol. 2151, p. 1, ff. 45–45v.
105. Peralta, *¡Chile tiene fiesta!*, 136–42.

Chapter Four

1. Report of Lazcano in the trial of Esponda, 1814, ANFMG, vol. 6.
2. For this broad definition of iconoclasm, see Fureix, *Œil blessé*; and Clay, *Iconoclasm in Revolutionary Paris*. The iconoclasm I study here is different from what Freedberg calls "ontological" iconoclasm; that is, the hatred of images per se. See Freedberg, *Power of Images*, 378–428. I do not address in this chapter the destruction or rejection of religious images.
3. Duschinsky, "Pure and Impure," 141–42, for the quote. For a more detailed elaboration, see Arnal and McCutcheon, *Sacred Is Profane*.
4. Agamben, *Profanations*, 73.
5. Luhmann, *Theory of Society*, 1:138–49, 141 and 142 for the quotes.
6. On the distinction between political and "pre-political" modes of establishing authority, see Arendt, *On Revolution*, 171–206.
7. Agamben, *Profanations*, 74.
8. Historian Emmanuel Fureix has recently argued that new ideas about sovereignty (as accessible and modifiable) transformed how people in postrevolutionary France related to the visible world and particularly to iconoclasm. Here I complement Fureix's thesis by insisting on how iconoclasm itself contributed to revolutionize what we may call the social experience of political sovereignty. Fureix, *Œil blessé*.
9. Canetti, *Masa y poder*, 20–21.
10. Vista of Márquez de la Plata, 23 January 1781, ANFRA, vol. 1664, p. 2, fs. 274v-75.
11. Ibid., ff. 271v–76. For the practice of *damnatio memoriae*, see Calomino, *Defacing the Past*.
12. Testimony of Vergne, 17 January 1781, ANFRA, vol. 1644, p. 2, f. 218.
13. The sentence the attorney recommended was not carried out. Crown officials proposed similar punishments for rebels in other Spanish American colonies. See, for example, Phelan, *People and King*, 228.
14. Calderón and Thibaud, *Majestad de los pueblos*, 29 and 50. See also the scholastic idea of "majesty as mistery" explored in Cañeque, *King's Living Image*, 36–50, 45 for the quote.

15. Hespanha, *Ordem do mundo*, 17–90; Tomás y Valiente, *Manual de historia*, 284–89; Garriga, "Orden jurídico"; Lempérière, "Constitution," 9; Leal Curiel, *Discurso de la fidelidad*, 194–203.
16. Palti, *¿Ideas fuera de lugar?*, 31, 52, and 54; Palti, *Archaeology of the Political*, esp. 80–81. For descriptions produced in Chile of the king as a transcendent and infallible deliverer of justice, see Meza Villalobos, *Conciencia política chilena*, 170–77.
17. Lefort, *Essais sur le politique*, 17–32 and 275–329.
18. The Spanish legislation explicitly stated that attacks against the king were sacrilegious. See Tomás y Valiente, *Derecho penal*, 238–42. Another example of this concept being used to describe challenges against royal sovereignty in late colonial Spanish America in Phelan, *People and the King*, 212–17.
19. Pérez Uriondo, 15 January 1781, ANFRA, vol. 1644, p. 2, f. 204.
20. I give examples of these attitudes toward the royal portrait in chapter 3.
21. As defined by William Reddy, an emotional regime is a set of norms prescribing emotional expression. See Reddy, *The Navigation of Feeling*. For a recent appraisal of this model, see Boddice, *The History of Emotions*, 70–77.
22. Cañeque, "The Emotions of Power."
23. See, for example, the undated religious reflection, probably written by philosopher Juan Egaña, in ANFV, vol. 791, ff. 32–32v. For a detailed analysis of how these emotional values shaped the colony's official discourse on honor, see Undurraga, *Los rostros del honor*, 219–55. For more on the value ascribed to humility in discourses about justice, race, and gender in colonial Chile, see Cornejo, *Manuela Orellana*, 61–71; Albornoz Vásquez, *Experiencias de conflicto*, 33; Araya, "Sirvientes contra amos."
24. Méndez, *Plebeian Republic*, 95; Hespanha, *Ordem do mundo*, 103–6; Fisher, "Keeping and Losing One's Head."
25. Delumeau, *Le péché et la peur*, 211–35.
26. Higgins to De la Cuadra, 18 April 1795, ANFCG, vol. 784, ff. 204v–5. See also Leal Curiel, *Discurso de la fidelidad*, esp. 210–28.
27. On pride as the source of rebellion against the crown, see Calderón and Thibaud, *Majestad de los pueblos*, 44; Voekel, *Alone before God*, 167; and Jaffary, *False Mystics*, 154.
28. For this concept see Hartog, *Regimes of Historicity*, esp. 16–20.
29. For examples of this argument being made in relation to Chile, see Ovalle to the President, 28 May 1810, in CHDICH, 30:93–99; and, more veiled, Villodres, *Carta pastoral*, 9.
30. See, for example, the marquis of Montepío to the officers of the regiment of the Prince, Santiago, 1806, ANSFL, vol. 27, p. 18.
31. See the anonymous and undated reflection (most probably written by Juan Egaña) in ANFV, vol. 791, ff. 22–24v, as well as Sellers-García, *Woman on the Windowsill*, 177–79.
32. For these multiple forms of future-making in colonial Mexico, see O'Hara, *History of the Future*.
33. See, for example, Cohen-Aponte, "Imagining Insurgency Peru," 202; Walker, *The Tupac Amaru Rebellion*, 258–59; Serulnikov, *Revolution in the Andes*, 136.
34. The most dramatic manifestations of such doubts took place during the expulsion of the Jesuits in 1767 and subsequent years. See Barros Arana, *Historia Jeneral de Chile*, 6:289–91; Kordic, *Epistolario*, 448; Morales to Arriaga,

29 October 1772, ANFCG, vol. 777, f. 99; Amunátegui, *Precursores de la independencia*, 1:245–48. For the need to reinforce the distinction between the sacred and the profane, see, for example, *Synodo Diocesana*; and Vicuña Mackenna, *Historia crítica*, 2:516–18.

35. Undurraga, "'Valentones'"; Undurraga, *Los rostros del honor*, 219–343. For the concept of "emotional community" see Rosenwein, *Emotional Communities*, 1–31.
36. Rozas, 1777, ANFCG, vol. 305, p. 9, ff. 401v and 404. For similar descriptions of the period as an "Age of Enlightenment," see the speeches written by Zerdán in 1778, AGI, Chile, 315; Salas (attributed) in 1801, in Amunátegui, *Precursores de la independencia*, 3:385–99; and Egaña in 1804, ANFV, vol. 274, ff. 124–34.
37. Valenzuela, *Fiesta*, 275–83; and Amunátegui, *Precursores de la independencia*, 1:82–94.
38. Álvarez de Acevedo to Carrera and Toro y Zambrano, 23 July 1787, ANFCG, vol. 778, ff. 27v–28v.
39. Higgins to Martínez de Aldunate, 5 November 1788, ANFCG, vol. 778, f. 102.
40. See Bellion, *Iconoclasm in New York*; Fureix, *Iconoclasme et révolutions*.
41. Cohen-Aponte, "Imagining Insurgency."
42. Peralta, "Entre la fidelidad y la incertidumbre," 140; Fraser, *Napoleon's Cursed War*, 36–38.
43. Jiménez Guerra to the court, 1811, ANFSFL, vol. 30, p. 4, ff. 14v–15.
44. Bredekamp, *Acte d'image*, 189–97.
45. Solans, "Milagros"; Cid, "'Señales últimos tiempos'"; and, more generally, Fernández Sebastián, *Historia conceptual*, 399–470.
46. O'Hara, *History of the Future*, 153.
47. Ferrer, *Freedom's Mirror*, 271–328; Coronado, *World Not to Come*, esp. 181–212, 264–351.
48. See, among others, Guerra, *Modernidad e independencias*; Adelman, *Sovereignty and Revolution*; Portillo Valdés, *Crisis atlántica*.
49. Serrano, "La representación"; Jocelyn-Holt, "El escenario juntista chileno," 272–75; Vargas Cariola, "Reacciones chilenas," 180–83.
50. Testimony of Rojas, 27 June 1810, in CHDICH, 30:132.
51. Olaguer Feliú, *Relación de lo ocurrido*, 27.
52. Salas to Martínez de Rozas, 18 September 1810, ANFV, vol. 964, ff. 79–79v.
53. See the trial of Escuseiro, 1811, ANFSFL, vol. 70, p. 8; Talavera, "Revoluciones de Chile," in CHDICH, 29:191; and the anonymous letter to Martínez de Rozas, 4 March 1811, ANFV, vol. 964, ff. 96–96v.
54. Thibaud, "Sacrer la République," 130–32.
55. Johnston, *Letters written*, 79–81; Talavera, "Revoluciones de Chile," in CHDICH, 29:643–51; Martínez, "Memoria Histórica," in CHDICH, 41(2):87–89.
56. On this door, see Guarda, *El arquitecto*, 190; Pereira Salas, *Historia del arte*, 210–11.
57. Talavera, "Revoluciones de Chile," in CHDICH, 29:648.
58. *Aurora de Chile*, 1 October 1812.
59. Acedo and Prieto are not explicitly named in the sources. I have deduced they were the ones involved by cross-referencing the information in the sources cited above with Acedo to the Supreme Director, 1826, in SCL, 30:283; and Ramírez Espíndola, "Ejército regular," 148.

60. Martínez, "Memoria Histórica," in CHDICH, 41(2):88; Talavera, "Revoluciones de Chile," in CHDICH, 29:649.
61. Thibaud, "Sacrer la République," 137–39.
62. For a thorough exploration of the regimes of historicity involved in references to Native groups during this period, see Thibaud, "La ley y la sangre."
63. Carrera to Díaz de Valdés, 15 November 1814, ANFV, vol. 238-B, ff. 174–75.
64. Like other politically engaged women, Javiera Carrera framed her activities in relation to multiple gender roles (as sister, wife, and eventually matriarch). See Chambers, *Families in War*, 29–61.
65. Hunt, "Iconoclasme et temps," 50.
66. See, for example, the sermon preached in Santiago by friar José María Romo on 29 August 1810, reproduced in Talavera, "Revoluciones de Chile," in CHDICH, 29:50–53, esp. 52.
67. Zapata, "Mistica Junta que se hiso en Esta Ciudad de Santiago de Chile a 18 del mes de Julio del presente año de 810," ANFA, vol. 34, p. 21.
68. Another woman, Ventura Pradel, had at least an indirect role in the destruction of a silver royal coat of arms, as discussed below.
69. Osorio to the Secretary of State and the Indies, 15 September 1815, AGI, Chile, 207. Historian Diego Barros Arana provides a different account. See Barros Arana, *Historia Jeneral de Chile*, 8:344.
70. Decree, 20 May 1813, in *El Monitor Araucano*, 25 May 1813. The pyramid was never built.
71. Osorio to the Secretary of State and the Indies, 15 September 1815, AGI, Chile, 207. See also the files concerning Ventura Pradel's request for reimbursement in ANFRA, vol. 3235, p. 1.
72. Decree of 1 September 1813, copied in Osorio to the Secretary of State and the Indies, 15 September 1815, AGI, Chile, 207.
73. Ibid. The crimes of lèse-majesté and counterfeiting money were explicitly linked in the important medieval code called the Siete Partidas. See Tomás y Valiente, *Derecho penal*, 206.
74. Enemy flags were a particularly prized war trophy. See Valenzuela, *Fiesta*, 289–92.
75. *El Monitor Araucano*, 2 May 1813.
76. Aldunate to Irigoyen, 14 May 1814, AGI, Diversos, 3; Carrera, *Manifiesto*, 15. For these desecrations, see chapter 3.
77. Barros Arana, *Historia Jeneral de Chile*, 9:545.
78. Barros Arana, "Rasgos biográficos," 261.
79. See the anonymous list of insurgents of Valparaíso, 1817, in CHDICH, 35:683.
80. Cañeque, *King's Living Image*.
81. See Freedberg, *Power of Images*, 378–428.
82. Esponda's case is analyzed in detail in chapter 3.
83. Report of Concha, 13 October 1814, in CHDICH, 35:136.
84. Crown attorney of the Council of the Indies, 14 February 1816, AGI, Chile, 313.
85. Decree of Osorio, 30 December 1814, ANFRA, vol. 3235, p. 1, ff. 2–2v.
86. Guerrero Lira, *Contrarrevolución de la independencia*, 213–40; Cid, *Pensar la revolución*, 97–98, 120–27.
87. Osorio to the Marquis of Concordia, 14 April 1815, AGI, Diversos, 4.
88. Report of the Surveillance Tribunal of Concepción, 22 June 1816, and Santiago's city council to Marcó del Pont, 1 July 1816, AGI, Chile, 207.

89. Committee of Surveillance and Public Safety to Marcó del Pont, 13 July 1816, AGI, Chile, 207.
90. Although royalists in Chile did not execute people as punishment for their iconoclastic "regicides," as happened in New Granada. See Gutiérrez, *Restauración en Nueva Granada*, 209–11.
91. See Barros Arana, *Historia Jeneral de Chile*, 10:616–17.
92. Valenzuela, *Fiesta*, 272–73. For how colonists and colonial officers used royal portraits to assert an imperial history of continued royal sovereignty and colonial rule, see Engel, *Pictured Politics*, 37–56 and 87–89.
93. Higgins to Santiago's city council, 20 June 1788, ANFCG, vol. 778, f. 59v.
94. Concha, "Manifiesto documentado," 20 January 1820, in CHDICH, 10:18–19; files concerning Ventura Pradel's request for reimbursement, 1817–1823, ANFRA, vol. 3235, p. 1.
95. Bladh, *La República de Chile*, 41–42; Mandiola, "Apuntes sobre la vida," esp. 248; Vicuña Mackenna, *Relaciones históricas*, 2:531; Eyzaguirre, *Viejas imágenes*, 55–70; Pereira Salas, *Historia del arte*, 314–15.
96. *Viva la Patria. Gazeta del Supremo Gobierno de Chile*, 11 June 1817.
97. See the testimonies of Gálvez and Arriagada in the trial of Ventura Astete, 21 June 1817, ANFMG, vol. 6.
98. Decree of O'Higgins, 22 March 1817, in *Boletin de las leyes, 1817–1818*, 31.
99. Barros Arana, *Historia Jeneral de la Independencia*, 4:17–18; Barros Arana, *Historia Jeneral de Chile*, 11:52; Montt, *Bibliografía chilena*, 3:45–46.
100. They would have been led by a renowned supporter of the Carrera family, Bartolo Araos. See Vicuña Mackenna, *Historia crítica*, 2:423.
101. Eyzaguirre, *Viejas imágenes*, 68–69.
102. Pinto and Valdivia, *¿Chilenos todos?*, 144–51; Cruz, *Patrimonio artístico*, 162–65.
103. As the intendancy's official newspaper explained. *Boletín de Policía*, 1 February 1825.
104. Decree of 20 January 1825, in *Boletín de Policía*, 1 February 1825. The only colonial street that was permanently modified was "King Street," already known as "State Street" by 1818. There were some precedents to this measure in Chile. See Cid, "Ritos," 31, 34; Cruz, *Patrimonio artístico*, 258–61.
105. Juan Egaña to Mariano Egaña, 30 January 1825, in Egaña, *Cartas*, 98.
106. On Gil de Castro see Majluf, *José Gil de Castro*.
107. Jocelyn-Holt, *Peso de la noche*, 85–92; Cruz, *Patrimonio artístico*, 43–67.
108. Majluf, "Cómo reemplazar." Majluf is skeptical of drawing broad conclusions based on this portrait. I believe that, while it may not have been intentionally iconoclastic, the portrait is illustrative of the new regime of historicity then emerging.
109. Jocelyn-Holt, *La Independencia de Chile*, 309–10; Peralta, *¡Chile tiene fiesta!*; Silva, *Identidad y nación*; Cid, "Ritos"; Valenzuela, *Fiesta*. For the celebration of heroes, see chapter 5. Some also considered establishing a monarchy in Chile. See Cid, *Pensar la revolución*, 139–50.
110. For the notion of a "transfer of sacrality" between colonial and revolutionary politics, see Thibaud, *Libérer le nouveau monde*, esp. 225–444. The term goes back to Mona Ozouf's influential *Festivals and the French Revolution*.
111. See, among others, Núñez Rius, "Estado"; Salazar, *Labradores*; Collier, *Chile*; Illanes, *Chile Des-centrado*; Grez, *"Regeneración del pueblo"*; Salazar, *Mercaderes*; Heise, *Años de formación*, 207–23.

112. I take the idea of the destruction of the sovereign's transcendent body from Foucault, "Les têtes de la politique," 9–10.
113. Defense of Mardones (also signed by another lawyer, José Gregorio Calderón), 1813, in CHDICH, 22:102–51.
114. Cf. Palti, *Archaeology of the Political*, esp. 101–3, Palti, *¿Ideas fuera de lugar?*, 31; and Dedieu, *Après le Roi*, esp. 103–5.
115. See Cid, "Ritos."
116. Juan Egaña to Mariano Egaña, 29 July 1824, in Egaña, *Cartas*, 48–49. This episode is also mentioned in Concha y Toro, *Chile durante los años*, 13, who follows Egaña so closely it seems he had access to his letter.
117. Juan Egaña to Mariano Egaña, 29 July 1824, in Egaña, *Cartas*, 49.
118. On the construction of O'Higgins and San Martín as heroes, see chapter 5.
119. Juan Egaña to Mariano Egaña, 29 July 1824, in Egaña, *Cartas*, 49.
120. Juan Egaña, "Memorias para la historia de la constitucion de Chile promulgada en 823," ANFV, vol. 792, p. 2, f. 56v.
121. Other than in Egaña's letter, Cañas was also described as African-descended in a list of supporters of General José Miguel Carrera written in 1817, in CHDICH, 43:411–13. He is mentioned as a "tailor" in Stuardo Ortíz and Eyzaguirre Escobar, *Santiago*, 8; and Grez, *"Regeneración del pueblo,"* 223–24. In 1817 he described his trade as shoemaker. See testimony of Cañas, 6 October 1817, and petition of Cañas, 1817, in CHDICH, 43:504 and 558. Cañas had achieved the status of a "master" artisan already in 1813, as can be appreciated in a list of donations to the government published that year. See *El Monitor Araucano*, 10 April 1813.
122. Testimony of Cañas, 6 October 1817, in CHDICH, 43:503–5. In early 1813 Cañas donated a large sum of money (12 pesos, which was closer to what rich men and women donated) to finance Carrera-led war efforts against royalists in Concepción. See *El Monitor Araucano*, 10 April 1813, as well as the files regarding donations in ANFSFL, vol. 27, p. 22.
123. Petition of Cañas, 1817, in CHDICH, 43:558–59.
124. Testimony of Cañas, 6 October 1817, in CHDICH, 43:503–5.
125. On perceptions of self-worth and the negotiation of racial relations in Spanish America, see, for example, Twinam, *Purchasing Whiteness*; Twinam, *Public Lives*; and Vinson, *Bearing Arms*.
126. Petition of Cañas, 1817, in CHDICH, 43:558–59.
127. Decree, 20 October 1817, in CHDICH, 43:559. Cañas did not stay out of trouble for long: in late 1823 he was imprisoned in one of Santiago's military headquarters for an undetermined "scandal." Santiago's intendant to the commander of the eighth battalion, 19 September 1823, ANFIS, vol. 1, f. 590v.
128. For more information on this organization and its political goals, see Grez, *"Regeneración del pueblo,"* 220–26, and Wood, *Society of Equality*, 48–78.
129. Cañas's participation is referenced in *Aviso importantísimo*.
130. *Refutación al aviso importantisimo*. They were not the only ones to mention Infante's role in the abolition of slavery during the presidential campaign. See *El Penquisto*, 7 April 1829, and *El Sepulturero*, 21 April 1829. For the association between his candidacy and equality, see also Wood, *Society of Equality*, 55–60.
131. Contreras, "Artesanos mulatos y soldados beneméritos"; Arancibia, "Soldado de la Independencia."
132. Nineteenth-century historian Benjamín Vicuña Mackenna claimed that his

father, Pedro Félix Vicuña, apparently a firsthand witness to these events, communicated this anecdote to him. See Vicuña Mackenna, *Vida del Capitán Jeneral*, 656.

133. Cf. Barros Arana, *Historia Jeneral de Chile*, 14:355–67; Barros Borgoño, *Misión del vicario apostólico*.
134. In 1821, for example, he read a poem praising O'Higgins during a ceremony organized by the government to celebrate Santiago's Afro-descendant military unit. Later, in 1823, liberals accused him of supporting a conservative faction during the elections. In 1824 he was in charge of the protection of the apostolic vicar then visiting Chile. See *Gazeta Ministerial de Chile*, 8 September 1821; Francisco Muñoz Bezanilla, Santiago Muñoz Bezanilla, and Orjera to the senate, 1823, in SCL, 7:237; Barros Borgoño, *Misión del vicario apostólico*, 141–42.
135. I thus disagree with historian María Eugenia Albornoz Vásquez, who has argued Romero offered "the ideal model for mixed-race Black men [*mestizos negros*]" in postcolonial Chile, which would have been to serve the country while "remaining in their proper place." Albornoz Vásquez, *Experiencias de conflicto*, 116–17.
136. Fureix, *Œil blessé*, 9.

Chapter Five

1. On imperial "emulation" see Paquette, *Enlightenment*, 30–55; and Adelman, "Mimesis and Rivalry."
2. *Semanario Republicano*, 18 November 1813.
3. *El Crisol*, 2 August 1829.
4. Lurquin to the junta, 30 September 1811, ANFSFL, vol. 32, p. 8.
5. Santiago's city council to the Minister of Government, February 1822, ANFRA, vol. 2160, ff. 169–70.
6. F. J. del C. O., *El precursor*, 10. The last sentence seems to be a quote from an unidentified source.
7. Pardo, "Cartilla del espejo, y desengaño," 1824, ANFV, vol. 30, ff. 2, 3, 5–5v, for the quotes, and 58–61v for similar ideas.
8. For similar views in late medieval and early modern France, see Merlin, *Public et littérature*, 61–70.
9. Valenzuela, *Maleficio*, 45; *Gazeta Ministerial de Chile*, 11 September and 2 October 1819.
10. Pastoral letter of Navarro, 1 June 1810, ANFSFL, vol. 103, p. 12.
11. *El Avisador de Valparaíso*, 2 July 1829.
12. Contreras, "Milicias de pardos," 114–16.
13. Fragment of a poem in praise of Manuela Larraín and her husband, Estanislao Portales, ANFV, vol. 259, ff. 36–49v, here 45.
14. On the representation of virtue and hierarchy in portraits, see chapter 2.
15. See Orrego to the Supreme Director, 1 January 1819, and Gormaz to the Supreme Director, 22 January 1819, ANFMI, vol. 7, ff. 46 and 48.
16. Decree of O'Higgins, 28 January 1819, ANFMI, vol. 7, ff. 48–48v.
17. Report of Pérez de Uriondo, 27 June 1805, in CHDICH, 43:75.
18. González Undurraga, "En busca de la libertad"; Pardo, "Cartilla del espejo, y desengaño," 1824, ANFV, vol. 30, f. 81v.; *El Agricultor*, February, 1842.
19. Benavides to the governor of Valdivia, 8 March 1782, ANFCG, vol. 774, f. 47.

20. Urra to the Audiencia, 1801, ANFRA, vol. 2162, p. 2, f. 58.
21. See the trial of Ovalle, 1816, ANFSFL, vol. 34, p. 12.
22. See, for example, the trial of eight enslaved men in Santiago in 1764–1765, ANFRA, vol. 297, ff. 1–58, further discussed in chapter 6, and the case against an enslaved man named Antonio in 1767–1768, reproduced in Arancibia, Cornejo, and González, *Pena de muerte*, 131–212.
23. See Leal Curiel, *Discurso de la fidelidad*, 203–10; Lempérière, *Entre Dieu et le Roi*, 211–14; Delgado, *Laywomen and Making Colonial Catholicism*, 119–23; Sellers-García, *Woman on the Windowsill*, 50–52, 84–85, and 221–22.
24. Fossier, "'Propter vitandum scandalum.'"
25. Bowen Silva, *Experimentar el cuerpo*, 52–57.
26. *El amigo social y verdadero ciudadano*, 13.
27. Quoted in Cornejo, *Manuela Orellana*, 37.
28. I examine alternative modes of assessing the public import of people's actions in chapter 8.
29. "Don Ignacio Francisco de Milán. Autos por injurias contra Manuel Fernández," reproduced in Contreras, "Usos y abusos." Milán's use of the concept of scandal was clearly strategic. Although he insisted that Fernández's insults were a "scandal," not all witnesses in the trial agreed. For disputes over the categorization of events as scandals or scandalous, see also Rojas, *Voces de la justicia*, 146–53 and 249–51.
30. Altolaguirre to the President, 1783, ANFCG, vol. 146, p. 9, ff. 224–24v.
31. Ugarte to the President, 14 September 1813, ANFSFL, vol. 33, p. 17. For more examples, see Santiago's intendant to the Supreme Director, 30 August 1819 and 26 July 1820, ANFIS, vol. 1, ff. 296v and 353v–54v.
32. See Gárate's complaint as well as Ustáriz's testimony in the case against Gacitúa, 1802, ANFRA, vol. 2625, p. 5, ff. 110–11 and 116v; García to Osorio, 12 January 1815, ANFSFL, vol. 33, p. 17; Santiago's intendant to the government, 21 May 1820, ANFIS, vol. 1, ff. 336v–37; and Tapia to the governor-intendant of Concepción, 1 June 1825, ANFIC, vol. 68, p. 11, f. 330.
33. Vicuña Mackenna, *Relaciones históricas*, 2:324; Santiago's intendant to Sánchez, 25 April 1823, ANFIS, vol. 1, ff. 455–55v; decree of Echeverría, 2 December 1813, AGI, Chile, 315; Otaolaurruchi to the interim commissioner, 1801, ANFRA, vol. 1444, p. 3, f. 85v.
34. While the content and emphasis of imperial propaganda changed according to official and diplomatic needs, the king was always presented as a hero. See, for example, Víctor Mínguez, "Del rey pacífico." Colonial groups often interpreted the king's heroism according to their own interests. During royal funerals, for example, religious authorities seized the opportunity to present the deceased monarch as an example of religiosity and respect for the church, virtues they sometimes argued were lacking among local secular authorities. Cruz, *La muerte*, 192–230; Valenzuela, "Sermones contra la autoridad."
35. Valenzuela, *Fiesta*, 27–64.
36. See, for example, "Theatro del dolor," ca. 1761, ANFV, vol. 259, ff. 8–32; Egaña, "Oracion inaugural para la apertura de los Estudios de la Real Universidad de San Felipe," 1804, ANFV, vol. 274, ff. 124–34; Santiago's royal university to the President, 7 May 1808, ANFV, vol. 418, ff. 184–84v.
37. Fernández Sebastián, *Historia conceptual*, 299–307.
38. Project of regulation of the press, 1817, ANFSFL, vol. 38, p. 3, ff. 2–2v.
39. Monteagudo, *Relacion de la gran fiesta*, 6–8.

40. Gazmuri, "Los modelos políticos."
41. According to Amunátegui, *Crónica de 1810*, 1:139–41, who saw the manuscript.
42. Claro to Montt, 26 January [1831], ANFVM, vol. 112, ff. 79–80.
43. On the contested fabrication of Washington as a hero in postcolonial United States, see Newman, *Parades and Politics*.
44. *Semanario Republicano*, 30 October 1813; *El Avisador Chileno*, 10 April 1824.
45. *Semanario de Policía*, 22 October 1817.
46. On this elite reinterpretation of Native history as part of Chile's history, see Casanova, "Entre la ideología y la realidad."
47. Cf. Pagden, *Spanish Imperialism*; Cañizares-Esguerra, *How to Write History*.
48. "Apuntes auto-biográficos del Jeneral don Francisco Antonio Pinto," BNMSBA, vol. 98.
49. For this discourse of "race war," see Thibaud, "La ley y la sangre."
50. Collier, *Ideas and Politics*, 212–17; Casanova, "Entra la ideología y la realidad"; Gallardo, "Héroes indómitos"; Pinto, *Formación del Estado*, 88–130; Peralta, "Ni por la razón"; Pinto and Valdivia, *¿Chilenos todos?*, 58–61; Stuven and Cid, *Debates republicanos en Chile*, 2:429–505; Enríquez, "La República chilena"; Cartes, "¿Bárbaros o ciudadanos?."
51. On these heroes, see Huidobro, *El imaginario*, 271–95.
52. Egaña, *Almanak nacional*, 5–23.
53. Peralta, "Ni por la razón"; Marimán Quemenado, "La República."
54. Earle, *Return of the Native*.
55. *El Valdiviano Federal*, 8 July 1831.
56. Rojas to Buenos Aires' Junta, 29 December 1811, in Ministerio de Relaciones Exteriores y Culto, *Diplomacia de la Revolución*, 2:199.
57. *Méritos del cura Uribe* [1840?]. This printed brochure can be found in ANFMI, vol. 3, ff. 179–80.
58. *El Monitor Araucano*, 25 May and 19 August 1813. Similar references to heroic or martyred officers deceased during the war can be found in *El Monitor Araucano*, 22 June, 22 July, 24 August, and 20 November 1813.
59. *El Monitor Araucano*, 11 March 1814.
60. Juan Egaña to Mariano Egaña, 19 February 1825, in Egaña, *Cartas*, 102. See also *El Correo de Arauco*, 14 July 1824.
61. *El Monitor Araucano*, 31 August 1813. On this event and Ezeiza's posterity as a royalist hero, see Betancourt Castillo, *Ezeiza*, 287–306.
62. Report of Santiago's city council, 9 December 1814, ANFMG, vol 6, p. 1.
63. See *Viva el Rey. Gazeta del Gobierno de Chile*, 6 December 1816.
64. See, *Gazeta Extraordinaria del Gobierno de Chile*, 19 December 1814; and the issues of *Viva el Rey. Gazeta del Gobierno de Chile*, 17 August and 28 December 1815, 27 August, 10 September, 27 September, 8 October, 22 October, and 6 December 1816, 3 January 1817.
65. Ossa, *Armies*, 57–58.
66. See, for example, *Gazeta Ministerial de Chile*, 13 and 20 June, 31 October, and 12 December 1818, 10 April 1819, 15, 21, 23, 25 August, 13 and 20 October 1821, and 28 July 1822; *El Telégrafo*, 18 February 1820; O'Higgins, *Manifiesto del Capitán General*; *Mercurio de Chile*, nums. 4 and 9, 1822; *El Cosmopolita*, 20 December 1822.
67. There were nevertheless some efforts to present them as heroes. See *El Observador de Chile*, 16 July 1823; *El Patriota Chileno*, 3 February and 22 July 1826; and *El Penquisto*, 7 April 1829.

68. The phrase "our hero" can be found in Claro to Arís, 1832, in ANFVM, vol. 112, f. 112; and Claro to Albano, 27 July 1832, ANFVM, vol. 92, f. 140. The pasquinades, which are dated 1824 and 1825, can be found in ANFVM, vol. 92, ff. 16–17v and 24–24v. See also *Clamor de la Patria* 3 May 1823; and *El O'Higginista*, 18 January, 1 and 12 February 1831. For criticisms of O'Higgins, see *El Tizón Republicano*, 5 and 12 May 1823; *El Avisador Chileno*, 10 April 1824; *El Patriota Chileno*, 10 August 1826; and *El Insurgente Araucano*, 10 February 1827.
69. Examples in *El Tizón Republicano*, 5 May 1823; *El Avisador Chileno*, 11 August 1824; *El Correo de Arauco*, 9 October 1824; Juan Egaña to Mariano Egaña, 19 February 1825, in Egaña, *Cartas*, 102–3; *El Monitor Imparcial*, 10 October 1827; *El Minero de Coquimbo*, 3 May 1828; *La Clave*, 17 February 1829. Criticisms of these figures can be found in *Clamor de la Patria*, 14 May 1823; and *El Indicador*, 14 February 1827.
70. See particularly *La Clave*, 16 June 1828; Arís to O'Higgins, 19 June 1828, in ABO 33:34; *El Vijía*, 26 June 1828; *Premio postumo*; *Suplemento al Vijía*.
71. *Premio postumo*.
72. Varas, *Lecciones elementales de moral*, 44.
73. I take the concept of mimetic drive from Schaeffer, *Pourquoi la fiction?*
74. Cano, *La mujer en el Reyno de Chile*, esp. 519–649; Figueroa, "El honor femenino"; Serrano and Correa, "Patriota o sarracena"; Undurraga, *Los rostros del honor*, 189–97. Although not the subject of this chapter, it should be noted that women used models of religious and domestic virtues in heterodox and unexpected ways. See, for example, Kordic, *Epistolario*; and Araya, "Beatas en Chile colonial."
75. For this ideal of radiating influence, see Serrano, "Religiosas modernas," 88.
76. For concerns about royalist women, see *Viva la Patria. Gazeta del Supremo Gobierno de Chile*, 11 June 1817; *Gazeta de Santiago de Chile*, 18 June 1817; *Semanario de Policía*, 20 March 1818; [Verdugo], *Clamor de la justicia*; [Verdugo], *Clamor de la justicia: continuación del diálogo*.
77. *Gazeta de Santiago de Chile*, 18 June 1817.
78. Decree of Quintana, 8 August 1817, *Gazeta de Santiago de Chile*, 23 August 1817; Patricia Peña, ". . . Y las mujeres." Many other women also petitioned for funds as widows, wives, or mothers of virtuous male citizens. See Serrano and Correa, "Patriota o sarracena."
79. Decree of O'Higgins, 2 December 1818, in *Gazeta Ministerial de Chile*, 5 December 1818.
80. Rosales del Solar to the director, 18 December 1817, *Gazeta de Santiago de Chile*, 24 January 1818. For the importance of lint, see the government's call to women to donate lint in early 1818 in *Gazeta de Santiago de Chile*, 7 March 1818.
81. Decree of Cruz, 20 December 1817, *Gazeta de Santiago de Chile*, 24 January 1818.
82. Anonymous, *Ilustres Americanas*.
83. Pérez de Arza remained in Santiago in charge of her husband's trade. Her position was described by one of her adversaries in 1828 as that of a modest merchant. See Errázuriz, *Segundo manifiesto*.
84. Petition of Pérez de Arza, 12 December 1814, AGI, Chile, 208; and petition of Pérez de Arza, n.d., AGI, Diversos, 4.
85. Decree of Osorio, 13 January 1815, AGI, Diversos, 4.
86. Petition of Pérez de Arza, 28 February 1815, AGI, Diversos, 4.

87. Pérez de Arza to the viceroy, 13 March 1815, AGI, Diversos, 4.
88. See *Mercurio de España*, March 1807; *Romance*.
89. Pérez de Arza to the viceroy, 13 March 1815, AGI, Diversos, 4.
90. For these gendered views of political participation, see Chambers, *Families in War*.
91. Petition of Pérez de Arza, 28 February 1815, AGI, Diversos, 4.
92. Pérez de Arza to the viceroy, n.d. [1815], AGI, Diversos, 4.
93. Pérez de Arza to the viceroy, 11 July 1815, AGI, Diversos, 4.
94. See the journal of Salas in *Escritos de don Manuel de Salas*, 2:37 and 42.
95. Montt, *Bibliografía chilena*, 3:81.
96. Errázuriz, *Segundo manifiesto*.
97. Petition of Arza, [1819], ANFCG, vol. 1050, ff. 313–13v.
98. See Pérez de Arza, *Maria Ana Pérez de Arza*; and Pérez de Arza, *Contestacion al segundo manifiesto*.

Chapter Six

1. *Viva el Rey. Gazeta del Gobierno de Chile*, 16, 23, 30 January; 6, 13, 22, 27 February; 5, 12, 19, 29 March; and 9 April 1816. For more on this gazette and the royalist discourse, see Guerrero Lira, *Contrarrevolución de la independencia*, 213–40; Cid, *Pensar la revolución*, 93–102.
2. See, among a vast literature, Schultz, *Tropical Versailles*, 101–49; Williams, "'Who Induced?'"; Fradkin, *Historia de una montonera*; Malandain, *L'introuvable complot*.
3. Ferrer, *Freedom's Mirror*, esp. 46–47; Polasky, *Revolutions without Borders*, esp. 136–71; Soriano, *Tides of Revolution*, esp. 91, 256–57; Marks, *Black Freedom*.
4. Malandain, *L'introuvable complot*. For reason-giving as a social and political activity, see also Tilly, *Why?*; and Boltanski, *Énigmes et complots*.
5. See Fossier, "La contagion des péchés." The origins of this notion of contagion as the dangerous transmission of unorthodox beliefs can be traced back to ancient Greece. See Jarcho, *Concept of Contagion*.
6. See Nesvig, *Ideology and Inquisition*; Stearns, *Infectious Ideas*, esp. 52–54.
7. See, for example, the communications of Santiago's intendant to various authorities in August 1825, ANFIS, vol. 1, ff. 773v–75. Ordinary people similarly feared and took measures to avoid being contaminated by contagious diseases. See Caffarena Barcenilla, *Viruela y vacuna*.
8. Ibid., 45–51 and 68–81.
9. Blest, *Ensayo sobre las causas*. For similar appraisals of the origins of diseases and how to treat them, see *Aurora de Chile*, 5 March 1812; *Mercurio de Chile*, no. 5, 1822; *El Mercurio Chileno*, 1 July 1828; *El Mercurio de Valparaíso*, 13 September 1828.
10. To quote Bourdieu's reflection on the notion of class "What Makes a Social Class?," 8. For the body as a political concept in the Iberian Atlantic during the Age of Revolutions, see Fernández Sebastián, *Historia conceptual*, 333–39; and, for an earlier period, Leal Curiel, *Discurso de la fidelidad*, 221–55.
11. Talavera, "Revoluciones de Chile," in CHDICH, 29:38–39.
12. Rodríguez Zorilla to Rodríguez, 26 August 1810, in CHDICH, 9:48.
13. *La Antorcha*, 20 October 1839. A similar view in *El Interrogante y Respondente*, 13 March 1823; and *El Tizón Republicano*, 5 May 1823.
14. See *Clamor del estado religioso*; and Rodríguez Zorilla to Rodríguez, 27 August 1810, in CHDICH, 9:50 for the quotes. See also Carrera to the junta,

11 May 1812, in CHDICH, 23:31–34; the decree of the junta, 17 February 1813, in CHDICH, 24:273–274; Marcó del Pont to the Marquis of Concordia, 20 May 1816, AGI, Diversos, 4; Vial to the Interim Director, 2 May 1817, in ABO, 22:212–14; and the report of Quintana, Santiago, 15 September 1817, in CHDICH, 43:466.

15. See, among many similar examples, García Carrasco to the Viceroy of Peru, 19 October 1810, in CHDICH, 9:34; O'Higgins to the senate, 14 December 1818, SCL, 2:139–40; Freire, *El Director Supremo*, 3; Chillán's city council to Santiago's Junta, 11 February 1830, ANFMI, vol. 16, f. 255. This schema matched that of the Roman Catholic church in the Spanish realms, as discussed in chapter 7.
16. Salas to Rojas, 4 June 1774, ANFV, vol. 118, ff. 49–50v, f. 50 for the quote. See also the letters Salas sent to Rojas dated 4 October and 2 December 1774, 30 January and 9 September 1776, 28 March 1782, as well as two incomplete and undated letters, in ANFV, vol. 118, ff. 53–54, 55–55v, 61–68, 73–74v, 93–94, 106–7v, and 114–15v.
17. Egaña, "Oracion inaugural para la apertura de los Estudios de la Real Universidad de San Felipe," ANFV, vol. 274, ff. 124–34.
18. Egaña, "Discurso sobre el ámor de la Patria," BNSM, A-36-2(32) p. 10.
19. Talavera, "Revoluciones de Chile," in CHDICH, 29:35.
20. Talavera, "Revoluciones de Chile," in CHDICH, 29:317.
21. See Torres, "Advertencias precautorias a los habitantes de Chile," in Amunátegui, *Crónica de 1810*, 1:187, for the quote.
22. See, for example, the manifesto of Concha, 2 April 1813, AGI, Chile, 207; García to the President, 11 December 1816, ANFSFL, vol. 33, p. 50.
23. Barros Arana, *Historia Jeneral de Chile*, 9:628–34.
24. Royal order of 31 July 1814, copied in Osorio to Martínez, 23 May 1815, AGI, Chile, 313.
25. Martínez, "Memoria Histórica," in CHDICH, 42(1):11–26.
26. Vigarello, *Pratiques de santé*, 57.
27. Higgins to Campo de Alange, 6 December 1790, ANFCG, vol. 786, ff. 134–36v.
28. Adelman, "The Rites of Statehood," 396–99; Rosas Lauro, *Del trono a la guillotina*, 167–77, 181–93; Ferrer, *Freedom's Mirror*; Soriano, *Tides of Revolution*, esp. 85–91.
29. See the testimony of Calvo, 12 June 1795; and those of Álvarez, Maurichanis, and Durán, all taken 15 June 1795, in ANFJLS, leg. 64, p. 7.
30. "Pastoral del Obispo de la Concepcion Don Diego Antonio Navarro Martin de Villodres al hacerse cargo de su obispado en 1° de junio de 1810," ANFSFL, vol. 103, p. 12. See also Guardino, *The Time of Liberty*, 126 and 131; and Schultz, *Tropical Versailles*, 111–12.
31. Petition of García, n.d. [1813], in AGI, Lima, 746, no. 66.
32. García Carrasco to the king, 27 August and 8 September 1810, in CHDICH, 9:3–31.
33. See, for example, José María Esponda to Antonio Esponda, 12 December 1811, in ANFMG, vol. 6.
34. Talavera, "Revoluciones de Chile," 3, 417, 464–65, and 527.
35. "Catecismo Politico para instruccion de la juventud del Reyno de Chile," ca. 1810, AGI, Diversos, 2; Talavera, "Revoluciones de Chile," in CHDICH, 29:274–75.
36. I follow here the testimony of the emissary himself, Estanislao Varela, 9 May 1815, ANFSFL, vol. 35, p. 13.

37. Aldunate to Irigoyen, 14 May 1814, AGI, Diversos, 3; Santiago's merchant guild to the king, 20 July 1815, AGI, Chile, 445.
38. Talavera, "Revoluciones de Chile," in CHDICH, 29:341 for the quotes. I have translated as "devil" the more specific word "Belial" that Talavera uses to describe the government of Buenos Aires. See also ibid., 47, 165–66, 172, 247, 317, 529, and 640–41 for more examples of Talavera's interest in agents sent by Napoleon and Buenos Aires's government.
39. Proclamation, 15 July 1811, in ibid., 345. Reactions to Carlota's plans in Chile are analyzed in more detail in Amunátegui, *Crónica de 1810*, 1:312–24; Meza Villalobos, *Actividad política*, 59–60 and 77–78; and Hernández Ponce, "Carlota Joaquina de Borbón," 137–65.
40. For similar fears elsewhere in Spanish America, see Guardino, *The Time of Liberty*, 183–86; Méndez, *Plebeian Republic*, 60–62.
41. Freire to Cauquenes's city council, 26 January 1819, ANFMI, vol. 15, f. 66.
42. Freire to the Supreme Director, 26 January 1819, ANFMI, vol. 15, f. 68v. Prieto was a supporter of the Carrera family and in 1819 led an unsuccessful armed insurrection against the O'Higgins government.
43. Lynch to O'Higgins, 20 January 1825, ANFVM, vol. 88, f. 74v; petition of González, 1827, ANFV, vol. 121, ff. 81–81v; Claro to Prieto, 28 July 1829, ANFVM, vol. 97, ff. 73–84v. For similar though less explicit examples, see *La Clave*, 16 August and 12 October 1827, and *El Sepulturero*, 16 and 22 August 1828.
44. Mongey, "Vagabonds de la république"; Guardino, *Time of Liberty*, 128–31.
45. See the communications of these agents in Ministerio de Relaciones Exteriores y Culto, *Diplomacia de la Revolución*.
46. Collier and Feliú Cruz, *Primera misión*, 32–57.
47. For Carlota's politics and Dowling's mission in Chile, see Ternavasio, *Candidata a la corona*, esp. 97–98; Amunátegui, *Crónica de 1810*, 1:312–24; and Hernández Ponce, "Carlota Joaquina de Borbón," 137–65.
48. Talavera, "Revoluciones de Chile," in CHDICH, 29:640–41.
49. Castro to the Junta of the United Provinces of the Río de la Plata, 11 October 1811, in Ministerio de Relaciones Exteriores y Culto, *Diplomacia de la Revolución*, 2:51.
50. Castro to the Junta of Río de la Plata, 9 December 1811, in ibid., 2:173–74.
51. Vera to the government of Río de la Plata, 10 January 1812, in ibid., 2:208.
52. Trial of Castilla (alias Antonio Cantuarias), 1821, ANFJSC, leg. 1596, p. 2.
53. Petition of Marín, 1819, ANFCG, vol. 335, p. 5, ff. 295–96.
54. Ossa, *Armies*, 96–102.
55. Vera, "Relacion de las cosas que noté y advertí en el Puerto de San Carlos de Chiloe y de las noticias que adquiri por informes reservados," 12 February 1822, ANFV, vol. 127, ff. 63–63v; friar Almirall to O'Higgins, 13 August 1826, ANFVM, vol. 88, ff. 120–20v; "Diario de campaña de Guillermo de Vic Tupper," in Tupper, *Memorias del Coronel Tupper*, 118.
56. Petition of Campos [Coñuepan], 1825, ANFIC, vol. 84. I would like to thank Hugo Contreras for showing me this document. On Coñuepan's political activities, see León, *O'Higgins y la cuestión mapuche*; Zarley, "Lof and Liberators"; and Pairican, *Toqui*. In 1816, royalist governor Marcó del Pont feared that Coñuepán might persuade other Mapuche people to join the revolutionary camp. See Ossa, *Armies*, 74. Claude Gay, who traveled extensively among the Mapuches later, reproduced what he claimed was one of

Coñuepan's oral interventions in favor of the new regime in late 1823 in Gay, *Historia física*, 8:288–89.

57. "Instrucciones reservadas que deberá observar el Capitan General del Egército de los Andes Don José de San Martin en las operaciones de la campaña destinada a la reconquista de Chile," 21 December 1816, BNMSBA, vol. 2. A similar reference from the government of Río de la Plata can be found in Ossa, *Armies*, 95.
58. Beauchef, *Memorias de Jorge Beauchef*, 139.
59. This tactic and its distorting effects in the documentation are further examined in Patch, *Maya Revolt*; and Penry, *People are King*. For additional discussions about how colonial trials construct leadership narratives, see Van Young, *Other Rebellion*, esp. 91–125; and Finch, *Rethinking Slave Rebellion*, esp. 168–98.
60. Although this question is not recorded in the transcript, reading the witnesses' testimonies makes it clear that Zañartu asked it of all the prisoners.
61. Trial of several enslaved men, Santiago, 1764, ANFCG, vol. 297, ff. 1–58.
62. See the legal proceedings concerning this case in ANFRA, vol. 2162, p. 2, ff. 44–100v, ff. 76–79 for the quote.
63. Echavarría to Recabarren, 21 March 1818, ANFICO, vol. 6.
64. See Echavarría to Recabarren, 30 March 1818, for the quotes, as well as Vicuña to Recabarren, 30 and 31 March, 4 April 1818, and the criminal investigation into the events in Illapel, 1818, all in ANFICO, vol. 6; Orrego to the Supreme Director, 23 March 1818, ANFMI, vol. 7, ff. 17v–19; and O'Higgins to the senate, 22 January 1819, SCL, 2:230–31.
65. Trial for conspiracy, 1814, CHDICH, 9:321–82; trial of Gaspar and others, Concepción, 1817, ANFMG, vol. 7; trial of Tagle, Quillota, 1817, ANFCG, vol. 336, p. 12; trial of Mena, Quillota, 1818, ANFCG, vol. 334, p. 2, ff. 51–62; trial of Bazán, Cauquenes, 1819, ANFJCA, caja 3, p. 16; trial of Cerda, Los Andes, 1819, ANFMI, vol. 5, ff. 87–89v; trial of González and others, San Fernando, 1823, ANFCG, vol. 337, p. 2; trial of several men accused of sedition, Quillota, 1825, ANFCG, vol. 337, p. 6; trial of several men involved in a mutiny, San Fernando, 1828, ANFRA, vol. 2460, p. 11; trial of the students of Santiago's National Institute, Santiago, 1833, ANFCG, vol. 338, p. 1; trial of Bazán and others, Santiago, 1840, ANFJSC, leg. 1588, p. 1; trial of Baes, Soloaga, and Castillo, Santiago, 1841, ANFJSC, leg. 1588, p. 2.
66. Testimony of Pacheco, 11 October 1825, ANFCG, vol. 337, p. 6, ff. 194–195, 195 for the quote.
67. Criminal investigation of Barrera and others, 1824, ANFIC, vol. 68, p. 10, ff. 172–329v, f. 328 for the quote.
68. Vista of Rodríguez Aldea, 1 July 1815, in CHDICH, 35:220–22. The wider population was aware of this. See Fernández, "Sangre por sangre"; and, for neighboring Buenos Aires, Fradkin, "Cultura política," 48–50.
69. Kuethe and Andrien, *Spanish Atlantic World*, 91. For the application of this strategy during the revolutionary period see Van Young, *Other Rebellion*, 111–25.
70. *Voto consultivo* (legal opinion) of the Audiencia to the president, 27 July 1815, in CHDICH, 35:149–52; Guerrero Lira, *Contrarrevolución de la independencia*, 137–85.
71. Abascal, "Instrucciones que deberá observar el coronel don Mariano Osorio en el mando del ejército real de Concepción de Chile," 18 July 1814, in CHDICH, 4:148–60, 156 for the quote. A detailed study of exile in Juan Fernández during

the royalist government in Guerrero Lira, *Contrarrevolución de la independencia*, 119–35.

72. Ossa, *Armies*, 60–61.
73. Royal decree of 1 February 1816, in CHDICH, 35:163–64.
74. *Voto consultivo* of the Audiencia to the president, 27 July 1815, and vista of Rodríguez Aldea, 18 January 1816, in CHDICH, 35:149 and 194. See also the vista of Rodríguez Aldea, 1 July 1815, in CHDICH, 35:220–22.
75. Real cédula, 1 February 1816, in CHDICH, 35:163–64. The discussions leading to the royal pardon in Collar to Chile's president, 23 January 1816, ANFSFL, vol. 33, p. 21.
76. For Pérez de Arza, see chapter 5. Reyes was an influential colonial official. Esterripa was the widow of former governor Luis Muñoz de Guzmán and had important political connections in the colony. Gaínza was the leader of the royalist army until the arrival in Chile of Mariano Osorio. For their participation in this political faction, see Pérez de Arza to the viceroy of Perú, [1815], 17 June, 11 July, and 31 October 1815, and María Ana Pérez de Arza, Manuela de Arza, Dolores de Arza, and Miguel de Arza to the Marquis of Concordia, 16 April 1816, AGI, Diversos, 4.
77. See Ossa, *Armies*, 66. For the governor's attitude toward political repression, see Marcó del Pont to Abascal, 20 January, 15 April, 20 May, 18 June, 10 September 1816, and 28 January 1817, AGI, Diversos, 4.
78. Cf. Guerrero Lira, *Contrarrevolución de la independencia*, 161–67.
79. Marcó del Pont, "Razon de los individuos comprometidos en la revolucion de este Reino," 30 October 1816, AGI, Chile, 208.
80. "Testimonio de varios informes sobre el indulto concedido por S.M. a los rebolucionarios del año 00," 7 January 1817, AGI, Chile, 206.

Chapter Seven

1. Benavides to Higgins, 19 July 1784, ANFCG, vol. 775, ff. 117–17v; "Noticia de los principales acahecimientos"; Walker, *Tupac Amaru Rebellion*, 253–55; Moreno, "'Si se hiciera lo de acá se extinguiría en todas partes,'" esp. 42–45; Ortíz Sotelo, *La Real Armada*, esp. 145–47; Moreno Cebrián and Chauca García, "Los ecos indianos."
2. Quoted in Moreno, "'En todas partes,'" 44.
3. Minutes of the meeting in Los Ángeles, 28 November 1781, ANFMV, vol. 20, ff. 18–23v, here 19v. See also the minutes of the meeting in Los Ángeles, April 1781, ANFMV, vol. 20, ff. 7–9v.
4. Cf. Schwartz, *All Can Be Saved*; Martínez, *Genealogical Fictions*; Nesvig, *Ideology and Inquisition*.
5. The order reached towns as remote as San Juan Bautista, a frontier outpost south of Concepción. See the dossier concerning this royal order in ANFV, vol. 913, p. 8, ff. 132–33. Antonio Vergne describes what appears to have been a copy of this book being seized by authorities in Santiago in early 1780. See "No. 2. Copia del segundo borrador," ANFRA, vol. 1664, p. 2, f. 365v.
6. Thomson, "Sovereignty Disavowed," 407–13.
7. See chapter 6.
8. Domergue, *Le livre en Espagne*. While censorship decreased after 1792, the idea that the revolutionary contagion needed to be contained was never abandoned.

9. Rosas Lauro, *Del trono a la guillotina*, 181–93. For Chile, see Amunátegui, *Precursores de la independencia*, 1:248–51; Higgins to López de Lerena, 14 November 1791, and to Gardoqui, 8 December 1793, ANFCG, vol. 786, ff. 447v and 541; Higgins to the governors of Concepción and Valparaíso, and to the administrator of the customs office, 10 December 1791, ANFCG, vol. 782, f. 544; Higgins to Chile's military governors, the administrator of the customs office, and the commissioner of Coquimbo, 7 December 1793, ANFCG, vol. 783, ff. 478–78v.
10. On this increased traffic, see Amunátegui, *Precursores de la independencia*, 1:293–305; Donoso, *El Marqués de Osorno*, 254–69; and Pereira Salas, *Primeros contactos*.
11. Higgins to the governors of Juan Fernández, Valdivia, and Valparaíso, and the intendant of Concepción, 30 January 1792, ANFCG, vol. 782, ff. 546v–50v. See also Higgins to Porlier, 5 April 1791, ANFCG, vol. 786, ff. 5v–10.
12. Muñoz de Guzmán to "Citizen Fhalir" [William Shaler?], 13 April 1802, ANFCG, vol. 789, ff. 134–34v, 134 for the quotes; Barros Arana, *Historia Jeneral de Chile*, 7:37–38; Pereira Salas, *Primeros contactos*, 308–9.
13. Multiple such orders can be found in ANFCG, vols. 782 and 783. For overviews of these efforts, see Donoso, *El Marqués de Osorno*, 254–69; and Pereira Salas, *Primeros contactos*.
14. Donoso, *El Marqués de Osorno*, 259–60, and 264.
15. Higgins to the governor of Valparaíso, 29 February and 11 March 1792, to the intendant of Concepción, 5 and 9 March 1792, ANFCG, vol. 782, ff. 155–56v, 159, and 407v–9; Higgins to Godoy, 10 March and 12 April 1792, ANFCG, vol. 786, 199v–202v, and 217v–18v.
16. Higgins to Llaguno, 17 September 1795, ANFCG, vol. 786, ff. 101–1v.
17. Higgins to the guard of the principal road of the Andes, 9 April 1795, ANFCG, vol. 784, ff. 154v–55, for the quote. See also Higgins to the governor of Valparaíso, the commissioner of Coquimbo, bishop Marán, and the guard of the road of Portillo, 9 April 1795, ANFCG, vol. 784, ff. 102, 155–55v, 16v–17, and 204.
18. See Higgins to the governor of Valparaíso, 29 August and 26 November 1794, to González, 26 November 1794, ANFCG, vol. 783, ff. 172v–73, 182–82v, and 244v; Higgins to González, 5 and 13 January 1795, ANFCG, vol. 784, f. 142v and 144. For the expulsion of Trimalle and Porré from Perú, see Rosas Lauro, *Del trono a la guillotina*, 202–3.
19. Higgins to Marán, 16 January 1796, ANFCG, vol. 784, ff. 52–52v.
20. All quotes come from a petition García addressed to the government, n.d. [1813], AGI, Lima, 746, no. 66. See also the dossier concerning García's merits in AGI, Lima, 746, no. 66.
21. For the mail, see, for example, García Carrasco to the king, 8 September 1810, AGI, Chile, 206; Talavera, "Revoluciones de Chile," in CHDICH, 29:59, 108–9, 515–16, 545–46. For the 1813 ban, see Junta to the Customs Administrator, 6 April 1813, in *El Monitor Araucano*, 8 April 1813. For the prophylactic logic behind such measures, see "Plan presentado al congreso para reforma del nuevo gobierno," 1811, reproduced in Talavera, "Revoluciones de Chile," in CHDICH, 29:425–30.
22. There are multiple examples of these efforts in ANFMI vols. 5, 7, 9, 10, 13, and 15. See also the trial against the Carrera brothers and their accomplices, 1817, in CHDICH, 43:373–565.

23. See, for example, the efforts to enforce spatial segregation between the Spanish and Natives in Guarda, *Historia urbana*, 189–90. For studies of spatial segregation and race in colonial Spanish America, see Nemser, *Infrastructures of Race*; and García, *Beyond the Walled City*. For a critical reassessment of the actual relevance and implementation of colonial segregation policies, see Masters, "The Two."
24. Ruiz, "Comunidades y cacicazgos."
25. Report of Mascayano and Jiménez, 2 July 1823, ANFRA, vol. 2629, p. 1, ff. 36–37v, 36 for the quote.
26. On the virtues of deportation in the official discourse, see Cordero Fernández, "Destierro a la isla," 439–49.
27. Vigarello, *Pratiques de santé*, 91–108, 119–20.
28. Talavera, "Revoluciones de Chile," in CHDICH, 29:522.
29. Gandarillas to Benavente, 22 February 1825, ANFV, vol. 821, f. 134.
30. Edict of Guill y Gonzaga, 5 February 1764, ANFV, vol. 321, ff. 32–33; edict of Jáuregui, 7 June 1773, ANFV, vol. 111, ff. 8–15; "Bando de buen gobierno," 62, 66.
31. See Valenzuela, *Maleficio*, 48 and 55; Cornejo, *Manuela Orellana*, 127; the trial for conspiracy against several men in Santiago, 1811, ANFV, vol. 156; the vistas of Crown attorney Rodríguez Aldea, 1815–1816, in CHDICH, 35:169–378; Zenteno to O'Higgins, 23 December 1828, ANFVM, vol. 92, ff. 62–63v; "Razon de los reos prosesados por el Jues del Crimen desde el mes de Marzo del año pasado de ochocientos treinta y uno con instruccion de sus delitos y penas," 6 September 1833, ANFIS, vol. 3, esp. f. 86.
32. Araya, *Ociosos*, 60–62.
33. See, among multiple examples, the edict of Guill y Gonzaga, 24 March 1763, ANFV, vol. 321, ff. 21–22; Benavides to the Audiencia, 20 July 1785, ANFCG, vol. 776, ff. 26–28; Higgins to the Audiencia, 26 June 1788, to the commissioners of Talca, Colchagua, Rancagua, Melipilla, Quillota, and Aconcagua, 24 October 1788, and to Jaraquemada, 9 December 1788, ANFCG, vol. 778, ff. 61v, 416v–17v, 114v–15v; Higgins to the commissioner of Colchagua, 2 November 1790, and to the commissioner of Rancagua, 11 December 1790, ANFCG, vol. 780, ff. 439v and 441v; Higgins to the Audiencia, 2 April 1794, ANFCG, vol. 783, ff. 98v–99; Higgins to Rezabal, 1 September 1795, to Alava, 7 March 1796, to the commissioners of Colchagua, Rancagua, and Aconcagua, 2 April 1796, and Avilés to the commissioners of Curicó and Cauquenes, 28 November 1796, ANFCG, vol. 784, ff. 37, 274v, 401, and 413v–14; and Muñoz de Guzmán to the Audiencia, 27 August 1803, ANFCG, vol. 789, f. 69v–71. Eva Maria Mehl found a similar pattern in her study of deportations in colonial Mexico. See Mehl, *Forced Migration*, esp. 119–93.
34. Report of the notaries of the Audiencia, 19 June 1798, AGI, Chile, 226.
35. Valparaíso, Chiloé, and Concepción also served as penal colonies, although they were of lesser importance. See Guarda, *Historia urbana*, 137.
36. León, *Encierro y corrección*, 1:116–25 and 2:273–94; Guarda, *Historia de Valdivia*, 166–70; Cordero Fernández, "Destierro a la isla."
37. See Benavides to Valdivieso, 9 May 1783, ANFCG, vol. 775, ff. 241v–42; and Benavides to Álvarez Acevedo, 17 February 1785, ANFCG, vol. 776, f. 9v. Similar cases can be found in Pereira Larraín, *Afectos e intimidades*, 267–68.
38. Higgins to Vicente, 26 August 1789, ANFCG, vol. 780, ff. 191v–92, for the quotes.

39. All quotes come from documentation cited in Araya, *Ociosos*, 66.
40. Sentence of Zañartu, 25 March 1765, ANFCG, vol. 297, ff. 53–53v.
41. Quoted in León, *Encierro y corrección*, 2:305–6.
42. Two representative examples in council of war of Valdivia, 21 March 1812, in CHDICH, 23:42–54; and the testimony of Mapuche logko Mariluan, 9 October 1827, ANFIC, vol. 68, p. 20, ff. 489–91.
43. Examples of deportations such as these abound. See Talavera to Quiroz, 15 September 1811, in CHDICH, 30:ccc–cccx; "Reos que existen presos en varios puntos," 1813, and "Lista de los Sarracenos presos," 23 July 1814, in CHDICH, 23:179–91 and 451–53; O'Higgins, "Instrucciones reservadas que ha de observar el Coronel graduado Don Jorje Beaucheff," 18 March 1822, ANFV, vol. 127, ff. 73–73v; trial of Calvo and others, 1823, ANFRA, vol. 2629, p. 1; *Espediente importantisimo*.
44. See the files in ABO, 16:276–320; as well as numerous petitions in ANFCG vol. 1050.
45. The first political prisoner in Juan Fernández was Damián Seguí in 1811. See his trial in ANFSFL, vol. 27, p. 14. For the experience of political exile in Juan Fernández, see León, *Encierro y corrección*, 2:273–94; Guerrero Lira, *Contrarrevolución de la independencia*, 119–35; and Vicuña Mackenna, *Juan Fernández*.
46. See *Real Cédula*, 1 February 1816, and vista of Rodríguez Aldea, 22 April 1815, in CHDICH, 35:163 and 170; and the sentence of San Bruno, 23 April 1816, ANFSFL, vol. 34, p. 13, ff. 19–21.
47. Vista of Rodríguez Aldea, 16 November 1816, ANFSFL, vol. 33, p. 59.
48. Vista of Rodríguez Aldea, 27 April 1816, in CHDICH, 35:361.
49. While it is unclear how often people were sentenced to death in colonial Chile, we do know that executions became much more common during and after the imperial civil wars. See Arancibia, Cornejo, and González, "Estudio preliminar"; Correa Gómez, *El último suplicio*; León, *Ni realistas ni patriotas*.
50. Santiago's city council to the president, 22 May 1827, ANFRA, vol. 2161, ff. 121–21v.
51. Van Deusen, *Between the Sacred*; Nemser, *Infrastructures of Race*, 65–100; Abercrombie, *Passing to América*, 55–95; Delgado, *Laywomen and Making Colonial Catholicism*.
52. Ibid., 261.
53. See report of the Treasury, 15 January 1768, AGI, Chile, 229; Benavides to Alcázar, 19 August 1782, ANFCG, vol. 774, ff. 170–70v; Avilés to Petorca's magistrate, 20 June 1797, ANFCG, vol. 787, f. 202; and the dossier concerning San Fernando and Talca in 1798 and 1799 in ANFRA, vol. 2942, p. 1.
54. Undurraga, *Los rostros del honor*, 81–82.
55. See the litigation of Jáuregui, 1757, in González, *Esclavos y esclavas*, 131–56, 137 for the quote. For slaveholders using the concept of recogimiento to justify the continued enslavement of African-descended women, see also Araya, "Sirvientes contra amos"; and Mejías Navarrete, "Esclavitud doméstica," esp. 125.
56. Abercrombie, *Passing to América*, 55–95.
57. See, for example, Higgins to Porlier, 11 November 1790, ANFCG, vol. 785, ff. 399v–401v; the summary of the report of the bishop of Concepción, 1792, AGI, Chile, 454; the report of bishop Sobrino y Minayo, 12 October 1793, AGI, Chile, 460. For a similar reference to recogimiento, see *Semanario de Policía*, 4 February 1818.

58. Legal action of Alonso, 1770, in González, *Esclavos y esclavas*, 72–73.
59. See, among a vast literature, Van Deusen, *Between the Sacred*; Mezan Algranti, *Honradas e devotas*; Ghirardi and Vassallo, "El encierro femenino"; Uchanier Lecoña, "Monasterios y recogimientos"; Porta, "Control social."
60. Ibid., xiii for the quote.
61. Delgado, *Laywomen and Making of Colonial Catholicism*, 6.
62. The exact date of inauguration of the Casa is unclear, but it was operative by 1727. On this institution, see Laval, "La casa de recogidas," 353–63; Cano Roldán, *La mujer*, 416–20; Salinas, *Chilenas de la colonia*, 75–81; Peña González, "Casa de Recogidas"; León, *Encierro y corrección*, 2:344–54; León, "'Reducidas a un decente recogimiento'"; Onetto, "Ideales y transgresiones."
63. Santiago's Audiencia to the king, 28 April 1704, BNMM, vol. 172, p. 3628. The Dominican friar Tadeo Silva would repeat this argument more than a century later when discussing the enclosement of secular women in convents in his newspaper *El Observador Eclesiástico*, 3 November 1823.
64. "Constituciones y ordenanzas que han de observar las Beatas Colegialas," 1735, BNMM, vol. 183, p. 4076.
65. Araya, "Beatas en Chile colonial."
66. Nemser, *Infrastructures of Race*, 65–100.
67. Petition of the recogidas, 3 February 1740, BNMM, vol. 185, p. 4133.
68. See the files in ANFRA, vol. 325, p. 4, especially Urbano to the president, 1802, ANFRA, vol. 325, p. 4, ff. 260–61.
69. Figueroa, "El honor femenino," 87.
70. See Orders of Irarrázaval, 1774, ANFRA, vol. 2770, p. 1; Astorga, "Razon de las Mugeres que se hallan presas en la Casa de Recogidas," 6 March 1781, ANFRA, vol. 2839, p. 13, ff. 200–ov; the case of Contreras, 1783, ANFCG, vol. 530, p. 8, ff. 65–67v; the dossier on the number of recogidas in 1789, ANFRA, vol. 492, p. 2; Cornejo, *Manuela Orellana*, esp. 127 and 132; Pereira Larraín, *Afectos e intimidades*, 211; Contreras, "Usos y abusos"; Laval, "La casa de recogidas," 363; León, *Encierro y corrección*, 2:352. In 1796 the Casa was transformed into an asylum for women accused of immoral behavior, a discipline center for unruly women, and a regular prison for women serving fixed terms. See "Relacion de gobierno," 468, and Cornejo, *Manuela Orellana*, 145.
71. Dossier regarding the number of recogidas in 1789, ANFRA, vol. 492, p. 2.
72. Peña González, "Casa de corrección"; León, *Encierro y corrección*, 2:354–77; Neira, "Castigo femenino."
73. Report of Salas, 1824, quoted in León, *Encierro y corrección*, 2:358. See also Neira, "Jeremy Bentham," 291.
74. *La Lucerna*, 18, 25 July; 1, 15 August; and 5 September 1832.
75. References to these asylums, in which actors often used the language of recogimiento, include de Alday to the king, 2 May 1759 and 8 February 1769, in Lizana, *Colección de documentos*, 1:542–43 and 629–30; Guarda, *Historia urbana*, 204; and the dossier concerning Santiago's asylum in the early nineteenth century in ANFSFL, vol. 27, p. 9.
76. Zúñiga to Higgins, 19 January 1790, ANFCG, vol. 504, ff. 158–74v. For more on this institution, see Hanisch, *Peumo*, 89–92; and Araya, "Beatas en Chile colonial," 39–40.
77. This was the case, for example, with María del Rosario Arellana, who in 1799 was imprisoned there to prevent her from marrying a man her family

rejected. See Avilés to Marán, to the judge of Cáhuil, and to Zúñiga, 5 January 1799, ANFCG, vol. 788, ff. 3–3v, 301, and 301–1v, respectively.

78. Zúñiga to Higgins, 19 January 1790, ANFCG, vol. 504, ff. 158–74v.
79. For an example of these sentences, see the case of Manuela Fernández de Rebolledo, 1800, in ANFRA, vol. 2140, p. 1; Albornoz Vásquez, *Experiencias de conflicto*, 51–70; and Dougnac Rodríguez, "Algunas manifestaciones."
80. Espejo to Calvo Encalada, n.d., ANFSM, A3398.
81. Figueroa, "El honor femenino," 85.
82. There were multiple forms of depósito during this period. Here I focus exclusively on those with an avowed prophylactic purpose. For general studies of this practice, see Delgado, *Laywomen and Making Colonial Catholicism*; Ghirardi and Vassallo, "El encierro femenino"; Kanter, *Hijos del Pueblo*, 82–96; Penyak, "Safe Harbors."
83. For examples of this kind of depósito in Chile, see Benavides to Higgins, 7 April and 31 August 1785, ANFCG, vol. 776, ff. 234–34v and 249v–250; Avilés to the governor of Valparaíso, 17 November 1798, ANFCG, vol. 787, f. 175v.
84. Salazar, *Labradores*, 294–96; Araya, "Sirvientes contra amos"; Chambers, *Families in War*, 182–212; Rojas, *Historia de la infancia*, 74–75.
85. Araya, "Beatas en Chile colonial," 39.
86. Higgins to the commissioner of Rancagua, 26 October 1789, ANFCG, vol. 780, f. 418.
87. Del Pino to the commissioner of Melipilla, 6 October 1800, ANFCG, vol. 788, f. 326. See also the case of José Cruz Salinas in 1829, discussed in Chambers, *Families in War*, 208–9; and Araya, "Sirvientes contra amos," 176–78.
88. See the dossier in ANFCG, vol. 19, p. 12.
89. Yécora to the junta, 23 September 1811, ANFRA, vol. 2477, p. 5, ff. 73–74, 73 for the quote.
90. Decree of Yécora, 17 September 1811, ANFRA, vol. 2477, p. 5, ff. 63–63v.
91. See the files concerning this case in ANFCG, vol. 504, ff. 122–84v.
92. Zúñiga to Higgins, 19 January 1790, ANFCG, vol. 504, ff. 158–74v.
93. Criminal investigation against Tomás Pomaire, 1811, ANFRA, vol. 2477, p. 5. For a more detailed description of this event, see León, "'Los indios.'"
94. Valenzuela, "Esclavos mapuches"; Obregón and Zavala, "Abolición y persistencia"; Chueca, "'Cosa cierta por precio cierto'"; Poblete, "El trabajo de niños."
95. Avilés to the intendant of Concepción, 25 September 1798, ANFCG, vol. 787, ff. 396v–97.
96. Beauchef, *Memorias de Jorge Beauchef*, 214.
97. Journal of Figueroa, 1792, reproduced in Vicuña Mackenna, *El coronel don Tomás de Figueroa*, 31.
98. Higgins to the governor of Valdivia, 13 March 1793, ANFCG, vol. 783, ff. 413v–14.
99. See, for example, the files concerning the fate of an unnamed Mapuche man, sold in Valparaíso for thirty pesos in 1773, ANFCG, vol. 307, p. 16, ff. 276–78v.
100. Villalobos, *Vida fronteriza*, 107.
101. The quote is from the representación of Martina Prado, Santiago, 1817, ANFCG, vol. 103, p. 27, ff. 196–98v.
102. Certificate of depósito, 28 November 1817, ANFCG, vol. 103, p. 27, f. 200.
103. Files concerning the freedom of Martina Prado's children, ANFCG, vol. 103, p. 27, ff. 191–212v.
104. Pereira Larraín, *Afectos e intimidades*, 122–24, 211, 220, 240.

105. The quotes are taken from the vista of Crown attorney Del Campo, 19 January 1799, ANFRA, vol. 2942, p. 1, ff. 2–3v.
106. Guzmán to the President and Audiencia, 8 October 1798, ANFRA, vol. 2942, p. 1, ff. 2–3.
107. Neira, "Castigo femenino."
108. For an excellent example of an elite woman negotiating her depósito, see the files concerning Manuela Sierra's depósito in Copiapó, 1790–1791, ANFJCO, caja 69, leg. 77, pp. 12 and 13. More generally on the ability of women to shape this institution, see Delgado, *Laywomen and Making Colonial Catholicism*.
109. Cited in Cornejo, *Manuela Orellana*, 78.
110. Real Academia Española, *Diccionario*, 1732, 681. On spiritual exercises and their role in early modern Catholicism, see Sluhovsky, *Becoming a New Self*, esp. 67–95; and Molina, *To Overcome Oneself*, esp. 24–49.
111. See, for instance, "Constituciones y ordenanzas que han de observar las Beatas Colegialas," 1735, BNMM, vol. 183, p. 4076; Pardo to Recabarren, 19 March 1747 in Vergara, *Cartas de mujeres*, 8–13; Alday to the king, 5 September 1768, and Sobrino y Minayo to the king, 14 October 1793, in Lizana, *Colección de documentos*, 1:623 and 710–20; Del Río to Eyzaguirre, 29 May 1820, ANFJE, vol. 7, f. 51; *El Observador Eclesiástico*, 15 and 29 November 1823; and Juan Egaña to Mariano Egaña, 1 May 1827, in Egaña, *Cartas*, 213–14.
112. For a list of casas de ejercicios during this period see Guarda, *Edad Media de Chile*, 256–57. Guarda does not mention the casas de ejercicios of Quillota and Talca. References to the latter two can be found in Higgins to the commissioner of Quillota, 14 June 1790, ANFCG, vol. 780, f. 306v; and Rancagua's city council to the Supreme Director, 2 December 1820, ANFMI, vol. 10, ff. 150–51.
113. Higgins to Llaguno, 17 September 1795, ANFCG, vol. 786, ff. 102–3.
114. Santa Cruz, "Noticia de Santiago," 8 April 1790, in Sagredo and González, *La Expedición Malaspina*, here 474–75.
115. Alday to the king, 17 October 1767, and Sobrino y Minayo to the king, 14 October 1793, in Lizana, *Colección de documentos*, 1:612–17 and 710–20; Hanisch, *Peumo*, 86. Hanisch later provides a different estimation of the number of people accepted in each round of ejercicios—one hundred women and eighty men per round.
116. Zúñiga to Higgins, 19 January 1790, and Sobrino y Minayo to Higgins, 22 September 1791, ANFCG, vol. 504, ff. 158–74v, and 184–84v.
117. Alday to the king, 5 February 1767, in Lizana, *Colección de documentos*, 1:590–91; Arís to O'Higgins, 8 May 1835, in ABO, 34:580.
118. Hanisch, *Peumo*, 86.
119. See, for example, Zúñiga to Higgins, 19 January 1790, ANFCG, vol. 504, ff. 158–74v; Bladh, *La República de Chile*, 55–56.
120. Adriana Montt to José María Montt, 1822, in Montt, *Recuerdos de familia*, 585–89.
121. Guill y Gonzaga to Arriaga, 10 May 1765, reproduced in Amunátegui, *Precursores de la independencia*, 1:154–57.
122. Verdugo to Carrera, 9 March 1796, in Vergara, *Cartas de mujeres*, 48.
123. Lurquin to the president, 28 May 1808, ANFCG, vol. 69, p. 1, ff. 3–3v.
124. For an explicit rendition of this argument, see Bustamante [pseud.], *Paco y Manolo*, 14.
125. Santa Cruz, "Noticia de Santiago," 8 April 1790, in Sagredo and González, *La Expedición Malaspina*, 474–75.

126. Álvarez de Acevedo to Gálvez, 7 September 1787, ANFCG, vol. 781, ff. 490v–91. Other people also connected ejercicios and the concept of recogimiento. See Zúñiga to Higgins, 19 January 1790, ANFCG, vol. 504, ff. 158–74v; Del Río to Eyzaguirre, 29 May 1820, ANFJE, vol. 7, f. 51; *El Mercurio de Valparaíso*, 17 November 1829.
127. Such skeptical views can be found in *El Monitor Imparcial*, 10 November 1827; Gay, *Diario*, 222; *El Valdiviano Federal*, 1 September 1835; *El Valdiviano Federal*, 12 November 1841.
128. *Cartas Pehuenches*, 14 January 1819.
129. Neira, "Castigo femenino"; León, *Encierro y corrección*, 2:373.
130. Santiago's city council to the president, 22 May 1827, ANFRA, vol. 2161, ff. 121–21v. Church tribunals also sentenced people to attend ejercicios as penance for their transgressions. See Pereira Larraín, *Afectos e intimidades*, 123.
131. José Ignacio Eyzaguirre to Alejo Eyzaguirre, 2 and 14 November 1822, and María Juana [Eyzaguirre] to Alejo Eyzaguirre, 28 November 1822, ANFJE, vol. 7, ff. 21–21v, 22–23, and 75–76v.
132. Quoted in Salinas, *Canto a lo divino*, 275–76.
133. Bustamante [pseud.], *Paco y Manolo*, 14.
134. Cited in Amunátegui, *Precursores de la independencia*, 1:189–90.
135. Higgins to Seco y Santa Cruz, 1 October 1793, ANFCG, vol. 783, ff. 62–62v.
136. "Noticia de las mujeres que han estado en captura en la casa de ejercicios," 1813, in CHDICH, 23:191–95; instructions of O'Higgins to Quintana, 18 April 1817, reproduced in Melfi, "La Prensa O'Higginista," 29–30; *Semanario de Policía*, 1 October 1817; trial of Velásquez, 1817, ANFMG, vol. 6; summary of a letter written by Rodríguez Zorrilla, 12 February 1818, AGI, Chile, 313; Grez, *Mujeres de la independencia*, 35–36; Peña, ". . . Y las mujeres," 240, 248, and 249.
137. García Ferrer, "Razón de lo que he presenciado," 159.
138. Chambers, *Families in War*, 75–88.
139. "Noticia de las mujeres que han estado en captura en la casa de ejercicios," 1813, in CHDICH, 23:193.
140. Unsigned communication to the governor-intendant of Santiago, 26 April 1817, in ABO, 16:266–67. The sentence was later changed to confinement in the beaterio of La Calera. See intendant of Santiago to Ruiz-Tagle, 30 April 1817, in ABO, 16:267.
141. *Semanario de Policía*, 1 October 1817; *Gazeta de Santiago de Chile*, 21 March 1818. The government had threatened women with imprisoning them in an institution of "correction" in August 1817. See *Gazeta de Santiago de Chile*, 2 and 23 August 1817.
142. Report of Pérez de Arza, 12 September 1815, AGI, Chile, 208.
143. Pérez de Arza to the Viceroy of Peru, 13 March 1815, AGI, Diversos, 4.
144. Egaña, *Coleccion de algunos escritos*, 5:44.
145. As he was legally bound to, per the will of the previous owner, Ana Vicuña. See Hanisch, "La filosofía," 175.
146. Juan Egaña to Mariano Egaña, 1 May 1827, in Egaña, *Cartas*, 213–14. Juan Egaña revisited this project in a second letter to his son Mariano, signed in Santiago on 28 July 1827, in ibid., 230.

Chapter Eight

1. Aguilar Rivera, *En pos de la quimera*; Portillo, "La revolución constitucional";

Annino and Ternavasio, *El laboratorio constitucional iberoamericano*. Several of Chile's codes, for example, were modeled after the influential Spanish charter of 1812. Ossa, "De Cádiz a la América del Sur"; Cartes, "La constitución de Cádiz."

2. Luengo and Dalmau, "Writing Spanish History"; Jaksić and Posada Carbó, *Liberalismo y poder*.
3. Dedieu, *Après le Roi*, 39. This notion of publicness, Annick Lempérière has noted, was founded on Catholic notions of salvation and sin, according to which members of a community shared responsibility for the salvation of others. Lempérière, *Entre Dieu et le Roi*, 206–11.
4. Cf. Chambers, "Private Crimes."
5. "Instruccion de el Ministerio y Facultades de los Alcaldes de Barrio." For a detailed analysis of the boundaries between the public and the nonpublic in similar instructions drafted in Guatemala City, see Sellers-Garcia, *Woman on the Windowsill*, 221–22, which invites us "to think of 'public' as something on a spectrum" rather than as the mere opposite of the nonpublic.
6. Quoted in Barros Arana, *Historia Jeneral de Chile*, 6:400. For an analysis of the complex boundaries between the public and the nonpublic in this document, see Sellers-Garcia, *Woman on the Windowsill*, 221.
7. Decree of Osorio, 16 August 1815, AGI, Chile, 226. A regulation of 1819 created a new figure called "inspectors," who would similarly be in charge of "cutting dissensions among neighbors and even within families, if these are public and scandalous." See *Gazeta Ministerial de Chile*, 2 October 1819.
8. The following discussion is based on Tomás y Valiente, *Derecho penal*; Tomás y Valiente, *Tortura judicial*; Tomás y Valiente, *Manual de historia*, 383–98; Clavero, *Historia del derecho*; and Ramos Vásquez, "La represión."
9. Opposition to these views is discussed in Astigarraga, "La Ilustración napolitana imputada."
10. Chiaramonte, *Fundamentos intelectuales y políticos*.
11. Vista of Pérez de Uriondo, 20 January 1781, ANFRA, vol. 1644, p. 2, f. 265v.
12. Vista of Márquez de la Plata, 23 January 1781, ANFRA, vol. 1644, ff. 271v–76, here 273.
13. Moreover, there was evidence that the two Frenchmen had a plan and that they had asked others to follow them. Petition of Pérez de Uriondo, 6 February 1781, ANFRA, vol. 1644, p. 2, ff. 290–95, 292v for the quote.
14. For the conflict of jurisdiction between Ambrosio Higgins and Santiago's bishop, Francisco José Marán, see Dougnac Rodríguez, "Algunas manifestaciones," 67–80.
15. Higgins to Marán, 27 May 1795, ANFCG, vol. 784, ff. 24v–25.
16. Decree, 12 June 1795, in ANFJLS, leg. 64, p. 7.
17. Higgins to the Audiencia, 3 August 1795, ANFCG, vol. 784, f. 31v.
18. Agreement of the Audiencia, 12 August 1795, reproduced in Amunátegui, *Precursores de la independencia*, 3:283–85.
19. Prodi, *Historia de la justicia*.
20. For the public sphere in Spanish America, see the works cited in the introduction. On the role of "public opinion" as a principle of legitimation in the Atlantic and Spanish America, see Habermas, *Structural Transformation*; Baker, *Inventing the French Revolution*; Fernández Sebastián and Chassin, eds., *Avènement de l'opinion*; Palti, *Tiempo de la política*, 161–202; Goldman, "Legitimidad y deliberación."

21. Stuven and Cid, *Debates republicanos en Chile*, 2:343–71; Stuven, *La seducción*; and González Bernaldo de Quirós, "Literatura injuriosa."
22. Wetters, *Opinion System*, esp. xv.
23. I follow here what Wetters has called "the four conceptual paradigms for the idea of opinion" in Western Europe. See ibid., 15 for the quote. For examples, see Jáuregui to Gálvez, 7 February 1780, ANFCG, vol. 779, ff. 297v–99; Higgins to the commissioner of Colchagua, 14 October 1795, ANFCG, vol. 784, ff. 209v–10v; Muñoz de Guzmán to Valparaíso's governor, 19 July 1802, ANFCG, vol. 789, ff. 151–51v; model letter of citizenship, [n.d., ca. 1810–1814], AGI, Chile, 207; report of Portales, 2 January 1811, ANFV, vol. 281, p. 99, ff. 252–66v; "Educacion," *Aurora de Chile*, 9 April 1812; Varas, *Lecciones elementales de moral*, 33.
24. Stuven and Cid, *Debates republicanos en Chile*, 2:343–71.
25. Egaña, "Discurso sobre el ámor de la Patria," 1807, BNSM, A-36-2(32) p. 10.
26. Zenteno to O'Higgins, 2 February 1825, ANFVM, vol. 92, ff. 59–60v, here 59v.
27. A few examples in the communication of Velasco, 20 September 1811, ANFSFL, vol. 30, p. 22; decree of the Vindication Committee, 6 February 1815, AGI, Chile, 207; testimony of Osses, 25 September 1827, ANFIC, vol. 68, p. 20, ff. 486v–87v; Claro to O'Higgins, 5 February 1833, ANFVM, vol. 97, ff. 151–52v.
28. See, for example, testimony of Garfias, 20 August 1812, ANFSFL, vol. 40, p. 22, f. 18; trial of Caro and Villaseñor, 1817, ANFMG, vol. 6; trial of Bruna and Gaona, 1818, ANFJSC, leg. 1587, p. 1; testimony of Orellana, 31 October 1820, ANFCG, vol. 335, p. 4, ff. 163–65; and trial of Bustos and others, 1820, ANFJSC, leg. 1587, p. 4.
29. Santa María de Oro to Acosta, 3 December 1814, AGN, Sala VII, legajo 61.
30. See, for example, the junta to Santiago's city council, [n.d., ca. April 1811], ANFV, vol. 238-A, f. 21; edict of the junta, 17 February 1813, in CHDICH, 24:273–74; "Reos que existen presos en varios puntos," 1813, in CHDICH, 23:179–91.
31. Decree of 23 June 1813, *Boletin de las leyes, 1810–1814*, 243–47, here 243. Examples of similar references in *El Monitor Araucano*, 27 November and 15, 22, 25 July 1813; [Gandarillas], *A los escritores*; *El Sol de Chile*, 3 and 10 July 1818; *El Cosmopolita*, 5 October 1822; *El Despertador Araucano*, 17 May 1823; *La Estrella de Chile*, 18 November 1826; *El Insurgente Araucano*, 19 February 1827; *El Indicador*, 24 February 1827; *El Fanal*, 17 June 1829.
32. To give but a few examples, see García Carrasco to Aldunate, 19 September 1808, in CHDICH, 8:49–50; Santiago's Merchant's Guild to the king, 20 July 1815, AGI, Chile, 445; vista of Villegas, 21 October 1819, and vista of Vial, 11 December 1819, both in ANFJCA, caja 3, p. 16.
33. Decree of 24 November 1812, in *Boletin de las leyes, 1810–1814*, 187.
34. See the communications of April and May 1810 between García Carrasco and the viceroy of Río de la Plata, in CHDICH, 8:259–266.
35. Decree of García Carrasco, 18 May 1808, in CHDICH, 30:3–4.
36. Decree of García Carrasco, 24 May 1810, in CHDICH, 30:241–43, 242 for the quote.
37. Decree of the Audiencia, 26 May 1810, in CHDICH, 30:22–25.
38. The city council, probably inspired by Montesquieu's writings, argued that "words" reported by witnesses constituted unreliable evidence. Santiago's city council to the president, 28 May 1810, in CHDICH, 30:82–87.

39. Testimony of Ovalle, 26 June 1810, testimony of Rojas, 27 June 1810, testimony of Vera, 28 June 1810, in CHDICH, 30:116–54.
40. Petition Vera, n.d. [29 June 1810], in CHDICH, 30:157–63, here 162.
41. Petition of Vera, 6 October 1810, CHDICH, 30:316–64.
42. Partida VII, title XXXI, law II, in Burns, S.J. *Las Siete Partidas*, 5:1463–64.
43. These arguments deviated from the spirit of the law of the Siete Partidas, as the code's main argument was not that thoughts and their expression were not punishable per se but rather that magistrates needed to prove that criminals had willingly accepted them in order to punish them.
44. Sentence of the junta, 15 October 1810, in CHDICH, 30:367–70.
45. Petition of Santibáñez, 23 November 1810, ANFSFL, vol. 27, p. 14.
46. Legal defense of Argomedo, 6 December 1811, ANFV, vol. 156, ff. 43–46, 44 for the quote.
47. Defense of Garfias, 25 August 1812, ANFSFL, vol. 40, p. 22.
48. Defense of Salamanca, January 1812, BNMSBA, vol. 38, ff. 645–59.
49. Trial of Salamanca, 1812, BNMSBA, vol. 38, ff. 540–692.
50. Vista of Vial and Villegas, 23 February 1813, in CHDICH, 21:273–74.
51. Defense of Astorga, 1813, in CHDICH, 22:185–98, 190 for the quote.
52. Defense of Rodríguez, Urra, and Espejo, in CHDICH, 22:102–51. Mardones apparently worked with Calderón, who also signed this submission. A copy of this text can be found in Juan Egaña's personal archives as well, suggesting he either helped Mardones and Calderón draft it or wrote it himself. The latter option is the most likely, as Egaña kept copies of his own works in this archive. See the manuscript in ANFV, vol. 120-A, ff. 104–11v.
53. Defense of Argomedo, 1813, in CHDICH, 22:65–101.
54. In fact, after again one more turn in government, a new administration nullified this and other sentences in cases of conspiracy that had transpired since the Carreras took power in 1811. Decree of 18 February 1814 in *El Monitor Araucano*, 25 February 1814.
55. For versions of this argument and/or of its implicit logic, see testimony of Urra, 10 October 1817, in CHDICH, 43:522–26; petition of Lurquin, 1817, ANFSFL, vol. 38, p. 17; *Acta definitorial de Franciscanos de 17 de octubre de 1820*; *Gazeta Ministerial de Chile*, 19 June 1819, 25 November 1820, 20 January, 17 February, and 5 May 1821; *El Criticón Médico*, 5 June 1830; *El Cosmopolita*, 1 May 1833; and *El Constitucional*, 14 August 1833.
56. [Verdugo], *El patriotismo*. A similar logic in *Gazeta Ministerial de Chile*, 19 June 1819 and 25 November 1820; *El Criticón Médico*, 5 June 1830.
57. Testimony of Esponda, 28 September 1814, ANFMG, vol. 6.
58. Plan for regulation of the press, 1817, ANFSFL, vol. 38, p. 3, f. 5 for the quote.
59. *Viva la Patria. Gazeta del Supremo Gobierno de Chile*, 7 May 1817.
60. See the trial of Pavez, Santander, and Martínez, 1825, ANFIC, vol. 68, p. 14; *Extracto de la causa criminal*; and *Alcance al numero 165*.
61. Vista of the legal adviser to Santiago's Surveillance Committee, 4 May 1816, ANFSFL, vol. 34, p. 13.
62. Piwonka, *Orígenes de la libertad*; Stuven and Cid, *Debates republicanos en Chile*, 2:343–71; Cid, *Pensar la revolución*, 312–17.
63. *Mercurio de Chile*, nums. 4 and 6, 1822; *El Patriota Chileno*, 5 January 1827; *La Clave*, 9 February 1828; *El Crepúsculo*, 19 September 1829; *El Defensor de los Militares Denominados Constitucionales*, 24 July 1830.

64. *El Valdiviano Federal*, 20 July 1829.
65. *El Insurgente Araucano*, 10, 13, 19, and 24 February, 5, 17 March, 1827; *El Valdiviano Federal*, 20 July 1829; *El Espectador Chileno*, 21 August 1829; *El Crepúsculo*, 3 October 1829.
66. Castillo, *Creación de la República*.
67. Portillo, *Crisis atlántica*.
68. Amor de la Patria [pseud.], "Catesismo politico christiano."
69. Collier, *Ideas and Politics*, 150–55; Bravo Lira, *Estado de Derecho*; Stuven and Cid, *Debates republicanos en Chile*, 2:17–47; Stuven, "De la autonomía"; San Francisco, "El primer constitucionalismo chileno"; Cid, *Pensar la revolución*, 184–224.
70. "Proyecto de una constitucion que pudiera adaptarse Al Pays de Chile," 1811, ANFV, vol. 276, p. 13. This code was published with some modifications in 1813. Egaña, *Proyecto de Constitución*. For how this document was drafted and published, see Silva Castro, *Egaña en la Patria Vieja*, 69–91.
71. Egaña, *Proyecto de Constitución*, 5. This notion was similarly hailed as a republican precept in the official newspaper *El Monitor Araucano*, 27 November 1813.
72. Egaña, *Proyecto de Constitución*, 4.
73. *Constitucion politica del Estado*, 1822.
74. "Proyecto de Garantias," March 1825, SCL, 11:27–29. Although this law was not published, other authorities similarly expressed their desire to issue laws enshrining individual liberties. See *Rol de Policía*, 9 July 1827. See also Cid, *Pensar la revolución*, 312–17 for debates over censorship and public liberties during these years.
75. *Proyecto de Constitucion*, 25 for the quote.
76. *Constitución política de la República*.
77. Junta Gubernativa to Freire, 26 December 1829, ANFMI, vol. 1, f. 36v; vista of Egaña, 1830, ANFV, vol. 159, f. 40.
78. *La Lucerna*, 16 November 1832. For this shift in perspectives regarding constitutions, see also Stuven and Cid, *Debates republicanos en Chile*, 2:39–42; Cid, "Terminar la revolución"; Lacueva Muñoz, Saldaña Fernández, and Varela Norambuena, "Revolución."
79. See, for example, *La Opinión*, 14 October and 12 November 1830; *Correo Mercantil*, 25 May 1832; *El Cosmopolita*, 1 May 1833.
80. *Constitución de la República*, 7, 42.
81. *El Araucano*, 6 September 1833, for the quotes. The controversy began with an article in *El Mercurio de Valparaíso*, 4 September 1833. That it concerned legal protections over inner dispositions became evident in the subsequent discussion. See *El Araucano*, 16 September and 5 October 1833, as well as more indirectly the issues of 3 and 29 November 1833; *El Mercurio de Valparaíso*, 31 September 1833; and, most of all, *Alcance al numero 165*.
82. Portales to Garfias, 6 December 1834, in Fariña Vicuña, *Epistolario*, 2:590–92.
83. Donoso, *Ideas políticas en Chile*.

Conclusion

1. Vicuña Mackenna, *D. Diego Portales*; Sotomayor Valdés, *Historia de Chile*; Donoso, *Ideas políticas en Chile*; Núñez Rius, "Estado"; Villalobos, *Portales*; Collier, *Ideas and Politics*, 323–60; León, *Encierro y corrección*, esp. 2:294–321;

Grez, *"Regeneración del pueblo,"* 233–48; Wood, *Society of Equality*; Pinto et al., *El orden y el bajo pueblo*.

2. See, in addition to the references mentioned in the previous note, Stuven, *La seducción*; Illanes, *Chile Des-centrado*; Goicovic, "Consideraciones teóricas"; Salinas, "Espacio urbano"; Serrano, *¿Qué hacer con Dios?*; Castillo and Fernández, *Republicanismo popular*; Serrano del Pozo, *Chile contra la Confederación*; Catepillán Tessi, *La "Provincia de Chile."*
3. Lefort, *Essais sur le politique*. Palti similarly sees these the loss of a transcendent source of authority as locating "the Latin American political system within a democratic horizon." See Palti, *Archaeology of the Political*, 95–103.

Bibliography

Archival Sources

CHILE

Archivo Nacional Histórico

Fondo Antiguo
Fondo Capitanía General
Fondo Intendencia de Concepción
Fondo Intendencia de Coquimbo
Fondo Intendencia de Santiago
Fondo Jaime Eyzaguirre
Fondo Judicial de Cauquenes
Fondo Judicial de Copiapó
Fondo Judicial de La Serena
Fondo Judicial de Los Andes
Fondo Judicial de Santiago, Criminales
Fondo Ministerio de Guerra
Fondo Ministerio del Interior
Fondo Morla Vicuña
Fondo Municipalidad de Santiago
Fondo Real Audiencia
Fondo Reynals Bruguera
Fondo Salvador Trucíos
Fondo Santa María
Fondo Sergio Fernández Larraín
Fondo Varios
Fondo Vicuña Mackenna

Biblioteca Nacional

Sala Medina. Manuscritos Diego Barros Arana
Sala Medina. Manuscritos Medina

ARGENTINA

Archivo General de la Nación

Sala VII

SPAIN

Archivo General de Indias

Sección Chile
Sección Diversos
Sección Lima
Sección Ultramar

Newspapers Cited

Aurora de Chile
Boletín de Policía
Cartas Pehuenches
Clamor de la Patria
Clamor del Pueblo Chileno
Correo Mercantil
Diario de la Convención de Chile
El Agricultor
El Almirez
El Apagador
El Amigo de la Verdad
El Avisador Chileno
El Avisador de Valparaíso
El Censor de la Revolución
El Constitucional
El Correo de Arauco
El Cosmopolita (1822)
El Cosmopolita (1833)
El Crepúsculo
El Crisol
El Criticón Médico
El Defensor de los Militares Denominados Constitucionales
El Descamizado
El Despertador Araucano
El Fanal
El Indicador
El Insurgente Araucano
El Interrogante y Respondente
El Juicio
El Liberal
El Mercurio Chileno
El Mercurio de Valparaíso
El Minero de Coquimbo

El Monitor Araucano
El Monitor Imparcial
El Nuevo Corresponsal
El O'Higginista
El Observador de Chile
El Observador de Valparaíso
El Observador Eclesiástico
El Patriota Chileno
El Penquisto
El Pipiolo
El Redactor del Senado
El Sepulturero
El Sol de Chile
El Sufragante
El Telégrafo
El Tizón Republicano
El Valdiviano Federal
El Verdadero Liberal
El Vijía
Gazeta de Santiago de Chile
Gazeta Ministerial de Chile
La Antorcha
La Clave
La Estrella de Chile
La Lucerna
La Miscelánea Chilena
La Opinión
Mercurio de Chile
Mercurio de España
Registro Municipal
Rol de Policía
Semanario de Policía
Semanario Republicano
Viva el Rey. Gazeta del Gobierno de Chile
Viva la Patria. Gazeta del Supremo Gobierno de Chile

Published Primary Sources

Acta definitorial de Franciscanos de 17 de octubre de 1820. Santiago: Imprenta de Valles, y Vilugrón, 1820.
Alcance al numero 165 del Araucano. Santiago: Imprenta de la Opinión, 1833.
Amor de la Patria, José [pseud]. "Catesismo politico christiano." 1810.

Biblioteca Nacional de Chile. *Memoria Chilena*. http://www.memoriachilena.gob.cl/602/w3-article-92740.html.

Anonymous. *Ilustres Americanas*. Paris: Libreria de la Viuda de Wincop, 1825.

Arancibia, Claudia, José Tomás Cornejo, and Carolina González, eds. *Pena de muerte en Chile colonial: Cinco casos de homicidio de la Real Audiencia*. Santiago: RIL Editores/Centro de Investigaciones Diego Barros Arana, 2003.

Archivo de Don Bernardo O'Higgins. 37 vols. Santiago: Editorial Nascimento/Imprenta Universitaria/Instituto Geográfico Militar/Editorial Universidad Católica/Editorial del Pacífico, 1946–2008.

Aviso importantísimo. Santiago: Imprenta Republicana, 1829.

Bando de buen gobierno. Santiago: n.p., 1812.

"Bando de buen gobierno, 1799." *Revista Chilena de Historia y Geografía* 98 (1941): 60–78.

Bladh, C. E. *La República de Chile, 1821–1828*. Translated by Elisabeth de Vylder de Lundberg. Santiago: Imprenta Universitaria, [1951].

Blest, Guillermo. *Ensayo sobre las causas comunes y activas de las enfermedades que se padecen en Santiago de Chile con indicaciones de los mejores medios para evitar su destructora influencia*. Santiago: Imprenta de R. Rengifo, 1828.

Beauchef, Jorge. *Memorias de Jorge Beauchef*. Edited by Patrick Puigmal. Santiago: Dirección de Bibliotecas, Archivos y Museos, 2005.

Boletin de las leyes i decretos del gobierno, 1810–1814. Santiago: Imprenta Nacional, 1898.

Boletin de las leyes i decretos del gobierno, 1817–1818. Santiago: Imprenta Nacional, 1898.

Boletin de las leyes i decretos del gobierno, 1819–1820. Santiago: Imprenta Nacional, 1900.

Boletín de las leyes y de las órdenes y decretos del gobierno. Santiago: Imprenta de la Independencia, 1839.

Boletín de las leyes, y de las órdenes y decretos del gobierno. Vol. 2. Valparaíso: Imprenta del Mercurio, 1846.

Burns, Robert I., S.J. *Las Siete Partidas*. 5 vols. Philadelphia: University of Pennsylvania Press, 2012.

Bustamante, Miguel [pseud.]. *Paco y Manolo o fragmento de los dialogos sobre las cosas del dia*. Santiago: Imprenta Nacional, [1823].

Caldcleugh, Alexander. *Travels in South America, during the Years 1819–20–21*. 2 vols. London: John Murray, 1825.

Carrera, José Miguel. "Diario del Brigadier General José Miguel Carrera."

Museo Histórico Nacional. http://www.museohistoriconacional.cl/618/w3-article-55475.html.
———. *Manifiesto que hace a los pueblos de Chile el ciudadano José Miguel Carrera*. [Montevideo]: n.p., 1818.
Carta contextacion al autor del Independiente. Santiago: Imprenta del Gobierno, 1821.
Carvallo y Goyeneche. "Descripción histórico-geográfica del Reino de Chile." In *Colección de Historiadores de Chile y documentos relativos a la Historia nacional*. Vols. 8–10. Santiago: Imprenta de la Librería del Mercurio/Imprenta de "La Estrella de Chile," 1875–1876.
Cienfuegos, José Ignacio. *Catón cristiano-politico para el uso de las escuelas de la República de Chile*. 5th ed. Valparaíso: Imprenta Europea, 1847.
Clamor del estado religioso. Santiago: Imprenta de Gobierno, [1814].
Colección de Historiadores y de Documentos relativos a la Independencia de Chile. 43 vols. Santiago: Imprenta Cervantes, 1900–1966.
Constitución de la República de Chile. Santiago: Imprenta de la Opinión, 1833.
Constitucion politica del Estado de Chile. Santiago: Imprenta del Estado, 1822.
Constitución política de la República de Chile. Santiago: Imprenta de R. Rengifo, 1828.
De la Touanne, Edmond Bigot. *Album pittoresque de la frégate la Thétis et de la corvette L'Espérance*. Paris: Chez Bulla, 1828
Diccionario portatil, filosofico-politico-moral. Santiago: Imprenta de los Ciudadanos Valles y Vilugrón, 1820.
Domeyko, Ignacio. *Mis viajes: memorias de un exiliado*. 2 vols. Santiago: Ediciones de la Universidad de Chile, 1978.
Egaña, Juan. *Almanak nacional para el Estado de Chile en el año bisiesto de 1824*. Santiago: Imprenta Nacional, 1824.
———. *Cartas de don Juan Egaña a su hijo Mariano, 1824–1828*. Santiago: Sociedad de Bibliófilos Chilenos, 1946.
———. *Coleccion de algunos escritos politicos, morales, poéticos, y filosoficos*. 6 vols. London: Imprenta Manuel Calero/Imprenta de la Sa. Va. Laplace y Baume, 1826–1836.
———. *Proyecto de Constitución para el Estado de Chile*. Santiago: Imprenta del Gobierno, 1813.
El amigo social y verdadero ciudadano. Santiago: Imprenta Nacional, [1823].
"El Reglamento de Teatros y el precio de las localidades á principios del siglo diecinueve." *Revista Chilena de Historia y Geografía* 3 (1911): 489–91.
Errázuriz, Fernando. *Segundo manifiesto que hace al público Fernando Errázuriz*. [Santiago]: Imprenta de R. Rengifo, [1828].

Escritos de don Manuel de Salas y documentos relativos a él y su familia. 3 vols. Santiago: Imprenta Cervantes, 1900–1914.

Espediente importantisimo seguido por el Sr. Fiscal de la Exma. Corte Suprema de Justicia por la violacion de garantias individuales en el destierro de D. José Santiago Muñoz Bezanilla &. Santiago: Imprenta Republicana, 1830.

Espejo, Juan de Dios, Toribio Espejo and Juan Manuel Garay. *Contesto que dan los que suscriben a la imputacion que les ha hecho el inspector Nicolas Martinez de Ureta*. Santiago: Imprenta de la Independencia, 1829.

Extracto de la causa criminal seguida ante la comandancia jeneral de armas contra Don Jose Lave. Santiago: Imprenta Nacional, 1832.

Fariña Vicuña, Carmen, ed. *Epistolario de don Diego Portales*. 2 vols. Santiago: Ediciones Universidad Diego Portales, 2007.

F. J. del C. O. *El precursor del Sr. Nuncio*. Santiago: Imprenta de D. Estevan Valles, por Perez, 1824.

Freire, Ramón. *El Director Supremo a los pueblos de la República*. Santiago: Imprenta Nacional, 1825.

[Gandarillas, Manuel José]. *A los escritores del pais*. Santiago: P. D. J. C. Gallardo, [1814].

Gandarillas, Manuel José. *Don Bernardo O'Higgins. Apuntes históricos sobre la revolución de Chile*. Santiago: Guillermo E. Miranda, 1905.

García Ferrer, Manuel Gregorio. "Razón de lo que he presenciado y mucha parte que no e bisto mean contado personas honrradas de una y otra parte, desde el año dies y para que lo sepan lo pongo en este cuaderno." *Revista Chilena de Historia y Geografía* 51, no. 55 (1925–1926): 151–69.

Gardiner, Allen F. *A Visit to the Indians of the Frontiers of Chili*. London: R. B. Seeley y W. Burnside, 1840.

Gay, Claudio. *Atlas de la historia física y política de Chile*. 2 vols. Paris: E. Thunot, 1854.

———. *Diario de su primer viaje a Chile. Manuscrito inédito*. Edited by Luis Mizón. n.p.: Fundación Claudio Gay, 2008.

———. *Historia física y física de Chile: según documentos adquiridos en esta república durante doce años de residencia en ella*. Paris/Chile: En casa del autor/Museo de Historia Natural de Santiago, 1844–1871.

Gonzalez Undurraga, Carolina. *Esclavos y esclavas demandando justicia. Chile, 1740–1823: Documentación judicial por carta de libertad y papel de venta*. Santiago: Universitaria, 2014.

Graham, Maria. *Journal of a Residence in Chile, During the Year 1822*. London: Longman, Hurst, Rees, Orme, Brown, Green, and John Murray, 1824.

Haenke, Thaddaeus Peregrinus. *Descripción del Reyno de Chile*. Santiago: Nascimento, 1942.

Hall, Basil. *Extracts from a Journal, Written on the Coasts of Chili, Peru, and Mexico, in the Years 1820, 1821, 1822*. 4th ed. 2 vols. Edinburgh: Archibald Constable and Co., 1825.

"Instruccion de el Ministerio y Facultades de los Alcaldes de Barrio." 31 August 1780. *Memoria Chilena*, http://www.memoriachilena.gob.cl/602/w3-article-10366.html.

Johnston, Samuel B. *Letters Written During a Residence of Three Years in Chili Containing an Account of the Most Remarkable Events in the Revolutionary Struggles of That Province*. Erie, PA: R. I. Curtis, 1816.

Kordic, Raissa, ed. *Epistolario de Sor Dolores Peña y Lillo (Chile, 1763–1769)*. Madrid: Universidad de Navarra/Iberoamericana/Vervuert, 2008.

"La sociedad colonial. Epistolario de la familia Bernales." *Revista Chilena de Historia y Geografía* 57 (1928): 169–93.

Lizana, Elías. *Colección de documentos históricos recopilados del Archivo del Arzobispado de Santiago*. 4 vols. Santiago: Imprenta de San José, 1919–1921.

Los Populares. *A los pueblos de la provincia de Santiago*. Santiago: Imprenta de la Federación, 1829.

Marín del Solar, Mercedes. *Poesias de la señora Da. Mercedes Marin del Solar*. Edited by Enrique del Solar. Santiago: Imprenta Andres Bello, 1874.

Milet-Mureau, Louis Antoine. *Atlas du voyage de La Pérouse*. Paris: Imprimerie de la République, 1797.

Miller, John. *Memoirs of General Miller, in the Service of the Republic of Peru*. 2nd ed., 2 vols. London: Longman, Rees, Orme, Brown, and Green, 1829.

Ministerio de Relaciones Exteriores y Culto. *Diplomacia de la Revolución: Chile*. 4 vols. Buenos Aires: n.p., 1958–1963.

Molina Hernández, Jorge Javier. *Vida de un soldado. Desde la Toma de Valdivia (1820) a la Victoria de Yungay (1839)*. Santiago: RIL Editores, 2009.

Monteagudo, Bernardo. *Memoria sobre los principios políticos que seguí en la administración del Perú, y acontecimientos posteriores a mi separación*. Santiago: Imprenta Nacional, 1823.

———. *Relacion de la gran fiesta civica celebrada en Chile el 12 de febrero de 1818*. Santiago: Imprenta del Estado, 1818.

Motivos que ocasionaron la instalacion de la Junta de gobierno en Chile. Cadix: Imprenta de la Junta Superior de Gobierno, 1811.

"Noticia de los principales acahecimientos experimentados por el gefe de esquadra don Josef de Cordova." 10 August 1784. Archivo Museo Naval de Madrid. http://bibliotecavirtualdefensa.es/BVMDefensa/i18n/catalogo_imagenes/grupo.cmd?path=72918

Norambuena, Carmen, and Olga Uliánova, eds. *Viajeros rusos al sur del mundo*. Santiago: Centro de Investigaciones Diego Barros Arana/IDEA Universidad de Santiago, 2000.

O'Higgins, Bernardo. *Manifiesto del Capitán General Don Bernardo O'Higgins a los pueblos que dirige*. Santiago: Imprenta del Gobierno, 1820.

Olaguer Feliú, Manuel. *Relación de lo ocurrido en el Reyno de Chile desde el 25 de Mayo de 1810 hasta la erección de su Junta Gubernativa*. Santiago: Instituto O'Higginiano de Chile, 1989.

Pérez de Arza, María Ana. *Contestacion al segundo manifiesto de D. Fernando Errazuriz*. [Santiago]: Impr. de N. Ambrosy y Cia. por E. Molinari, 1828.

———. *Maria Ana Pérez de Arza contesta a D. Fernando Errázuriz: su papel de fecha 12 de Junio*. [Santiago]: n.p., [1828].

Pérez Rosales, Vicente. *Recuerdos del pasado (1814–1860)*. Santiago: Andrés Bello, 1980.

Premio postumo a los ilustres jenerales Juan Jose, Jose Miguel, y Luis de Carrera, contenido en la siguiente mocion. Santiago: Imprenta de N. Ambrosy & Ca., 1828.

Proyecto de Constitucion. [Santiago]: Imprenta de la Biblioteca, 1826.

Real Academia Española. *Diccionario de la lengua castellana*. 5 vols. Madrid: Imprenta de Francisco del Hierro/Imprenta de la Real Academia Española, 1726–1739.

———. *Diccionario de la lengua castellana*. Madrid: Joaquin Ibarra, 1780.

———. *Diccionario de la lengua castellana compuesto por la Real Academia Española*. Madrid: Joaquin Ibarra, 1783.

———. *Diccionario de la lengua española*. Madrid: Joaquin Ibarra, 1791.

———. *Diccionario de la lengua castellana*. Madrid: por la viudad de don Joaquín Ibarra, 1803.

———. *Diccionario de la lengua castellana*. 5th ed. Madrid: Imprenta Real, 1817.

Recopilación de los decretos expedidos por el Exmo. Sr. Director Supremo. Santiago: Imprenta de Gobierno, 1819.

Refutación al aviso importantisimo de los artesanos. Santiago: Imprenta de la Independencia, 1829.

Reglamento constitucional provisorio del Pueblo de Chile. Santiago: Imprenta del Gobierno, 1812.

"Relacion de gobierno que dejó el señor marqués de Avilés." *Anales de la Universidad de Chile* 47 (1875): 445–77.

Romance hecho en que se hace relacion circunstanciada de la gloriosa reconquista de la Ciudad de Buenos-Ayres. Buenos Aires: Real Imprenta de los Niños Expósitos, 1807.

Rugendas, Mauricio. *Album de Trajes Chilenos*. Santiago: Imprenta Litografica de J. B. Lebas, 1838.

Sagredo, Rafael. *De la Colonia a la República: los catecismos políticos americanos, 1811–1827*. Madrid: MAPFRE/Doce Calles, 2009.

Sagredo, Rafael, and José Ignacio González. *La Expedición Malaspina en la frontera austral del imperio español*. Santiago: Editorial Universitaria/Centro de Investigaciones Diego Barros Arana, 2004.

Schmidtmeyer, Peter. *Travels into Chile, over the Andes, in the years 1820 and 1821*. London: S. McDowall/Longman, Hurst, Rees, Orme, Brown, & Green, 1824.

Sesiones de los Cuerpos Lejislativos de la República de Chile, 1811 a 1845. 37 vols. Santiago: Imprenta Cervantes, 1887–1908.

Synodo Diocesana. Lima: En la Oficina de la Calle de la Encarnacion, 1764.

Suplemento al Vijía N. 3. Santiago: n.p., 1828.

Tornero, Recaredo Santos. *Chile ilustrado: Guía descriptivo del territorio de Chile, de las capitales de provincia, y de los puertos principales*. Valparaíso: Librerias i Ajencias del Mercurio, 1872.

Tupper, Ferdinand B. *Memorias del Coronel Tupper (1800–1830)*. Buenos Aires: Editorial Francisco de Aguirre, 1972.

Uriondo, Pedro. *El Ciudadano Pedro de Uriondo Gobernador Local del Departamento de Santiago*. Santiago: Imprenta de la Opinión, 1830.

Varas, José Miguel. *Lecciones elementales de moral*. Santiago: Imprenta de la Independencia, 1828.

[Verdugo, Manuel José]. *Clamor de la justicia e idioma de la verdad*. Santiago: Imprenta del Estado, 1818.

———. *Clamor de la justicia e idioma de la verdad: continuación del diálogo entre Paulino y Rosa*. Santiago: Imprenta del Estado, 1818.

Vergara, Sergio, ed. *Cartas de mujeres en Chile, 1630–1885*. Santiago: Editorial Andrés Bello, 1987.

Villodres, Diego Antonio. *Carta pastoral del Illmo. señor D. D. Diego Antonio Navarro Martin de Villodres*. Lima: Imprenta de los huérfanos, 1814.

Vowell, Richard Longeville. *Campaigns and Cruises in Venezuela and New Grenada*. 3 vols. London: Longman and Co., 1831.

Zapiola, José. *Recuerdos de treinta años*. 8th ed. Santiago: Zig-Zag, 1945.

Secondary Sources

Abercrombie, Thomas A. *Passing to América: Antonio (Née María) Yta's Transgressive, Transatlantic Life in the Twilight of the Spanish Empire*. University Park: Pennsylvania State University Press, 2018.

Adelman, Jeremy. "Mimesis and Rivalry: European Empires and Global Regimes." *Journal of Global History* 10, no. 1 (2015): 77–98.

———. *Sovereignty and Revolution in the Iberian Atlantic*. Princeton, NJ: Princeton University Press, 2006.

———. "The Rites of Statehood: Violence and Sovereignty in Spanish America, 1789–1821." *Hispanic American Historical Review* 90, no. 3 (2010): 391–422.

Adelman, Joseph M. *Revolutionary Networks: The Business and Politics of Printing the News, 1763–1789*. Baltimore: Johns Hopkins University Press, 2019.

Agamben, Giorgio. *Profanations*. New York: Zone Books, 2007.

Aguilar Rivera, José Antonio. *En pos de la quimera: reflexiones sobre el experimento constitucional atlántico*. Mexico: Centro de Investigación y Docencia Económicas/Fondo de Cultura Económica, 2000.

Albornoz Vásquez, María Eugenia. *Experiencias de conflicto: Subjetividades, cuerpos y sentimientos en Chile, siglos XVIII y XIX*. Santiago: Acto Editores, 2015.

———. "Seguir un delito a lo largo del tiempo: interrogaciones al cuerpo documental de pleitos judiciales por injuria en Chile, siglos XVIII y XIX." *Nuevo Mundo Mundos Nuevos* 2007. http://journals.openedition.org/nuevomundo/13033.

Amunátegui, Domingo. *Mayorazgos i títulos de Castilla*. 3 vols. Santiago: Imprenta, Litografía y Encuadernación Barcelona, 1901–1904.

Amunátegui, Miguel Luis. *La crónica de 1810*. 3 vols. Santiago: Imprenta de la República de Jacinto Núñez/Imprenta Elzeviriana de J. T. Medina, 1876–1899.

———. *Los precursores de la independencia de Chile*. 3 vols. Santiago: Imprenta de la República, 1870–1872.

Andermann, Jens. *The Optics of the State: Visuality and Power in Argentina and Brazil*. Pittsburgh: University of Pittsburgh Press, 2007.

Annino, Antonio, and Marcela Ternavasio, eds. *El laboratorio constitucional iberoamericano: 1807/1808–1830*. Madrid: Iberoamericana/Vervuert, 2012.

Arancibia, Claudia. "Un soldado de la Independencia." *Revista de Historia Militar* 4 (2005): 14–16.

Arancibia, Claudia, José Tomás Cornejo, and Carolina González. "Estudio preliminar." In *Pena de muerte en Chile colonial: Cinco casos de homicidio de la Real Audiencia*, edited by Claudia Arancibia, José Tomás Cornejo, and Carolina González, 9–30. Santiago: RIL Editores/Centro de Investigaciones Diego Barros Arana, 2003.

Araya, Alejandra. "Azotar. El cuerpo, prácticas de dominio colonial e imaginarios del Reino a la República de Chile." In *Formas de control y disciplinamiento: Chile, América y Europa, siglos XVI–XIX*, edited by Verónica Undurraga and Rafael Gaune, 194–215. Santiago: Uqbar Editores, 2014.

———. "El castigo físico: el cuerpo como representación de la persona, un capítulo en la historia de la occidentalización de América, siglos XVI–XVIII." *Historia* 39, no. 2 (2006): 349–67.

———. "Imaginario sociopolítico e impresos modernos: de la plebe al pueblo en proclamas, panfletos y folletos. Chile, 1813–1823." *Fronteras de la Historia* 16, no. 2 (2011): 297–326.

———. "La fundación de una memoria colonial: la construcción de sujetos y narrativas en el espacio judicial del siglo XVIII." In *Justicia, poder y sociedad en Chile: recorridos históricos*, edited by Tomás Cornejo and Carolina González, 185–216. Santiago: Ediciones Universidad Diego Portales, 2007.

———. "Las beatas en Chile colonial: en el corazón de lo social y en el margen de la historiografía." *Dimension Histórica de Chile* 19 (2004–2005): 13–46.

———. *Ociosos, vagabundos y malentretenidos en Chile colonial*. Santiago: Dirección de Bibliotecas, Archivos y Museos, 2001.

———. "Petronila Zúñiga contra Julián Santos por estupro, rapto y extracción de Antonia Valenzuela, su hija . . . el uso de los textos judiciales en el problema de la identidad como problema de sujetos históricos." *Anuario de Postgrado* 3 (1999): 219–41.

———. "Registrar a la plebe o el color de las castas: 'calidad', 'clase' y 'casta' en la Matrícula de Alday (Chile, siglo XVIII)." In *América colonial: denominaciones, clasificaciones e identidades*, edited by Alejandra Araya and Jaime Valenzuela, 331–61. Santiago: RIL Editores, 2010.

———. "Sirvientes contra amos: las heridas en lo íntimo propio." In *Historia de la vida privada en Chile*, vol. 1, edited by Rafael Sagredo and Cristián Gazmuri, 161–97. Santiago: Taurus, 2005.

Arendt, Hannah. *On Revolution*. New York: Penguin Books, 2006.

———. *The Promise of Politics*. Edited by Jerome Kohn. New York: Shocken Books, 2005.

Arnal, William E., and Russell T. McCutcheon. *The Sacred Is the Profane: The Political Nature of "Religion."* Oxford: Oxford University Press, 2013.

Astigarraga, Jesús. "La Ilustración napolitana imputada. Críticas y censuras a la Scienza della legislazione de G. Filangieri en la España de finales del siglo XVIII." *Nuevo Mundo Mundos Nuevos*, Workshops, 2007. http://journals.openedition.org/nuevomundo/6911.

Austin, Shawn Michael. *Colonial Kinship: Guaraní, Spaniards, and Africans in Paraguay*. Albuquerque: University of New Mexico Press, 2020.

Baker, Keith M. *Inventing the French Revolution: Essays on French Political Culture in the Eighteenth Century*. Cambridge: Cambridge University Press, 1990.

Barbier, Jacques A. "Elites and Cadres in Bourbon Chile." *Hispanic American Historical Review* 52, no. 3 (1972): 416–35.

———. *Reform and Politics in Bourbon Chile, 1755–1796*. Ottawa: University of Ottawa Press, 1980.

Barros Arana, Diego. *Historia Jeneral de Chile*. 16 vols. Santiago: Rafael Jover, 1884–1902.

———. *Historia Jeneral de la Independencia de Chile*. 4 vols. Santiago: Imprenta del Ferrocarril, 1854–1858.

———. "Rasgos biográficos de don Melchor de Santiago Concha (1799–1883)." In Diego Barros Arana, *Obras completas*, vol. 12, 255–306. Santiago: Imprenta Cervantes/Imprenta Barcelona, 1908–1914.

Barros Borgoño, Luis. *La misión del vicario apostólico Don Juan Muzi: notas para la historia de Chile (1823–1825)*. Santiago: Imprenta de "La Época," 1883.

Bauer, Arnold J. *Chilean Rural Society from the Spanish Conquest to 1930*. Cambridge: Cambridge University Press, 1975.

Bellion, Wendy. *Iconoclasm in New York: Revolution to Reenactment*. University Park: The Pennsylvania State University Press, 2019.

Bengoa, José. *Historia social de la agricultura chilena*. 2 vols. Santiago: Ediciones Sur, 1988–1990.

Benton, Lauren. *A Search for Sovereignty: Law and Geography in European Empires, 1400–1900*. New York: Cambridge University Press, 2010.

Bernand, Carmen. "El color de los criollos: de las naciones a las castas, de las castas a la nación." In *Huellas de África en América: Perspectivas para Chile*, edited by Celia Cussen, 13–34. Santiago: Universitaria, 2009.

Betancourt Castillo, Francisco. *Ezeiza, falsificador y realista. Negocios, sociabilidad y política en Chile a fines del período colonial*. Valparaíso: Ediciones Universitarias de Valparaíso, 2022.

Blanchard, Peter. *Fearful Vassals: Urban Elite Loyalty in the Viceroyalty of Río de la Plata, 1776–1810*. Pittsburgh: University of Pittsburgh Press, 2020.

Boccara, Guillaume. *Los vencedores: historia del pueblo mapuche en la época colonial*. Translated by Diego Milos. San Pedro de Atacama: IIAM, 2007.

Boddice, Rob. *The History of Emotions*. Manchester: Manchester University Press, 2018.

Boltanski, Luc. *Énigmes et complots: une enquête à propos d'enquêtes*. Paris: Gallimard, 2012.

Borucki, Alex. *From Shipmates to Soldiers: Emerging Black Identities in the Río de la Plata*. Albuquerque: University of New Mexico Press, 2015.

Bourdieu, Pierre. "What Makes a Social Class? On the Theoretical and Practical Existence of Groups." *Berkeley Journal of Sociology* 32 (1987): 1–17.

Bowen Silva, Martín. *Experimentar el cuerpo y escribir los pecados: la confesión general de José Ignacio Eyzaguirre (1799–1804)*. Lima: Instituto Francés de Estudios Andinos/Instituto de Estudios Peruanos, 2014.

Bravo Lira, Bernardino. *El Estado de Derecho en la historia de Chile: por la razón o la fuerza*. Santiago: Ediciones Universidad Católica de Chile, 1996.

Bredekamp, Horst. *Théorie de l'acte d'image*. Translated by Frédéric Jolly. Paris: La Découverte, 2015.

Bridikhina, Eugenia. *Theatrum mundi: entramados del poder en Charcas colonial*. Lima: Instituto Francés de Estudios Andinos/Plural, 2007.

Brubaker, Rogers, and Frederick Cooper. "Beyond 'Identity.'" *Theory and Society* 29 (2000): 1–47.

Caffarena Barcenilla, Paula. *Viruela y vacuna: difusión y circulación de una práctica médica. Chile en el contexto hispanoamericano 1780–1830*. Santiago: Universitaria, 2016.

Cáceres, Jorge. "Republicanismo bíblico independentista. El caso de la 'instrucción' de Antonio Berney (Santiago, 1780–1781)." *Revista de Humanidades* 36 (2017): 69–96.

Calderón, María Teresa, and Clément Thibaud. *La majestad de los pueblos en la Nueva Granada y Venezuela (1780–1832)*. Bogotá: Universidad del Externado de Colombia/Taurus, 2010.

Calomino, Dario. *Defacing the Past: Damnation and Desecration in Imperial Rome*. London: Spink, 2016.

Camp, Stephanie M. H. *Closer to Freedom: Enslaved Women and Everyday Resistance in the Plantation South*. Chapel Hill: University of North Carolina Press, 2004.

Canetti, Elias. *Masa y poder*. 3rd ed. Madrid: Alianza Editorial, 2018.

Cano Roldán, Imelda. *La mujer en el Reyno de Chile*. Santiago: Municipalidad de Santiago, 1981.

Cañeque, Alejandro. "The Emotions of Power: Love, Anger, and Fear, or How to Rule the Spanish Empire." In *Emotions and Daily Life in Colonial Mexico*, edited by Javier Villa-Flores and Sonya Lipsett-Rivera, 89–121. Albuquerque: University of New Mexico Press, 2014.

———. *The King's Living Image: The Culture and Politics of Viceregal Power in Colonial Mexico*. New York: Routledge, 2004.

Cañizares-Esguerra, Jorge. *How to Write the History of the New World: Histories, Epistemologies, and Identities in the Eighteenth-Century Atlantic World*. Stanford, CA: Stanford University Press, 2001.

Carayon, Céline. *Eloquence Embodied: Nonverbal Communication among French and Indigenous Peoples in the Americas*. Williamsburg, VA: Omohundro Institute of Early American History and Culture/University of North Carolina Press, 2019.

Carmagnani, Marcello. *Los mecanismos de la vida económica en una sociedad colonial: Chile, 1680–1830*. Santiago: Dirección de Bibliotecas, Archivos y Museos, 2001.

Cartes, Armando. "¿Bárbaros o ciudadanos? Los Mapuches en el albor Republicano." In *Ciudadanía: temas y debates*, 221–48. Santiago: Centro de Estudios Bicentenario, 2015.

———. *Concepción contra Chile. Consensos y tensiones regionales en la Patria Vieja*. 2nd ed. Santiago: Ediciones Centro de Estudios Bicentenario, 2016.

———. "La constitución de Cádiz de 1812. Derroteros americanos, transferencias y perspectivas." *Cuadernos de Historia* 47 (2017): 39–58.

Casanova, Holdenis. "Entre la ideología y la realidad: la inclusión de los mapuche en la nación chilena (1810–1830)." *Revista de Historia Indígena* 4 (2000): 9–48.

Castillo, Vasco. *La creación de la República. La filosofía pública en Chile, 1810–1830*. Santiago: LOM, 2009.

Castillo, Vasco, and Camilo Fernández. *Republicanismo popular: escritos de Santiago Ramos, "El Quebradino."* Santiago: LOM, 2017.

Castoriadis, Cornelius. *L'institution imaginaire de la société*. Paris: Seuil, 1975.

Catepillan Tessi, Ezequiel. *La "Provincia de Chile": Construcción del Estado-Nación en Chiloé, 1830–1880*. PhD diss., Ciudad de México: El Colegio de México, 2017.

———. "Pu peñi en la cadena." In *Awükan ka kuxankan zugu Wajmapu mew. Violencias coloniales en Wajmapu*, edited by Enrique Antileo Baeza, Luis Cárcamo-Huechante, Margarita Calfío Montalva, and Herson Huinca-Piutrin, 57–86. Temuco, Chile: Ediciones Comunidad de Historia Mapuche, 2015.

Cavieres, Eduardo. *La Serena en el s. XVIII: las dimensiones del poder local en una sociedad regional*. Valparaíso: Ediciones Universitarias de Valparaíso, 1993.

———. *Sobre la independencia en Chile: el fin del Antiguo Régimen y los orígenes de la representación moderna*. Valparaíso: Ediciones Universitarias de Valparaíso, 2012.

Chambers, Sarah C. *Families in War and Peace: Chile from Colony to Nation*. Durham, NC: Duke University Press, 2015.

———. *From Subjects to Citizens: Honor, Gender, and Politics in Arequipa, Peru, 1780–1854*. University Park: Pennsylvania State University Press, 1999.

———. "Private Crimes, Public Order: Honor, Gender, and the Law in Early Republican Peru." In *Honor, Status, and Law in Modern Latin America*, edited by Sueann Caulfield and Sarah C. Chambers, 27–49. Durham, NC: Duke University Press, 2005.

Chiaramonte, José Carlos. *Fundamentos intelectuales y políticos de las independencias: notas para una nueva historia intelectual de Iberoamérica*. Buenos Aires: Teseo, 2010.

———. *Nación y Estado en Iberoamérica. El lenguaje politico en tiempos de la independencia*. Buenos Aires: Editorial Sudamericana, 2004.

Chueca, Ignacio. "'Venta es dar una cosa cierta por precio cierto.' Cultura jurídica y esclavitud infantil en pleitos fronterizos chilenos (1763–1775)." In *Cultura legal y espacios de justicia en América, siglos XVI–XIX*, edited by Macarena Cordero, Rafael Gaune, and Rodrigo Moreno, 167–94. Santiago: Universidad Adolfo Ibáñez, Departamento de Historia/ Dirección de Bibliotecas, Archivos y Museos, Centro de Investigaciones Diego Barros Arana, 2017.

Cid, Gabriel. "'Las señales de los últimos tiempos.' Laicidad y escatología en el pensamiento católico hispanoamericano del siglo XIX." *Hispania Sacra* 66, no. 133 (2014): 179–207.

———. "Un ícono funcional: la invención del *roto* como símbolo nacional, 1870–1888." In *Nación y nacionalismo en Chile. Siglo XIX*, volume 1, edited by Gabriel Cid and Alejandro San Francisco, 221–54. Santiago: Centro de Estudios Bicentenario, 2009.

———. *Pensar la revolución: historia intelectual de la independencia de Chile*. Santiago: Ediciones Universidad Diego Portales, 2019.

———. "Ritos para una nueva legitimidad: ceremoniales constitucionales y republicanismo en Chile (1812–1833)." *Historia Crítica* 47 (2012): 17–43.

———. "Terminar la revolución: el debate político-constitucional en Chile, 1829–1833." *Revista de Estudios Políticos* 176 (2017): 17–45.

Clavero, Bartolomé. *Historia del derecho: derecho común*. Salamanca: Ediciones Universidad de Salamanca, 1994.

Clay, Richard S. *Iconoclasm in Revolutionary Paris: The Transformation of Signs*. Oxford: Voltaire Foundation, 2012.

Cohen-Aponte, Ananda. "Imagining Insurgency in Late Colonial Peru." In *Visual Culture and Indigenous Agency in the Early Americas*, edited by Alessia Frassani, 188–210. Leiden: Brill, 2021.

Colivoro, Juan, and Ignacio Álamos. *Población indígena en el Santiago colonial. Fines del siglo XVIII*. Santiago: Ediciones del Mate, 2012.

Collier, Simon. *Ideas and Politics of Chilean Independence, 1808–1833*. Cambridge: Cambridge University Press, 1967.

———. *Chile: The Making of a Republic, 1830–1865: Politics and Ideas*. Cambridge: Cambridge University Press, 2003.

Collier, William Miller, and Guillermo Feliú Cruz. *La primera misión de los Estados Unidos de América en Chile*. Santiago: Imprenta Cervantes, 1926.

Concha, Manuel. *Crónica de La Serena desde su fundación hasta nuestros días (1549–1870)*. 2nd ed. Santiago: Universidad de Chile, 1979.

Concha y Toro, Melchor. *Chile durante los años de 1824 a 1828*. Santiago: Imprenta Nacional, 1862.

Contreras, Hugo. "Artesanos mulatos y soldados beneméritos. El Batallón de Infantes de la Patria en la Guerra de Independencia de Chile, 1795–1820." *Historia* 44, no. 1 (2011): 51–89.

———. "Contextos sociales y culturales de un pintor mulato a principios del siglo XIX." In *José Gil de Castro: Pintor de Libertadores*, edited by Natalia Majluf, 20–33. Lima: Museo de Arte de Lima, 2014.

———. "Las milicias de pardos y morenos libres en Santiago de Chile en el siglo XVIII, 1760–1800." *Cuadernos de Historia* 25 (2006): 93–117.

———. "Oficios, milicias y cofradías. Éxito económico, prestigio y redes sociales afromestizas en Santiago de Chile, 1780–1820." *Revista de Historia Social y de las Mentalidades* 17, no. 2 (2013): 43–74.

———. "Usos y abusos del fuero militar entre los milicianos pardos de Santiago de Chile durante la segunda mitad del siglo XVIII: un aporte documental." *El Taller de la Historia* 8, no. 8 (2016). https://revistas.unicartagena.edu.co/index.php/eltallerdelahistoria/article/view/1339.

Cornejo, José Tomás. *Manuela Orellana, la criminal: género y cultura en el Chile del siglo XVIII*. Santiago: Tajamar Editores/Centro de Investigación Diego Barros Arana, 2006.

Coronado, Jorge. *The Andes Imagined: Indigenismo, Society, and Modernity*. Pittsburgh: University of Pittsburgh Press, 2009.

Coronado, Raúl. *A World Not to Come: A History of Latino Writing and Print Culture*. Cambridge, MA: Harvard University Press, 2013.

Correa Gómez, Antonio. *El último suplicio: ejecuciones públicas en la formación republicana de Chile, 1810–1843*. Santiago: Ocho Libros Editores, 2007.

Costeloe, Michael P. *The Central Republic in Mexico, 1835–1846: "Hombres de Bien" in the Age of Santa Anna*. Cambridge: Cambridge University Press, 1993.

Cordero Fernández, Macarena. "Destierro a la isla de Juan Fernández a fines del siglo XVIII: Civilización, corrección y exclusión social." In *América en diásporas: esclavitudes y migraciones forzadas en Chile y otras regiones americanas (siglos XVI-XIX)*, edited by Jaime Valenzuela Márquez, 439–67. Santiago: RIL Editores/Instituto de Historia, Pontificia Universidad Católica de Chile, 2017.

Corvalán, Nicolás. "Amores, intereses y violencias en la familia de Chile tradicional. Una mirada histórica a la cultura afectiva de niños y jóvenes." *Contribuciones Científicas y Tecnológicas* 114 (1996): 57–78.

Craig, Robert T. "How We Talk about How We Talk: Communication Theory in the Public Interest." *Journal of Communication* 55, no. 4 (December 2005): 659–67.

Cromwell, Jesse. *The Smugglers' World: Illicit Trade and Atlantic Communities in Eighteenth-Century Venezuela*. Chapel Hill: University of North Carolina Press, 2018.

Cruz, Isabel. *El traje: transformaciones de una segunda piel*. Santiago: Ediciones Universidad Católica de Chile, 1996.

———. "El traje como signo de los nuevos tiempos: la Revolución Francesa y la moda en Chile, 1800–1820." In *La Revolución Francesa y Chile*, edited by Ricardo Krebs and Cristián Gazmuri, 179–223. Santiago: Editorial Universitaria, 1990.

———. *La fiesta: metamorfosis de lo cotidiano*. Santiago: Ediciones de la Universidad Católica de Chile, 1995.

———. *La muerte: transfiguración de la vida*. Santiago: Ediciones de la Universidad Católica de Chile, 1998.

———. *Patrimonio artístico en Chile: De la Independencia a la República, 1790–1840*. Santiago: Origo Ediciones, 2016.

Darnton, Robert. *Poetry and the Police: Communication Networks in Eighteenth-Century Paris*. Cambridge, MA: Belknap Press of Harvard University Press, 2010.

De Certeau, Michel. *L'invention du quotidien*. Vol. 1. Paris: Gallimard, 1990.

De Ramón, Armando. *Santiago de Chile (1541–1991). Historia de una sociedad urbana*. Santiago: Sudamericana, 2000.

De Ramón, Armando, and José Manuel Larraín. *Orígenes de la vida económica chilena, 1659–1808*. Santiago: Centro de Estudios Públicos, 1982.

De Ramón, Emma. "Demandas por igualdad en Chile colonial." In *Historias de racismo y discriminación en Chile*, edited by Rafael Gaune and Martín Lara, 193–223. Santiago: Uqbar Editores, 2009.

Dedieu, Jean-Pierre. *Après le Roi. Essai sur l'effondrement de la monarchie espagnole*. Madrid: Casa de Velázquez, 2010.

Del Águila, Alicia. *Los velos y las pieles: cuerpo, género y reordenamiento social en el Perú republicano (Lima, 1822–1872)*. Lima: Instituto de Estudios Peruanos, 2003.

Delgado, Jessica L. *Laywomen and the Making of Colonial Catholicism in New Spain, 1630–1790*. Cambridge: Cambridge University Press, 2018.

Delumeau, Jean. *Le péché et la peur. La culpabilisation en Occident (XIIIe–XVIIIe siècles)*. Paris: Fayard, 1983.

Desramé, Céline. "La comunidad de lectores y la formación del espacio público en Chile revolucionario: de la cultura del manuscrito al reino de la prensa (1808–1833)." In *Los espacios públicos en Iberoamérica: ambigüedades y problemas. Siglos XVIII–XIX*, 273–99. Mexico: Centro Francés de Estudios Mexicanos/Fondo de Cultura Económica, 1998.

Di Meglio, Gabriel. *¡Viva el bajo pueblo! La plebe urbana de Buenos Aires y la política entre la Revolución de Mayo y el rosismo (1810–1829)*. Buenos Aires: Prometeo, 2007.

Diener, Pablo. *Rugendas: su viaje por Chile, 1834–1842*. Santiago: Origo Ediciones, 2012.

———. "Lo pintoresco como categoría estética en el arte de viajeros: apuntes para la obra de Rugendas." *Historia* 40, no. 2 (2007): 285–309.

Diggs, Irene. "Zambo-Peluca." *Phylon* 13, no. 1 (1952): 43–47.

Domergue, Lucienne. *Le livre en Espagne au temps de la Révolution française*. Lyon: Presses Universitaires de Lyon, 1984.

Donoso, Ricardo. *El Marqués de Osorno Don Ambrosio Higgins, 1720–1801*. Santiago: Publicaciones de la Universidad de Chile, 1941.

———. *Las ideas políticas en Chile*. Mexico: Fondo de Cultura Económica, 1946.

———. *Un letrado del siglo XVIII. El Dr. José Perfecto de Salas*. 2 vols. Buenos Aires: Universidad de Buenos Aires, Facultad de Filosofía y Letras, 1963.

Donoso Fritz, Karen. "'Fue famosa la chingana . . . '. Diversión popular y cultura nacional en Santiago de Chile, 1820–1840." *Revista de Historia Social y de las Mentalidades* 13, no. 1 (2009): 87–119.

Dougnac Rodríguez, Antonio. "Algunas manifestaciones del regalismo borbónico a fines del siglo XVIII." *Boletín de la Academia Chilena de la Historia* 102 (1991–1992): 43–94.

Dubcovsky, Alejandra. *Informed Power: Communication in the Early American South*. Cambridge, MA: Harvard University Press, 2016.

Duschinsky, Robbie. "Pure and Impure in the Philosophy of Giorgio Agamben." *Telos* 160 (2012): 139–64.

Earle, Rebecca. *The Return of the Native: Indians and Myth-Making in Spanish America, 1810–1930*. Durham, NC: Duke University Press, 2007.

Echeverri, Marcela. *Indian and Slave Royalists in the Age of Revolution: Reform, Revolution, and Royalism in the Northern Andes, 1780–1825*. New York: Cambridge University Press, 2016.

Edwards, Erika Denise. *Hiding in Plain Sight: Black Women, the Law, and the Making of a White Argentine Republic*. Tuscaloosa: University of Alabama Press, 2020.

Eller, Anne. *We Dream Together: Dominican Independence, Haiti, and the Fight for Caribbean Freedom*. Durham, NC: Duke University Press, 2016.

Elliott, John. *Empires of the Atlantic World: Britain and Spain in America, 1492–1830*. New Haven, CT: Yale University Press, 2007.

Engel, Emily. *Pictured Politics: Visualizing Colonial History in South American Portrait Collections*. Austin: University of Texas Press, 2020.

Enríquez, Lucrecia. "Familia local y política imperial: la élite de Santiago de Chile en la monarquía española (siglo XVIII)." *Temas Americanistas* 20 (2008): 77–91.

———. "La reforma de los regulares en la naciente república chilena (1817–1824)." In *Tradición y reforma en la Iglesia Hispanoamericana*, edited by Lucrecia Enríquez, Rodolfo Aguirre, and Francisco Cervantes Bello, 51–84. Santiago: Centro de Estudios Bicentenario/Instituto de Ciencias Sociales y Humanidades "Alfonso Vélez Pliego," Benemérita Universidad Autónoma de Puebla/Instituto de Investigaciones sobre la Universidad y la Educación, UNAM, 2015.

———. "La República chilena ante la cuestión indígena (1810–1830)." *Hispania Sacra* 63, no. 128 (2011): 627–52.

Errázuriz, Federico. *Chile bajo el imperio de la Constitucion de 1828*. Santiago: Imprenta Chilena, 1861.

Esposito, Roberto. *Categorías de lo impolítico*. Translated by Roberto Raschella. Buenos Aires: Katz, 2006.

———. *Diez pensamientos acerca de la política*. Translated by Luciano Padilla López. Buenos Aires: Fondo de Cultura Económica, 2012.

———. *Instituting Thought: Three Paradigms of Political Ontology*. Translated by Mark William Epstein. Medford, MA: Polity Press, 2021.

Eyzaguirre, Jaime. "El Doctor don Miguel de Eyzaguirre, Universitario y Magistrado. 1770–1821." *Boletín de la Academia Chilena de la Historia* 52 (1955): 71–132.

———. *Viejas imágenes*. Santiago: Editorial Difusión, 1947.

Feliú Cruz, Guillermo. *La abolición de la esclavitud en Chile: proceso histórico y social*. 2nd ed. Santiago: Universitaria, 1973.

Fernández, Marcos. "'La mano del plebeyo levantada, es la montaña que se despeña.' La conceptualización del *pueblo* en tiempos de transformación. Chile, 1750–1850." *Historia* 42, no. 1 (2009): 109–39.

———. "Sangre por sangre: la retórica judicial y la veracidad documental como problema heurístico en las solicitudes de indulto." In *Justicia, poder y sociedad en Chile: recorridos históricos*, edited by Tomás Cornejo and Carolina González, 219–40. Santiago: Ediciones Universidad Diego Portales, 2007.

Fernández Sebastián, Javier. *Historia conceptual en el Atlántico ibérico: lenguajes, tiempos, revoluciones*. Madrid: Fondo de Cultura Económica, 2021.

Fernández Sebastián, Javier, and Joëlle Chassin, eds. *L'avènement de l'opinion publique. Europe et Amérique XVIII-XIX*e *siècles*. Paris: L'Harmattan, 2004.

Ferrer, Ada. *Freedom's Mirror: Cuba and Haiti in the Age of Revolution*. New York: Cambridge University Press, 2014.

Figueroa, Consuelo. "El honor femenino: ideario colectivo y práctica cotidiana." In *Perfiles revelados: Historias de mujeres en Chile, siglos XVIII–XX*, edited by Diana Veneros, 63–90. Santiago: Ediciones Universidad de Santiago, 1997.

Figueroa, Virgilio. *Diccionario histórico, biográfico y bibliográfico de Chile*. Santiago: Impr. y Litogr. La Ilustración, 1925–1931.

Finch, Aisha K. *Rethinking Slave Rebellion in Cuba: La Escalera and the Insurgencies of 1841–1844*. Chapel Hill: University of North Carolina Press, 2015.

Fisher, Andrew B. "Keeping and Losing One's Head: Composure and

Emotional Outbursts as Political Performance in Late-Colonial Mexico." In *Emotions and Daily Life in Colonial Mexico*, edited by Javier Villa-Flores and Sonya Lipsett-Rivera, 168–97. Albuquerque: University of New Mexico Press, 2014.

Flores, Leyla. "Mujeres del bajo pueblo y la construcción de una sociabilidad propia: la experiencia de las pulperías en Santiago, Valparaíso y el Norte Chico (1750–1830)." *Dimensión Histórica de Chile* 13–14 (1997–1998): 13–32.

Fogel, Michèle. *Les cérémonies de l'information dans la France du XVIe siècle au milieu du XVIIIe siècle*. Paris: Fayard, 1989.

Forment, Carlos A. *Democracy in Latin America, 1760–1900*. Vol. 1. Chicago: University of Chicago Press, 2003.

Fossier, Arnaud. "La contagion des péchés (XIe–XIIIe siècles). Aux origines canoniques du biopouvoir." *Tracés* 21 (2011): 23–39.

———. "'*Propter vitandum scandalum*': Histoire d'une catégorie juridique (XIIIe–XVe siècle)." *Mélanges de l'Ecole française à Rome. Moyen Âge* 121, no. 2 (2009): 317–48.

Foucault, Michel. "Les têtes de la politique." In *Dits et écrits*, vol. 2, 9–13. Paris: Gallimard, 2001.

Fradkin, Raúl O. "Cultura política y acción colectiva en Buenos Aires (1806–1829): un ejercicio de exploración." In *¿Y el pueblo dónde está? Contribuciones para una historia popular de la Revolución de Independencia en el Río de la Plata*, 2nd ed., edited by Raúl O. Fradkin, 25–60. Ciudad Autónoma de Buenos Aires: Prometeo Libros, 2015.

———. *La historia de una montonera: Bandolerismo y caudillismo en Buenos Aires, 1826*. Buenos Aires: Siglo Veintiuno Editores, 2006.

Frank, Jason. *Constituent Moments: Enacting the People in Postrevolutionary America*. Durham, NC: Duke University Press, 2010.

———. *The Democratic Sublime: On Aesthetics and Popular Assembly*. New York: Oxford University Press, 2021.

Fraser, Ronald. *Napoleon's Cursed War: Popular Resistance in the Spanish Peninsular War, 1808–1814*. London: Verso, 2008.

Freedberg, David. *The Power of Images: Studies in the History and Theory of Response*. Chicago: University of Chicago Press, 1989.

Frontaura, José Manuel. *Historia del Convictorio Carolino (Apuntes para la historia de los antiguos colegios de Chile)*. Santiago: Imprenta Nacional, 1889.

———. *Noticias históricas sobre las escuelas públicas de Chile á fines de la era colonial*. Santiago: Imprenta Nacional, 1892.

Fureix, Emmanuel, ed. *Iconoclasme et révolutions de 1789 à nos jours*. Ceyzérieu, France: Champ Vallon, 2014.

———. *L'œil blessé. Politiques de l'iconoclasme après la Révolution française*. Ceyzérieu, France: Champ Vallon, 2019.

Gallardo, Viviana. "Héroes indómitos, bárbaros y ciudadanos chilenos: el discurso sobre el indio en la construcción de la identidad nacional." *Historia Indígena* 5 (2001): 119–34.

García, Guadalupe. *Beyond the Walled City: Colonial Exclusion in Havana*. Oakland: University of California Press, 2016.

Garrido, Pablo. *Historial de la cueca*. Valparaíso: Ediciones Universitarias de Valparaíso, 1979.

Garriga, Carlos. "Orden jurídico y poder político en el Antiguo Régimen." In *Cádiz, 1812: La constitución jurisdiccional*, edited by Carlos Garriga and Marta Llorente, 43–72. Madrid: Centro de Estudios Políticos y Constitucionales, 2007.

Gauchet, Marcel. *L'avènement de la démocratie*. 4 vols. Paris: Gallimard, 2007–2017.

———. *Le désenchantement du monde: une histoire politique de la religion*. Paris: Gallimard, 1985.

Gazmuri, Susana. "Los modelos políticos de la antigüedad clásica y su papel en los discursos republicanos en Chile (1810–1833)." *Estudios Avanzados* 27 (2017): 37–53.

Ghirardi, Mónica, and Jaqueline Vassallo. "El encierro femenino como práctica. Notas para el ejemplo de Córdoba, Argentina, en el contexto de Iberoamérica en los siglos XVIII y XIX." *Revista de Historia Social y de las Mentalidades* 14, no. 2 (2010): 73–101.

Godoy Orellana, Milton. "Fiestas, construcción de Estado nacional y resignificación del espacio público en Chile: Norte Chico, 1800–1840." *Cuadernos de Historia* 37 (2012): 51–73.

Goicovic, Igor. "Consideraciones teóricas sobre la violencia social en Chile (1850–1930)." *Última Década* 21 (2005): 121–45.

———. "De la indiferencia a la resistencia. Los sectores populares y la Guerra de Independencia en el norte de Chile (1817–1823)." *Revista de Indias*, 74, no. 260 (2014): 129–60.

———. "Es tan corto el amor y es tan largo el olvido . . . Seducción y abandono en Chile tradicional, 1750–1880." *Contribuciones Científicas y Tecnológicas* 114 (1996): 25–56.

———. *Relaciones de solidaridad y estrategia de reproducción social en la familia popular del Chile tradicional (1750–1860)*. Madrid: Consejo Superior de Investigaciones Científicas/Instituto de Historia, 2006.

Goicovic, Igor, and Andrea Armijo. "Tierras en disputa. El traslado de los pueblos de indios de Melipilla, siglos XVIII–XIX." *Historia y Sociedad* 39 (2020): 24–50.

Goldman, Noemí. "Legitimidad y deliberación: el concepto de opinión pública en Iberoamérica, 1750–1850." In *Diccionario politico y social del mundo americano: la era de las revoluciones, 1750–1850*, edited by Javier Fernández Sebastián, 981–98. Madrid: Fundación Carolina/Sociedad Estatal de Conmemoraciones Culturales/ Centro de Estudios Políticos y Constitucionales, 2009.

González Bernaldo de Quirós, Pilar. *Civilidad y política en los orígenes de la nación argentina: las sociabilidades en Buenos Aires, 1829–1862*. Buenos Aires: Fondo de Cultura Económica, 2008.

———. "Literatura injuriosa y opinión pública en Santiago de Chile durante la primera mitad del siglo XIX." *Estudios Públicos* 76 (Spring 1999): 233–62.

González Undurraga, Carolina. "En busca de la libertad: la petición judicial como estrategia política. El caso de las esclavas negras (1750–1823)." In *Justicia, poder y sociedad en Chile: recorridos históricos*, edited by Tomás Cornejo and Carolina González, 57–83. Santiago: Ediciones Universidad Diego Portales, 2007.

Grez, Sergio. *De la "regeneración del pueblo" a la huelga general: génesis y evolución histórica del movimiento popular en Chile (1810–1890)*. 2nd ed. Santiago: RIL Editores, 2007.

Grez, Vicente. *Las mujeres de la independencia*. Santiago: Imprenta Gutenberg, 1878.

Groebner, Valentin. *Who Are You?: Identification, Deception, and Surveillance in Early Modern Europe*. Translated by Mark Kyburz and John Peck. New York: Zone Books, 2007.

Guarda, Fernando. *Historia de Valdivia, 1552–1952*. Santiago: Imprenta Cultura, 1953.

Guarda, Gabriel. *El arquitecto de la Moneda: Joaquín Toesca, 1752–1799: una imagen del imperio español en América*. Santiago: Ediciones Universidad Católica de Chile, 1997.

———. *Historia urbana del reino de Chile*. Santiago: Andrés Bello, 1978.

———. *La ciudad chilena del siglo XVIII*. Buenos Aires: Centro Editor de América Latina, 1968.

———. *La Edad Media de Chile: Historia de la Iglesia desde la fundación de Santiago a la incorporación de Chiloé, 1541–1826*. Santiago: Ediciones Universidad Católica de Chile, 2016.

Guardino, Peter. *The Time of Liberty: Popular Political Culture in Oaxaca, 1750–1850*. Durham, NC: Duke University Press, 2005.

Guerra, François-Xavier. *Modernidad e independencias: ensayo sobre las revoluciones hispánicas*. 2nd ed. Mexico: MAPFRE/Fondo de Cultura Económica, 1993.

Guerra, François-Xavier, and Annick Lempérière. "Introducción." In François-Xavier Guerra et al. *Los espacios públicos en Iberoamérica: ambigüedades y problemas. Siglos XVIII–XIX*, 5–21. Mexico: Centro Francés de Estudios Mexicanos/Fondo de Cultura Económica, 1998.

Guerra, François-Xavier, et al. *Los espacios públicos en Iberoamérica: ambigüedades y problemas. Siglos XVIII–XIX*. Mexico: Centro Francés de Estudios Mexicanos/Fondo de Cultura Económica, 1998.

Guerra Acuña, Alejandra. *Pensar como no se debe: las ideas en crisis. Conspiradores e ilustrados en Santiago de Chile (1780–1810)*. Valparaíso: Ediciones Universitarias de Valparaíso, 2013.

Guerrero Lira, Cristián. *La contrarrevolución de la independencia en Chile*. Santiago: Editorial Universitaria/Dirección de Bibliotecas, Archivos y Museos, 2002.

Guevara, Tomás. *Los Araucanos en la revolución de la Independencia*. Santiago: Imprenta Cervantes, 1910.

Gutiérrez, Daniel. *La Restauración en la Nueva Granada (1815–1819)*. Bogotá: Universidad Externado de Colombia, 2016.

Habermas, Jürgen. *The Structural Transformation of the Public Sphere: An Inquiry into a Category of Bourgeois Society*. Translated by Thomas Burger. Cambridge, MA: MIT Press, 1989.

Hamnett, Brian. *The End of Iberian Rule on the American Continent (1770–1830)*. Cambridge: Cambridge University Press, 2017.

Hanisch, Walter. "La filosofía de don Juan Egaña." *Historia* 3 (1964): 164–310.

———. *Peumo: Historia de una Parroquia, 1662–1962*. Santiago: Instituto de Historia, Pontificia Universidad Católica de Chile, 1963.

Hanks, William F. *Converting Words: Maya in the Age of the Cross*. Berkeley: University of California Press, 2010.

Hartog, François. *Regimes of Historicity: Presentism and the Experiences of Time*. Translated by Saskia Brown. New York: University of Columbia Press, 2015.

Heise, Julio. *Años de formación y aprendizaje políticos: 1810–1833*. Santiago: Universitaria, 1978.

Helg, Aline. *Liberty and Equality in Caribbean Colombia, 1770–1835*. Chapel Hill: University of North Carolina Press, 2004.

Hernández Ponce, Roberto. "Carlota Joaquina de Borbón. Apuntes en torno al episodio carlotino y a un epistolario chileno inédito, 1808–1816." *Historia* 20 (1985): 137–65.

———. "La Guardia Nacional de Chile. Apuntes sobre su origen y organización, 1808–1848," *Historia* 19 (1984): 53–113.

Herzog, Tamar. *Defining Nations: Immigrants and Citizens in Early Modern Spain and Spanish America*. New Haven, CT: Yale University Press, 2003.

Hespanha, António Manuel. *A ordem do mundo e o saber dos juristas: Imaginários do antigo direito europeu*. n.p., 2017.

———. *Como os juristas viam o mundo. 1550–1750: direitos, estados, pessoas, coisas, contratos, ações e crimes*. Lisbon: n.p., 2015.

Huidobro, María Gabriela. *El imaginario de la guerra de Arauco: mundo épico y tradición clásica*. Santiago: Fondo de Cultura Económica/ Universidad Nacional Andrés Bello, 2017.

Hunt, Lynn. "L'iconoclasme et le temps en revolution." In *Iconoclasme et révolutions de 1789 à nos jours*, edited by Emmanuel Fureix, 50–55. Ceyzérieu, France: Champ Vallon, 2014.

Hurtado, María de la Luz. "Cuerpo y mujer chilena en la urbe ilustrada del siglo XIX." In *Historia de las mujeres en Chile*, vol. 1, edited by Ana María Stuven and Joaquín Fermandois, 375–425. Santiago: Taurus, 2011.

Iglesias, Margarita. "Las recaderas de la Colonia o las sirvientas de razón." *Nomadías. Monográficas* 1 (1999): 49–59.

Illanes, María Angélica. *Chile Des-centrado: Formación socio-cultural republicana y transición capitalista, 1810–1910*. Santiago: LOM, 2003.

Jaffary, Nora. *False Mystics: Deviant Orthodoxy in Colonial Mexico*. Lincoln: University of Nebraska Press, 2004.

Jaksić, Iván, and Eduardo Posada Carbó, eds. *Liberalismo y poder: Latinoamérica en el siglo XIX*. Santiago: Fondo de Cultura Económica, 2011.

Jarcho, Saul. *The Concept of Contagion in Medicine, Literature, and Religion*. Malabar, FL: Krieger, 2000.

Jiménez, Christina M. *Making an Urban Public: Popular Claims to the City in Mexico, 1879–1932*. Pittsburgh: University of Pittsburgh Press, 2019.

Jocelyn-Holt, Alfredo. "El escenario juntista chileno, 1808–1810." In *1808. La eclosión juntera en el mundo hispano*, edited by Manuel Chust, 269–85. Mexico: Fondo de Cultura Económica/Colmex, 2007.

———. *El peso de la noche: nuestra frágil fortaleza histórica*. Argentina: Ariel, 1997.

———. *La Independencia de Chile. Tradición, modernización y mito*. 3rd ed. Santiago: Planeta, 2001.

Johnson, Sara E. *The Fear of French Negroes: Transcolonial Collaboration in the Revolutionary Americas*. Berkeley: University of California Press, 2012.

Jouhaud, Christian, and Alain Viala. "Introduction." In *De la publication: entre Renaissance et Lumières*, edited by Christian Jouhaud and Alain Viala, 5–24. Paris: Fayard, 2002.

Kagan, Richard L. "A World Without Walls: City and Town in Colonial Spanish America." In *City Walls: The Urban Enceinte in Global Perspective*, edited by James D. Tracy, 117–52. Cambridge: Cambridge University Press, 2000.

———. *Urban Images of the Hispanic World, 1493–1793*. New Haven, CT: Yale University Press, 2000.

Kanter, Deborah E. *Hijos del Pueblo: Gender, Family, and Community in Rural Mexico, 1730–1850*. Austin: University of Texas Press, 2008.

Kinsbruner, Jay. *The Colonial Spanish-American City: Urban Life in the Age of Atlantic Capitalism*. Austin: University of Texas Press, 2005.

Kroen, Sheryl. *Politics and Theater: The Crisis of Legitimacy in Restoration France, 1815–1830*. Berkeley: University of California Press, 2000.

Kuethe, Allan J., and Kenneth J. Andrien. *The Spanish Atlantic World in the Eighteenth Century: War and the Bourbon Reforms, 1713–1796*. New York: Cambridge University Press, 2014.

Laclau, Ernesto, and Chantal Mouffe. *Hegemony and Socialist Strategy: Towards a Radical Democratic Politics*. 2nd ed. London: Verso, 2014.

Lacoste, Pablo, and Michelle Malén Lacoste Adunka. "Chamantos, Ponchos y Balandres en Colchagua y Rancagua (siglos XVII-XIX)." *Estudios Atacameños* 57 (2018): 97–118.

Lacueva Muñoz, Jaime J., José Saldaña Fernández, and Johanan A. Varela Norambuena. "Revolución, constitución y orden: lecturas del Julio francés en la prensa chilena (1830–1833)." *Pasado y Memoria* 21 (2020): 21–40.

Landavazo, Marco Antonio. *La máscara de Fernando VII: Discurso e imaginario monárquicos en una época de crisis. Nueva España, 1808–1822*. Mexico, D.F.: El Colegio de México, Centro de Estudios Históricos/Universidad Michoacana de San Nicolás de Hidalgo/El Colegio de Michoacán, 2001.

Landers, Jane G. "*Cimarrón* and Citizen: African Ethnicity, Corporate Identity, and the Evolution of Free Black Towns in the Spanish Circum-Caribbean." In *Slaves, Subjects, and Subversives: Blacks in Colonial Latin America*, edited by Jane G. Landers and Barry M. Robinson, 111–145. Albuquerque: University of New Mexico Press, 2006.

Lara, María Pía. *The Disclosure of Politics: Struggles over the Semantics of Secularization*. New York: Columbia University Press, 2013.

Lasso, Marixa. *Myths of Harmony: Race and Republicanism during the Age of Revolution, Colombia 1795–1831*. Pittsburgh: University of Pittsburgh Press, 2007.

Lastarria, José Victorino. "Situación moral de Santiago en 1858." In *Estampas del Nuevo Extremo: antología de Santiago, 1541–1941*, edited by Ricardo Latcham, 117–24. Santiago: Editorial Nascimento, 1941.

Latour, Bruno. "Il n'y a pas de monde commun: il faut le composer." *Multitudes* 45 (2011): 38–41.

Laval, Enrique. "La casa de recogidas." *Boletín de la Academia Chilena de la Historia* 3, no. 6 (1935): 353–63.

———. *Noticias sobre los médicos en Chile en los siglos XVI, XVII y XVIII*. Santiago: Universidad de Chile/Centro de Investigación de Historia de la Medicina, 1953.

Leal Curiel, Carole. *El discurso de la fidelidad: Construcción social del espacio como símbolo del poder regio (Venezuela, siglo XVIII)*. Caracas: Academia Nacional de la Historia, 1990.

Lefebvre, Henri. *La production de l'espace*. 4th ed. Paris: Anthropos, 2000.

Lefort, Claude. *Essais sur le politique: XIXe–XXe siècles*. Paris: Seuil, 2001.

Lempérière, Annick. "Constitution, juridiction, codification. Le libéralisme hispano-américain au miroir du droit." *Almanack* 15 (2017): 1–43.

———. *Entre Dieu et le Roi, la République*. Paris: Les Belles Lettres, 2004.

Lenz, Rodolfo. *Diccionario etimológico de las voces chilenas derivadas de lenguas indígenas americanas*. Edited by Mauricio Podestá. Santiago: Seminario de Filología Hispánica, Universidad de Chile, n.d.

León, Leonardo. *Apogeo y ocaso del* toqui *Ayllapangui de Malleco, Chile. 1769–1776*. Santiago: Dirección de Bibliotecas, Archivos y Museos, 1999.

———. "El malón de Curiñamcu: el surgimiento de un cacique araucano (1764–1767)." *Proposiciones* 19 (1990): 18–43.

———. "'Los indios en el día aumentan su desvergüenza . . . ' Rebeldía, disputas y conflictos en el 'pueblo de indios' de Pomaire (Chile central), 1790–1811." *Cuadernos de Historia* 35 (2011): 93–134.

———. "Monarquistas hasta el ocaso: Los 'indios' de Chile central en los preámbulos de 1810." In *Las revoluciones americanas y la formación de los estados nacionales*, edited by Jaime Rosenblitt, 271–331. Santiago: Dirección de Bibliotecas, Archivos y Museos, 2013.

———. *Ni realistas ni patriotas: el bajo pueblo durante la Independencia de Chile, 1810–1822*. Santiago: Dirección de Bibliotecas, Archivos y Museos, 2011.

———. *O'Higgins y la cuestión Mapuche, 1817–1818*. Santiago: Akhilleus, 2014.

———. *Plebeyos y patricios en Chile colonial, 1750–1772: la gesta innoble*. Santiago: Universitaria, 2014.

León, Marco Antonio. *Encierro y corrección. La configuración de un sistema de prisiones en Chile (1800–1911)*. 3 vols. Santiago: Universidad Central de Chile, Facultad de Ciencias Jurídicas y Sociales, 2003.

———. "Entre lo público y lo privado: acercamientos a las *tapadas* y *cubiertas* en España, Hispanoamérica y Chile." *Boletín de la Academia Chilena de Historia* 103 (1993): 273–311.

———. "'Reducidas a un decente recogimiento.' La Casa de Recogidas-Corrección de mujeres de Santiago y la penalidad femenina en Chile (s. XVIII–XIX)." *Dimension Histórica de Chile* 19 (2004–2005): 47–80.

Lipsett-Rivera, Sonya. *Gender and the Negotiation of Daily Life in Mexico, 1750–1856*. Lincoln: University of Nebraska Press, 2012.

———. *The Origins of Macho: Men and Masculinity in Colonial Mexico*. Albuquerque: University of New Mexico Press, 2019.

López, Adalberto. *The Colonial History of Paraguay: The Revolt of the Comuneros, 1721–1735*. Abingdon, UK: Routledge, 2017.

Loraux, Nicole. *La tragédie d'Athènes. La politique entre l'ombre et l'utopie*. Paris: Seuil, 2005.

———. *The Divided City: On Memory and Forgetting in Ancient Athens*. Translated by Corinne Pache and Jeff Fort. New York: Zone Books, 2002.

Lorenzo, Santiago. *De lo rural a lo urbano: Chile en el siglo XVIII*. Valparaíso: Ediciones Universitarias de Valparaíso, 2014.

———. *Origen de las ciudades chilenas: las fundaciones del siglo XVIII*. 2nd ed. Santiago: Ediciones Universitarias de Valparaíso, 2013.

Lorenzo, Santiago, and Rodolfo Urbina. *La política de poblaciones en Chile durante el siglo XVIII*. Quillota: El Observador, 1978.

Luengo, Jorge, and Pol Dalmau. "Writing Spanish History in the Global Age: Connections and Entanglements in the Nineteenth Century." *Journal of Global History* 13 (2018): 425–45.

Luhmann, Niklas. *Theory of Society*. 2 vols. Translated by Rhodes Barrett. Palo Alto, CA: Stanford University Press, 2012.

Luque Azcona, Emilio José. *Ciudad y poder: la construcción material y simbólica del Montevideo colonial (1723–1810)*. Sevilla: Secretariado de Publicaciones de la Universidad de Sevilla/Consejo Superior de Investiaciones Científicas/Deputación de Sevilla, 2007.

Majluf, Natalia. "De cómo reemplazar a un rey: retrato, visualidad y poder en la crisis de la independencia (1808–1830)." *Histórica* 37, no. 1 (2013): 73–108.

Majluf, Natalia, ed. *José Gil de Castro: Pintor de Libertadores*. Lima: Museo de Arte de Lima, 2014.

Malandain, Gilles. *L'introuvable complot. Attentat, enquête et rumeur dans la France de la Restauration*. Paris: Éditions de l'École des hautes études en sciences sociales, 2011.

Mannarelli, María Emma. *Private Passions and Public Sins: Men and Women in Seventeenth-Century Lima*. Translated by Sidney Evans and Meredith D. Dodge. Albuquerque: University of New Mexico Press, 2007.

Mandiola, Francisco Javier. "Apuntes sobre la vida y obras de don Ignacio Andía y Varela." *Boletín de la Academia Chilena de la Historia* 2, no. 3 (1934): 243–58.

Marchart, Oliver. *Post-Foundational Political Thought: Political Difference in Nancy, Lefort, Badiou and Laclau*. Edinburgh: Edinburgh University Press, 2007.

———. *Thinking Antagonism: Political Ontology after Laclau*. Edinburgh: Edinburgh University Press, 2018.

Marks, John Garrison. *Black Freedom in the Age of Slavery: Race, Status, and Identity in the Urban Americas*. Columbia: South Carolina Univeristy Press, 2020.

Mariman, Pablo, Fabiana Nahuelquir, José Millalen, Margarita Calfío, and Rodrigo Levil. *¡Allkütunge, wingka! ¡ka kiñechi! Ensayos sobre historias Mapuche*. Temuco, Chile: Ediciones Comunidad de Historia Mapuche, 2019.

Marimán Quemenado, Pablo. "La República y los Mapuche: 1819–1828." In *Ta iñ fijke xipa rakizuameluwün. Historia, colonialismo y resistencia desde el país Mapuche*, edited by Comunidad de Historia Mapuche, 63–87. Temuco, Chile: Ediciones Comunidad de Historia Mapuche, 2013.

Martínez, María Elena. *Genealogical Fictions: Limpieza de Sangre, Religion, and Gender in Colonial Mexico*. Stanford, CA: Stanford University Press, 2008.

McFarlane, Anthony. *War and Independence in Spanish America*. New York: Routledge, 2014.

Masters, Adrian. "A Thousand Invisible Architects: Vassals, the Petition and Response System, and the Creation of Spanish Imperial Caste Legislation." *Hispanic American Historical Review* 98, no. 3 (August 2018): 377–406.

———. "The Two, the One, the Many, the None: Rethinking the Republics of Spaniards and Indians in the Sixteenth-Century Spanish Indies." *The Americas* 78, no. 1 (January 2021): 3–36.

Maturana, Víctor. *Historia de los Agustinos en Chile*. Santiago: Imprenta de Valparaíso de F. T. Lathrop, 1904.

McDonnell, Michael A. "Rethinking the Age of Revolution." *Atlantic Studies* 13, no. 3 (2016): 301–14.

Medina, José Toribio. *Bibliografía de la imprenta en Santiago de Chile desde sus orígenes hasta febrero de 1817*. Santiago: Fondo Histórico y Bibliográfico José Toribio Medina, 1961.

———. *Diccionario biográfico colonial*. Santiago: Imprenta Elzeviriana, 1906.

Mehl, Eva Maria. *Forced Migration in the Spanish Pacific World: From Mexico to the Philippines, 1765–1811*. Cambridge: Cambridge University Press, 2016.

Mejías Navarrete, Elizabeth. "La esclavitud doméstica en sus prácticas: los esclavos y su constitución en personas. Chile 1750–1820." *Fronteras de la Historia* 12 (2007): 119–50.

Melfi, Domingo. "La Prensa O'Higginista." *Anales de la Universidad de Chile* 92, no. 15 (1934): 24–39.

Mellafe, Rolando. "Alma y utopía: Santiago colonial." *Cuadernos de Historia* 15 (1995): 37–48.

Mellafe, Rolando, and Lorena Loyola. *La memoria de América colonial: inconsciente colectivo y vida cotidiana*. Santiago: Editorial Universitaria, 1994.

Mellafe, Rolando, and René Salinas. *Sociedad y población rural en la formación de Chile actual: La Ligua 1700–1850*. Santiago: Ediciones de la Universidad de Chile, 1988.

Méndez, Cecilia. *The Plebeian Republic: The Huanta Rebellion and the Making of the Peruvian State, 1820–1850*. Durham, NC: Duke University Press, 2005.

Merlin, Hélène. *Public et littérature en France au XVIIe siècle*. Paris: Les Belles Lettres, 1994.

Meza Villalobos, Néstor. *La actividad política del Reino de Chile entre 1806 y 1808*. Santiago: Publicación del Instituto de Investigaciones Histórico-Culturales, Facultad de Filosofía y Eduación, Universidad de Chile, [1956].

———. *La conciencia política chilena durante la monarquía*. Santiago: Instituto de Investigaciones Histórico-Culturales, Facultad de Filosofía y Educación, Universidad de Chile, 1958.

Mezan Algranti, Leila. *Honradas e devotas. Mulheres da colônia: condição feminina nos conventos e recolhimentos do Sudeste do Brasil, 1750–1822*. 2nd ed. Rio de Janeiro: José Olympio, 1999.

Milton, Cynthia E. *The Many Meanings of Poverty: Colonialism, Social*

Compacts, and Assistance in Eighteenth-Century Ecuador. Stanford, CA: Stanford University Press, 2007.

Minchom, Martin. *The People of Quito, 1690–1810: Change and Unrest in the Underclass*. London: Routledge, 2019.

Mínguez, Víctor. "Del rey pacífico a los héroes de la guerra. Propaganda e ideología en dos exequias novohispanas (1762–1808)." In *Insurgencia y republicanismo*, edited by Jesús Navarro García, 47–65. Seville, Spain: CSIC, 2006.

Molina, J. Michelle. *To Overcome Oneself: The Jesuit Ethic and Spirit of Global Expansion, 1520–1767*. Berkeley: University of California Press, 2013.

Molina, Raúl. "Pueblos de Indios del Norte Chico. Los diaguita actuales/Indian Towns of the Norte Chico and Chile's Present-day Diaguitas." In *El arte de ser diaguita/The Art of Being Diaguita*, edited by C. Sinclaire, 81–108. Santiago: Museo Chileno de Arte Precolombino, 2016.

Molina Otárola, Raúl, and Luis Campos Muñoz. "Confín geográfico, refugio indígena, pueblo de indios y etnogénesis en el Huasco Alto, (Chile)." *Revista de Geografía Norte Grande* 68 (2017): 123–40.

Mongey, Vanessa. "Les vagabonds de la république: les révolutionnaires européens aux Amériques, 1780–1820." In *Les empires atlantiques des Lumières au libéralisme (1763–1865)*, edited by Federica Morelli, Clément Thibaud, and Geneviève Verdo, 67–82. Rennes, France: Presses Universitaires de Rennes, 2009.

Montt, Luis. *Bibliografía chilena*. 3 vols. Santiago: Imprenta Universitaria, 1918–1921.

———. *Recuerdos de familia*. Santiago: Imprenta Universitaria, 1943.

Moreno, Daniel. "'Si se hiciera lo de acá se extinguiría en todas partes.' Conflictos, tensiones y autoridad: la acción de la justicia frente a la amenaza de la viruela en la frontera sur de Chile, 1785." *Fronteras de la Historia* 19, no. 2 (2014): 38–68.

Moreno Cebrián, Alfredo, and Jorge Chauca García. "Los ecos indianos del gran levantamiento de Tupac Amaru y su proyección peninsular: un episodio olvidado." *Revista de Indias* 80, no. 279 (2020): 317–44.

Morse, Richard M. "Cities as People." In *Rethinking the Latin American City*, edited by Richard M. Morse and Jorge Enrique Hardoy, 3–19. Washington, DC: Woodrow Wilson Center Press/Johns Hopkins University Press, 1992.

Mouffe, Chantal. *Agonistics: Thinking the World Politically*. London: Verso, 2013.

———. *On the Political*. London: Routledge, 2005.

Moyano, Cristina, and Alejandro San Francisco. "Liberalismo: Chile." In *Diccionario político y social del mundo iberoamericano: la era de las revoluciones, 1750–1850*, edited by Javier Fernández Sebastián, 756–69. Madrid: Fundación Carolina/Centro de Estudios Políticos y Constitucionales, 2009.

Neira, Marcelo. "Castigo femenino en Chile durante la primera mitad del siglo XIX." *Historia* 37, no. 2 (2004): 367–90.

———. "Jeremy Bentham y el liberalismo en Chile durante la primera mitad del siglo XIX." *Boletín de la Academia Chilena de la Historia* 113 (2004): 285–313.

Nemser, Daniel. *Infrastructures of Race: Concentration and Biopolitics in Colonial Mexico*. Austin: University of Texas Press, 2017.

Nesvig, Martin. *Ideology and Inquisition: The World of the Censors in Early Mexico*. New Haven, CT: Yale University Press, 2009.

Newman, Simon P. *Parades and the Politics of the Street: Festive Culture in the Early American Republic*. Philadelphia: University of Pennsylvania Press, 1997.

Núñez Rius, Jorge. "Estado, crisis de hegemonía y guerra en Chile 1830–1841." *Andes* 4, no. 6 (1987): 137–89.

O'Hara, Matthew D. *A Flock Divided: Race, Religion, and Politics in Mexico, 1749–1857*. Durham, NC: Duke University Press, 2010.

———. *The History of the Future in Colonial Mexico*. New Haven, CT: Yale University Press, 2018.

Obregón, Jimena, and José Manuel Zavala. "Abolición y persistencia de la esclavitud indígena en Chile colonial: estrategias esclavistas en la frontera araucano-mapuche." *Memoria Americana* 17, no. 1 (2009): 17–31.

Ogborn, Miles. *The Freedom of Speech: Talk and Slavery in the Anglo-Caribbean World*. Chicago: University of Chicago Press, 2019.

Onetto, Mauricio. "De ideales y transgresiones en medio de una precariedad: la casa de recogidas de Santiago de Chile, siglos XVII–XVIII." *Revista de Historia Social y de las Mentalidades* 13, no. 1 (2009): 159–200.

Ortíz Sotelo, Jorge. *La Real Armada en el Pacífico sur: el Apostadero Naval del Callao, 1746–1824*. Madrid: Bonilla Artigas Editores/UNAM, Instituto de Investigaciones Históricas, 2015.

Ossa, Juan Luis. *Armies, Politics and Revolution: Chile, 1808–1826*. Liverpool: Liverpool University Press, 2014.

———. "De Cádiz a la América del Sur: el viaje de una ilusión constitucional." In *Entre Mediterráneo y Atlántico: circulaciones, conexiones y miradas*, edited by Antonino de Francesco, Luigi

Mascilli Migliorini, and Raffaele Nocera, 255–78. Chile: Fondo de Cultura Económica, 2014.

Osorio, Alejandra B. *Inventing Lima: Baroque Modernity in Peru's South Sea Metropolis*. New York: Palgrave Macmillan, 2008.

———. "Of National Boundaries and Imperial Geographies: A New Radical History of the Spanish Habsburg Empire." *Radical History Review* 130 (2018): 100–30.

Ozouf, Mona. *Festivals and the French Revolution*. Translated by Alan Sheridan. Cambridge, MA: Harvard University Press, 1994.

Pagden, Anthony. *Spanish Imperialism and the Political Imagination: Studies in European and Spanish-American Social and Political Theory, 1513–1830*. New Haven, CT: Yale University Press, 1990.

Pairican Padilla, Fernando. *Toqui: guerra y tradición en el siglo XIX*. Santiago: Pehuén, 2020.

Palti, Elías José. *¿Las ideas fuera de lugar? Estudios y debates en torno a la historia político-intelectual latinoamericana*. Buenos Aires: Prometeo, 2014.

———. *An Archaeology of the Political: Regimes of Power from the Seventeenth Century to the Present*. New York: Columbia University Press, 2017.

———. *El tiempo de la política: el siglo XIX reconsiderado*. Buenos Aires: Siglo Veintiuno Editores, 2007.

Paquette, Gabriel. *Enlightenment, Governance, and Reform in Spain and Its Empire, 1759–1808*. Basingstoke, UK: Palgrave Macmillan, 2008.

———. "The Dissolution of the Spanish Atlantic Monarchy." *The Historical Journal* 52, no. 1 (March 2009): 175–212.

Patch, Robert W. *Maya Revolt and Revolution in the Eighteenth Century*. Abingdon, UK: Routledge, 2015.

Penry, S. Elizabeth. *The People Are King: The Making of an Indigenous Andean Politics*. New York: Oxford University Press, 2019.

Penyak, Lee M. "Safe Harbors and Compulsory Custody: *Casas de Depósito* in Mexico, 1750–1865." *Hispanic American Historical Review* vol. 79, no. 1 (1999): 83–99.

Peña González, Patricia. " . . . Y las mujeres, ¿Dónde estuvieron? Mujeres en el proceso independentista chileno." *Anuario de Postgrado*. Santiago: La Escuela, 1997.

———. "La casa de corrección de mujeres: una 'unidad de producción.'" In *Mujeres ausentes, miradas presentes: IV jornadas de investigación en historia de la mujer*, edited by Patricia Peña and Paulina Zamorano, 109–32. Santiago: Universidad de Chile, Facultad de Filosofía y Humanidades, [2000].

———"La Casa de Recogidas de Santiago, un hospital de almas." In *Descorriendo el Velo: II y III Jornadas de Investigaciones en Historia de la mujer*, edited by Sergio Vergara, Paulina Zamorano, and Zvonimir Martinic, 117–130. [Santiago]: Universidad de Chile, Facultad de Filosofía y Humanidades, [1998].

Peralta, Paulina. *¡Chile tiene fiesta! El origen del 18 de septiembre (1810–1837)*. Santiago: LOM, 2007.

———. "Ni por la razón ni por la fuerza. El fallido intento del Estado Nacional por incorporar a los pueblos mapuche y pehuenche (1810–1835)." *Revista de Historia Social y de las Mentalidades* 13, no. 1 (2009): 55–85.

Peralta, Víctor. "Entre la fidelidad y la incertidumbre: el virreinato del Perú entre 1808 y 1810." In *1808. La eclosión juntera en el mundo hispano*, edited by Manuel Chust, 138–61. Mexico: Fondo de Cultura Económica/Colmex, 2007.

Pereira Larraín, Teresa. *Afectos e intimidades: el mundo familiar en los siglos XVII, XVIII y XIX*. Santiago: Ediciones Universidad Católica de Chile, 2007.

Pereira Salas, Eugenio. *Historia del arte en el Reino de Chile*. Santiago: Ediciones de la Universidad de Chile, 1965.

———. *Historia del teatro en Chile desde sus orígenes hasta la muerte de Juan Casacuberta, 1849*. Santiago: Ediciones de la Universidad de Chile, 1974.

———. *Juegos y alegrías coloniales en Chile*. Santiago: Zig-Zag, 1947.

———. *Los primeros contactos entre Chile y los Estados Unidos, 1778–1809*. Santiago: Editorial Andrés Bello, 1971.

Peters, John Durham. *Speaking into the Air: A History of the Idea of Communication*. Chicago: University of Chicago Press, 2000.

———. *The Marvelous Clouds: Toward a Philosophy of Elemental Media*. Chicago: University of Chicago Press, 2016.

Phelan, John Leddy. *The People and the King: The Comunero Revolution in Colombia, 1781*. Madison: University of Wisconsin Press, 1978.

Piccato, Pablo. "Public Sphere in Latin America: A Map of the Historiography." *Social History* 35, no. 2 (May 2010): 165–92.

Pinto, Jorge. *La formación del Estado y la nación, y el pueblo mapuche: de la inclusión a la exclusion*. Santiago: Dirección de Bibliotecas, Archivos y Museos, 2003.

Pinto, Julio, and Verónica Valdivia. *¿Chilenos todos? La construcción social de la nación (1810–1840)*. Santiago: LOM, 2009.

Pinto, Julio et al. *El orden y el bajo pueblo: los regímenes de Portales y Rosas frente al mundo popular, 1829–1852*. Santiago: LOM, 2015.

Piwonka, Gonzalo. "Juan José Echeverría y Pedro Nicolás de Chopitea, dos cordiales empresarios y profundos adversarios politicos." *Dimensión Histórica de Chile* 15–16 (1999–2000): 101–66.

———. "Opinión pública. Chile." In *Diccionario politico y social del mundo americano: la era de las revoluciones, 1750–1850*. Edited by Javier Fernández Sebastián, 1024–36. Madrid: Fundación Carolina/Sociedad Estatal de Conmemoraciones Culturales/Centro de Estudios Políticos y Constitucionales, 2009.

———. *Orígenes de la libertad de prensa en Chile: 1823–1830*, Santiago: RIL Editores/Dirección de Bibliotecas, Archivos y Museos/Centro de Investigaciones Diego Barros Arana, 2000.

Plot, Martín, ed. *Claude Lefort: Thinker of the Political*. Basingstoke: Palgrave Macmillan, 2013.

Poblete, María Pía. "El trabajo de niños y niñas mapuche-huilliches como 'mocitos' y 'chinitas' de servicio (Valdivia, siglos XVIII y XIX)." *Revista Chilena de Antropología* 40 (2019): 221–37.

Poirier, Nicolas. *Introduction à Claude Lefort*. Paris: La Découverte, 2020.

Polasky, Janet. *Revolutions without Borders: The Call to Liberty in the Atlantic World*. New Haven, CT: Yale University Press, 2015.

Ponce Vázquez, Juan José. *Islanders and Empire: Smuggling and Political Defiance in Hispaniola, 1580–1690*. Cambridge: Cambridge University Press, 2020.

Poole, Deborah. *Vision, Race, and Modernity: A Visual Economy of the Andean Image World*. Princeton, NJ: Princeton University Press, 1997.

Porta, Adriana. "Control social y espacio virreinal: la Casa de Recogidas de la Residencia." In *Ideologías, prácticas y discursos: la construcción cultural del mundo social, siglos XVII–XIX*, edited by Jaime Peire, Mariano Di Pasquale, and Arrigo Amadori, 251–91. Sáenz Peña, Argentina: Universidad Nacional Tres de Febrero, 2013.

Portillo, José María. *Crisis atlántica: autonomía e independencia en la crisis de la monarquía hispánica*. Madrid: Fundación Carolina/Centro de Estudios Hispánicos e Iberoamericanos/Marcial Pons Historia, 2006.

———. "La revolución constitucional en el mundo hispano." In *Pueblos, Nación, Constitución (en torno a 1812)*, Bartolomé Clavero et al., 53–99. Vitoria-Gasteiz, Spain: Ikusager Ediciones, 2004.

Premo, Bianca. *The Enlightenment on Trial: Ordinary Litigants and Colonialism in the Spanish Empire*. New York: Oxford University Press, 2017.

Prodi, Paolo. *Una historia de la justicia: de la pluralidad de fueros al dualismo moderno entre conciencia y derecho*. Translated by Luciano Padilla López. Buenos Aires: Katz Editores, 2008.

Purcell, Fernando. *Diversiones y juegos populares. Formas de sociabilidad y crítica social: Colchagua, 1850–1880*. Santiago: Dirección de Bibliotecas, Archivos y Museos/LOM, 1997.

———. "La chingana como espacio privado de diversión popular. Colchagua 1850–1880." In *Lo público y lo privado en la historia americana*, 197–224. Santiago: Fundación Mario Góngora, 2000.

Rabinovich, Alejandro M. "Las órdenes militares en tiempos revolucionarios. El republicanismo y la posibilidad de una aristocracia militar. Río de la Plata, Chile y Perú, 1810–1824." *Revista Universitaria de Historia Militar* 5, no. 9 (2016): 15–32.

Ramírez Espíndola, Manuel. "Ejército regular y élites locales en la Intendencia de Concepción a fines del período colonial. Una aproximación desde la prosopografía y el análisis de redes sociales." *Tiempo y Espacio* 28 (2012): 107–49.

Ramos Vásquez, Isabel. "La represión de los delitos atroces en el Derecho Castellano de la Edad Moderna." *Estudios Histórico-Jurídicos* 26 (2004): 255–99.

Reddy, William. *The Navigation of Feeling: A Framework for the History of Emotions*. Cambridge: Cambridge University Press, 2001.

Ricketts, Mónica. *Who Should Rule? Men of Arms, the Republic of Letters, and the Fall of the Spanish Empire*. New York: Oxford University Press, 2017.

Rodríguez O., Jaime E. "Atlantic Revolutions." In *The Cambridge World History*, vol. 7, part 2, edited by J. R. McNeill and Kenneth Pomeranz, 273–98. Cambridge: Cambridge University Press, 2015.

———. *The Independence of Spanish America*. Cambridge: Cambridge University Press, 1998.

———. *"We Are Now the True Spaniards": Sovereignty, Revolution, Independence, and the Emergence of the Federal Republic of Mexico, 1808–1824*. Stanford, CA: Stanford University Press, 2012.

Rojas, Jorge. *Historia de la infancia en Chile republicano, 1810–2010*. Santiago: JUNJI, 2010.

Rojas, Mauricio F. *Las voces de la justicia. Delito y sociedad en Concepción (1820–1875): Atentados sexuales, pendencias, bigamia, amancebamiento e injurias*. Santiago: Dirección de Bibliotecas, Archivos y Museos, 2008.

Rojas Mix, Miguel. *La Plaza Mayor: el urbanismo, instrumento de dominio colonial*. Barcelona: Muchnik, 1978.

Rosales, Justo Abel. *La cañadilla de Santiago: su historia y sus tradiciones,*

1541–1887. Santiago: Establecimiento Tipográfico de La Época, 1887.

Rosas Lauro, Claudia. *Del trono a la guillotina. El impacto de la Revolución Francesa en el Perú (1789–1808)*. Lima: Instituto Francés de Estudios Andinos/Fondo Editorial de la Pontificia Universidad Católica del Perú/Embajada de Francia en el Perú, 2006.

Rosenwein, Barbara. *Emotional Communities in the Early Middle Ages*. Ithaca, NY: Cornell University Press, 2006.

Ruiz, Carlos. "Comunidades y cacicazgos de Choapa." In *Estudios Coloniales I*, edited by Julio Retamal, 79–128. Santiago: Universidad Nacional Andrés Bello/RIL Editores, 2000.

Sábato, Hilda. *Republics of the New World: The Revolutionary Political Experiment in 19th-Century Latin America*. Princeton, NJ: Princeton University Press, 2018.

Salazar, Gabriel. *Construcción de Estado en Chile (1800–1837). Democracia de los "pueblos," militarismo ciudadano, golpismo oligárquico*. Santiago: Sudamericana, 2005.

———. *Labradores, peones y proletarios: Formación y crisis de la sociedad popular chilena del siglo XIX*. 3rd ed. Santiago: LOM, 2000.

———. *Mercaderes, empresarios y capitalistas (Chile, siglo XIX)*. Santiago: Sudamericana, 2009.

Salinas, Cecilia. *Las chilenas de la colonia: virtud sumisa, amor rebelde*. Santiago: LOM, 1994.

Salinas, Maximiliano. *Canto a lo divino y religión popular en Chile hacia 1900*. Santiago: Rehue, [1991].

Salinas, René. "Caracteres generales de la evolución demográfica de un centro urbano chileno: Valparaíso, 1685–1830." *Historia* 10 (1971): 177–204.

———. "Del maltrato al uxoricidio: la violencia 'puertas adentro' en la aldea chilena tradicional (siglo XIX)." *Revista de Historia Social y de las Mentalidades* 7, no. 2 (2003): 95–113.

———. "Espacio urbano y revueltas populares. El motín de Santiago en 1858." *Revista de Historia Social y de las Mentalidades* 7, no. 1 (2003): 13–39.

———. "Fama pública, rumor y sociabilidad." In *Lo público y lo privado en la historia americana*, 133–53. Santiago: Fundación Mario Góngora, 2002.

———. "Violencias sexuales e interpersonales en Chile tradicional." *Revista de Historia Social y de las Mentalidades* 4, no. 1 (Winter 2000): 13–49.

Salinas, René, and Nicolás Corvalán. "Transgresores sumisos, pecadores felices. Vida afectiva y vigencia del modelo matrimonial en Chile tradicional, siglos XVIII–XIX." *Cuadernos de Historia* 16 (1996): 9–39.

San Francisco, Alejandro. "El primer constitucionalismo chileno, 1810–1828." *Anuario de Historia Regional y de las Fronteras* 12, no. 1 (2007): 339–61.

Scavino, Dardo. "La metafísica y la metáfora del lazo social." In *Palabras que atan: Metáforas y conceptos del vínculo social en la historia moderna y contemporánea*, edited by François Godicheau and Pablo Sánchez León, 129–47. Madrid: Fondo de Cultura Económica/Université Bordeaux Montaigne, 2015.

Schaeffer, Jean-Marie. *Pourquoi la fiction?* Paris: Seuil, 1999.

Schmitt, Carl. *Political Theology: Four Chapters on the Concept of Sovereignty*. Translated by George Schwab. Chicago: University of Chicago Press, 1985.

Schultz, Kirsten. *Tropical Versailles: Empire, Monarchy, and the Portuguese Royal Court in Rio de Janeiro, 1808–1821*. New York: Routledge, 2001.

Schwartz, Stuart B. *All Can Be Saved: Religious Tolerance and Salvation and Salvation in the Iberian Atlantic World*. New Haven, CT: Yale University Press, 2008.

Scott, Julius. *The Common Wind: Afro-American Currents in the Age of the Haitian Revolution*. London: Verso, 2018.

Segre, Erica. *Intersected Identities: Strategies of Visualisation in Nineteenth- and Twentieth-century Mexican Culture*. New York: Berghahn Books, 2007.

Seibel, Beatriz. *Historia del teatro argentino. Desde los rituales hasta 1930*. Buenos Aires: Corregidor, 2002.

Sellers-García, Sylvia. *The Woman on the Windowsill: A Tale of Mystery in Several Parts*. New Haven, CT: Yale University Press, 2020.

Serrano, Sol. *¿Qué hacer con Dios en la República? Política y secularización en Chile (1845–1885)*. Santiago: Fondo de Cultura Económica, 2008.

———. "La definición de lo público en un Estado católico. El caso chileno. 1810–1855." *Estudios Públicos* 76 (Spring 1999): 211–32.

———. "La representación en el reino de Chile: 1808–1814." In *Las experiencias de 1808 en Iberoamérica*, edited by Alfredo Ávila and Juan Ramón de la Fuente, 492–508. Alcalá de Henares, Spain: Universidad de Alcalá/Universidad Nacional Autónoma de México, 2008.

———. "Religiosas modernas en el siglo XIX." In *Mujeres chilenas: fragmentos de una historia*, edited by Sonia Montecino, 87–96. Santiago: Catalonia, 2008.

Serrano, Sol, and Antonio Correa. "De patriota o sarracena a madre republicana. Las mujeres en la independencia de Chile." *Tiempos de América* 17 (2010): 119–30.

Serrano, Sol, Macarena Ponce de León, and Francisca Rengifo, eds. *Historia de la educación en Chile (1810– 2010)*. 3 vols. Santiago: Taurus, 2012–2018.

Serrano del Pozo, Gonzalo. *Chile contra la Confederación. La guerra en povincias: 1836–1839*. Santiago: RIL Editores, 2017.

Serulnikov, Sergio. *Revolution in the Andes: The Age of Túpac Amaru*. Translated by David Frye. Durham, NC: Duke University Press, 2013.

———. *Subverting Colonial Authority: Challenges to Spanish Rule in Eighteenth-Century Southern Andes*. Durham, NC: Duke University Press, 2003.

Sharples, Jason T. "Discovering Slave Conspiracies: New Fears of Rebellion and Old Paradigms of Plotting in Seventeenth-Century Barbados." *American Historical Review* 120, 3 (2015): 811–43.

Silva, Bárbara. *Identidad y nación entre dos siglos: Patria Vieja, Centenario y Bicentenario*. Santiago: LOM, 2008.

Silva Castro, Raúl. *Egaña en la Patria Vieja: 1810–1814*. Santiago: Andrés Bello, 1959.

Silva Vargas, Fernando. "La composición social del Chile republicano." In *Historia de la República de Chile*, vol. 1, edited by Fernando Silva Vargas and Juan Eduardo Vargas Cariola, 51–78. Santiago: Zig-Zag, 2013.

———. "Una aproximación a la demografía." In *Historia de la República de Chile*, vol. 1, edited by Fernando Silva Vargas and Juan Eduardo Vargas Cariola, 29–49. Santiago: Zig-Zag, 2013.

Sluhovsky, Moshe. *Becoming a New Self: Practices of Belief in Early Modern Catholicism*. Chicago: University of Chicago Press, 2017.

Smith H., Brian, and Hugo Rueda R. *El retrato en miniatura: imagen íntima*. Santiago: Dirección de Bibliotecas, Archivos y Museos/ Museo Histórico Nacional, n.d.

Solans, Francisco Javier Ramón. "Milagros, visiones apocalípticas y profecías. Una lectura sobrenatural de la Guerra de la Independencia." *Ayer* 96 (2014): 83–104.

Soriano, Cristina. *Tides of Revolution: Information, Insurgencies, and the Crisis of Colonial Rule in Venezuela*. Albuquerque: University of New Mexico Press, 2018.

Soto, Rosa. *Esclavas negras en Chile colonial*. Santiago: Bravo y Allende Editores, 2011.

Sotomayor Valdés, Ramón. *Historia de Chile bajo el gobierno del Jeneral D.*

Joaquín Prieto. 2nd ed. 4 vols. Santiago: Imprenta "Esmeralda," 1900–1903.

Stearns, Justin K. *Infectious Ideas: Contagion in Pre-modern Islamic and Christian Thought in the Western Mediterranean*. Baltimore: Johns Hopkins University Press, 2011.

Stuardo Ortíz, Carlos, and Juan Eyzaguirre Escobar. *Santiago: contribuyentes, autoridades, funcionarios, agentes diplomáticos y consulares, 1817–1819*. Santiago: Publicaciones de la Academia Chilena de la Historia, 1952.

Stuven, Ana María. "De la autonomía a la república: el debate constitucional en Chile, 1808–1833." In *El laboratorio constitucional iberoamericano: 1807/1808–1830*, edited by Antonio Annino and Marcela Ternavasio, 179–201. Madrid: Iberoamericana/Vervuert, 2012.

———. *La seducción de un orden: las elites y la construcción de Chile en las polémicas culturales y políticas del siglo XIX*. Santiago: Ediciones de la Universidad Católica de Chile, 2000.

Stuven, Ana María, and Gabriel Cid. *Debates republicanos en Chile. Siglo XIX*. 2 vols. Santiago: Ediciones Universidad Diego Portales, 2012–2013.

Ternavasio, Marcela. *Candidata a la corona: la Infanta Carlota Joaquina en el laberinto de las revoluciones hispanoamericanas*. Buenos Aires: Siglo Veintiuno Editores, 2015.

Thibaud, Clément. "La ley y la sangre. La 'guerra de razas' y la constitución en la América Bolivariana." *Almanack* 1 (2011): 5–23.

———. *Libérer le nouveau monde: la fondation des premières républiques hispaniques. Colombie et Vénézuela (1780–1820)*. Bécherel, France: Les Perséides, 2017.

———. "Sacrer la République: enjeux de l'iconoclasme révolutionnaire en Colombie bolivarienne au début du XIX siècle." In *Iconoclasme et révolutions de 1789 à nos jours*, edited by Emmanuel Fureix, 129–41. Ceyzérieu, France: Champ Vallon, 2014.

Thomson, Sinclair. "Sovereignty Disavowed: The Tupac Amaru Revolution in the Atlantic World." *Atlantic Studies* 13, no. 3 (2016): 407–31.

———. *We Alone Will Rule: Native Andean Politics in the Age of Insurgency*. Madison: University of Wisconsin Press, 2002.

Tilly, Charles. *Why?* Princeton, NJ: Princeton University Press, 2006.

Tomás y Valiente, Francisco. *El Derecho penal de la monarquía absoluta (siglos XVI, XVII y XVIII)*. 2nd ed. Madrid: Tecnos, 1992.

———. *La tortura judicial en España*. Barcelona: Editorial Crítica, 2000.

———. *Manual de historia del derecho español*. 4th ed. Madrid: Tecnos, 2013.

Torres Puga, Gabriel. *Opinión pública y censura en Nueva España: indicios de un silencio imposible, 1767–1794*. Mexico, D.F.: El Colegio de México, Centro de Estudios Históricos, 2010.

Trumper, Camilo D. *Ephemeral Histories: Public Art, Politics, and the Struggle for the Streets in Chile*. Oakland: University of California Press, 2016.

Tutino, John. *Mexico City, 1808: Power, Sovereignty, and Silver in an Age of War and Revolution*. Albuquerque: University of New Mexico Press, 2018.

Twinam, Ann. *Private Lives and Public Secrets: Gender, Honor, Sexuality, and Illegitimacy in Colonial Spanish America*. Stanford, CA: Stanford University Press, 1999.

———. *Purchasing Whiteness: Pardos, Mulattos, and the Quest for Social Mobility in the Indies*. Stanford, CA: Stanford University Press, 2015.

Uchanier Lecoña, Lourdes. "Monasterios y recogimientos en el control del comportamiento a finales de la época colonial, en la ciudad de La Paz." In *Historias de mujeres: mujeres, familias, historias*, edited by Ana María Lema Garrett, 35–44. Santa Cruz de la Sierra, Bolivia: El País, 2011.

Undurraga, Verónica. "El honor no es más que la buena opinión. Aproximación al honor a partir de la categoría de lo público en el Chile de 1792 a 1822." *Bicentenario. Revista de Historia de Chile y América* 4, no. 2 (2005): 17–35.

———. "Españoles oscuros y mulatos blancos: identidades múltiples y disfraces del color en el ocaso de la colonia chilena. 1778–1820." In *Historias de racismo y discriminación en Chile*, edited by Rafael Gaune and Martín Lara, 341–68. Santiago: Uqbar Editores, 2009.

———. "Fronteras sociales y sus intersticios: usos y abusos de las categorías 'caballeros,' 'dones,' y 'Españoles' en Santiago de Chile, siglo XVIII." In *América colonial: denominaciones, clasificaciones e identidades*, edited by Alejandra Araya and Jaime Valenzuela, 285–313. Santiago: RIL Editores, 2010.

———. *Los rostros del honor: normas culturales y estrategias de promoción social en Chile colonial, siglo XVIII*. Santiago: Dirección de Bibliotecas, Archivos y Museos, 2012.

———. "'Valentones,' alcaldes de barrio y paradigmas de civilidad. Conflictos y acomodaciones en Santiago de Chile, siglo XVIII." *Revista de Historia Social y de las Mentalidades* 14, no. 2 (2010): 35–71.

Urbina, Rodolfo. *Población indígena, encomienda y tributo en Chiloé: 1567–1813*. [Valparaíso]: Ediciones, Universitarias de Valparaíso, n.d.

Uribe-Uran, Victor M. *Fatal Love: Spousal Killers, Law, and Punishment in the Late Colonial Spanish Atlantic*. Stanford, CA: Stanford University Press, 2016.

———. "The Birth of a Public Sphere in Latin America During the Age of Revolution." *Comparative Studies in Society and History* 42, no. 2 (April 2000): 425–57.

———. "The Great Transformation of Law and Legal Culture: 'The Public' and 'the Private' in the Transition from Empire to Nation in Mexico, Colombia, and Brazil, 1750–1850." In *Empire to Nation: Historical Perspectives on the Making of the Modern World*, edited by Joseph W. Esherick, Hasan Kayali, and Eric Van Young, 68–105. Lanham, MD: Rowman & Littlefield, 2006.

Valencia Avaria, Luis. "Las banderas de Chile." *Boletín de la Academia Chilena de la Historia* 63 (1960): 12–57.

Valenzuela, Eduardo. *Maleficio. Historias de hechicería y brujería en el Chile colonial*. Santiago: Pehuén, 2013.

Valenzuela, Jaime. "Afán de prestigio y movilidad social: los espejos de la apariencia." In *Historia de la vida privada en Chile*, vol. 1, edited by Rafael Sagredo and Cristián Gazmuri, 285–313. Santiago: Taurus, 2005.

———. "Diversiones rurales y sociabilidad popular en Chile Central: 1850–1880." In *Formas de sociabilidad en Chile, 1840–1940*, Maurice Agulhon et al., 369–91. Santiago: Fundación Mario Góngora, 1992.

———. "Esclavos mapuches. Para una historia del secuestro y deportación de indígenas en la colonia." In *Historias de racismo y discriminación en Chile*, edited by Martín Lara and Rafael Gaune, 225–60. Santiago: Uqbar Editores, 2009.

———. *Fiesta, rito y política: del Chile borbónico al republicano*. Santiago: Dirección de Bibliotecas, Archivos y Museos, 2014.

———. *Las liturgias del poder. Celebraciones públicas y estrategias persuasivas en Chile colonial (1609–1709)*. Santiago: Dirección de Bibliotecas, Archivos y Museos/LOM, 2001.

———. "Sermones contra la autoridad: dos casos del siglo XVIII." In *Estudios coloniales II*, edited by Julio Retamal Ávila, 281–316. Santiago: Universidad Andrés Bello, 2002.

Van Deusen, Nancy. *Between the Sacred and the Worldly: The Institutional and Cultural Practice of Recogimiento in Colonial Lima*. Stanford, CA: Stanford University Press, 2002.

Van Young, Eric. *The Other Rebellion: Popular Violence, Ideology, and the Mexican Struggle for Independence, 1810–1821*. Stanford, CA: Stanford University Press, 2001.

Vargas Cariola, Juan Eduardo. "Del autonomismo al separatismo." In *Historia de la República de Chile*, vol. 1, edited by Fernando Silva Vargas and Juan Eduardo Vargas Cariola, 243–96. Santiago: Zig-Zag, 2013.

———. "Las reacciones chilenas ante los sucesos de España." In *Historia de la República de Chile*, vol. 1, edited by Fernando Silva Vargas and Juan Eduardo Vargas Cariola, 179–204. Santiago: Zig-Zag, 2013.

Vega, Alejandra. "Trajes del teatro del mundo: vestimenta, sujetos y diferencia americana en la primera modernidad." *Nuevo Mundo Mundos Nuevos*, Debates (June 2014). http://journals.openedition.org/nuevomundo/66794.

Vergara Quiroz, Sergio. *Historia Social del Ejército de Chile*. 2 vols. Santiago: Departamento Técnico de Investigación, Vicerrectoría Académica y Estudiantil, Universidad de Chile, 1993.

Vicuña Mackenna, Benjamín. *D. Diego Portales*, 2 vols. Valparaíso: Imprenta y Librería del Mercurio, 1863.

———. *El coronel don Tomás de Figueroa*. Santiago: Rafael Jover Editor, 1884.

———. *El ostracismo de los Carreras*. Santiago: Imprenta del Ferrocarril, 1857.

———. *El ostracismo del Jeneral D. Bernardo O'Higgins*. Valparaíso: Imprenta i Librería del Mercurio, 1860.

———. *Historia crítica y social de la ciudad de Santiago, desde su fundacion hasta nuestros dias, (1541–1868)*. 2 vols. Valparaíso: Imprenta del Mercurio, 1869.

———. *Juan Fernández: historia verdadera de la isla de Robinson Crusoe*. Santiago: Rafael Jover Editor, 1883.

———. *Relaciones históricas*. 2 vols. Santiago: Rafael Jover, 1878.

———. *Vida del Capitán Jeneral de Chile don Bernardo O'Higgins*. Santiago: Rafael Jover, 1882.

Vial Correa, Gonzalo. *El africano en el reino de Chile: ensayo histórico-jurídico*. Santiago: Universidad Católica de Chile, Facultad de Ciencias Jurídicas y Sociales, Instituto de Investigaciones Históricas, 1957.

———. "Los prejuicios sociales en Chile, al terminar el siglo XVIII. (Notas para su estudio)." *Boletín de la Academia Chilena de la Historia* 73 (1965): 14–29.

Vigarello, Georges. *Histoire des pratiques de santé. Le sain et le malsain depuis le Moyen Âge*. Paris: Seuil, 1999.

———. *Le propre et le sale: l'hygiène du corps depuis le Moyen Âge*. Paris: Seuil, 1985.

Villa-Flores, Javier. *Dangerous Speech: A Social History of Blasphemy in Colonial Mexico*. Tucson: University of Arizona Press, 2006.

Villalobos, Sergio. *Los pehuenches en la vida fronteriza*. Santiago: Ediciones Universidad Católica de Chile, 1989.

———. *Portales: una falsificación histórica*. 3rd ed. Santiago: Universitaria, 1990.

———. *Vida fronteriza en la Araucanía: el mito de la Guerra de Arauco*. Santiago: Editorial Andrés Bello, 1995.

Vinson, Ben, III. *Bearing Arms for His Majesty: The Free-Colored Militia in Colonial Mexico*. Stanford, CA: Stanford University Press, 2001.

Voekel, Pamela. *Alone before God: The Religious Origins of Modernity in Mexico*. Durham, NC: Duke University Press, 2002.

Walker, Charles F. *Shaky Colonialism: The 1746 Earthquake-Tsunami in Lima, Peru, and Its Long Aftermath*. Durham, NC: Duke University Press, 2008.

———. *Smoldering Ashes: Cuzco and the Creation of Republican Peru, 1780–1840*. Durham, NC: Duke University Press, 1999.

———. *The Tupac Amaru Rebellion*. Cambridge, MA: Belknap Press of Harvard University Press, 2014.

Walker, Tamara J. *Exquisite Slaves: Race, Clothing, and Status in Colonial Lima*. New York: Cambridge University Press, 2017.

Warner, Michael. *Publics and Counterpublics*. New York: Zone Books, 2005.

Warner, William B. *Protocols of Liberty: Communication Innovation and the American Revolution*. Chicago: University of Chicago Press, 2013.

Warren, Richard A. *Vagrants and Citizens: Politics and the Masses in Mexico City from Colony to Republic*. Lanham, MD: Rowman & Littlefield, 2007.

Weber, David J. *Bárbaros: Spaniards and Their Savages in the Age of Enlightenment*. New Haven: Yale University Press, 2005.

Wetters, Kirk. *The Opinion System: Impasses of the Public Sphere from Hobbes to Habermas*. New York: Fordham University Press, 2008.

Williams, Derek. "'Who Induced the Indian Communities?': The Los Pastos Uprising and the Politics of Ethnicity and Gender in Late-Colonial New Granada." *Colonial Latin American Historical Review* 10, no. 3 (2001): 276–309.

Wood, James. *The Society of Equality: Popular Republicanism and Democracy in Santiago de Chile, 1818–1851*. Albuquerque: University of New Mexico Press, 2011.

Yachnin, Paul, and Marlene Eberhart, eds. *Forms of Association: Making Publics in Early Modern Europe*. Amherst: University of Massachusetts Press, 2015.

Yokota, Kariann Akemi. *Unbecoming British: How Revolutionary America Became a Postcolonial Nation*. Oxford: Oxford University Press, 2011.

Zaldívar, Trinidad, and Macarena Sánchez. "Símbolos, emblemas y ritos en la construcción de la nación. La fiesta cívica republicana: Chile 1810–1830." In *Nación y nacionalismo en Chile. Siglo XIX*, vol. 2, edited by Gabriel Cid and Alejandro San Francisco, 73–115. Santiago: Centro de Estudios Bicentenario, 2009.

Zamorano Varea, Paulina. "'Ganarse la vida' en la Colonia. Mujeres y oficios." In *Mujeres chilenas: fragmentos de una historia*, edited by Sonia Montecino, 63–75. Santiago: Catalonia, 2008.

———. "Mujeres, violencia y espacio público en el Santiago del siglo XVIII." *Revista Chilena de Historia y Geografía* 169 (2008): 101–17.

Zañartu, Sady. *Santiago: calles viejas*. Santiago: Gabriela Mistral, 1975.

Zarley, Jesse. "Between the Lof and the Liberators: Mapuche Authority in Chile's *Guerra a Muerte* (1819–1825)." *Ethnohistory* 66, no. 1 (2019): 117–39.

Zavala Cepeda, José Manuel. *Los mapuches del siglo XVIII: dinámica interétnica y estrategias de resistencia*. 2nd ed. Temuco, Chile: Ediciones Universidad Católica de Temuco, 2011.

INDEX

Page numbers in *italic text* indicate figures. Page numbers followed by an *m* indicate maps.

CPSIA information can be obtained
at www.ICGtesting.com
Printed in the USA
LVHW041238150323
741632LV00001B/1

9 780826 364814